D. H. LAWRENCE

Kangaroo

WITH AN INTRODUCTION BY
RICHARD ALDINGTON

WILLIAM HEINEMANN LTD
MELBOURNE :: LONDON :: TORONTO

FIRST PUBLISHED 1923
REPRINTED 1923, 1928, 1930, 1932, 1950
RESET IN THE PHOENIX EDITION, 1955
REPRINTED 1960

PRINTED IN GREAT BRITAIN
AT THE WINDMILL PRESS
KINGSWOOD, SURREY

CONTENTS

KANGAROO

INTRODUCTION BY RICHARD ALDINGTON

THE writing of *Kangaroo* was an extraordinary *tour de force* of rapid composition, comparable with the almost fabulous creation of *Guy Mannering* in six weeks. Although some characters and episodes in the book are imaginary or transferred to Australia from elsewhere, much of the writing deals with Lawrence's experiences of Australia—with the unique result that he was remembering and setting down with extreme accuracy and vividness one set of experiences while actually undergoing others, themselves destined to be remembered and written as he found new ones. All that Australian part of the book was lived and written, not so much simultaneously, as successively during his brief visit.

The chance preservation of a fragment of personal diary and of several letters (most of them not included in the Huxley edition of *Letters*) now enable us to trace the period of writing accurately. Lawrence and his wife reached Perth, in Western Australia, by ship from Ceylon at the beginning of May, 1922. They stayed with friends at Darlington, about sixteen miles from Perth, and on May 15th Lawrence wrote that they had been "a fortnight" in Australia, but were leaving for Sydney, by the s.s. *Malwa*. A letter, undated but written on the liner, to his American friend, E. H. Brewster, contains a statement by Lawrence: "I am not thinking of any work." Therefore *Kangaroo* was not even thought of before the arrival in Sydney (which starts the book) on May 26th, 1922.

Although the first four chapters of *Kangaroo* are set in Sydney, the Lawrences in fact spent only Saturday and Sunday there, and on Monday, May 28th, were already installed in a bungalow jocosely called "Wyework" at Thirroul, a small mining village about thirty miles south of Sydney. He wrote two letters that very first day, in one of which he announced "a bitter, burning nostalgia for Europe and for Sicily", and a repudiation of Australian "conveniences"—"they can keep their conveniences". The bungalow had been taken for a month, and they would have to stay until a ship sailed on July 6th. By June 3rd we come already on the typical Laurentian change of mood, for he wrote Mable Dodge Luhan in Taos: "I have started a novel and if I can go on with it, I shall stay till I've finished it—till about the end of August." He was able to go on with it, and mentions his book to Brewster in letters dated June 5th and 13th. On June 9th he told his mother-in-law: "Suddenly I am writing again, a wild novel of Australia," and tells his sister-in-law a few days later that the book is "a queer show". On June 22nd he wrote his friend, Catherine Carswell, that he had "half done it—funny sort of novel where nothing happens and such a lot of things *should* happen: scene Australia". On July 3rd his private diary has the entry: "Have nearly written *Kangaroo*." About five weeks then saw the 150,000 words of *Kangaroo* conceived and written, except for the last brief chapter which was added in September, at Taos, New Mexico.

Kangaroo, then, is not one of Lawrence's worked-over novels, which he wrote and re-wrote over and over with such energy. It was "improvised", as most of his novels were, in the sense that he began to write the book without having planned it and without even knowing where it would take him. *Kangaroo*, like *Aaron's Rod*, he gave to the printer in its first draft, without bothering to reconstruct. What the book lacks in conventional form and grouping is more than atoned for by its magical freshness and vividness, that immediate feeling of life which Lawrence's writings had more abundantly than any author of his time. Nobody else gives you that sense that you yourself have actually experienced what he has written. An Australian friend, Mr. Adrian Lawlor, writes me that he has never seen that coast south of Sydney, but "after reading Lawrence, God! I've *been* there."

But the reader must be warned that some of these Australian characters and the scenes between people are wholly imagined or imaginatively transported from the outside world. Whenever Lawrence is evoking the Australian spirit of place and anonymous people going about their everyday lives and so coming casually in contact with Somers and Harriet, then it is all "real" as children say, it actually happened—the Sydney taximan, the garbage man, the bus conductor, and so on. But the named characters and all that happens with them were imagined. For in Australia Lawrence met nobody socially. "I don't present any letters of introduction, we don't know a soul on this side of the continent: which is almost a triumph in itself. For the first time in my life I feel how lovely it is to know nobody in the whole country: and nobody can come to the door, except the tradesmen who bring the bread and meat and so on, and who are very unobtrusive." Jack and Victoria and Jaz are probably founded on memories of Australians Lawrence met on liners between Naples and Sydney. Dr. Eder is said to have given hints for the character of Kangaroo, and though Lawrence vehemently denied this, the reason may have been the English novelist's dread of the libel action—particularly haunting to Lawrence who was accustomed to draw such recognisable yet unflattering portraits of his acquaintances. The minor character of William James is a recollection of Lawrence's days in Cornwall.

Yet so convincing are these imagined scenes that Lawrence was bitterly blamed for refusing to tell the dying 'Roo that he loved him—though no such person and no such scene ever existed! Where did he get the vivid scenes of political contest between the Diggers and the socialists? Not from his favourite periodical, *The Sydney Bulletin*, for at that time no such political violence occurred in Australia. Probably they were a transference to the Australian scene of the bitter contests between fascists and communists Lawrence had seen in Italy in 1920–22. Lawrence himself was greatly interested in the nature of power, and many pages and scenes of *Kangaroo* will show the strange battle of wills between himself and his wife when, after nearly ten years marriage, he laboured and battled unavailingly to prove to her that the basis of marriage is not perfect love, but perfect submission of the wife to the husband. This Somers–Harriet contest is one of the major themes of the book, and marvellously true to the characters of Lawrence and his wife. But Lawrence, mistaking perhaps his power as a writer for power as a leader, was constantly brooding over the thought of himself as a leader of men in action— only to recoil violently and instinctively from any such part the moment he sensed—or his "daimon" sensed—that it would interfere with his power as a writer, which required pure individualism and isolation. Out of this in turn came the two astonishing chapters of reminiscence of Lawrence's life in wartime England when he felt himself threatened with having to submit to crude bullying power in the humblest of positions, and revolted angrily from the threat. In fact, he was never in any danger of conscription since he was so ill with consumption that he was instantly exempted; but the spiritual battle was to be fought, and he did not shrink. As Lawrence Powell says, those two chapters are "an impassioned chronicle of the hatred and persecution visited upon individuals who do not succumb to the madness of wartime propaganda". But in the end as in the beginning, it must be insisted that, with all its other achievements, the supreme achievement of *Kangaroo* lies in its unforgettably vivid and accurate pictures of the Australian continent, in which no other English writer has approached Lawrence.

Kangaroo was first published in September, 1923, by Martin Secker in England and by Thomas Seltzer in America. I am told that it received only two reviews in Australian periodicals, one of them written by P. R. Stephensen, the printer, who years later issued the reproductions of Lawrence's paintings.

CHAPTER I

TORESTIN

A BUNCH of workmen were lying on the grass of the park beside Macquarie Street, in the dinner-hour. It was winter, the
end of May, but the sun was warm, and they lay there in shirt-
sleeves, talking. Some were eating food from paper packages.
They were a mixed lot—taxi-drivers, a group of builders who
were putting a new inside into one of the big houses opposite,
and then two men in blue overalls, some sort of mechanics.
Squatting and lying on the grassy bank beside the broad tarred
road where taxis and hansom cabs passed continually, they had
that air of owning the city which belongs to a good Australian.

Sometimes, from the distance behind them, came the faintest
squeal of singing from out of the "fortified" Conservatorium
of Music. Perhaps it was one of these faintly wafted squeals
that made a blue-overalled fellow look round, lifting his thick
eyebrows vacantly. His eyes immediately rested on two figures
approaching from the direction of the conservatorium, across
the grass lawn. One was a mature, handsome, fresh-faced
woman, who might have been Russian. Her companion was
a smallish man, pale-faced, with a dark beard. Both were well-
dressed, and quiet, with that quiet self-possession which is
almost unnatural nowadays. They looked different from other
people.

A smile flitted over the face of the man in the overalls—or
rather a grin. Seeing the strange, foreign-looking little man
with the beard and the absent air of self-possession walking
unheeding over the grass, the workman instinctively grinned.
A comical-looking bloke! Perhaps a Bolshy.

The foreign-looking little stranger turned his eyes and caught
the workman grinning. Half-sheepishly, the mechanic had
eased round to nudge his mate to look also at the comical-
looking bloke. And the bloke caught them both. They wiped
the grin off their faces. Because the little bloke looked at them
quite straight, so observant, and so indifferent. He saw that
the mechanic had a fine face, and pleasant eyes, and that the

grin was hardly more than a city habit. The man in the blue overalls looked into the distance, recovering his dignity after the encounter.

So the pair of strangers passed on, across the wide asphalt road to one of the tall houses opposite. The workman looked at the house into which they had entered.

"What d'you make of them, Dug?" asked the one in the overalls.

"Dunnow! Fritzies, most likely."

"They were talking English."

"Would be, naturally—what yer expect?"

"I don't think they were Germans."

"Don't yer, Jack? Mebbe they weren't then."

Dug was absolutely unconcerned. But Jack was piqued by the funny little bloke.

Unconsciously he watched the house across the road. It was a more or less expensive boarding-house. There appeared the foreign little bloke dumping down a gladstone bag at the top of the steps that led from the porch to the street, and the woman, the wife apparently, was coming out and dumping down a black hat-box. Then the man made another excursion into the house, and came out with another bag, which he like-wise dumped down at the top of the steps. Then he had a few words with the wife, and scanned the street.

"Wants a taxi," said Jack to himself.

There were two taxis standing by the kerb near the open grassy slope of the park, opposite the tall brown houses. The foreign-looking bloke came down the steps and across the wide asphalt road to them. He looked into one, and then into the other. Both were empy. The drivers were lying on the grass smoking an after-luncheon cigar.

"Bloke wants a taxi," said Jack.

"Could ha' told *you* that," said the nearest driver. But nobody moved.

The stranger stood on the pavement beside the big, cream-coloured taxi, and looked across at the group of men on the grass. He did not want to address them.

"Want a taxi?" called Jack.

"Yes. Where are the drivers?" replied the stranger in un-mistakeable English: English of the old country.

"Where d'you want to go?" called the driver of the cream-coloured taxi, without rising from the grass.

"Murdoch Street."

"Murdoch Street? What number?"

"Fifty-one."

"Neighbour of yours, Jack," said Dug, turning to his mate.

"Taking it furnished, four guineas a week," said Jack in a tone of information.

"All right," said the driver of the cream-coloured taxi, rising at last from the grass. "I'll take you."

"Go across to 120 first," said the little bloke, pointing to the house. "There's my wife and the bags. But look!" he added quickly. "You're not going to charge me a shilling each for the bags."

"What bags? Where are they?"

"There at the top of the steps."

"All right, I'll pull across and look at 'em."

The bloke walked across, and the taxi at length curved round after him. The stranger had carried his bags to the foot of the steps: two ordinary-sized Gladstones, and one smallish square hat-box. There they stood against the wall. The taxi-driver poked out his head to look at them. He surveyed them steadily. The stranger stood at bay.

"Shilling apiece, them bags," said the driver laconically.

"Oh no. The tariff is threepence," cried the stranger.

"Shilling *apiece*, them bags," repeated the driver. He was one of the proletariat that has learnt the uselessness of argument.

"All right, if you don't want to pay the fare, don't engage the car, that's all. Them bags is a shilling apiece."

"Very well, I don't want to pay so much."

"Oh, all right. If you don't, you won't. But they'll cost you a shilling apiece on a taxi, an' there you are."

"Then I don't want a taxi."

"Then why don't you say so. There's no harm done. I don't want to charge you for pulling across here to look at the bags. If you don't want a taxi, you don't. I suppose you know your own mind."

Thus saying he pushed off the brakes and the taxi slowly curved round on the road to resume its previous stand.

The strange little bloke and his wife stood at the foot of the steps beside the bags, looking angry. And then a hansom-cab came clock-clocking slowly along the road, also going to draw up for the dinner hour at the quiet place opposite. But the driver spied the angry couple.

"Want a cab, sir?"

"Yes, but I don't think you can get the bags on."

"How many bags?"

"Three. These three," and he kicked them with his toe angrily.

The hansom-driver looked down from his Olympus. He was very red-faced, and a little bit humble.

"Them three? Oh yes! Easy! Easy! Get 'em on easy. Get them on easy, no trouble at all." And he clambered down from his perch, and resolved into a little red-faced man, rather beery and hen-pecked looking. He stood gazing at the bags. On one was printed the name: "R. L. Somers".

"*R. L. Somers!* All right, you get in, sir and madam. You get in. Where d'you want to go? Station?"

"No. Fifty-one Murdoch Street."

"All right, all right, I'll take you. Fairish long way, but we'll be there under an hour."

Mr. Somers and his wife got into the cab. The cabby left the doors flung wide open, and piled the three bags there like a tower in front of his two fares. The hat-box was on top, almost touching the brown hairs of the horse's tail, and perching gingerly.

"If you'll keep a hand on that, now, to steady it," said the cabby.

"All right," said Somers.

The man climbed to his perch, and the hansom and the extraneous tower began to joggle away into the town. The group of workmen were still lying on the grass. But Somers did not care about them. He was safely jogging with his detested baggage to his destination.

"Aren't they *vile!*" said Harriet, his wife.

"It's God's Own Country, as they always tell you," said Somers. "The hansom-man was quite nice."

"But the taxi-drivers! And the man charged you eight shillings on Saturday for what would be two shillings in London!"

"He rooked me. But there you are, in a free country, it's the man who makes you pay who is free—free to charge you what he likes, and you're forced to pay it. That's what freedom amounts to. They're free to charge, and you are forced to pay."

In which state of mind they jogged through the city, catching a glimpse from the top of a hill of the famous harbour spreading out with its many arms and legs. Or at least they saw one bay with warships and steamers lying between the houses and the wooded, bank-like shores, and they saw the centre of the harbour, and the opposite squat cliffs—the whole low wooded table-land reddened with suburbs and interrupted by the pale spaces of the many-lobed harbour. The sky had gone grey, and the low table-land into which the harbour intrudes squatted dark-looking and monotonous and sad, as if lost on the face of the earth: the same Australian atmosphere, even here within the area of huge, restless, modern Sydney, whose million inhabitants seem to slip like fishes from one side of the harbour to another.

Murdoch Street was an old sort of suburb, little squat bungalows with corrugated iron roofs, painted red. Each little bungalow was set in its own hand-breadth of ground, surrounded by a little wooden palisade fence. And there went the long street, like a child's drawing, the little square bungalows dot-dot-dot, close together and yet apart, like modern democracy, each one fenced round with a square rail fence. The street was wide, and strips of worn grass took the place of kerb-stones. The stretch of macadam in the middle seemed as forsaken as a desert, as the hansom clock-clocked along it.

Fifty-one had its name painted by the door. Somers had been watching these names. He had passed "Elite", and "Très Bon" and "The Angels of Roost" and "The Better 'Ole". He rather hoped for one of the Australian names. Wallamby or Wagga-Wagga. When he had looked at the house and agreed to take it for three months, it had been dusk, and he had not noticed the name. He hoped it would not be U-An-Me, or even Stella Maris.

"Forestin," he said, reading the flourishing T as an F. "What language do you imagine that is?"

"It's T, not F," said Harriet.

"Torestin," he said, pronouncing it like Russian. "Must be a native word."

"No," said Harriet. "It means *To rest in*." She didn't even laugh at him. He became painfully silent.

Harriet didn't mind very much. They had been on the move for four months, and she felt if she could but come to anchor somewhere in a corner of her own, she wouldn't much care where it was, or whether it was called Torestin or Angels' Roost or even Très Bon.

It was, thank heaven, quite a clean little bungalow, with just commonplace furniture, nothing very preposterous. Before Harriet had even taken her hat off she removed four pictures from the wall, and the red plush table-cloth from the table. Somers had disconsolately opened the bags, so she fished out an Indian sarong of purplish shot colour, to try how it would look across the table. But the walls were red, of an awful deep bluey red, that looks so fearful with dark-oak fittings and furniture: or dark-stained jarrah, which amounts to the same thing; and Somers snapped, looking at the purple sarong—a lovely thing in itself:

"Not with red walls."

"No, I suppose not," said Harriet, disappointed. "We can easily colour-wash them white—or cream."

"What, start colour-washing walls?"

"It would only take half a day."

"That's what we come to a new land for—to God's Own Country—to start colour-washing walls in a beastly little suburban bungalow? That we've hired for three months and mayn't live in three weeks!"

"Why not? You must have walls."

"I suppose you must," he said, going away to inspect the two little bedrooms, and the kitchen, and the outside. There was a scrap of garden at the back, with a path down the middle, and a fine Australian tree at the end, a tree with pale bark and no leaves, but big tufts of red, spikey flowers. He looked at the flowers in wonder. They were apparently some sort of bean flower, in sharp tufts, like great red spikes of stiff wisteria, curving upwards, not dangling. They looked handsome against the blue sky: but again, extraneous. More like scarlet cockatoos perched in the bare tree, than natural growing flowers. Queer burning red, and hard red flowers! They call it coral tree.

There was a little round summer-house also, with a flat roof and steps going up. Somers mounted, and found that from the lead-covered roof of the little round place he could look down the middle harbour, and even see the low gateway, the low headlands with the lighthouse, opening to the full Pacific. There was the way out to the open Pacific, the white surf breaking. A tramp steamer was just coming in, under her shaft of black smoke.

But near at hand nothing but bungalows—street after street. This was one of the old-fashioned bits of Sydney. A little farther off the streets of proper brick houses clustered. But here on this hill the original streets of bungalow places remained almost untouched, still hinting at the temporary shacks run up in the wilderness.

Somers felt a little uneasy because he could look down into the whole range of his neighbours' gardens and back premises. He tried not to look at them. But Harriet had come climbing after him to survey the world, and she began:

"Isn't it lovely up here! Do you see the harbour?—and the way we came in! Look, look, I remember looking out of the port-hole and seeing that lighthouse, just as we came in—and those little brown cliffs. Oh, but it's a wonderful harbour. What it must have been when it was first discovered. And now all these little dog-kennely houses, and everything. But this next garden is lovely; have you seen the—what are they, the lovely flowers?"

"Dahlias."

"But did ever you see such dahlias! Are you sure they're dahlias? They're like pink chrysanthemums—and like roses—oh, lovely! But all these little dog-kennels—awful piggling suburban place—and sort of lousy. Is this all men can do with a new country? Look at those tin cans!"

"What do you expect them to do. Rome was not built in a day."

"Oh, but they might make it nice. Look at all the little backs: like chicken-houses with chicken-runs. They call this making a new country, do they?"

"Well, how would you start making a new country yourself?" asked Somers, a little impatiently.

"I wouldn't have towns—and corrugated iron—and millions of little fences—and empty tins."

"No, you'd have old chateaus and Tudor manors."

They went down, hearing a banging at the back door, and seeing a tradesman with a basket on his arm. And for the rest of the day they were kept busy going to the door to tell the inexhaustible tradespeople that they were now fixed up with grocer and butcher and baker and all the rest. Night came on, and Somers sat on his tub of a summer-house looking at the

lights glittering thick in swarms in the various hollows down
to the water, and the lighthouses flashing in the distance, and
ship lights on the water, and the dark places thinly sprinkled
with lights. It wasn't like a town, it was like a whole country
with towns and bays and darknesses. And all lying mysteriously
within the Australian underdark, that peculiar lost, weary
aloofness of Australia. There was the vast town of Sydney.
And it didn't seem to be real, it seemed to be sprinkled on the
surface of a darkness into which it never penetrated.

Somers sighed and shivered and went down to the house. It
was chilly. Why had he come? Why, oh why? What was he
looking for? Reflecting for a moment, he imagined he knew
what he had come for. But he wished he had not come to
Australia, for all that.

He was a man with an income of four hundred a year, and
a writer of poems and essays. In Europe, he had made up his
mind that everything was done for, played out, finished, and
he must go to a new country. The newest country: young
Australia! Now he had tried Western Australia, and had
looked at Adelaide and Melbourne. And the vast, uninhabited
land frightened him. It seemed so hoary and lost, so unapproachable. The sky was pure, crystal pure and blue, of a
lovely pale blue colour: the air was wonderful, new and unbreathed: and there were great distances. But the bush, the
grey, charred bush. It scared him. As a poet, he felt himself
entitled to all kinds of emotions and sensations which an
ordinary man would have repudiated. Therefore he let himself feel all sorts of things about the bush. It was so phantom-
like, so ghostly, with its tall pale trees and many dead trees,
like corpses, partly charred by bush fires: and then the foliage
so dark, like grey-green iron. And then it was so deathly still.
Even the few birds seemed to be swamped in silence. Waiting,
waiting—the bush seemed to be hoarily waiting. And he could
not penetrate into its secret. He couldn't get at it. Nobody
could get at it. What was it waiting for?

And then one night at the time of the full moon he walked
alone into the bush. A huge electric moon, huge, and the tree-
trunks like naked pale aborigines among the dark-soaked
foliage, in the moonlight. And not a sign of life—not a vestige.

Yet something. Something big and aware and hidden! He
walked on, had walked a mile or so into the bush, and had just
come to a clump of tall, nude, dead trees, shining almost

phosphorescent with the moon, when the terror of the bush overcame him. He had looked so long at the vivid moon, without thinking. And now, there was something among the trees, and his hair began to stir with terror, on his head. There was a presence. He looked at the weird, white, dead trees, and into the hollow distances of the bush. Nothing! Nothing at all. He turned to go home. And then immediately the hair on his scalp stirred and went icy cold with terror. What of? He knew quite well it was nothing. He knew quite well. But with his spine cold like ice, and the roots of his hair seeming to freeze, he walked on home, walked firmly and without haste. For he told himself he refused to be afraid, though he admitted the icy sensation of terror. But then to experience terror is not the same thing as to admit fear into the conscious soul. Therefore he refused to be afraid.

But the horrid thing in the bush! He schemed as to what it would be. It must be the spirit of the place. Something fully evoked to-night, perhaps provoked, by that unnatural West-Australian moon. Provoked by the moon, the roused spirit of the bush. He felt it was watching, and waiting. Following with certainty, just behind his back. It might have reached a long black arm and gripped him. But no, it wanted to wait. It was not tired of watching its victim. An alien people—a victim. It was biding its time with a terrible ageless watchfulness, waiting for a far-off end, watching the myriad intruding white men.

This was how Richard Lovat Somers figured it out to himself, when he got back into safety in the scattered township in the clearing on the hill-crest, and could see far off the fume of Perth and Freemantle on the sea-shore, and the tiny sparkling of a farther-off lighthouse on an island. A marvellous night, raving with moonlight—and somebody burning off the bush in a ring of sultry red fire under the moon in the distance, a slow ring of creeping red fire, like some ring of fireflies, upon the far-off darkness of the land's body, under the white blaze of the moon above.

It is always a question whether there is any sense in taking notice of a poet's fine feelings. The poet himself has misgivings about them. Yet a man ought to feel something, at night under such a moon.

Richard S. had never quite got over that glimpse of terror in the Westralian bush. Pure foolishness, of course, but there's no telling where a foolishness may nip you. And, now that night had settled over Sydney, and the town and harbour were sparkling unevenly below, with reddish-seeming sparkles, whilst overhead the marvellous Southern Milky Way was tilting uncomfortably to the south, instead of crossing the zenith; the vast myriads of swarming stars that cluster all along the milky way, in the Southern sky, and the Milky Way itself leaning heavily to the south, so that you feel all on one side if you look at it; the Southern sky at night, with that swarming Milky Way all bushy with stars, and yet with black gaps, holes in the white star-road, while misty blotches of star-mist float detached, like cloud-vapours, in the side darkness, away from the road; the wonderful Southern night-sky, that makes a man feel so lonely, alien: with Orion standing on his head in the west, and his sword-belt upside down, and his Dog-star prancing in mid-heaven, high above him; and with the Southern Cross insignificantly mixed in with the other stars, democratically inconspicuous; well then, now that night had settled down over Sydney, and all this was happening overhead, for R. L. Somers and a few more people, our poet once more felt scared and anxious. Things seemed so different. Perhaps everything *was* different from all he had known. Perhaps if St. Paul and Hildebrand and Darwin had lived south of the equator, we might have known the world all different, quite different. But it is useless iffing. Sufficient that Somers went indoors into his little bungalow, and found his wife setting the table for supper, with cold meat and salad.

"The only thing that's really cheap," said Harriet, "is meat. That huge piece cost two shillings. There's nothing to do but to become savage and carnivorous—if you can."

"The kangaroo and the dingo are the largest fauna in Australia," said Somers. "And the dingo is probably introduced."

"But it's very good meat," said Harriet.

"I know that," said he.

The hedge between number fifty-one and number fifty was a rather weary hedge with a lot of dead branches in it, on the Somers' side. Yet it grew thickly, with its dark green, slightly glossy leaves. And it had little pinky-green flowers just coming out: sort of pink pea-flowers. Harriet went nosing round for flowers. Their garden was just trodden grass with the remains of some bushes and a pumpkin vine. So she went picking sprigs from the intervening hedge, trying to smell a bit of scent in them, but failing. At one place the hedge was really thin, and so of course she stood to look through into the next patch.

"Oh, but these dahlias are really marvellous. You *must* come and look," she sang out to Somers.

"Yes, I know, I've seen them," he replied rather crossly, knowing that the neighbours would hear her. Harriet was so blithely unconscious of people on the other side of hedges. As far as she was concerned, they ought not to be there: even if they were in their own garden.

"You must come and look, though. Lovely! Real plum colour, and the loveliest velvet. You must come."

He left off sweeping the little yard, which was the job he had set himself for the moment, and walked across the brown grass to where Harriet stood peeping through the rift in the dead hedge, her head tied in a yellow, red-spotted duster. And of course, as Somers was peeping beside her, the neighbour who belonged to the garden must come backing out of the shed and shoving a motor-cycle down the path, smoking a short little pipe meanwhile. It was the man in blue overalls, the one named Jack. Somers knew him at once, though there were now no blue overalls. And the man was staring hard at the dead place in the hedge, where the faces of Harriet and Richard were seen peeping. Somers then behaved as usual on such occasions, just went stony and stared unseeing in another direction; as if quite unaware that the dahlias had an owner with a motor-cycle: any other owner than God, indeed. Harriet nodded a confused and rather distant "Good morning." The man just touched his cap, very cursorily, and nodded, and said good morning across his pipe, with his teeth clenched, and strode round the house with his machine.

"Why must you go yelling for other people to hear you?" said Somers to Harriet.

"Why shouldn't they hear me!" retorted Harriet.

The day was Saturday. Early in the afternoon Harriet went to the little front gate because she heard a band: or the rudiments of a band. Nothing would have kept her indoors when she heard a trumpet, not six wild Somerses. It was some very spanking Boy Scouts marching out. There were only six of them, but the road was hardly big enough to hold them. Harriet leaned on the gate in admiration of their dashing

broad hats and thick calves. As she stood there she heard a
voice:

"Would you care for a few dahlias? I believe you like
them."

She started and turned. Bold as she was in private, when
anybody addressed her in the open, any stranger, she wanted
to bolt. But it was the fifty neighbour, the female neighbour,
a very good-looking young woman, with loose brown hair and
brown eyes and a warm complexion. The brown eyes were
now alert with question and with offering, and very ready to
be huffy, or even nasty, if the offering were refused. Harriet
was too well-bred.

"Oh, thank you very much," she said, "but isn't it a pity to
cut them."

"Oh, not at all. My husband will cut you some with pleasure.
Jack!—Jack!" she called.

"Hello!" came the masculine voice.

"Will you cut a few dahlias for Mrs.—er—I don't know
your name"—she flashed a soft, warm, winning look at
Harriet, and Harriet flushed slightly. "For the people next
door," concluded the offerer.

"Somers—S-O-M-E-R-S." Harriet spelled it out.

"Oh, Somers!" exclaimed the neighbour woman, with a
gawky little jerk, like a schoolgirl. "Mr. and Mrs. Somers,"
she reiterated, with a little laugh.

"That's it," said Harriet.

"I saw you come yesterday, and I wondered—we hadn't
heard the name of who was coming." She was still rather
gawky and school-girlish in her manner, half shy, half brusque.

"No, I suppose not," said Harriet, wondering why the girl
didn't tell her own name now.

"That's your husband who has the motor-bike?" said Harriet.

"Yes, that's right. That's him. That's my husband, Jack, Mr.
Callcott."

"Mr. Callcott, oh!" said Harriet, as if she were mentally
abstracted trying to spell the word.

Somers, in the little passage inside his house, heard all this
with inward curses. "That's done it!" he groaned to himself.
He'd got neighbours now.

And sure enough, in a few minutes came Harriet's gushing
cries of joy and admiration: "Oh, how lovely! how marvellous! but can they really be dahlias? I've never seen such

dahlias! they're really too beautiful! But you shouldn't give them me, you shouldn't."

"Why not?" cried Mrs. Callcott in delight.

"So many. And isn't it a pity to cut them?" This, rather wistfully, to the masculine silence of Jack.

"Oh no, they want cutting as they come, or the blooms gets smaller," said Jack, masculine and benevolent.

"And scent!—they have scent!" cried Harriet, sniffing at her velvety bouquet.

"They have a little—not much though. Flowers don't have much scent in Australia," deprecated Mrs. Callcott.

"Oh, I must show them to my husband," cried Harriet, half starting from the fence. Then she lifted up her voice:

"Lovat!" she called. "Lovat! You *must* come. Come here! Come and see! Lovat!"

"What?"

"Come. Come and see."

This dragged the bear out of his den: Mr. Somers, twisting sour smiles of graciousness on his pale, bearded face, crossed the veranda and advanced towards the division fence, on the other side of which stood his Australian neighbour in shirt-sleeves, with a comely young wife very near to him, whilst on this side stood Harriet with a bunch of pink and purple ragged dahlias, and an expression of joyous friendliness, which Somers knew to be false, upon her face.

"Look what Mrs. Callcott has given me! Aren't they exquisite?" cried Harriet, rather exaggerated.

"Awfully nice," said Somers, bowing slightly to Mrs. Callcott, who looked uneasy, and to Mr. Callcott—otherwise Jack.

"Got here all right in the hansom, then?" said Jack.

Somers laughed—and he could be charming when he laughed —as he met the other man's eye.

"My wrist got tired, propping up the luggage all the way," he replied.

"Ay, there's not much waste ground in a hansom. You can't run up a spare bed in the parlour, so to speak. But it saved you five bob."

"Oh, at least ten, between me and a Sydney taxi-driver."

"Yes, they'll do you down if they can—that is, if you let 'em. I have a motor-bike, so I can afford to let 'em get the wind up. Don't depend on 'em, you see. That's the point."

"It is, I'm afraid."

The two men looked at each other curiously. And Mrs. Callcott looked at Somers with bright, brown, alert eyes, like a bird that has suddenly caught sight of something. A new sort of bird to her was this little man with a beard. He wasn't handsome and impressive like his wife. No, he was odd. But then he had a touch of something, the magic of the old world that she had never seen, the old culture, the old glamour. She thought that, because he had a beard and wore a little green house-jacket, he was probably a socialist.

The Somers now had neighbours: somewhat to the chagrin of Richard Lovat. He had come to this new country, the youngest country on the globe, to start a new life and flutter with a new hope. And he started with a rabid desire not to see anything and not to speak one single word to any single body—except Harriet, whom he snapped at hard enough. To be sure, the mornings sometimes won him over. They were so blue and pure: the blue harbour like a lake among the land, so pale blue and heavenly, with its hidden and half-hidden lobes intruding among the low, dark-brown cliffs, and among the dark-looking tree-covered shores, and up to the bright red suburbs. But the land, the ever-dark bush that was allowed to come to the shores of the harbour! It was strange that, with the finest of new air dimming to a lovely pale blue in the distance, and with the loveliest stretches of pale blue water, the tree-covered land should be so gloomy and lightless. It is the sun-refusing leaves of the gum trees that are like dark, hardened flakes of rubber.

He was not happy, there was no pretending he was. He longed for Europe with hungry longing: Florence, with Giotto's pale tower: or the Pincio at Rome: or the woods in Berkshire—heavens, the English spring with primroses under the bare hazel bushes, and thatched cottages among plum blossom. He felt he would have given anything on earth to be in England. It was May—end of May—almost bluebell time, and the green leaves coming out on the hedges. Or the tall corn under the olives in Sicily. Or London Bridge, with all the traffic on the river. Or Bavaria with gentian and yellow globe flowers, and the Alps still icy. Oh God, to be in Europe, lovely, lovely Europe that he had hated so thoroughly and abused so vehemently, saying it was moribund and stale and finished. The fool was himself. He had got out of temper, and so had called Europe moribund: assuming that he himself, of course, was not moribund, but sprightly and chirpy and too vital, as the Americans would say, for Europe. Well, if a man wants to make a fool of himself, it is as well to let him.

Somers wandered disconsolate through the streets of Sydney, forced to admit that there were fine streets, like Birmingham for example; that the parks and the Botanical Gardens were handsome and well-kept; that the harbour, with all the two-decker brown ferry-boats sliding continuously from the Circular Quay, was an extraordinary place. But oh, what did he care about it all! In Martin Place he longed for Westminster, in Sussex Street he almost wept for Covent Garden and St. Martin's Lane, at the Circular Quay he pined for London Bridge. It was all London without being London. Without any of the lovely old glamour that invests London. This London of the Southern Hemisphere was all, as it were, made in five minutes, a substitute for the real thing. Just a substitute —as margarine is a substitute for butter. And he went home to the little bungalow bitterer than ever, pining for England.

But if he hated the town so much, why did he stay? Oh, he had a fanciful notion that if he was really to get to know anything at all about a country, he must live for a time in the principal city. So he had condemned himself to three months at least. He told himself to comfort himself that at the end of three months he would take the steamer across the Pacific, homewards, towards Europe. He felt a long navel string fastening him to Europe, and he wanted to go back, to go home. He would stay three months. Three months' penalty for having forsworn Europe. Three months in which to get used to this Land of the Southern Cross. Cross indeed! A new crucifixion. And then away, homewards!

The only time he felt at all happy was when he had re-assured himself that by August, by August he would be taking his luggage on to a steamer. That soothed him.

He understood now that the Romans had preferred death to exile. He could sympathise now with Ovid on the Danube, hungering for Rome and blind to the land around him, blind to the savages. So Somers felt blind to Australia, and blind to the uncouth Australians. To him they were barbarians. The most loutish Neapolitan loafer was nearer to him in pulse than these British Australians with their aggressive familiarity. He surveyed them from an immense distance, with a kind of horror.

Of course he was bound to admit that they ran their city very well, as far as he could see. Everything was very easy, and there was no fuss. Amazing how little fuss and bother there was—on the whole. Nobody seemed to bother, there seemed to be no policemen and no authority, the whole thing went by itself, loose and easy, without any bossing. No real authority—no superior classes—hardly even any boss. And everything rolling along as easily as a full river, to all appearances.

That's where it was. Like a full river of life, made up of drops of water all alike. Europe is really established upon the aristocratic principle. Remove the sense of class distinction, of higher and lower, and you have anarchy in Europe. Only nihilists aim at the removal of all class distinction, in Europe.

But in Australia, it seemed to Somers, the distinction was already gone. There was really no class distinction. There was a difference of money and of "smartness". But nobody felt *better* than anybody else, or higher; only better-off. And there is all the difference in the world between feeling *better* than your fellow man, and merely feeling *better-off*.

Now Somers was English by blood and education, and though he had no antecedents whatsoever, yet he felt himself to be one of the *responsible* members of society, as contrasted with the innumerable *irresponsible* members. In old, cultured, ethical England this distinction is radical between the responsible members of society and the irresponsible. It is even a categorical distinction. It is a caste distinction, a distinction in the very being. It is the distinction between the proletariat and the ruling classes.

But in Australia nobody is supposed to rule, and nobody does rule, so the distinction falls to the ground. The proletariat appoints men to administer the law, not to rule. These ministers are not really responsible, any more than the housemaid is responsible. The proletariat is all the time responsible, the only source of authority. The will of the people. The ministers are merest instruments.

Somers for the first time felt himself immersed in real democracy—in spite of all disparity in wealth. The instinct of the place was absolutely and flatly democratic, *à terre* democratic. Demos was here his own master, undisputed, and therefore quite calm about it. No need to get the wind up at all over it; it was a granted condition of Australia, that Demos was his own master.

And this was what Richard Lovat Somers could not stand. You may be the most liberal Liberal Englishman, and yet you cannot fail to see the categorical difference between the responsible and the irresponsible classes. You cannot fail to admit the necessity for *rule*. Either you admit yourself an anarchist, or you admit the necessity for *rule*—in England. The working classes in England feel just the same about it as do the upper classes. Any working man who sincerely feels himself a responsible member of society feels it his duty to exercise authority in some way or other. And the irresponsible working man likes to feel there is a strong boss at the head, if only so that he can grumble at him satisfactorily. Europe is established on the instinct of authority: "Thou shalt." The only alternative is anarchy.

Somers was a true Englishman, with an Englishman's hatred of anarchy, and an Englishman's instinct for authority. So he felt himself at a discount in Australia. In Australia authority was a dead letter. There was no giving of orders here; or, if orders were given, they would not be received as such. A man in one position might make a suggestion to a man in another position, and this latter might or might not accept the suggestion, according to his disposition. Australia was not yct in a state of anarchy. England had as yet at least nominal authority. But let the authority be removed, and then! For it is notorious, when it comes to constitutions, how much there is in a name.

Was all that stood between Australia and anarchy just a name?—the name of England, Britain, Empire, Viceroy, or Governor General, or Governor? The shadow of the old sceptre, the mere sounding of a name? Was it just the hollow word "Authority", sounding across seven thousand miles of sea, that kept Australia from Anarchy? Australia—Authority—Anarchy: a multiplication of the alpha.

So Richard Lovat cogitated as he roamed about uneasily. Not that he knew all about it. Nobody knows all about it. And those that fancy they know *almost* all about it are usually most wrong. A man must have *some* ideas about the thing he's up against, otherwise he's a simple wash-out.

But Richard *was* wrong. Given a good temper and a genuinely tolerant nature—both of which the Australians

seem to have in a high degree—you can get on for quite a
long time without "rule". For quite a long time the thing
just goes by itself.

Is it merely running down, however, like a machine running
on but gradually running down?

Ah, questions!

CHAPTER II

NEIGHBOURS

THE Somers–Callcott acquaintance did not progress very
rapidly, after the affair of the dahlias. Mrs. Callcott asked
Mrs. Somers across to look at their cottage, and Mrs. Somers
went. Then Mrs. Somers asked Mrs. Callcott back again. But
both times Mr. Somers managed to be out of the way, and
managed to cast an invisible frost over the *rencontre*. He was
not going to be dragged in, no, he was not. He very much
wanted to borrow a pair of pincers and a chopper for an hour,
to pull out a few nails, and to split his little chunks of kindling
that the dealer had sent too thick. And the Calcotts were very
ready to lend anything, if they were only asked for it. But no,
Richard Lovat wasn't going to ask. Neither would he buy a
chopper, because the travelling expenses had reduced him to
very low water. He preferred to wrestle with the chunks of
jarrah every morning.

Mrs. Somers and Mrs. Callcott continued, however, to have
a few friendly words across the fence. Harriet learned that
Jack was foreman in a motor-works place, that he had been
wounded in the jaw in the war, that the surgeons had not been
able to extract the bullet, because there was nothing for it to
"back up against"—and so he had carried the chunk of lead in
his gizzard for ten months, till suddenly it had rolled into his
throat and he had coughed it out. The jeweller had wanted
Mrs. Callcott to have it mounted in a brooch or a hatpin. It
was a round ball of lead, from a shell, as big as a marble, and
weighing three or four ounces. Mrs. Callcott had recoiled from
this suggestion, so an elegant little stand had been made, like a
little lamp-post on a polished wood base, and the black little
globe of lead dangled by a fine chain like an arc-lamp from the
top of the toy lamp-post. It was now a mantelpiece ornament.

All this Harriet related to the indignant Lovat, though she wisely supressed the fact that Mrs. Callcott had suggested that "perhaps Mr. Somers might like to have a look at it."

Lovat was growing more used to Australia—or to the "cottage" in Murdoch Road, and the view of the harbour from the tub-top of his summer-house. You couldn't call that all "Australia"—but then one man can't bite off a continent in a mouthful, and you must start to nibble somewhere. He and Harriet took numerous trips in the ferry steamers to the many nooks and corners of the harbour. One day their ferry steamer bumped into a collier that was heading for the harbour outlet—or rather, their ferry-boat headed across the nose of the collier, so the collier bumped into them and had his nose put out of joint. There was a considerable amount of yelling, but the ferry-boat slid flatly away towards Manly, and Harriet's excitement subsided.

It was Sunday, and a lovely sunny day of Australian winter. Manly is the bathing suburb of Sydney—one of them. You pass quite close to the wide harbour gate, The Heads, on the ferry steamer. Then you land on the wharf, and walk up the street, like a bit of Margate with sea-side shops and restaurants, till you come out on a promenade at the end, and there is the wide Pacific rolling in on the yellow sand: the wide fierce sea, that makes all the built-over land dwindle into non-existence. At least there was a heavy swell on, so the Pacific belied its name and crushed the earth with its rollers. Perhaps the heavy, earth-despising swell is part of its pacific nature.

Harriet, of course, was enraptured, and declared she could not be happy till she had lived beside the Pacific. They bought food and ate it by the sea. Then Harriet was chilled, so they went to a restaurant for a cup of soup. When they were again in the street Harriet realised that she hadn't got her yellow scarf: her big, silky yellow scarf that was so warm and lovely. She declared she had left it in the eating-house, and they went back at once for it. The girls in the eating-house—the waitresses —said, in their cheeky Cockney Australian that they "hedn't seen it", and that the "next people who kyme arfter must 'ev tyken it".

Anyhow, it was gone—and Harriet furious, feeling as if there had been a thief in the night. In this unhappy state of affairs Somers suggested they should sit on the tram-car and go somewhere. They sat on the tram-car and ran for miles along a coast with ragged bush loused over with thousands of small promiscuous bungalows, built of everything from patchwork of kerosene tin up to fine red brick and stucco, like Margate. Not far off the Pacific boomed. But fifty yards inland started these bits of swamp, and endless promiscuity of "cottages".

The tram took them five or six miles, to the terminus. This was the end of everywhere, with new "stores"—that is, fly-blown shops with corrugated-iron roofs—and with a tram-shelter, and little house-agents' booths plastered with signs—and more "cottages"; that is, bungalows of corrugated-iron or brick—and bits of swamp or "lagoon" where the sea had got in and couldn't get out. The happy couple had a drink of sticky aerated waters in one of the "stores", then walked up a wide sand-road dotted on either side with small bungalows, beyond the backs of which lay a whole aura of rusty tin cans chucked out over the back fence. They came to the ridge of sand, and again the pure, long-rolling Pacific.

"I love the sea," said Harriet.

"I wish," said Lovat, "it would send a wave about fifty feet high round the whole coast of Australia."

"You are so bad-tempered," said Harriet. "Why don't you see the lovely things!"

"I do, by contrast."

So they sat on the sands, and he peeled pears and buried the peel in the yellow sand. It was winter, and the shore was almost deserted. But the sun was warm as an English May.

Harriet felt she absolutely must live by the sea, so they wandered along a wide, rutted space of deep sand, looking at the "cottages" on either side. They had impossible names. But in themselves, many of them were really nice. Yet there they stood like so many forlorn chicken-houses, each on its own oblong patch of land, with a fence between it and its neighbour. There was something indescribably weary and dreary about it. The very ground the houses stood on seemed weary and drabbled, almost asking for rusty tin cans. And so many pleasant little bungalows set there in an improvised road, wide and weary—and then the effort had lapsed. The tin shacks were almost a relief. They did not call for geraniums and lobelias, as did the pretty Hampstead Garden Suburb "cottages". And these latter might call, but they called in vain. They got bits of old paper and tins.

Yet Harriet absolutely wanted to live by the sea, so they

stopped before each bungalow that was to be let furnished. The estate agents went in for abbreviations. On the boards at the corner of the fences it said either "4 Sale" or "2 Let". Probably there was a colonial intention of jocularity. But it was almost enough for Somers. He would have died rather than have put himself into one of those cottages.

The road ended on the salt pool where the sea had ebbed in. Across was a state reserve—a bit of aboriginal Australia, with gum trees and empty spaces beyond the flat salt waters. Near at hand a man was working away, silently loading a boat with beach-sand, upon the lagoon. To the right the sea was rolling on the shore, and spurting high on some brown rocks. Two men in bathing-suits were running over the spit of sand from the lagoon to the surf, where two women in "waders", those rubber paddling-drawers into which we bundle our children at the seaside, were paddling along the fringe of the foam. A blond young man wearing a jacket over his bathing-suit walked by with two girls. He had huge massive legs, astonishing. And near at hand Somers saw another youth lying on the warm sand-hill in the sun. He had rolled in the dry sand while he was wet, so he was hardly distinguishable. But he lay like an animal on his face in the sun, and again Somers wondered at the thick legs. They seemed to run to leg, these people. Three boys, one a lad of fifteen or so, came out of the warm lagoon in their bathing-suits to roll on the sand and play. The big lad crawled on all fours and the little one rode on his back, and pitched off into the sand. They were extraordinarily like real young animals, mindless as opossums, lunging about.

This was Sunday afternoon. The sun was warm. The lonely man was just pushing off his boat on the lagoon. It sat deep in the water, half full of sand. Somers and Harriet lay on the sand-bank. Strange it was. And it *had* a sort of fascination. Freedom! That's what they always say. "You feel free in Australia." And so you do. There is a great relief in the atmosphere, a relief from tension, from pressure. An absence of control or will or form. The sky is open above you, and the air is open around you. Not the old closing-in of Europe.

But what then? The *vacancy* of this freendom is almost terrifying. In the openness and the freedom this new chaos, this litter of bungalows and tin cans scattered for miles and miles, this Englishness all crumpled out into formlessness and chaos. Even the heart of Sydney itself—an imitation of London and New York, without any core or pith of meaning. Business going on full speed: but only because it is the other end of English and American business.

The absence of any inner meaning: and at the same time the great sense of vacant spaces. The sense of irresponsible freedom. The sense of do-as-you-please liberty. And all utterly uninteresting. What is more hopelessly uninteresting than accomplished liberty? Great swarming, teeming Sydney flowing out into these myriads of bungalows, like shallow waters spreading, undyked. And what then? Nothing. No inner life, no high command, no interest in anything, finally.

Somers turned over and shut his eyes. New countries were more problematic than old ones. One loved the sense of release from old pressure and old tight control, from the old world of water-tight compartments. This was Sunday afternoon, but with none of the surfeited dreariness of English Sunday afternoons. It was still a raw loose world. All Sydney would be out by the sea or in the bush, a roving, unbroken world. They all rushed from where they were to somewhere else, on holidays. And to-morrow they'd all be working away, with just as little meaning, working without any meaning, playing without any meaning; and yet quite strenuous at it all. It was just dazing. Even the rush for money had no real pip in it. They really cared very little for the power that money can give. And except for the sense of power, that had no real significance here. When all is said and done, even money is not much good where there is no genuine culture. Money is a means to rising to a higher, subtler, fuller state of consciousness, or nothing. And when you flatly don't want a fuller consciousness, what good is your money to you? Just to chuck about and gamble with. Even money is a European invention—European and American. It has no real magic in Australia.

Poor Richard Lovat wearied himself to death struggling with the problem of himself, and calling it Australia. There was no actual need for him to struggle with Australia: he must have done it in the hedonistic sense, to please himself. But it wore him to rags.

Harriet sat up and began dusting the sand from her coat— Lovat did likewise. Then they rose to be going back to the tram-car. There was a motor-car standing on the sand of the road near the gate of the end house. The end house was called St. Columb, and Somers's heart flew to Cornwall. It was quite a nice little place, standing on a bluff of sand sideways above the lagoon.

"I wouldn't mind that," said Harriet, looking up at St. Columb.

But Somers did not answer. He was shut against any of these humiliating little bungalows. "Love's Harbour" he was just passing by, and it was "4 Sale". It would be. He ploughed grimly through the sand. "Arcady"—"Stella Maris"—"Rack-etty-Coo".

"I say!" called a voice from behind.

It was Mrs. Callcott running unevenly over the sand after them, the colour high in her cheeks. She wore a pale grey crêpe-de-chine dress and grey suède shoes. Some distance behind her Jack Callcott was following, in his shirt-sleeves.

"Fancy you being here!" gasped Mrs. Callcott, and Harriet was so flustered she could only cry:

"Oh, how do you do!"—and effusively shake hands, as if she were meeting some former acquaintance on Piccadilly. The shaking hands quite put Mrs. Callcott off her track. She felt it almost an affront, and went red. Her husband sauntered up and put his hands in his pockets, to avoid mistakes.

"Ha, what are *you* doing here," he said to the Somers pair. "Wouldn't you like a cup of tea?"

Harriet glanced at Richard Lovat. He was smiling faintly.

"Oh, we should *love* it," she replied to Mr. Callcott "But where?—have you got a house here?"

"My sister has the end house," said he.

"Oh, but—will she want us?" cried Harriet, backing out.

The Callcotts stood for a moment silent.

"Yes, if you like to come," said Jack. And it was evident he was aware of Somers's desire to avoid contact.

"Well, I should be awfully grateful," said Harriet. "Wouldn't you, Lovat?"

"Yes," he said, smiling to himself, feeling Jack's manly touch of contempt for all this hedging.

So off they went to "St. Columb". The sister was a brown-eyed Australian with a decided manner, kindly, but a little suspicious of the two newcomers. Her husband was a young Cornishman, rather stout and short and silent. He had his hair cut round at the back, in a slightly rounded line above a smooth, sunburnt, reddened nape of the neck. Somers found out later that this young Cornishman—his name was Trewhella

—had married his brother's widow. Mrs. Callcott supplied Harriet later on with all the information concerning her sister-in-law. The first Trewhella, Alfred John, had died two years ago, leaving his wife with a neat sum of money and this house, "St. Columb", and also with a little girl named Gladys, who came running in shaking her long brown hair just after the Somers appeared. So the present Trewhellas were a newly-married couple. The present husband, William James, went round in a strange, silent fashion helping his wife Rose to prepare tea.

The bungalow was pleasant, a large room facing the sea, with verandas and other little rooms opening off. There were many family photographs, and a framed medal and ribbon and letter praising the first Trewhella. Mrs. Trewhella was alert and watchful, and decided to be genteel. So the party sat around in basket chairs and on the settles under the windows, instead of sitting at table for tea. And William James silently but willingly carried round the bread and butter and the cakes.

He was a queer young man, with an Irish-looking face, rather pale, an odd kind of humour in his grey eye and in the corners of his pursed mouth. But he spoke never a word. It was hard to decide his age—probably about thirty—a little younger than his wife. He seemed silently pleased about something—perhaps his marriage. Somers noticed that the whites of his eyes were rather bloodshot. He had been in Australia since he was a boy of fifteen—he had come with his brother—from St. Columb, near Newquay—St. Columb Major. So much Somers elicited.

"Well, how do you like Sydney?" came the inevitable question from Mrs. Trewhella.

"The harbour, I think, is wonderful," came Somers's invariable answer.

"It is a fine harbour, isn't it. And Sydney is a fine town. Oh yes, I've lived there all my life."

The conversation languished. Callcott was silent, and William James seemed as if he were never anything else. Even the little girl only fluttered into a whisper and went still again. Everybody was a little embarrassed, rather stiff: too genteel, or not genteel enough. And the men seemed absolute logs.

"You don't think much of Australia, then?" said Jack to Somers.

"Why," answered the latter, "how am I to judge! I haven't even seen the fringe of it."

"Oh, it's mostly fringe," said Jack. "But it hasn't made a good impression on you?"

"I don't know yet. My feelings are mixed. The *country* seems to me to have a fascination—strange——"

"But you don't take to the Aussies, at first sight. Bit of a collision between their aura and yours," smiled Jack.

"Maybe that's what it is," said Somers. "That's a useful way of putting it. I can't help my aura colliding, can I?"

"Of course you can't. And if it's a tender sort of aura, of course it feels the bump."

"Oh, don't talk about it," cried Harriet. "He must be just one big bump, by the way he grumbles."

They all laughed—perhaps a trifle uneasily.

"I thought so," said Jack. "What made you come here? Thought you'd like to write about it?"

"I thought I might like to live here—and write here," replied Somers smiling.

"Write about the bush-rangers and the heroine lost in the bush and wandering into a camp of bullies?" said Jack.

"Maybe," said Somers.

"Do you mind if I ask you what sort of things you do write?" said Jack, with some delicacy.

"Oh—poetry—essays."

"Essays about what?"

"Oh—rubbish mostly."

There was a moment's pause.

"Oh, Lovat, don't be so silly. You *know* you don't think your essays rubbish," put in Harriet. "They're about life, and democracy, and equality, and all that sort of thing," Harriet explained.

"Oh, yes?" said Jack. "I'd like to read some."

"Well," hesitated Harriet. "He can lend you a volume—you've got some with you, haven't you?" she added, turning to Somers.

"I've got one," admitted that individual, looking daggers at her.

"Well, you'll lend it to Mr. Callcott, won't you?"

"If he wants it. But it will only bore him."

"I might rise up to it, you know," said Jack laconically, "if I bring all my mental weight to bear on it."

Somers flushed, and laughed at the contradiction in metaphor.

"It's not the loftiness," he said, rather amused. "It's that people just don't care to hear some things."

"Well, let me try," said Jack. "We're a new country—and we're out to learn."

"That's exactly what we're not," broke out William James, with a Cornish accent and a blurt of a laugh. "We're out to show to everybody that we know everything there is to be known."

"That's some of us," said Jack.

"And most of us," said William James.

"Have it your own way, boy. But let us speak for the minority. And there's a minority that knows we've got to learn a big lesson—and that's willing to learn it."

Again there was silence. The women seemed almost effaced.

"There's one thing," thought Somers to himself, "when these Colonials *do* speak seriously, they speak like men, not like babies." He looked up at Jack.

"It's the world that's got to learn a lesson," he said. "Not only Australia." His tone was acid and sinister. And he looked with his hard, pale blue eyes at Callcott. Callcott's eyes, brown and less concentrated, less hard, looked back curiously at the other man.

"Possibly it is," he said. "But my job is Australia."

Somers watched him. Callcott had a pale, clean-shaven, lean face with close-shut lips. But his lips weren't bitten in until they just formed a slit, as they so often are in Colonials. And his eyes had a touch of mystery, of aboriginal darkness.

"Do you care very much for Australia?" said Somers, a little wistfully.

"I believe I do," said Jack. "But if I was out of a job like plenty of other unlucky diggers, I suppose I should care more about getting a job."

"But you care very much about your Australia?"

"My Australia? Yes, I own about seven acres of it, all told. I suppose I care very much about that. I pay my taxes on it, all right."

"No, but the future of Australia."

"You'll never see me on a platform shouting about it."

The Lovats said they must be going.

"If you like to crowd in," said Jack, "we can take you in the car. We can squeeze in Mr. Somers in front, and there'll be plenty of room for the others at the back, if Gladys sits on her dad's knee."

This time Somers accepted at once. He felt the halting refusals were becoming ridiculous.

They left at sunset. The west, over the land, was a clear gush of light up from the departed sun. The east, over the Pacific, was a tall concave of rose-coloured clouds, a marvellous high apse. Now the bush had gone dark and spectral again, on the right hand. You might still imagine inhuman presences moving among the gum trees. And from time to time, on the left hand, they caught sight of the long green rollers of the Pacific, with the star-white foam, and behind that the dusk-green sea glimmered over with smoky rose, reflected from the eastern horizon where the bank of flesh-rose colour and pure smoke-blue lingered a long time, like magic, as if the sky's rim were cooling down. It seemed to Somers characteristic of Australia, this far-off flesh-rose bank of colour on the sky's horizon, so tender and unvisited, topped with the smoky, beautiful blueness. And then the thickness of the night's stars overhead, and one star very brave in the last effulgence of sunset, westward over the continent. As soon as night came, all the raggle-taggle of amorphous white settlements disappeared, and the continent of the Kangaroo reassumed its strange, unvisited glamour, a kind of virgin sensual aloofness.

Somers sat in front between Jack and Victoria Callcott, because he was so slight. He made himself as small as he could, like the ham in the sandwich. When he looked her way, he found Victoria watching him under her lashes, and as she met his eyes, she flared into smile that filled him with wonder. She had such a charming, innocent look, like an innocent girl, naïve and a little gawky. Yet the strange exposed smile she gave him in the dusk. It puzzled him to know what to make of it. Like an offering—and yet innocent. Perhaps like the sacred prostitutes of the temple: acknowledgment of the sacredness of the act. He chose not to think of it, and stared away across the bonnet of the car at the fading land.

Queer, thought Somers, this girl at once sees perhaps the most real me, and most women take me for something I am not at all. Queer to be recognised at once, as if one were of the same family.

He had to admit that he was flattered also. She seemed to

see the wonder in him. And she had none of the European
women's desire to make a conquest of him, none of that
feminine rapacity which is so hateful in the old world. She
seemed like an old Greek girl just bringing an offering to the
altar of the mystic Bacchus. The offering of herself.

Her husband sat steering the car and smoking his short pipe
in silence. He seemed to have something to think about. At
least he had considerable power of silence, a silence which
made itself felt. Perhaps he knew his wife much better than
anyone else. At any rate, he did not feel it necessary to keep
an eye on her. If she liked to look at Somers with a strange,
exposed smile, that was her affair. She could do as she liked in
that direction, so far as he, Jack Callcott, was concerned. She
was his wife: she knew it, and he knew it. And it was quite
established and final. So long as she did not betray what was
between her and him, as husband and wife, she could do as
she liked with the rest of herself. And he could, quite rightly,
trust her to be faithful to that undefinable relation which subsisted between them as man and wife. He didn't pretend and
didn't want to occupy the whole field of her consciousness.

And in just the same way, that bond which connected himself with her, he would always keep unbroken for his part.
But that did not mean that he was sworn body and soul to
his wife. Oh no. There was a good deal of him which did not
come into the marriage bond, and with all this part of himself
he was free to make the best he could, according to his own
idea. He loved her, quite sincerely, for her naïve sophisticated
innocence which allowed him to be unknown to her, except
in so far as they were truly and intimately related. It was
the innocence which has been through the fire, and knows its
own limitations. In the same way he quite consciously chose
not to know anything more about her than just so much as
entered into the absolute relationship between them. He quite
definitely did not want to absorb her, or to occupy the whole
field of her nature. He would trust her to go her own way,
only keeping her to the pledge that was between them. What
this pledge consisted in he did not try to define. It was something indefinite: the field of contact between their two per-
sonalities met and joined, they were one, and pledged to
permanent fidelity. But that part of each in them which did
not belong to the other was free from all enquiry or even from
knowledge. Each silently consented to leave the other in large

part unknown, unknown in word and deed and very being. They didn't *want* to know—too much knowledge would be like shackles.

Such marriage is established on a very subtle sense of honour and of individual integrity. It seems as if each race and each continent has its own marriage instinct. And the instinct that develops in Australia will certainly not be the same as the instinct that develops in America. And each people must follow its own instinct, if it is to live, no matter whether the marriage law be universal or not.

The Callcotts had come to no agreement, verbally, as to their marriage. They had not thought it out. They were Australians, of strongly, subtly-developed desire for freedom, and with considerable indifference to old formulæ and the conventions based thereon. So they took their stand instinctively. Jack had defined his stand as far as he found necessary. If his wife was good to him and satisfied him in so far as *he* went, then he was pledged to trust her to do as she liked outside his ken, outside his range. He would make a cage for nobody. This he openly propounded to his mates: to William James, for example, and later to Somers. William James said yes, but thought the more. Somers was frankly disturbed, not liking the thought of applying the same prescription to his own marriage.

They put down the Trewhellas at their house in North Sydney, and went on to Murdoch Road over the ferry. Jack had still to take the car down to the garage in town. Victoria said she would prepare the high tea which takes the place of dinner and supper in Australia, against his return. So Harriet boldly invited them to this high tea—a real substantial meal—in her own house. Victoria was to help her prepare it, and Jack was to come straight back to Torestin. Victoria was as pleased as a lamb with two tails over this arrangement, and went in to change her dress.

Somers knew why Harriet had launched this invitation. It was because she had had a wonderfully successful cooking morning. Like plenty of other women, Harriet had learned to cook during war-time, and now she loved it, once in a while. This had been one of the whiles. Somers had stoked the excellent little stove, and peeled the apples and potatoes and onions and pumpkin, and looked after the meat and the sauces, while Harriet had lashed out in pies and tarts and little cakes and

baked custard. She now surveyed her prize Beeton shelf with
love, and began to whisk up a mayonnaise for potato salad.

Victoria appeared in a pale gauze dress of pale pink with
little dabs of gold—a sort of tea-party dress—and with her
brown hair loosely knotted behind, and with innocent sophisti-
cation pulled a bit untidy over her womanly forehead, she
looked winsome. Her colour was very warm, and she was
gawkily excited. Harriet put on an old yellow silk frock, and
Somers changed into a dark suit. For tea there was cold roast
pork with first-class brown crackling on it, and potato salad,
beetroot, and lettuce, and apple chutney; then a dressed lobster
—or crayfish, very good, pink and white; and then apple-pie
and custard-tarts and cakes and a dish of apples and passion
fruits and oranges, a pineapple and some bananas: and of
course big cups of tea, breakfast-cups.

Victoria and Harriet were delighted, Somers juggled with
colour-schemes on the table, the one central room in the
bungalow was brilliantly lighted, and the kettle sang on the
hearth. After months of India, with all the Indian decorum
and two silent men-servants waiting at table: and after the
old-fashioned gentility of the P. and O. steamer, Somers and
Harriet felt this show rather a come-down maybe, but still
good fun. Victoria felt it was almost "society". They waited
for Jack.

Jack arrived bending forward rather in the doorway, a
watchful look on his pale, clean-shaven face, and that atmosphere of silence about him which is characteristic of many
Australians.

"Kept you waiting?" he asked.

"We were just ready for you," said Harriet.

Jack had to carve the meat, because Somers was so bad at
it and didn't like doing it. Harriet poured the great cups of
tea. Callcott looked with a quick eye round the table to see
exactly what he wanted to eat, and Victoria peeped through
her lashes to see exactly how Harriet behaved. As Harriet
always behaved in the vaguest manner possible, and ate her
sweets with her fish-fork and her soup with her pudding-spoon,
a study of her table manners was not particularly profitable.

To Somers it was like being back twenty-five years, back in
an English farm-house in the Midlands, at Sunday tea. He had
gone a long way from the English Midlands, and got out of
the way of them. Only to find them here again, with hardly

a change. To Harriet it was all novel and fun. But Richard Lovat felt vaguely depressed.

The pleasant heartiness of the life he had known as a boy now depressed him. He hated the promiscuous mixing in of all the company, the lack of reserve in manner. He had preferred India for that: the gulf between the native servants and the whites kept up a sort of tone. He had learned to be separate, to talk across a slight distance. And that was an immense relief to him, because it was really more his nature. Now he found himself soused again in the old familiar "jolly and cosy" spirit of his childhood and boyhood, and he was depressed.

Jack, of course, had a certain reserve. But of a different sort. Not a physical reserve. He did keep his coat on, but he might as well have sat there in his shirt-sleeves. His very silence was, so to speak, in its shirt-sleeves.

There was a curious battle in silence going on between the two men. To Harriet, all this familiar shirt-sleeve business was just fun, the charades. In her most gushing genial moments she was still only masquerading inside her class—the "upper" class of Europe. But Somers was of the people himself, and he had that alert *instinct* of the common people, the instinctive knowledge of what his neighbour was wanting and thinking, and the instinctive necessity to answer. With the other classes, there is a certain definite breach between individual and individual, and not much goes across except what is intended to go across. But with the common people, and with most Australians, there is no breach. The communication is silent and involuntary, the give and take flows like waves from person to person, and each one knows: unless he is foiled by speech. Each one knows in silence, reciprocates in silence, and the talk as a rule just babbles on, on the surface. This is the common people among themselves. But there is this difference in Australia. Each individual seems to feel himself pledged to put himself aside, to keep himself at least half out of count. The whole geniality is based on a sort of code of "You put yourself aside, and I'll put myself aside." This is done with a watchful will: a sort of duel. And above this, a great geniality. But the continual holding most of himself aside, out of count, makes a man go blank in his withheld self. And that, too, is puzzling.

Probably this is more true of the men than of the women.

Probably women change less, from land to land, play fewer "code" tricks with themselves. At any rate, Harriet and Victoria got on like a house on fire, and as they were both beautiful women, and both looking well as they talked, everything seemed splendid. But Victoria was really paying just a wee bit of homage all the time, homage to the superior class.

As for the two men: Somers *seemed* a gentleman, and Jack didn't want to be a gentleman. Somers *seemed* a real gentleman. And yet Jack recognised in him at once the intuitive response which only subsists, normally, between members of the same class: between the common people. Perhaps the best of the upper classes have the same intuitive understanding of their fellow-man: but there is always a certain reserve in the response, a preference for the non-intuitive forms of communication, for deliberate speech. What is not said is supposed not to exist: that is almost code of honour with the other classes. With the true common people, only that which is *not* said is of any vital significance.

Which brings us back to Jack and Somers. The one thing Somers had kept, and which he possessed in a very high degree, was the power of intuitive communication with others. Much as he wanted to be alone, to stand clear from the weary business of unanimity with everybody, he had never chosen really to suspend this power of intuitive response: not till he was personally offended, and then it switched off and became a blank wall. But the smallest act of real kindness would call it back into life again.

Jack had been generous, and Somers liked him. Therefore he could not withhold his soul from responding to him, in a measure. And Jack, what did he want? He saw this other little fellow, a gentleman, apparently, and yet different, not exactly a gentleman. And he wanted to know him, to talk to him. He wanted to get at the bottom of him. For there was something about Somers—he might be a German, he might be a bolshevist, he might be anything, and he *must* be something, because he was different, a gentleman and not a gentleman. He was different because, when he looked at you, he knew you more or less in your own terms, not as an outsider. He looked at you as if he were one of your own sort. He answered you intuitively as if he were one of your own sort. And yet he had the speech and the clear definiteness of a gentleman. Neither one thing nor the other. And he seemed to know a lot. Jack was sure that Somers knew a lot, and could tell him a lot, if he would but let it out.

If he had been just a gentleman, of course, Jack would never have thought of wanting him to open out. Because a gentleman has nothing to open towards a man of the people. He can only talk, and the working man can only listen, across a distance. But seeing that this little fellow was both a gentleman and not a gentleman; seeing he was just like one of yourselves, and yet had all the other qualities of a gentleman : why, you might just as well get the secret out of him.

Somers knew the attitude, and was not going to be drawn. He talked freely and pleasantly enough—but never as Jack wanted. He knew well enough what Jack wanted : which was that they should talk together as man to man—as pals, you know, with a little difference. But Somers would never be pals with any man. It wasn't in his nature. He talked pleasantly and familiarly—fascinating to Victoria, who sat with her brown eyes watching him, while she clung to Jack's arm on the sofa. When Somers was talking and telling, it was fascinating, and his quick, mobile face changed and seemed full of magic. Perhaps it was difficult to locate any definite *Somers*, any one individual in all this ripple of animation and communication. The man himself seemed lost in the bright aura of his rapid consciousness. This fascinated Victoria : she of course imagined some sort of God in the fiery bush. But Jack was mistrustful. He mistrusted all this bright quickness. If there was an individual inside the brightly-burning bush of consciousness, let him come out, man to man. Even if it was a sort of God in the bush, let him come out, man to man. Otherwise let him be considered a sort of mountebank, a showman, too clever by half.

Somers knew pretty well Jack's estimation of him. Jack, sitting there smoking his little short pipe, with his lovely wife in her pink georgette frock hanging on to his side, and the watchful look on his face, was the manly man, the consciously manly man. And he had just a bit of contempt for the brilliant little fellow opposite, and he felt just a bit uneasy because the same little fellow laughed at his "manliness", knowing it didn't go right through. It takes more than "manliness" to make a man.

Somers' very brilliance had an overtone of contempt in it, for the other man. The women, of course, not demanding any orthodox "manliness", didn't mind the knock at Jack's particular sort. And to them Somers' chief fascination lay in the fact that he was never "pals". They were too deeply women to care for the sham of pals.

So Jack went home after a whisky and soda with his nose a little bit out of joint. The little man was never going to be pals, that was the first fact to be digested. And he couldn't be despised as a softy, he was too keen; he just laughed at the other man's attempt at despising him. Yet Jack did want to get at him, somehow or other.

CHAPTER III

LARBOARD WATCH AHOY!

"What do you think of things in general?" Callcott asked of Somers one evening, a fortnight or so after their first encounter. They were getting used to one another: and they liked one another, in a special sort of way. When neither of them was on the war-path, they were quite happy together. They played chess together now and then, a wild and haphazard game. Somers invented quite brilliant attacks, and rushed in recklessly, occasionally wiping Jack off the board in a quarter of an hour. But he was very careless of his defence. The other man played at this. To give Callcott justice, he was more accustomed to draughts than to chess, and Somers had never played draughts, not to remember. So Jack played a draughts game, aiming at seizing odd pieces. It wasn't Somers' idea of chess, so he wouldn't take the trouble to defend himself. His men fell to this ambush, and he lost the game. Because at the end, when he had only one or two pieces to attack, Jack was very clever at cornering, having the draughts moves off by heart.

"But it isn't chess," protested Somers.

"You've lost, haven't you?" said Jack.

"Yes. And I shall always lose that way. I can't piggle with those draughtsmen dodges."

"Ah well, if I can win that way, I have to do it. I don't know the game as well as you do," said Jack. And there was a quiet sense of victory, "done you down", in his tones. Somers required all his dignity not to become angry. But he shrugged his shoulders.

Sometimes, too, if he suggested a game, Callcott would object that he had something he must do. Lovat took the slight rebuff without troubling. Then an hour or an hour and a half later, Callcott would come tapping at the door, and would enter saying:

"Well, if you are ready for a game."

And Lovat would unsuspectingly acquiesce. But on these occasions Jack had been silently, secretly accumulating his forces; there was a silence, almost a stealth in his game. And at the same time his bearing was soft as it were submissive, and Somers was put quite off his guard. He began to play with his usual freedom. And then Jack wiped the floor with his little neighbour: simply wiped the floor with him, and left him gasping. One, two, three games—it was the same every time.

"But I can't see the board," cried Somers, startled. "I can hardly distinguish black from white."

He was really distressed. It was true what he said. He was as if stupefied, as if some drug had been injected straight into his brain. For his life he could not gather his consciousness together—not till he realised the state he was in. And then he refused to try. Jack gave a quiet little laugh. There was on his face a subtle little smile of satisfaction. He had done his high-flying opponent down. He was the better man.

After the first evening that this had taken place, Somers was much more wary of his neighbour, much less ready to open towards him than he had been. *He never again invited Jack to a game of chess*. And when Callcott suggested a game, Somers played, but coldly, without the recklessness and the laughter which were the chief charm of his game. And Jack was once more snubbed, put back into second place. Then once he was reduced, Somers began to relent, and the old guerilla warfare started again.

The moment Somers heard this question of Jack's: "What do you think of things in general?"—he went on his guard.

"The man is trying to draw me, to fool me," he said to himself. He knew by a certain quiet, almost sly intention in Jack's voice, and a certain false deference in his bearing. It was this false deference he was most wary of. This was the Judas approach.

"How in general?" he asked. "Do you mean the cosmos?"

"No," said Jack, foiled in his first move. He had been through the Australian high-school course, and was accustomed to think for himself. Over a great field he was quite indifferent to thought, and hostile to consciousness. It seemed to him more manly to be unconscious, even blank, to most of the great questions. But on his own subjects, Australian politics, Japan, and machinery, he thought straight and manly enough. And when he met a man whose being puzzled him, he wanted to get at the bottom of that, too. He looked up at Somers with a searching, penetrating, inimical look, that he tried to cover with an appearance of false deference. For he was always aware of the big empty spaces of his own consciousness; like his country, a vast empty "desert" at the centre of him.

"No," he repeated. "I mean the world—economics and politics. The welfare of the world."

"It's no good asking me," said Somers. "Since the war burst my bubble of humanity I'm a pessimist, a black pessimist about the present human world."

"You think it's going to the bad?" said Jack, still drawing him with the same appearance of deference, of wanting to hear.

"Yes, I do. Faster or slower. Probably I shall never see any great change in my lifetime, but the tendency is all downhill, in my opinion. But then I'm a pessimist, so you needn't bother about my opinion."

Somers wanted to let it all go at that. But Callcott persisted.

"Do you think there'll be more wars? Do you think Germany will be in a position to fight again very soon?"

"Bah, you bolster up an old bogey out here. Germany is the bogey of yesterday, not of to-morrow."

"She frightened us out of our sleep before," said Jack, resentful.

"And now, for the time being, she's done. As a war machine she's done, and done for ever. So much scrap-iron, her iron fist."

"You think so?" said Jack, with all the animosity of a returned hero who wants to think his old enemy the one and only bugbear, and who feels quite injured if you tell him there's no more point in his old hate.

"That's my opinion. Of course I may be wrong."

"Yes, you may," said Jack.

"Sure," said Somers. And there was silence. This time Somers smiled a little to himself.

"And what do you consider, then, is the bogey of to-morrow?" asked Jack at length, in a rather small, unwilling voice.

"I don't really know. What should you say?"

"Me? I wanted to hear what you have to say."

"And I'd rather hear what you have to say," laughed Somers.

There was a pause. Jack seemed to be pondering. At last he came out with his bluff, manly Australian self.

"If you ask me," he said, "I should say that Labour is the bogey you speak of."

Again Somers knew that this was a draw. "He wants to find out if I'm socialist or anti," he thought to himself.

"You think Labour is a menace to society?" he returned.

"Well," Jack hedged. "I won't say that Labour is the menace, exactly. Perhaps the state of affairs forces Labour to be the menace."

"Oh, quite. But what's the state of affairs?"

"That's what nobody seems to know."

"So it's quite safe to lay the blame on," laughed Somers. He looked with real dislike at the other man, who sat silent and piqued and rather diminished: "Coming here just to draw me and get to know what's inside me!" he said to himself angrily. And he would carry the conversation no farther. He would not even offer Jack a whisky and soda. "No," he thought to himself. "If he trespasses on my hospitality, coming creeping in here, into my house, just to draw me and get the better of me, under-handedly, then I'll pour no drink for him. He can go back to where he came from." But Somers was mistaken. He only didn't understand Jack's way of leaving seven-tenths of himself out of any intercourse. Richard wanted the whole man there, openly. And Jack wanted his own way, of seven-tenths left out.

So that after a while Jack rose slowly, saying:

"Well, I'll be turning in. It's work to-morrow for some of us."

"If we're lucky enough to have jobs," laughed Somers.

"Or luckier still, to have the money so that we don't need a job," returned Jack.

"Think how bored most folks would be on a little money and no settled occupation," said Somers.

"Yes, I might be myself," said Jack, honestly admitting it, and at the same time slightly despising the man who had no job, and therefore no significance in life.

"Why, of course."

When Callcott came over to Torestin, either Victoria came with him or she invited Harriet across to Wyewurk. Wyewurk was the name of Jack's bungalow. It had been built by a man who had inherited from an aunt a modest income, and who had written thus permanently his retort against society on his door.

"Wyewurk?" said Jack. "Because you've jolly well got to."

The neighbours nearly always spoke of their respective homes by their elegant names. "Won't Mrs. Somers go across to Wyewurk, Vicky says. She's making a blouse or something, sewing some old bits of rag together—or new bits—and I expect she'll need a pageful of advice about it." This was what Jack had said. Harriet had gone with apparent alacrity, but with real resentment. She had never in all her life had "neighbours", and she didn't know what neighbouring really meant. She didn't care for it, on trial. Not after she and Victoria had said and heard most of the things they wanted to say and hear. But they liked each other also. And though Victoria could be a terribly venomous little cat, once she unsheathed her claws and became rather "common", still, so long as her claws were sheathed her paws were quite velvety and pretty, she was winsome and charming to Harriet, a bit deferential before her, which flattered the other woman. And then, lastly, Victoria had quite a decent piano, and played nicely, whereas Harriet had a good voice, and played badly. So that often, as the two men played chess or had one of their famous encounters, they would hear Harriet's strong, clear voice singing Schubert or Schumann or French or English folk songs, whilst Victoria played. And both women were happy, because though Victoria was fond of music and had an instinct for it, her knowledge or songs was slight, and to be learning these old English and old French melodies, as well as the German and the Italian songs, was a real adventure and a pleasure to her.

They were still singing when Jack returned.

"Still at it!" he said manfully, from the background, chewing his little pipe.

Harriet looked round. She was just finishing the joyous

moan of *Plaisir d'amour*, a song she loved because it tickled her so. "*Dure toute la vie—i—i—ie—i—e*," she sang the concluding words at him, laughing in his face.

"You're back early," she said.

"Felt a mental twilight coming on," he said, "so thought we'd better close down for the night."

Harriet divined that, to use her expression, Somers had been "disagreeable" to him".

"Don't you sing?" she cried.

"Me! Have you ever heard a cow at a gate when she wants to come in and be milked?"

"Oh, he does!" cried Victoria. "He sang a duet at the Harbour Lights Concert."

"There!" cried Harriet. "How exciting! What duet did he sing?"

"Larboard Watch Ahoy!"

"Oh! Oh! I know that," cried Harriet, remembering a farmer friend of Somers', who had initiated her into the thrilling harmony, down in Cornwall.

"There wasn't a soul left in the hall, when we'd finished, except Victoria and the other chap's wife," said Jack.

"Oh, what a fib. They applauded like anything, and made you give an encore."

"Ay, and we didn't know another bally duet between us, so we had to sing Larboard Watch over again. It was Larboard Alarum Clock by the time we got to the end of it, it went off with such a rattle."

"Oh, do let us sing it," said Harriet. "You must help me when I go wrong, because I don't know it well."

"What part do you want to sing?" said Jack.

"Oh, I sing the first part."

"Nay," said Jack. "I sing that part myself. I'm a high tenor, I am, once I get the wind up."

"I couldn't possibly sing the alto," said Harriet.

"Oh, Jack, do sing the alto," said Victoria. "Go on, do! I'll help you."

"Oh well, if you'll go bail for me, I don't care what I do," said Jack.

And very shortly Somers heard a gorgeous uproar in Wyewurk. Harriet breaking down occasionally, and being picked up. She insisted on keeping on till she had it perfect, and the other two banged and warbled away with no signs of fatigue.

So that they were still hailing the Larboard Watch Ahoy when the clock struck eleven.

Then when silence did ensue for a moment, Mrs. Callcott came flying over to Torestin.

"Oh, Mr. Somers, won't you come and have a drink with Jack? Mrs. Somers is having a glass of hop bitters."

When Somers entered the living-room of Wyewurk, Jack looked up at him with a smile and a glow in his dark eyes, almost like love.

"Beer?" he said.

"What's the alternative?"

"Nothing but gas-water."

"Then beer."

Harriet and Victoria were still at the piano, excitedly talking songs. Harriet was teaching Victoria to pronounce the words of a Schubert song: for there was still one person in the world unacquainted with: "Du bist wie eine Blume." And Victoria was singing it in a wavering, shy little voice.

"Let's drink our beer by the kitchen fire," said Jack. "Then we shall we able to hear ourselves speak, which is more than we can do in this aviary."

Somers solemnly followed into the tiny kitchen, and they sat in front of the still hot stove.

"The women will keep up the throat-stretching for quite a time yet," said Jack.

"If we let them. It's getting late."

"Oh, I've just started my second awakening—feel as sharp as a new tin-tack."

"Talking about pessimism," he resumed after a pause. "There's some of us here that feels things are pretty shaky, you know." He spoke in a subdued, important sort of voice.

"What is shaky—Australian finance?"

"Ay, Australian everything."

"Well, it's pretty much the same in every country. Where there's such a lot of black smoke there's not a very big fire. The world's been going to the dogs ever since it started to toddle, apparently."

"Ay, I suppose it has. But it'll get there one day. At least Australia will."

"What kind of dogs?"

"Maybe financial smash, and then hell to pay all round. Maybe, you know. We've got to think about it."

Somers watched him for some moments with serious eyes. Jack seemed as if he were a little bit drunk. Yet he had only drunk a glass of lager beer. He wasn't drunk. But his face had changed, it had a kind of eagerness, and his eyes glowed big. Strange, he seemed, as if in a slight ecstasy.

"It may be," said Somers slowly. "I am neither a financier nor a politician. It seems as if the next thing to come a cropper were capital: now there are no more kings to speak of. It may be the middle classes are coming smash—which is the same thing as finance—as capital. But also it may not be. I've given up trying to know."

"What will be will be, eh," said Jack with a smile.

"I suppose so, in this matter."

"Ay, but look here, I believe it's right what you say. The middles classes *are* coming down. What do they sit on?—they sit on money, on capital. And this country is as good as bankrupt, so then what have they left to stand on?"

"They say most countries are really bankrupt. But if they agree among themselves to carry on, the word doesn't amount to much."

"Oh, but it does. It amounts to a hell of a lot, here in this country. If it ever came to the push, and the state was bankrupt, there'd be no holding New South Wales in."

"The state never will be bankrupt."

"Won't it? Won't there be a financial smash, a proper cave-in, before we're much older? Won't there? We'll see. But look here, do you care if there is?"

"I don't know what it means, so I can't say. Theoretically I don't mind a bit if international finance goes bust: if it can go bust."

"Never mind about theoretically. You'd like to see the power of money, the power of capital, *broke*. Would you or wouldn't you?"

Somers watched the excited, handsome face opposite him, and answered slowly:

"Theoretically, yes. Actually, I really don't know."

"Oh to hell with your theoretically. Drown it. Speak like a man with some feeling in your guts. You either would or wouldn't. Don't leave your shirt-tail hanging out, with a theoretically. Would you or wouldn't you?"

Somers laughed.

"Why, yes, I would," he said, "and be damned to everything."

"Shake," cried Jack, stretching over. And he took Somers' small hand between both his own. "I knew," he said in a broken voice, "that we was mates."

Somers was rather bewildered.

"But you know," he said, "I never take any part in politics at all. They aren't my affair."

"They're not! They're not! You're quite right. You're quite right, you are. You're damned sight too good to be mixing up in any dirty politics. But all I want is that your feelings should be the same as mine, and they are, thank my stars, they are."

By this time Somers was almost scared.

"But why should you care?" he said, with some reserve. The other however did not heed him.

"You're not with the middle classes, as you call them, the money-men, as I call them, and I know you're not. And if you're not with them you're against them."

"My father was a working man. I come from the working people. My sympathy is with them, when it's with anybody, I assure you."

Jack stared at Somers wide-eyed, a smile gathering round his mouth.

"Your father was a working man, was he? Is that really so? Well, that is a surprise! And yet," he changed his tone, "no, it isn't. I might have known. Of course I might. How should I have felt for you as I did, the very first minute I saw you, if it hadn't been so. Of course you're one of us: same flesh and blood, same clay. Only you've had the advantages of a money-man. But you've stuck true to your flesh and blood, which is what most of them don't do. They turn into so much dirt, like the washings in the pan, a lot of dirt to a very little gold. Well, well, and your father was a working man! And you now being as you are! Wonderful what we may be, isn't it?"

"It is indeed," said Somers, who was infinitely more amazed at the present Jack, than ever Jack could be at him.

"Well, well, that brings us a great deal nearer than ever, that does," said Callcott, looking at Somers with glowing, smiling eyes which the other man could not quite understand, eyes with something desirous, and something perhaps fanatical in them. Somers could not understand. As for the being brought nearer to Callcott, that was apparently entirely a matter of Jack's own feeling. Somers himself had never felt more alone and far off. Yet he trembled at the other man's strange fervour. He vibrated helplessly in some sort of troubled response.

The vibration from the two men had by this time quite penetrated into the other room and into the consciousness of the two women. Harriet came in all wondering and full of alert curiosity. She looked from one to the other, saw the eyes of both men shining, saw the puzzled, slightly scared look on her husband's face, and the glowing handsomeness on Jack's, and she wondered more than ever.

"What are you two men talking about?" she asked pointedly. "You look very much moved about something."

"Moved!" laughed Jack. "We're doing fifty miles an hour, and not turning a hair."

"I'm glad I'm not going with you then," said Harriet. "It's much too late at night for me for that sort of thing."

Victoria went over to her husband and stood close at his side ruffling up his brown, short, crisp, bright hair.

"Doesn't he talk nonsense, Mrs. Somers, doesn't he talk nonsense," the young wife crooned, in her singing, contralto voice, as she looked down at him.

Harriet started at the sudden revelation of palpitating intimacy. She wanted to go away, quick. So did Somers. But neither Jack nor Victoria wanted them to go.

Jack was looking up at Victoria with a curious smile, touched with a leer. It gave his face, his rather long, clean-shaven face with the thick eyebrows, most extraordinarily the look of an old mask. One of those old Greek masks that give a fixed mockery to every feeling. Leering up at his young wife with the hearty leer of a player masked as a faun that is at home, on its own ground. Both Harriet and Somers felt amazed, as if they had strayed into the wrong wood.

"You talk all the sense, don't you, kiddie?" he said, with a strong Australian accent again. And as he spoke with his face upturned to her, his Adam's apple moved in his strong white throat as if it chuckled.

"Of course I do," she crooned in her mocking, crooning contralto. "Of course I do."

He put his arm round her hips. They continued to look into each other's faces.

"It's awfully late. We shall have simply to fly to bed. I'm so sleepy now. Good-night. Thank you so much for the singing. I enjoyed it awfully. Good-night!"

Victoria looked up with a brightly-flushed face, entirely unashamed, her eyes glowing like an animal's. Jack relaxed his grip of her, but did not rise. He looked at the Somers pair with eyes gone dusky, as if unseeing, and the mask-like smile lingering on his face like the reflection from some fire, curiously natural, not even grotesque.

"Find your way across all right?" he said. "Good-night! Good-night!" But he was as unaware of them, actually, as if they did not exist within his ken.

"Well," said Harriet, as they closed the door of Torestin. "I think they might have waited just *two* minutes before they started their love-making. After all, one doesn't want to be implicated, does one?"

"One emphatically doesn't," said Somers.

"Really, it was as if he'd got his arm round all the four of us! Horrid!" said Harriet resentfully.

"He felt he had, I'm sure," said Somers.

It was a period when Sydney was again suffering from a bubonic plague scare: a very mild scare, some fifteen cases to a million people, according to the newspapers. But the town was placarded with notices "Keep your town clean", and there was a stall in Martin Place where you could write your name down and become a member of a cleanliness league, or something to that effect.

The battle was against rats, fleas, and dirt. The plague affects rats first, said the notices, then fleas, and then man. All citizens were called upon to wage war with the vermin mentioned. Alas, there was no need to call on Somers to wage the war. The first morning they had awakened in Torestin, it was to a slight uneasy feeling of uncleanliness. Harriet, who hated the thought of contamination, found the apples gnawed, when she went to take one to eat before breakfast. And rat dirts, she said, everywhere.

Then had started such a cleaning, such a scouring, such a stopping of holes, as Torestin had never known. Somers sourly re-christened the house Toscrubin. And after that, every night he had the joyful business of setting two rat-traps, those traps with the powerful fly-back springs. Which springs were a holy terror to him, for he knew his fingers would break like pipe-stems if the spring flew back on them. And almost every morning he had the nauseous satisfaction of finding a rat pinned by its nose in the trap, its eyes bulging out, a blot of deep red blood just near. Sometimes two rats. They were not really ugly, save for their tails. Smallish rats, perhaps only half grown, and with black, silky fur. Not like the brown rats he had know in the English country.

But big or little, ugly or not ugly, they were very objectionable to him, and he hated to have to start the day by casting one or more corpses gingerly, by the tip of the tail, into the garbage-tin. He railed against the practice of throwing cans and everything promiscuously on to any bit of waste ground. It seemed to his embittered fancy that Sydney harbour, and all the coast of New South Wales, was moving with this pest. It reminded him of the land of Egypt, under the hand of the Lord: plagues of mice and rats and rabbits and snails and all manner of crawling things. And then he would say: "Perhaps it must be so in a new country." For all that, the words "new country" had become like acid between his teeth. He was always recalling what Flinders Petrie says somewhere: "A colony is no younger than the parent country." Perhaps it is even older, one step further gone.

This evening—or rather midnight—he went to the back kitchen to put every scrap of any sort of food beyond rat-reach, and to bait the two traps with bits of cheese-rind. Then he bent back the two murderous springs, and the traps were ready. He washed his hands hard from the contamination of them. Then he went into the garden, even climbed the tub-like summer-house, to have a last look at the world. There was a big slip of very bright moon risen, and the harbour was faintly distinct.

Now that night had fallen, the wind was from the land, and cold. He turned to go indoors. And as he did so he heard a motor-car run quickly along the road, and saw the bright lights come to a stop at the gate of Wyewurk. Wyewurk was in darkness already. But a man left the car and came along the path to the house, giving a peculiar whistle as he did so. He went round to the back door and knocked sharply, once, twice, in a peculiar way. Then he whistled and knocked again. After which he must have heard an answer, for he waited quietly.

In a few minutes more the lights switched on and the door opened; Jack was there in his pyjamas.

"That you, Jaz boy?" he said in a quiet tone. "Why the
blazes didn't you come half an hour sooner, or half a minute
later? You got me just as I'd taken the jump, and I fell all
over the bloomin' hedge. Come in. You'll make a nervous
wreck of me between you."

The figure entered. It was William James, the brother-in-
law. Somers heard him go again in about ten minutes. But
Harriet did not notice.

CHAPTER IV

JACK AND JAZ

THE following evening Somers could feel waves of friendliness
coming across the hedge, from Victoria. And she kept going
out to the gate to look for Jack, who was late returning home.
And as she went, she always looked long towards the veranda
of Torestin, to catch sight of the Somers.

Somers felt the yearning and amicable advance in the
atmosphere. For some time he disregarded it. Then at last he
went out to look at the nightfall. It was early June. The sun
had set beyond the land, casting a premature shadow of night.
But the eastern sky was very beautiful, full of pure, pure light,
the light of the southern seas, next the Antarctic. There was a
great massive cloud settling low, and it was all gleaming, a
golden physical glow. Then across the upper sky trailed a thin
line of little dark clouds, like a line of porpoises swimming in
the extremely beautiful clarity.

"Isn't it a lovely evening again?" Victoria called to him as
he stood on the summer-house top.

"Very lovely. Australia never ceases to be a wonderland
for me, at nightfall," he answered.

"Aha!" she said. "You are fond of the evening?"

He had come down from his point of vantage, and they stood
near together by the fence.

"In Europe I always like morning best—much best. I can't
say what it is I find so magical in the evening here."

"No!" she replied, looking upwards round the sky. "It's
going to rain."

"What makes you think so?" he asked.

"It looks like it—and it feels like it. I expect Jack will be here before it comes on."

"He's late to-night, is he?"

"Yes. He said he might be. Is it six o'clock?"

"No, it's only a little after five."

"Is it? I needn't be expecting him yet, then. He won't be home till quarter-past six." She was silent for a while. "We shall soon have the shortest day," she said. "I am glad when it has gone. I always miss Jack so much when the evening comes, and he isn't home. You see I was used to a big family, and it seems a bit lonely to me yet, all alone in the cottage. That's why we're so glad to have you and Mrs. Somers next door. We get on so well, don't we? Yes, it's surprsiing. I always felt nervous of English people before. But I love Mrs. Somers. she's lovely."

"You haven't been married long?" asked Somers.

"Not quite a year. It seems a long time in some ways. I wouldn't not be with Jack, not for anything. But I do miss my family. We were six of us all at home together, and it makes a difference, being all alone."

"Was your home in Sydney?"

"No, on the South Coast—dairy-farming. No, my father was a surveyor, so was his father before him. Both in New South Wales. Then he gave it up and started this farm down south. Oh yes, I liked it—I love home. I love going down home. I've got a cottage down there that father gave me when I got married. You must come down with us some time when the people that are in it go. It's right on the sea. Do you think you and Mrs. Somers would like it?"

"I'm sure we should."

"And will you come with us for a week-end? The people in it are leaving next week. We let it furnished."

"We should like to very much indeed," said Somers, being polite over it because he felt a little unsure still, whether he wanted to be so intimate. But Victoria seemed so wistful.

"We feel so ourselves with you and Mrs. Somers," said Victoria. "And yet you're so different from us, and yet we feel so much ourselves with you."

"But we're not different," he protested.

"Yes, you are—coming from home. It's mother who always called England home. She was English. She always spoke so prettily. She came from Somerset. Yes, she died about five years ago. Then I was mother of the family. Yes, I am the eldest, except Alfred. Yes, they're all at home. Alfred is a mining engineer—there are coal-mines down the South Coast. He was with Jack in the war, on the same job. Jack was a captain and Alfred was a lieutenant. But they drop all the army names now. That's how I came to know Jack: through Alfred. Jack always calls him Fred."

"You didn't know him before the war?"

"No, not till he came home. Alfred used to talk about him in his letters, but I never thought then I should marry him. They are great friends yet, the two of them."

The rain that she had prophesied now began to fall—big straight drops, that resounded on the tin roofs of the houses.

"Won't you come in and sit with us till Jack comes?" asked Somers. "You'll feel dreary, I know."

"Oh, don't think I said it for that," said Victoria.

"Come round, though," said Somers. And they both ran indoors out of the rain. Lightning had started to stab in the south-western sky, and clouds were shoving slowly up.

Victoria came round and sat talking, telling of her home on the south coast. It was only about fifty miles from Sydney, but it seemed another world to her. She was so quiet and simple, now, that both the Somers felt drawn to her, and glad that she was sitting with them.

They were talking still of Europe, Italy, Switzerland, England, Paris—the wonderworld to Victoria, who had never been out of New South Wales in her life, in spite of her name—which name her father had given her to annoy all his neighbours, because he said the State of Victoria was run like a paradise compared to New South Wales—although he too never went a yard out of his home state, if he could help it; they were talking still of Europe when they heard Jack's voice calling from the opposite yard.

"Hello," cried Victoria, running out. "Are you there, Jack? I was listening for the motor-bike. I remember now, you went by tram."

Sometimes she seemed a little afraid of him—physically afraid—though he was always perfectly good-humoured with her. And this evening she sounded like that—as if she feared his coming home, and wanted the Somers to shelter her.

"You've found a second home over there, apparently," said Jack, advancing towards the fence. "Well, how's things?"

It was dark, so they could not see his face. But he sounded different. There was something queer, unknown about him.

"I'll come over for a game of chess to-night, old man, if you'll say the word," he said to Somers. "And the ladies can punish the piano again meanwhile, if they feel like it. I bought something to sweeten the melodies with, and give us a sort of breathing-space now and then: sort of little ear-rest, you know."

"That means a pound of chocolates," said Victoria, like a greedy child. "And Mrs. Somers will come and help me to eat them. Good!" And she ran in home. Somers thought of a picture advertisement in the *Bulletin*:

"*Madge*: I can't think what you see in Jack. He is so un-intellectual."

"*Gladys*: Oh, but he always brings a pound of Billyer's chocolates."

Or else: "Sweets to the Sweet. Give her Billyer's chocolates"; or else: "Billyer's chocolates sweeten the home."

The game of chess was a very quiet one. Jack was pale and subdued, silent, tired, thought Somers, after his long day and short night. Somers too played without any zest. And yet they were satisfied, just sitting there together, a curious peaceful ease in being together. Somers wondered at it, the rich, full peace that there seemed to be between him and the other man. It was something he was not used to. As if one blood ran warm and rich between them. "Then shall thy peace be as a river."

"There was nothing wrong at the Trewhellas, was there, that made William James come so late?" asked Somers.

Jack looked up with a tinge of inquiry in his dark eyes at this question: as if he suspected something behind it. Somers flushed slightly.

"No, nothing wrong," said Jack.

"I beg your pardon for asking," said Somers hastily. I heard a whistle when I'd just done setting the rat-traps, and I looked out, and heard you speak to him. That's how I knew who it was. I only wondered if anything was wrong."

"No, nothing wrong," repeated Jack laconically.

"That's all right," said Somers. "It's your move. Mind your queen."

"Mind my queen, eh? She takes some minding, that lady does. I feel I need a special eye at the end of my nose, to keep track of her. Come out of it, old lady. I'm not very bright at handling royalty, that's a fact."

Somers was now silent. He felt he had made a *faux pas*, and was rebuffed. They played for some time, Jack talking to himself mostly in that facetious strain which one just had to get used to in him, though Somers occasionally found it tiring.

Then after a time Jack put his hands into his lap, and looked up at Somers.

"You mustn't think I get the wind up, you know," he said, "if you ask me a question. You can ask me what you like, you know. And when I can tell you, I'll tell you. I know you'd never come shoving your nose in like a rat from under the skirting-board when nobody's looking."

"Even if I *seem* to," said Somers, ironically.

"No, no, you don't seem to. And when I *can* tell you, I'll do so. *I* know I can trust you."

Somers looked up wondering, and met the meditative dark eyes of the other man resting on his face.

"There's some of us chaps," said Jack, "who've been through the war and had a lick at Paris and London, you know, who can tell a man by the smell of him, so to speak. If we can't see the *colour* of his aura, we can jolly well size up the *quality* of it. And that's what we go by. Call it instinct or what you like. If I like a man, slap out, at the first sight, I'd trust him into hell, I would."

"Fortunately you haven't anything *very* risky to trust him with," laughed Somers.

"I don't know so much about that," said Jack. "When a man feels he likes a chap, and trusts him, he's risking all he need, even by so doing. Because none of us likes to be taken in, and to have our feelings thrown back in our faces, as you may say, do we?"

"We don't," said Somers grimly.

"No, we don't. And you know what it means to *have* them thrown back in your face. And so do I. There's a lot of the people here that I wouldn't trust with a thank-you, I wouldn't. But then there's some that I would. And mind you, taking all for all, I'd rather trust an Aussie, I'd rather trust an Australian than an Englishman, I would, and a lot rather. Yet there's some of the rottenest people in Sydney that you'd find even if you sifted hell over. Rotten—absolute yellow rotten. And many of them in public positions, too. Simply white-anting society, that's what they're doing. Talk about public affairs in Sydney, talk about undercurrents of business in Sydney: the wickedest crew on God's earth, bar none. All the underhanded tricks of a Chink, a blooming yellow Chinaman, and all the barefaced fair talk of an Englishman. There you are. And yet, I'm telling you, I'd rather trust even a Sydney man, and he's a special sort of wombat, than an Englishman.".

"So you've told me before: for my good, I suppose," laughed Somers, not without irony.

"No, now don't you go running away with any wrong ideas," said Jack suddenly reaching out his hand and laying it on Somers' arm. "I'm not hinting at anything. If I was I'd ask you to kick me out of your house. I should deserve it. No, you're an Englishman. You're a European, perhaps I ought to say, for you've lived about all over that old continent, and you've studied it, and you've got tired of it. And you've come to Australia. Your instinct brought you here, however much you may rebel against rats and tin cans and a few other things like that. Your instinct brought you here—and brought you straight up against me. Now that I call fate."

He looked at Somers with dark, burning questioning eyes.

"I suppose following one's deepest instinct *is* one's fate," said Somers, rather flatly.

"There—you know what I mean, you see. Well then, instinct brings us together. I knew it the minute I set eyes on you when I saw you coming across from the Botanical Gardens, and you wanted a taxi. And then when I heard the address, 51, Murdoch Street, I said to myself, 'That chap is coming into my life.' And it is so. I'm a believer in fate, absolute."

"Yes," said Somers, non-committal.

"It's fate that you left Europe and came to Australia, bit by bit, and unwilling to come, as you say yourself. It's fate that brings you to Sydney, and makes me see you that dinner-hour coming from the Botanical Gardens. It's fate that brings you to this house. And it's fate that sets you and me here at this minute playing chess."

"If you call it playing chess," laughed Somers.

Jack looked down at the board.

"I'm blest if I know whose move it is," he said. "But never mind. I say that fate meant you and Mrs. Somers to come here: her as much as you. I say fate meant me and you and Victoria and her to mean a lot to one another. And when I feel my fate,

I absolutely give myself up to it. That's what I say. Do you think I'm right."

His hand, which held Somers' arm lightly, now gripped the biceps of that arm hard, while he looked into the other man's face.

"I should say so," said Somers, rather uncomfortably.

Jack hardly heeded the words. He was watching the face.

"You're a stranger here. You're from the old country. You're different from us. But you're a man we want, and you're a man we've got to keep. I know it. What? What do you say? I can't trust you, can't I?"

"What with?" asked Somers.

"What with?" Jack hesitated. "Why everything!" he blurted. "Everything! Body and soul and money and every blessed thing. I can trust you with *everything*! Isn't that right?"

Somers looked with troubled eyes into the dark, dilated, glowing eyes of the other man.

"But I don't know what it means," he stammered. "*Everything!* It means so much, that it means nothing."

Jack nodded his head slowly.

"Oh yes, it does," he reiterated. "Oh yes, it does."

"Besides," said Somers, "why should you trust me with *anything*, let alone everything. You've no occasion to trust me at all—except—except as one neighbour trusts another, in common honour."

"Common honour!" Jack just caught up the words, not heeding the sense. "It's more than common honour. It's most uncommon honour. But look here," he seemed to rouse himself. "Supposing I came to you, to ask you things, and tell you things, you'd answer me man to man, wouldn't you?—with common honour? You'd treat everything I say with common honour, as between man and man?"

"Why, yes, I hope so."

"I know you would. But for the sake of saying it, say it. I can trust you, can't I? Tell me now, can I trust you?"

Somers watched him. Was it any good making reservations and qualifications? The man was in earnest. And according to standards of commonplace honour, the so-called honour of man to man, Somers felt that he would trust Callcott, and that Callcott might trust him. So he said simply:

"Yes."

A light leaped into Jack's eyes.

"That means you trust me, of course?" he said.

"Yes," replied Somers.

"Done!" said Jack, rising to his feet and upsetting the chessmen. Somers also pushed his chair, and rose to his feet, thinking they were going across to the next house. But Jack came to him and flung an arm round his shoulder and pressed him close, trembling slightly, and saying nothing. Then he let go, and caught Somers by the hand.

"This is fate," he said, "and we'll follow it up." He seemed to cling to the other man's hand. And on his face was a strange light of purpose and of passion, a look at once exalted and dangerous.

"I'll soon bring the others to see it," he said.

"But you know I don't understand," said Somers, withdrawing his hand and taking off his spectacles.

"I know," said Jack. "But I'll let you know everything in a day or two. Perhaps you wouldn't mind if William James—if Jaz came here one evening—or you wouldn't mind having a talk with him over in my shack."

"I don't mind talking to anybody," said the bewildered Somers.

"Right you are."

They still sat for some time by the fire, silent; Jack was pondering. Then he looked up at Somers.

"You and me," he said in a quiet voice, "in a way we're mates and in a way we're not. In a way—it's different."

With which cryptic remark he left it. And in a few minutes the women came running in with the sweets, to see if the men didn't want a macaroon.

On Sunday morning Jack asked Somers to walk with him across to the Trewhellas. That is, they walked to one of the ferry stations, and took the ferry steamer to Mosman's Bay. Jack was a late riser on Sunday morning. The Somers, who were ordinary half-past seven people, rarely saw any signs of life in Wyewurk before half-past ten on the Sabbath—then it was Jack in trousers and shirt, with his shirt-sleeves rolled up, having a look at his dahlias while Vicky prepared breakfast.

So the two men did not get a start till eleven o'clock. Jack rolled along easily beside the smaller, quieter Somers. They were an odd couple, ill-assorted. In a colonial way, Jack was handsome, well-built, with strong, heavy limbs. He filled out his expensively tailored suit and looked a man who might be worth anything from five hundred to five thousand a year. The only lean, delicate part about him was his face. See him from behind, his broad shoulders and loose erect carriage and brown nape of the neck, and you expected a good square face to match. He turned, and his long, lean, rather pallid face really didn't seem to belong to his strongly animal body. For the face wasn't animal at all, except perhaps in a certain slow, dark, lingering look of the eyes, which reminded one of some animal or other, some patient, enduring animal with an indomitable but naturally passive courage.

Somers, in a light suit of thin cloth, made by an Italian tailor, and an Italian hat, just looked a foreign sort of little bloke— but a gentleman. The chief difference was that he looked sensitive all over, his body, even its clothing, and his feet, even his brown shoes, all equally sensitive with his face. Whereas Jack seemed strong and insensitive in the body, only his face vulnerable. His feet might have been made of leather all the way through, tramping with an insentient tread. Whereas Somers put down his feet delicately, as if they had a life of their own, mindful of each step of contact with the earth. Jack strode along: Somers seemed to hover along. There was decision in both of them, but oh, of such different quality. And each had a certain admiration of the other, and a very definite tolerance. Jack just barely tolerated the quiet finesse of Somers, and Somers tolerated with difficulty Jack's facetious familiarity and heartiness.

Callcott met quite a number of people he knew, and greeted them all heartily. "Hello, Bill, old man, how's things?" "New boots pinchin' yet, Ant'ny? Hoppy sort of look about you this morning. Right 'o! So long, Ant'ny!" "Different girl again, boy! Go on, Sydney's full of yer sisters. All right, good-bye, old chap." The same breezy intimacy with all of them, and the moment they had passed by, they didn't exist for him any more than the gull that had curved across in the air. They seemed to appear like phantoms, and disappear in the same instant, like phantoms. Like so many Flying Dutchmen the Australian's acquaintances seemed to steer slap through his consciousness, and were gone on the wind. What was the consecutive thread in the man's feelings? Not his feeling for any particular human beings, that was evident. His friends even his loves, were just a series of disconnected, isolated moments in his life. Somers always came again upon this gap in the other man's continuity. He felt that if he knew Jack for twenty years, and then went away, Jack would say: "Friend o' mine, Englishman, rum sort of bloke, but not a bad sort. Dunno where he's hanging out just now. Somewhere on the surface of the old humming-top, I suppose."

The only consecutive thing was that facetious attitude, which was the attitude of taking things as they come, perfected. A sort of ironical stoicism. Yet the man had a sort of passion, and a passionate identity. But not what Somers called human. And threaded on this ironical stoicism.

They found Trewhella dressed and expecting them. Trewhella was a coal and wood merchant, on the north side. He lived quite near the wharf, had his sheds at the side of the house, and in the front a bit of garden running down to the practically tideless bay of the harbour. Across the bit of blue water were many red houses, and new, wide streets of single cottages, seaside-like, disappearing rather forlorn over the brow of the low hill.

William James, or Jas, Jaz, as Jack called him, was as quiet as ever. The three men sat on a bench just above the brown rocks of the water's edge, in the lovely sunshine, and watched the big ferry steamer slip in and discharge its stream of summer-dressed passengers, and embark another stream: watched the shipping of the middle harbour away to the right, and the boats loitering on the little bay in front. A motor-boat was sweeping at a terrific speed, like some broom sweeping the water, past the little round fort away in the open harbour, and two tall white sailing-boats, all wing and no body, were tacking across the pale blue mouth of the bay. The inland sea of the harbour was all bustling with Sunday morning animation: and yet there seemed space, and loneliness. The low, coffee-brown cliffs opposite, too low for cliffs, looked as silent and as aboriginal as if white men had never come.

The little girl Gladys came out shyly. Somers now noticed that she wore spectacles.

"Hello, kiddie!" said Jack. "Come here and make a footstool of your uncle, and see what your Aunt Vicky's been thinking of. Come on then, amble up this road."

He took her on his knee, and fished out of his pocket a fine sort of hat-band that Victoria had contrived with ribbon and artificial flowers and wooden beads. Gladys sat for a moment or two shyly on her uncle's knee, and he held her there as if she were a big pillow he was scarcely conscious of holding. Her stepfather sat exactly as if the child did not exist, or were not present. It was neutrality brought to a remarkable pitch. Only Somers seemed actually aware that the child was a little human being—and to him she seemed so absent that he didn't know what to make of her.

Rose came out bringing beer and sausage-rolls, and the girl vanished away again, seemed to evaporate. Somers felt uncomfortable, and wondered what he had been brought for.

"You know Cornwall, do you?" said William James, the Cornish sing-song still evident in his Australian speech. He looked with his light-grey, inscrutable eyes at Somers.

"I lived for a time near Padstow," said Somers.

"Padstow! Ay, I've been to Padstow," said William James. And they talked for a while of the bleak, lonely northern coast of Cornwall, the black huge cliffs with the gulls flying away below, and the sea boiling, and the wind blowing in huge volleys: and the black Cornish nights, with nothing but the violent weather outside.

"Oh, I remember it, I remember it," said William James. "Though I was a half-starved youngster on a bit of a farm out there, you know, for everlasting chasing half a dozen heifers from the cliffs, where the beggars wanted to fall over and kill themselves, and hunting for a dozen sheep among the gorse bushes, and wading up to my knees in mud most part of the year, and then in summer, in the dry times, having to haul water for a mile over the rocks in a wagon, because the well had run dry. And at the end of it my father gave me one new suit in two years, and sixpence a week. Ay, that was a life for you. I suppose if I was there still he'd be giving me my keep and five shinnin' a week—if he could open his heart as wide as two half-crowns, which I'm doubting very much."

"You have money out here, at least," said Somers. "But there was a great fascination for me, in Cornwall."

"Fascination! And where do you find the fascination? In a little Wesleyan chapel of a Sunday night, and a girl with her father waiting for her with a strap if she's not in by nine o'clock? Fascination, did you say?"

"It had a great fascination for me—magic—a magic in the atmosphere."

"All the fairy-tales they'll tell you?" said William James,

looking at the other man with a smile of slow ridicule. "Why ye didn't go and believe them, did ye?"

"More or less. I could more easily have believed them there than anywhere else I've been."

"Ay, no doubt. And that shows what sort of a place it be. Lot of dum silly nonsense." He stirred on his seat impatiently.

"At any rate, you're well out of it. You're set up all right here," said Somers, who was secretly amused. The other man did not answer for some time.

"Maybe I am," he said at last. "I'm not pining to go back and work for my father, I tell you, on a couple of pasties and a lot of abuse. No, after that, I'd like you to tell me what's wrong with Australia."

"I'm sure I don't know," said Somers. "Probably nothing at all."

Again William James was silent. He was a short, thick man, with a little felt hat that sat over his brow with a half humorous flap. He had his knees wide apart, and his hands clasped between them. And he looked for the most part down at the ground. When he did cock up his eye at Somers, it was with a look of suspicion marked with humour and troubled with a certain desire. The man was restless, desirous, craving something—heaven knows what.

"You thinking of settling out here then, are you?" he asked.

"No," said Somers. "But I don't say I won't. It depends."

William James fidgetted, tapping his feet rapidly on the ground, though his body was silent. He was not like Jack. He, too, was sensitive all over, though his body looked so thick it was silently alive, and his feet were still uneasy. He was young too, with a youth that troubled him. And his nature was secretive, maybe treacherous. It was evident Jack only half liked him.

"You've got the money, you can live where you like and go where you like," said William James, looking up at Somers. "Well, I might do the same. If I cared to do it, I could live quietly on what I've got, whether here or in England." Somers recognised the Cornishman in this.

"You could very easily have as much as I've got," he said, laughing.

"The thing is, what's the good of a life of idleness?" said William James.

"What's the good of a life of work?" laughed Somers.

Shrewdly, with quick grey eye, Trewhella looked at the other man to see if he were laughing at him.

"Yet I expect you've got some purpose in coming to Australia," said William James, a trifle challenging.

"Maybe I had—or have—maybe it was just whim."

Again the other man looked shrewdly, to see if it were the truth.

"You aren't investing money out here, are you?"

"No, I've none to invest."

"Because if you was, I'd advise you not to." And he spat into the distance, and kept his hands clasped tight.

All this time Jack sat silent and as if unconcerned, but listening attentively.

"Australians have always been croakers," he said now.

"What do you think of this Irish business?" asked William James.

"I? I really don't think much at all. I don't feel Ireland is my job, personally. If I had to say, off-hand, what I'd do myself, why, if I could I'd just leave the Irish to themselves, as they want, and let them wipe each other out or kiss and make friends as they please. They bore me rather."

"And what about the Empire?"

"That again isn't my job. I'm only one man, and I know it. But personally, I'd say to India and Australia and all of them the same—if you want to stay in the Empire, stay; if you want to go out, go."

"And suppose they went out?"

"That's their affair."

"Supposing Australia said she was coming out of the Empire and governing herself, and only keeping a sort of entente with Britain. What do you think she'd make of it?"

"By the looks of things, I think she'd make a howling mess of it. Yet it might do her good if she were thrown entirely on her own resources. You've got to have something to keep you steady. England has really kept the world steady so far—as steady as it's been. That's my opinion. Now she's not keeping it very steady, and the world's sick of being bossed, anyhow. Seems to me you may as well sink or swim on your own resources."

"Perhaps we're too likely to find ourselves sinking."

"Then you'll come to your senses, after you've sunk for the third time."

"What, about England? Cling to England again, you mean?"

"No, I don't. I mean you can't put the brotherhood of man on a wage basis."

"That's what a good many people say here," put in Jack.

"You don't trust socialism then?" said Jaz, in a quiet voice.

"What sort of socialism? Trades unionism? Soviet?"

"Yes, any."

"I really don't care about politics. Politics is no more than your country's housekeeping. If I had to swallow my whole life up in housekeeping, I wouldn't keep house at all; I'd sleep under a hedge. Same with a country and politics. I'd rather have no money than be gulfed in politics and social stuff. I'd rather have the moon for a motherland."

Jaz was silent for a time, contemplating his knuckles.

"And that," he said, "is how the big majority of Australians feel, and that's why they care nothing about Australia. It's cruel to the country."

"Anyhow, no sort of *politics* will help the country," said Somers.

"If it won't, then nothing will," retorted Jaz.

"So you'd advise us all to be like seven-tenths of us here, not care a blooming hang about anything except your dinner and which horse gets in?" asked Jack, not without sarcasm.

Now Richard was silent, driven into a corner.

"Why," he said, "there's just this difference. The bulk of Australians don't care about Australia—that is, you say they don't. And why don't they? Because they care about nothing at all, neither in earth below or heaven above. They just blankly don't care about anything, and they live in defiance, a sort of slovenly defiance of care of any sort, human or inhuman, good or bad. If they've got one belief left, now the war's safely over, it's a dull, rock-bottom belief in obstinately not caring, not caring about anything. It seems to me they think it manly, the only manliness, not to care, not to think, not to attend to life at all, but just to tramp blankly on from moment to moment, and over the edge of death without caring a straw. The final manliness."

The other two men listened in silence, the distant, colonial silence that hears the voice of the old country passionately speaking against them.

"But if they're not to care about politics, what are they to care about?" asked Jaz, in his small, insinuating voice.

There was a moment's pause. Then Jack added his question:
"Do you yourself really care about anything, Mr. Somers?"

Richard turned and looked him for a moment in the eyes.
And then, knowing the two men were trying to corner him,
he said coolly:

"Why, yes. I care supremely."

"About what?" Jack's question was soft as a drop of water
falling into water, and Richard sat struggling with himself.

"That," he answered, "you either know or don't know. And
if you don't know, it would only be words my trying to tell."

There was a silence of check-mate.

"I'm afraid, for myself, I don't know," said Jack.

But Somers did not answer, and the talk, rather lamely, was
turned off to other things.

The two men went back to Murdoch Street rather silent,
thinking their own thoughts. Jack only blurted once:

"What do you make of Jaz, then?"

"I like him. He lives by himself and keeps himself pretty
dark—which is his nature."

"He's a cleverer man than you'd take him for—figures things
out in a way that surprises me. And he's better than a detective for getting to know things. He's got one or two Cornish
pals down town, you see—and they tip one another the wink.
They're like the Irish in many ways. And they're not un-
commonly unlike a Chink. I always feel as if Jaz had got a
bit of Chinese blood in him. That's what makes the women
like him, I suppose."

"But do the women like him?"

"Rose does. I believe he'd make any woman like him, if he
laid himself out to do it. Got that quiet way with him, you
know, and a sly sort of touch-the-harp-gently, that's what they
like on the quiet. But he's the sort of chap I don't exactly
fancy mixing my broth with, and drinking of the same can
with."

Somers laughed at the avowal of antipathy between the two
men.

They were not home till two o'clock. Somers found Harriet
looking rather plaintive.

"You've been a long time," she said. "What did you do?"

"Just talked."

"What about?"

"Politics."

"And did you like them?"

"Yes, quite well."

"And have you promised to see them again to-day?"

"Who?"

"Why, any of them—the Callcotts."

"No."

"Oh. They're becoming rather an institution."

"You like them too?"

"Yes, they're all right. But I don't want to spend my life with them. After all, that sort of people isn't exactly my sort—and I thought you used to pretend it wasn't yours."

"It isn't. But then no sort of people is my sort."

"Yes, it is. Any sort of people, so long as they make a fuss of you."

"Surely they make an even greater fuss of you."

"Do they! It's you they want, not me. And you go as usual, like a lamb to the slaughter."

"Baa!" he said.

"Yes, baa! You should hear yourself bleat."

"I'll listen," he said.

But Harriet was becoming discontented. They had been in their house only six weeks: and she had had enough of it. Yet it was paid for for three months: at four guineas a week. And they were pretty short of money, and would be for the rest of the year. He had already overdrawn.

Yet she began to suggest going away: away from Sydney. She felt humiliated in that beastly little Murdoch Street.

"What did I tell you?" he retorted. "The very look of it humiliated me. Yet you wanted it, and you said you liked it."

"I did like it—for the fun of it. But now there's all this intimacy and neighbouring. I just can't stand it. I just can't."

"But you began it."

"No, I didn't; you began it. And your beastly sweetness and gentleness with such people. I wish you kept a bit of it for me."

He went away in silence, knowing the uselessness of argument. And to tell the truth he was feeling also a revulsion from all this neighbouring, as Harriet called it, and all this talk. It was usually the same. He started by holding himself aloof, then gradually he let himself get mixed in, and then he had revulsions. And to-day was one of his revulsions. Coming home from Mosman's Bay, he had felt himself dwindle to a

c*

cipher in Jack's consciousness. Then, last evening, there had been all this fervour and protestation. And this morning all the cross-examination by Trewhella. And he, Somers, had plainly said all he thought. And now, as he walked home with Jack, Jack had no more use for him than for the stump of cigar which he chewed between his lips merely because he forgot to spit it away. Which state of affairs did not go at all well with *our* friend's sense of self-importance.

Therefore, when he got home, his eyes opened once more to the delicacy of Harriet's real beauty, which he knew as none else knew it, after twelve years of marriage. And once more he realised her gay, undying courage, her wonderful fresh zest in front of life. And all these other little people seemed so common in comparison, so common. He stood still with astonishment, wondering how he could have come to betray the essential reality of his life and Harriet's to the common use of these other people with their watchful, vulgar wills. That scene of last evening: what right had a fellow like Callcott to be saying these things to him? What right had he to put his arm round his, Richard's, shoulder, and give him a tight hug? Somers winced to think of it. And now Callcott had gone off with his Victoria in Sunday clothes to some other outing. Anything was as good as anything else; why not!

A gulf there was between them, really, between the Somers and the Callcotts. And yet the easy way Callcott flung a flimsy rope of intimacy across the gulf, and was embracing the pair of his neighbours in mid-air, as it were, without a grain of common foothold. And Somers let himself be embraced. So he sat pale and silent and mortified in the kitchen that evening thinking of it all, and wishing himself far away, in Europe.

"Oh, how I detest this treacly democratic Australia," he said. "It swamps one with a sort of common emotion like treacle, and before one knows where one is, one is caught like a fly on a fly-paper, in one mess with all the other buzzers. How I hate it! I want to go away."

"It isn't Australia," said Harriet. "Australia's lovely. It's just the people. And it isn't even the people—if you would only keep your proper distance, and not make yourself cheap to them and get into messes."

"No, it's the country. It's in the air. I want to leave it."

But he was not very emphatic. Harriet wanted to go down

to the South Coast, of which she had heard from Victoria.

"Think," she said, "it must be lovely there—with the mountain behind, and steep hills, and blackberries, and lovely little bays with sand."

"There'll be no blackberries. It's end of June—which is their mid-winter."

"But there'll be the other things. Let's do that, and never mind the beastly money for this pokey Torestin."

"They've asked us to go with them to Mullumbimby in a fortnight. Shall we wait till then and look?"

Harriet sat in silence for some moments.

"We might," she said reluctantly. She didn't want to wait. But what Victoria had told her of Mullumbimby, the township on the South Coast, so appealed to her that she decided to abide by her opportunity.

And then curiously enough, for the next week the neighbours hardly saw one another. It was as if the same wave of revulsion had passed over both sides of the fence. They had fleeting glimpses of Victoria as she went about the house. And when he could, Jack put in an hour at his garden in the evening, tidying it up finally for the winter. But the weather was bad, it rained a good deal; there were fogs in the morning, and fog-horns on the harbour; and the Somers kept their doors continually blank and shut.

Somers went round to the shipping agents and found out about boats to San Francisco, and talked of sailing in July, and of stopping at Tahiti or at Fiji on the way, and of cabling for money for the fares. He figured it all out. And Harriet mildly agreed. Her revulsion from Australia had passed quicker than his, now that she saw herself escaping from town and from neighbours to the quiet of a house by the sea, alone with him. Still she let him talk. Verbal agreement and silent opposition is perhaps the best weapon on such occasions.

Harriet would look at him sometimes wistfully, as he sat with his brow clouded. She had a real instinctive mistrust of other people—all other people. In her heart of hearts she said she wanted to live alone with Somers, and know nobody, all the rest of her life. In Australia, where one can be lonely, and where the land almost calls to one to be lonely—and then drives one back again on one's fellow-men in a kind of frenzy. Harriet would be quite happy by the sea, with a house and a little garden and as much space to herself as possible, knowing nobody, but having Lovat always there. And he could write, and it would be perfect.

But he wouldn't be happy—and he said so—and she knew it. She saw it like a doom on his brow.

"And why couldn't we be happy in this wonderful new country, living to ourselves. We could have a cow, and chickens—and then the Pacific, and this marvellous new country. Surely that is enough for any man. Why must you have more?"

"Because I feel I *must* fight out something with mankind yet. I haven't finished with my fellow-men. I've got a struggle with them yet."

"But what struggle? What's the good? What's the point of your struggle? And what's your struggle for?"

"I don't know. But it's inside me, and I haven't finished yet. To make some kind of an opening—some kind of a way for the afterwards."

"Ha, the afterwards will make its own way, it won't wait for you. It's a kind of nervous obstinacy and self-importance in you. You *don't* like people. You always turn away from them and hate them. Yet like a dog to his vomit you always turn back. And it will be the same old game here again as everywhere else. What are these people after all? Quite nice, but just common and—and not in your line at all. But there you are. You stick your head into a bush like an ostrich, and think you're doing wonders."

"I intend to move with men and get men to move with me before I die," he said. Then he added hastily, "Or at any rate, I'll try a bit longer yet. When I make up my mind that it's really no good, I'll go with you and we'll live alone somewhere together, and forget the world. And in Australia too. Just like a business man retiring. I'll retire away from the world, and forget it. But not yet. Not till I feel I've finished. I've got to struggle with men and the world of men for a time yet. When it's over I'll do as you say."

"Ah, you and your men, men! What do these Callcotts and these little Trewhella people mean to you after all? Are they men? They are only something you delude yourself about. And then you'll come a cropper, and fall back on me. Just as it always is. You fall back on me, and I'm expected to like it. I'm good enough to fall back on, when you've made a fool of yourself with a lot of tuppeny little people, imagining you're doing something in the world of *men*. Much men there is about it. Common little street people, that's all."

He was silent. He heard all she had to say : and he knew that, as far as the past went, it was all quite true. He had started off on his fiery courses: always, as she said, to fall back rather the worse for the attempt, on her. She had no use at all for fiery courses and efforts with the world of men. Let all that rubbish go.

"Well," he said. "It's my need to make these tries, yet. Wait till I've exhausted the need, and we'll have a little place of our own and forget the world, really. I know I can do it. I could almost do it now : and here in Australia. The country appeals to me that way : to lose oneself and have done with this side of life. But wait a bit longer."

"Ah, I suppose I shall have to," she said recklessly. "You'll have to go on making a fool of yourself till you're tired. Wives are *supposed* to have to take their husbands back a little damaged and repentant from their *love affairs* with other women. And I'm hanged if it wouldn't be more fun than this business of seeing you come back once more fooled from your attempts with *men*—the world of men, as you call it. If they *were* real men I wouldn't mind. But look at your Jack Callcott. Really, and you're supposed to have had some experience in life. 'Clip in, old man!'" She imitated Jack's voice and manner. "And you stand it all and think it's wonderful! Nay, men are too foolish for me to understand them; I give them up."

He laughed, realising that most of what she said was true.

"You see," he said, "I have the roots of my life with you. But I want if possible to send out a new shoot in the life of mankind—the effort man makes for ever, to grow into new forms."

She looked at him. And somehow she wanted to cry, because he was so silly in refusing to be finally disappointed in his efforts with mankind, and yet his silliness was pathetic, in a way beautiful. But then it *was* so silly—she wanted to shake him.

"Send out a new shoot then. Send it out. You do it in your writing already!" she cried. "But getting yourself mixed up with these impudent little people won't send any shoots, don't you think it. They'll nip you in the bud again, as they always do."

He pondered this also, stubbornly, and knew it was true. But he had set his will on something, and wasn't going to give way.

"I want to do something with living people, somewhere, somehow, while I live on the earth. I write, but I write alone. And I live alone. Without any connection whatever with the rest of men."

"Don't swank, you don't live alone. You've got *me* there safe enough, to support you. Don't swank to me about being alone, because it insults me, you see. I know how much alone you are, with me always there keeping you together."

And again he sulked and swallowed it, and obstinately held out.

"None the less," he retorted, "I do want to do something along with men. I *am* alone and cut off. As a man among men, I just have no place. I have my life with you, I know: *et praeterea nihil*."

"*Et praeterea nihil!* And what more do you want? Besides, you liar, haven't you your writing? Isn't that all you want, isn't that *doing* all there is to be done? Men! Much *men* there is about them! Bah, when it comes to that, I have to be even the only man as well as the only woman."

"That's the whole truth," said he bitingly.

"Bah, you creature, you ought to be grateful," cried Harriet.

William James arrived one morning when the Callcotts were both out, and brought a little basket of persimmons and passion fruits for Harriet. As it happened, Somers also was out.

"I remember you said you like these date-plums, Mrs. Somers. Over at our place we don't care for them, so if you like to have them you're welcome. And these are about the last of the passion fruits, seemingly."

The persimmons were good big ones, of that lovely suave orange-red colour which is perhaps their chief attraction, and they were just beginning to go soft. Harriet of course was enchanted. William James came in and sat down for a few minutes, wondering what had become of Victoria. He looked round the room curiously. Harriet had, of course, arranged it to her own liking, taken away all the pictures and ornaments, hung a Tunis curtain behind the couch, stood two tall red lacquer candlesticks on the mantelpiece, and altogether given the room that air of pleasant distinction which a woman who knows how to do it finds so easy, especially if she has a few shawls and cushion-covers and bits of interesting brass or china. Harriet insisted on travelling with a few such things. She was prepared to camp in a furnished bungalow or cottage on any continent, but a few of her own things she must have about her. Also she wore a dress of Bavarian peasant stuff, very thin black woollen material, sprinkled all over with tiny pink roses with green leaves. And on her feet she had heelless sandals of plaited strips of leather, from Colombo. William James noticed every one of these things. They had a glamour like magic for him.

"This is quite a pleasant room you have here," he said in his Cornish voice, with the alert, subtle, faintly smiling look of wonder on his face.

"It isn't bad," said Harriet. "But a bit poky."

"Poky you call it? Do you remember the little stone holes they have for rooms in those old stone Cornish cottages?"

"Yes—but we had a lovely one. And the great thick granite walls and the low ceilings."

"Walls always letting the damp in, can't keep it out, because all the chinks and spaces are just stuffed with plain earth, and a bit of mortar smeared over the outside like butter scraped on bread. Don't I remember it! I should think I do."

"Cornwall had a great charm for me."

"Well, I don't know where you found it, I'm sure. But I suppose you've got a way of your own with a place, let it be Cornwall or where it may, to make it look well. It all depends where you're born and where you come from."

"Perhaps," said Harriet.

"I've never seen an Australian cottage looking like this, now. And yet it isn't the number of things you've put into it."

"The number I've taken out," laughed Harriet.

William James sat there with his quiet, slumberous-seeming body, watching her: watching the quick radiance of her fair face, and the charm of her bearing. There was something quick and sure and, as it were, beyond the ordinary clay, about her, that exercised a spell over him. She was his real Cornish idea of a lady: simple, living among people as if one of themselves, and yet not one of themselves: a sort of magic about her. He could almost see a glow in the air around her. And he could see that for her he was just a nice fellow who lived in another world and on another plane than herself, and that he could never come up or she come down. She was the queen that slumbers somewhere in every Cornish imagination, the queen ungrudged. And perhaps, in the true Celtic imagination slumbers the glamorous king as well. The Celt needs the mystic glow of real kingliness. Hence his loneliness in the democratic world of industry, and his social perversity.

"I don't suppose Rose could ever learn to do this with a room, could she now?" he asked, making a slight gesture with his hand. He sat with his clear, queer, light grey eyes fixed on Harriet's face.

"I think so," cried Harriet; then she met the watchful eyes. "In her own way she could. Every woman has her own way, you know."

"Yes, I do know," he answered.

"And you see," said Harriet, "we're more or less lazy people who have no regular work in the world. If we had, perhaps we should live in a different way."

William James shook his head.

"It's what's bred into you," he said, "that comes out. Now if I was a really rich man, I think I could learn to carry it off with the best of them, out here. But when it comes to being the real thing, why, I know it would be beyond me, so there you are."

"But can one be sure?" she cried.

"I think I can. I can see the difference between common and uncommon. I can do more than that. I can see the difference between gentlemen who haven't got the gift, and those that have. Take Lord Washburn, for example. He's a gentleman all right—he comes of an old family, they tell me. But I doubt very much if he's any better than I am."

"Why should he be?" cried Harriet.

"What I mean is," said William James, "he hasn't got the gift, you know."

"The gift of what?" said Harriet, puzzled.

"How shall I put it? The gift that you've got, now: and that Mr. Somers has as well: and that people out here don't have."

"But that may only be manner," said Harriet.

"No, it's more than manner. It's the gift of being superior, there now: better than most folks. You understand me, I don't mean swank and money. That'll never give it you. Neither is it *thinking* yourself superior. The people that are superior don't think it, and don't even seem to feel it, in a way. And yet in a way they know it. But there aren't many of them out here.

And what there are go away. This place is meant for all one
dead level sort of people."

He spoke with curious sarcasm.

"But," said Harriet, "you are Australian yourself now,
aren't you? Or don't you feel it?"

"Oh yes, I suppose I feel it," he said, shifting uneasily on his
seat. "I *am* Australian. And I'm Australian partly because I
know that in Australia there *won't* be anybody any better
than me. There now."

"But," laughed Harriet, "aren't you glad then?"

"Glad?" he said. "It's not a matter of gladness. It's a fact.
But I'm not one of the fools who think there's nobody any
better than me in the world. I know there are."

"How queer to hear you say so?"

"But this isn't the place for them. Here in Australia we
don't want them. We want the new-fashioned sort of people
who are all dead-level as good as one another. You're going
to Mullumbimby this week-end with Jack and Victoria, aren't
you?"

"Yes. And I thought if we liked it we might stay down there
for a while—by the sea—away from the town."

"You please yourselves, of course. Perhaps better there than
here. But—it's no business of mine, you know that"—he
shrugged his shoulders. "But there's something comes over
me when I see Mr. Somers thinking he can live out here, and
work with the Australians. I think he's wrong—I really do.
They'll drag him down to their level, and make what use they
can of him—and—well, in my opinion you'd both be sorry
for it."

"How strange that you should say so, you who are one of
them."

"I am one of them, and I'm not. I'm not one of anybody.
But I haven't got only just the two eyes in my head that can
tell the kettle from the teapot. I've got another set of eyes inside me somewhere that can tell real differences, when there
are any. And that's what these people don't seem to have at
all. They've only got the outside eyes."

Harriet looked at him in wonder. And he looked at her—at
her queer, rather large, but thin-skinned, soft hands.

"You need a thick skin to love out here," he said.

But still she sat with her hands folded, lost in meditation.

"But Lovat wants so much to do something in the world,

with other men," she said at last. "It's not *my* urging, I assure you."

"He's making a mistake. He's making a mistake to come out here, tell him from me. They'll take him at their own level, not at his."

"But perhaps he wants to be taken at their level," said .Harriet, rather bitterly, almost loving the short, thick man opposite for his quiet, Cornish voice and his uncanny grey eyes, and his warning.

"If he does he makes the mistake of his life, tell him from me." And William James rose to his feet. "You'll excuse me for stopping talking like this, over things that's no business of mine," he added.

"It's awfully good of you," said Harriet.

"Well, it's not often I interfere with people's doings. But there was just something about you and Mr. Somers——"

"Awfully good of you."

He had taken his little black felt hat. He had an almost Italian or Spanish look about him—from one of the big towns, Barcelona or even Palermo.

"I suppose I'll have to be getting along," he said.

She held out her hand to him to bid him good-bye. But he shook hands in a loose, slack way, and was gone, leaving Harriet uneasy as if she had received warning of a hidden danger.

She hastened to show Somers the persimmons when he came home, and to tell of her visitor.

"And he's queer, Lovat, he's awfully queer—nice too. He told me we were superior people, and that we made a mistake coming here, because they'd bring us down to their level."

"Not if we don't let them."

"He says we can't help it."

"Why did he come to tell you that, I wonder."

They were going down to Mullumbimby in two days' time—and they had hardly see anything of Jack and Victoria since the Sunday at Mosman's Bay. But Victoria called across the fence, rather hesitatingly:

"You're going with us on Saturday, aren't you, Mrs. Somers?"

"Oh yes, we're looking forward to it immensely—if it really suits you."

"I'm so glad. I thought perhaps you didn't want to go."

That same evening Jack and Victoria came across for a few minutes.

"Look at the lovely *cacchi*," said Harriet, giving the persimmons their Italian name. "William James brought them me this morning."

"William James brought them!" cried Victoria and Jack in a breath. "Why, whatever have you done to him?"

"Nothing," laughed Harriet. "I hope not, I'm sure."

"You must have given him a glad eye," said Jack. "Did he come in?"

"Yes, he came in and talked to me quite a long time. He said he would see you to-morrow in town."

"Wonders never cease! I tell you, you've done it on him. What did he talk to you about, then?"

"Oh, Australia. He said he didn't think we should really like it."

"He did, did he! Wanted to warn you off, so to speak."

"Perhaps," laughed Harriet.

"The little mingo. He's as deep as a five-hundred-feet boring, and I've never got down to sweet water in him yet."

"Don't you trust him?" said Harriet.

"Trust him? Oh yes, he'd never pick my pocket."

"I didn't mean that."

"That's the only way I have of trusting folks," said Jack.

"Then you don't trust them far," mocked Harriet.

"Perhaps I don't. And perhaps I'm wise of it."

CHAPTER V

COO-EE

THEY went to Mullumbimby by the two o'clock train from Sydney on the Friday afternoon, Jack having managed to get a day off for the occasion. He was a sort of partner in the motor-works place where he was employed, so it was not so difficult. And work was slack.

Harriet and Victoria were both quite excited. The Somers had insisted on packing one basket of food for the house, and Victoria had brought some dainties as well. There were few people in the train, so they settled themselves right at the front, in one of those long open second-class coaches with many cane seats and a passage down the middle.

"This is really for the coal-miners," said Victoria. "You'll see they'll get in when we get farther down."

She was rather wistful, after the vague coolness that had subsisted between the two households. She was so happy that Somers and Harriet were coming with her and Jack. They made her feel—she could hardly describe it—but so safe, so happy and safe. Whereas often enough, in spite of the stalwart Jack, she felt like some piece of fluff blown about on the air, now that she was taken from her own home. With Somers and Harriet she felt like a child that is with its parents, so lovely and secure, without any need ever to look round. Jack was a man, and everything a man should be, in her eyes. But he was also like a piece of driftwood drifting on the strange unknown currents in an unexplored nowhere, without any place to arrive at. Whereas, to Victoria, Harriet seemed to be rooted right in the centre of everything, at last she could come to perfect rest in her, like a bird in a tree that remains still firm when the floods are washing everything else about.

If only Somers would let her rest in Harriet and him. But he seemed to have a strange vindictiveness somewhere in his nature, that turned round on her and terrified her worse than before. If he would only be fond of her, that was what she wanted. If he would only be fond of her, and not ever really leave her. Not love. When she thought of lovers, she thought of something quite different. Something rather vulgar, rather common, more or less naughty. Ah no, he wasn't like that. And yet—since all men are potential lovers to every woman— wouldn't it be terrible if he asked for love. Terrible—but wonderful. Not a bit like Jack—not a bit. Would Harriet mind? Victoria looked at Harriet with her quick, bright, shy brown eyes. Harriet looked so handsome and distant: she was a little afraid of her. Not as she was afraid of Somers. Afraid as one woman is of another fierce woman. Harriet was fierce, Victoria decided. Somers was demonish, but could be gentle and kind.

It came on to rain, streaming down the carriage windows. Jack lit a cigarette, and offered one to Harriet. She, though she knew Somers disliked it intensely when she smoked, particularly in a public place like this long, open railway carriage, accepted, and sat by the closed window smoking.

The train ran for a long time through Sydney, or the endless outsides of Sydney. The town took almost as much leaving as London does. But it was different. Instead of solid rows of houses, solid streets like London, it was mostly innumerable detached bungalows and cottages, spreading for great distances, scattering over hills, low hills and shallow inclines. And then waste marshy places, and old iron, and abortive corrugated iron "works"—all like the Last Day of creation, instead of a new country. Away to the left they saw the shallow waters of the big opening where Botany Bay is: the sandy shores, the factory chimneys, the lonely places where it is still Bush. And the weary half established straggling of more suburb.

"Como", said the station sign. And they ran on bridges over two arms of water from the sea, and they saw what looked like a long lake with wooded shores and bungalows: a bit like Lake Como, but oh, so unlike. That curious sombreness of Australia, the sense of oldness, with the forms all worn down low and blunt, squat. The squat-seeming earth. And then they ran at last into real country rather rocky, dark old rocks, and sombre bush with its different pale-stemmed dull-leaved gum trees standing graceful, and various healthy-looking undergrowth, and great spikey things like zuccas. As they turned south they saw tree ferns standing on one knobbly leg among the gums, and among the rocks ordinary ferns and small bushes spreading in glades and sharp hill-slopes. It was virgin bush, and as if unvisited, lost, sombre, with plenty of space, yet spreading grey for miles and miles, in a hollow towards the west. Far in the west, the sky having suddenly cleraed, they saw the magical range of the Blue Mountains. And all this hoary space of bush between. The strange, as it were, *invisible* beauty of Australia, which is undeniably there, but which seems to lurk just beyond the range of our white vision. You feel you can't *see*—as if your eyes hadn't the vision in them to correspond with the outside landscape. For the landscape is so unimpressive, like a face with little or no features, a dark face. It is so aboriginal, out of our ken, and it hangs back so aloof. Somers always felt he looked at it through a cleft in the atmosphere; as one looks at one of the ugly-faced, distorted aborigines with his wonderful dark eyes that have such incomprehensible ancient shine in them, across gulfs of unbridged centuries. And yet, when you don't have the feeling of ugliness or monotony, in landscape or in nigger, you get a sense of subtle, remote, *formless* beauty more poignant than anything ever experienced before.

"Your wonderful Australia!" said Harriet to Jack. "I can't tell you how it moves me. It feels as if no one had ever loved it. Do you know what I mean? England and Germany and Italy and Egypt and India—they've all been loved so passionately. But Australia feels as if it had never been loved, and never come out into the open. As if man had never loved it, and made it a happy country, a bride country—or a mother country."

"I don't suppose they ever have," said Jack.

"But they will?" asked Harriet. "Surely they will. I feel that if I were Australian, I should love the very earth of it—the very sand and dryness of it—more than anything."

"Where should we poor Australian wives be?" put in Victoria, leaning forward her delicate, frail face—that reminded one of a flickering butterfly in its wavering.

"Yes," said Harriet meditatively, as if they had to be considered, but were not as important as the other question.

"I'm afraid most Australians come to hate the Australian earth a good bit before they're done with it," said Jack. "If you call the land a bride, she's the sort of bride not many of us are willing to tackle. She drinks your sweat and your blood, and then as often as not lets you down, does you in."

"Of course," said Harriet, "it will take time. And of course a *lot* of love. A lot of fierce love, too."

"Let's hope she gets in," said Jack. "They treat the country more like a woman they pick up on the streets than a bride, to my thinking."

"I feel I could *love* Australia," declared Harriet.

"Do you feel you could love an Australian?" asked Jack, very much to the point.

"Well," said Harriet, arching her eyes at him, "that's another matter. From what I see of them I rather doubt it," she laughed, teasing him.

"I should say you would. But it's no good loving Australia if you can't love the Australian."

"Yes, it is. If as you say Australia is like the poor prostitute, and the Australian just bullies her to get what he can out of her and then treats her like dirt."

"It's a good deal like that," said Jack.

"And then you expect me to approve of you."

"Oh, we're not all alike, you know."

"It always seems to me," said Somers, "that somebody will have to water Australia with their blood bfeore it's a real man's country. The soil, the very plants seem to be waiting for it."

"You've got a lurid imagination, my dear man," said Jack.

"Yes, he has," said Harriet. "He's always so extreme."

The train jogged on, stopping at every little station. They were near the coast, but for a long time the sea was not in sight. The land grew steeper—dark, straight hills like cliffs, masked in sombre trees. And then the first plume of colliery smoke among the trees on the hill-face. But they were little collieries, for the most part, where the men just walked into the face of the hill down a tunnel, and they hardly disfigured the land at all. Then the train came out on the sea—lovely bays with sand and grass and trees, sloping up towards the sudden hills that were like a wall. There were bungalows dotted in most of the bays. Then suddenly more collieries, and quite a large settlement of bungalows. From the trains they looked down on many many pale-grey zinc roofs, sprinkled about like a great camp, close together, yet none touching, and getting thinner towards the sea. The chimneys were faintly smoking, there was a haze of smoke and a sense of home, home in the wilds. A little way off, among the trees, plumes of white steam betrayed more collieries.

A bunch of schoolboys clambered into the train with their satchels, at home as schoolboys are. And several black colliers, with tin luncheon boxes. Then the train ran for a mile and a half, to stop at another little settlement. Sometimse they stopped at beautiful bays in a hollow between hills, and no collieries, only a few bungalows. Harriet hoped Mullumbimby was like that She rather dreaded the settlements with the many many iron roofs, and the wide, unmade roads of sandy earth running between, down to the sea, or skirting swamp-like little creeks.

The train jogged on again—they were there. The place was half and half. There were many tin roofs—but not so many. There were the wide, unmade roads running so straight as it were to nowhere, with little bungalow homes half-lost at the side. But they were pleasant little bungalow homes. Then quite near, inland, rose a great black wall of mountain, or cliff, or tor, a vast dark tree-covered tor that reminded Harriet of

Matlock, only much bigger. The town trailed down from the foot of this mountain towards the railway, a huddle of grey and red-painted iron roofs. Then over the railways, towards the sea, it began again in a scattered, spasmodic fashion, rather forlorn bungalows and new "stores" and fields with rail fences, and more bungalows above the fields, and more still running down the creek shallows towards the hollow sea, which lay beyond like a grey mound, the strangest sight Harriet had ever seen.

Next to the railway was a field, with men and youths playing football for their lives. Across the road from the football field was a barber's shop, where a man on horseback was leaning chattering to the barber, a young intelligent gentleman in eye-glasses. And on the broad grass of the roadside grew the trees with the bright scarlet flowers perching among the grey twigs.

Going towards the sea they were going away from the town that slid down at the bush-covered foot of the dark tor. The sun was just sinking to this great hill-face, amid a curdle of grey-white clouds. The faintest gold reflected in the more eastern sky, in front. Strange and forlorn, the wide sandy-rutted road with the broad grass margin and just one or two bungalows. "Verdun" was the first, a wooden house painted dark red. But some had quite wide grass round them, inside their fences, like real lawns.

Victoria had to dart to the house-agent for the key. The other three turned to the left, up another wide road cut in the almost nothingness, past two straying bungalows perched on brick supports—then across a piece of grassland as yet unoccupied, where small boys were kicking a football—then round the corner of another new road, where water lay in a great puddle so that they had to climb on to the grass beside the fence of a big red-painted bungalow. Across the road was a big bungalow built with imitation timbered walls and a red corrugated roof and red huge water-tanks. The sea roared loudly, but was not in sight. Next along the forlorn little road nestled a real bright red-tiled roof among a high bushy hedge, and with a white gate.

"I do hope it's that," said Harriet to herself. She was so yearning to find another home.

Jack stood waiting at the corner on the tall bit of grassy land above the muddy, cut-out road. There came Victoria running in her eager way across the open space up the slight incline. Evening was beginning to fall.

"Got 'em?" called Jack.

"Yes. Mrs. Wynne was just washing herself, so I had to wait a minute." Victoria came panting up.

"Is that it?" said Harriet timidly at last, pointing to the bright red roof.

"Yes, that's it," said Victoria, pleased and proprietary. A boy from the big red bungalow called to ask if he should bring milk across. The big red bungalow was a dairy. But Harriet followed eagerly on Jack's footsteps across the road. She peeped over the white gate as he unfastened it. A real lovely brick house, with a roof of bright red tiles coming down very low over dark wooden verandas, and huge round rain-tanks, and a bit of grass and a big shed with double doors. Joy! The gate was open, and she rushed in, under the tall, over-leaning hedge that separated them from the neighbour, and that reached almost to touch the side of her house. A wooden side veranda with bedsteads—old rusty bedsteads patched with strip and rope—and then grass, a little front all of grass, with loose hedges on either side—and the sea, the great Pacific right there and rolling in huge white thunderous rollers not forty yards away, under her grassy platform of a garden. She walked to the edge of the grass. Yes, just down the low cliff, really only a bank, went her own little path, as down a steep bank, and then was smooth yellow sand, and the long sea swishing white up its incline, and rocks to the left, and incredible long rollers furling over and crushing down on the shore. At her feet! At her very feet, the huge rhythmic Pacific.

She turned to the house. There it crouched, with its long windows and its wide veranda and its various slopes of low, red-tiled roofs. Perfect! Perfect! The sun had gone down behind the great front of black mountain wall which she could still see over the hedge. The house inside was dark, with its deep verandas like dark eyelids half closed. Somebody switched on a light. Long cottage windows, and a white ceiling with narrow dark beams. She rushed indoors. Once more in search of a home, to be alone with Lovat, where he would be happy. How the sea thundered!

Harriet liked the house extremely. It was beautifully built, solid, in the good English fashion. It had a great big room with dark jarrah timbering on the roof and the walls: it had a dark jarrah floors, and doors, and some solid, satisfactory jarrah furniture, a big, real table and a sideboard and strong square chairs with cane seats. The Lord had sent her here, that was certain.

And how delighted Victoria was with her raptures. Jack whipped his coat off and went to the shed for wood and coal, and soon had a lavish fire in the open hearth. A boy came with milk, and another with bread and fresh butter and eggs, ordered by Mrs. Wynne. The big black kettle was on the fire. And Harriet took Lovat's arm, she was so moved.

Through the open seaward door, as they sat at the table, the near sea was glimmering pale and greenish in the sunset, and breaking with a crash of foam right, as it seemed, under the house. If the house had not stood with its little grassy garden some thirty or forty feet above the ocean, sometimes the foam would have flown to the doorstep, or to the steps of the loggia. The great sea roaring at one's feet!

After the evening meal the women were busy making up beds and tidying round, while the men sat by the fire. Jack was quiet, he seemed to brood, and only spoke abstractedly, vaguely. He just sucked his pipe and stared in the fire, while the sea boomed outside, and the voices of the women were heard eager in the bedrooms. When one of the doors leading on to the verandas was opened, the noise of the sea came in frightening, like guns.

The house had been let for seven months to a man and wife with eleven children. When Somers got up at sunrise, in the morning, he could well believe it. But the sun rose golden from a low fume of haze in the north-eastern sea. The waves rolled in pale and bluey, glass-green, wonderfully heavy and liquid. They curved with a long arch, then fell in a great hollow thud and a spurt of white foam and a long, soft, snow-pure rush of forward flat foam. Somers watched the crest of fine, bristling spume fly back from the head of the waves as they turned and broke. The sea was all yellow-green light.

And through the light came a low, black tramp steamer, lurching up and down on the waves, disappearing altogether in the lustrous water, save for her bit of yellow-banded funnel and her mast-tips: then emerging like some long, out-of-shape dolphin on a wave-top. She was like some lost mongrel running over a furrowed land. She bellowed and barked forlornly, and hung round on the up-and-down waves.

Somers saw what she wanted. At the south end of the shallow bay was a long, high jetty straddling on great tree-trunk poles out on to the sea, and carrying a long line of little red-coal trucks, the sort that can be tipped up. Beyond the straddling jetty was a spit of low, yellow-brown land, grassy, with a stiff little group of trees like ragged Noah's Ark trees, and farther in, a little farm-place with two fascinating big gum trees that stuck out their clots of foliage in dark tufts at the end of slim, up-starting branches.

But the lines from the jetty ran inland for two hundred yards, to where a tiny colliery was pluming steam and smoke from beyond a marsh-like little creek. The steamer wanted to land. She saw the line of little trucks full and ready. She bellowed like a miserable cow, sloping up and down and turning round on the waters of the bay. Near the jetty the foam broke high on some sheltering rocks. The steamer seemed to watch yearningly, like a dog outside a shut door. A little figure walked along the jetty slowly, unconcernedly. The steamer bellowed again. The figure reached the end of the jetty, and hung out a red flag. Then the steamer shouted no more, but slowly, fearfully turned and slunk up and down the waves back towards Sydney.

The jetty—the forlorn pale-brown grassy bank running out to sea, with the clump of sharp, hard-pointed dark conifers, trees of the Southern Hemisphere, stiff and mechanical; then the foreshore with yellow sand and rollers; then two bungalows and a bit of waste ground full of tins; that was the southern aspect. Northwards, next door, was the big imitation black and white bungalow, with a tuft of wind-blown trees and half-dead hedge between it and the Somers' house. That was north. And the sun was already sloping upwards and northwards. It gave Somers an uneasy feeling, the northward travelling of the climbing sun : as if everything had gone wrong. Inland, lit up dark grey with its plumy trees in the morning light, was the great mountain or tor, with bare, greying rock showing near the top, and above the ridge-top the pure blue sky, so bright and absolutely unsullied, it was always a wonder. There was an unspeakable beauty about the mornings, the great sun from the sea, such a big, untamed, proud sun, rising up into a sky of such tender delicacy, blue, so blue, and yet so frail that even blue seems too coarse a colour to describe it, more virgin than humanity can conceive; the land inward lit up, the prettiness of many painted bungalows with tin roofs clustering up the low up-slopes of the grey-treed bush; and then rising like a wall, facing the light and still lightless, the tor face, with its high-up rim so grey, having tiny trees feathering against the most beautiful frail sky in the world. Morning!

But Somers turned to the house. It stood on one of the regulation lots, probably fifty feet by a hundred and fifty. The bit of level grass in front was only fifty feet wide, and perhaps about the same from the house to the brim of the sea-bank, which dropped bushily down some forty feet to the sand and the flat shore-rocks and the ocean. But this grassy garden was littered with bits of rag, and newspapers, sea-shells, tins and old sponges. And the lot next to it was a marvellous con-stellation of tin cans in every stage of rustiness, if you peeped between the bushes.

"You'll take the ashes and the rubbish too?" said Somers to the sanitary-man who came to take the sanitary tin of the earth-closet every Monday morning.

"No," responded that individual briefly: a true Australian–Cockney answer, impossible to spell. A sort of *neow* sound.

"Does anybody take them?"

"Neow. We take no garbage."

"Then what do I do with them?"

"Do what you like with 'em." And he marched off with the can. It was not rudeness. It was a kind of colonial humour.

After this Somers surveyed the cans and garbage of the next lot, under the bushes and everywhere, with colonial hopeless-ness. But he began at once to pick up rags and cans from his own grass.

The house was very pretty, and beautifully built. But it showed all signs of the eleven children. On the veranda at the side, on either side of the "visitors'" door, was a bed: one a huge family iron bedstead with an indescribably rusty, saggy wire mattress, the other a single iron bedstead with the wire mattress all burst and so mended with a criss-cross of ropes. These beds were screened from the sea-wind by sacks, old pieces of awful carpeting, and pieces of linoleum tacked to the side of the veranda. The same happened on the third side of the house: two more rope-mended iron bedsteads, and a nailed-up lot of unspeakable rags to screen from the wind.

The house had three little bedrooms, one opening from each of the side verandas, and one from the big central room. Each

contained two saggy single beds. That was five people. Remained seven, with the father and mother. Three children
must have gone into the huge bed by the side entrance door,
and the other four must have been sprinkled over the other
three outside, rope-mended beds.

The bungalow contained only the big room with five doors:
one on each side of the fireplace, opening into the inner bedroom and the kitchen respectively, and on each of the other
three sides a door opening on to the veranda. From the kitchen
opened a little pantry and a zinc-floored cubby-hole fitted with
the inevitable Australian douche and a little sink-hole to carry
off the water. This was the bathroom. There it was, all com-
pact and nice, two outer bedrooms on the wings, and for the
central block, the big room in front, the bedroom and kitchen
at the back. The kitchen door opened on to the bit of grass at
the back, near the shed.

It was a well-built little place, amazing in a world of wood
and tin shacks. But Somers would not have liked to live in it
with a thirteen-people family. There were eleven white breakfast-cups, of which nine had smashed handles and broad tin
substitutes quite cannily put on. There were two saucers only.
And all the rest to match: seven large brown teapots, of which
five had broken spouts: not one whole dish or basin of any
sort, except a sauce-boat. And rats! *Torestin* was a clean and
ratless spot compared with *Coo-ee*. For the house was called
Coo-ee, to fetch the rats in, Jack said.

The women flew at the house with hot water and soda. Jack
and Somers spent the morning removing bedsteads into the
shed, tearing down the horrid rag-and-dirt screens, pulling out
the nails with which these screens had been held in place, and
pulling out the hundreds of nails which had nailed down the
dirt-grey, thin carpet as if for ever to the floor of the big room.
Then they banged and battered this thin old patternless carpet,
and washed it with soda and water. And then they banged and
battered the two sofas, that were like sandbags, so full of sand
and dust. And they took down all the ugly, dirt-filmed pictures
of the Dana Gibson sort, and the "My refuge is in God" text.

"I should think so," said Jack. "Away from the muck they'd
made down here."

Like demons the four of them flew at this *Coo-ee* house, and
afternoon saw Jack and Somers polishing floors with a stuff
called glowax, and Harriet and Victoria putting clean papers

on all the shelves, and arranging the battered remnant of well-washed white crockery.

"The crockery is the worst item here," said Victoria. "You pay three-and-six and four shillings for one of these cups and saucers, and four-and-six for a common brown quart jug, and twelve guineas for a white dinner service."

Harriet looked at the horrid breakable stuff aghast.

"I feel like buying a tin mug at once," she said.

But Victoria did not bother. She took it all as it came. The people with the eleven children had paid three and a half guineas a week for seven months for the house.

At three o'clock Victoria's brother, a shy youth of seventeen, arrived in a buggy and drove Jack and Victoria away the four miles to the home of the latter. Somers and Harriet had tea alone.

"But I love and adore the place," said Harriet. "Victoria says we can have it for thirty shillings a week, and if they'd let you off even half of the month for Torestin, we should be saving."

The Callcotts arrived home in the early dark.

"Oh, but doesn't the house smell different," cried Victoria.

"Beeswax and turps," said Jack. "Not a bad smell."

Again the evening passed quietly. Jack had not been his own boisterous self at all. He was silent, and you couldn't get at him. Victoria looked at him curiously, wondering, and tried to draw him out. He laughed and was pleasant enough, but relapsed into silence, as if he were sad, or gloomy.

In the morning sunlight Harriet and Somers were out first, after Somers had made the fire, having a frightened dip in the sandy foam. They kept far back from the great rollers, which, as the two sat in the dribbling backwash, reared up so huge and white and fanged in a front attack, that Harriet always rose and ran, and it was long before she got really wet. And then when they did venture to sit in a foot of water, up came a sudden flush and flung them helpless rolling a dozen yards in, and banged them against the pebbles. It was distinctly surprising. Somers had never known that he weighed so little, that he was such a scrap of unimportance. And he still dared not quite imagine the whole of the blind, invisible force of that water. It was so different being in it, even on the edge of it, from looking at it from the outside.

As they came trembling and panting up the bank to the

grass-plot, dripping and smelling so strong and sticky of the Pacific, they saw Jack standing smoking and watching.

"Are you going to try it?" said Somers.

He shook his head, and lit a cigarette.

"No. It's past my bathing season," he said.

They ran to the little tub-house and washed the sand and salt and sea-stickiness off with fresh water.

Somers wondered whether Jack was going to say anything to him or not. He was not sure. Perhaps Jack himself was not sure. And Somers had that shrinking feeling one has from going to see the doctor. In a quiet sort of way, the two men kept clear of one another. They loitered about in the sun and round the house during the morning, mending the broken deck-chairs and doing little jobs. Victoria and Harriet were cooking roast pork and apple sauce, and baking little cakes. It had already been arranged that the Somers should come and live in Coo-ee, and Victoria was quite happy and determined to leave a supply of nice eatables behind her.

In the afternoon they all went strolling down the sands, Somers and Victoria, Jack and Harriet. They picked up big, iridescent abalone shells, such as people had on their mantel-pieces at home: and bits of purplish coral stuff. And they walked across two fields to have a look at an aeroplane which had come down with a broken propeller. Jack of course had to talk about it to the people there, while Somers hung back and tried to make himself invisible, as he always did when there were strange onlookers.

Then the four turned home. Jack and Victoria were leaving by the seven train next morning, Somers and Harriet were staying on a few days, before they returned to Sydney to pack up. Harriet was longing to have the house to themselves. So was Somers. He was also hoping that Jack wouldn't talk to him, wouldn't want anything of him. And at the same time he was waiting for some sort of approach.

The sea's edge was smoking with the fume of the waves like a mist, and the high shore ahead, with the few painted red-roofed bungalows, was all dim, like a Japanese print. Tier after tier of white-frost foam piled breaking towards the shore, in a haste. The tide was nearly high. Somers could hardly see beyond over the white wall-tops of the breaking waves, only on the clear horizon, far away, a steamer like a small black scratch, and a fantastic thread of smoke.

He lingered behind the rest, they were nearly home. They were at the wide sandy place where the creek left off. Its still, brackish waters just sank into the sands, without ever running to meet the waves. And beyond the sands was a sort of marsh, bushes and tall stark dead gum trees, and a few thin-tufted trees. Half-wild ponies walked heavily from the bush to the sands, and across to the slope where the low cliff rose again. In the depths of the marsh-like level was the low chimney of the mine, and tips of roofs: and beyond, a long range of wire-like trees holding up tufts of foliage in handfuls, in front of the pale blue, diminishing range of the hills in the distance. It was a weird scene, full of definite detail, fascinating detail, yet all in the funeral-grey monotony of the bush.

Somers turned to the piled-up, white-fronted sea again. On the tip of a rock above him sat a little bird with hunched up shoulders and a long beak: an absurd silhouette. He went towards it, talking to it. It seemed to listen to him: really to listen. That is another of the charms of Australia: the birds are not really afraid, and one can really communicate with them. In West Australia Somers could sit in the bush and talk to the flocks of big, handsome, black-and-white birds that they call magpies, but which are a sort of butcher bird, apparently. And they would gurgle little answers in their throats, and cock their heads on one side. Handsome birds they were, some with mottled grey breasts like fish. And the boldest would even come and take pieces of bread from his hands. Yet they were quite wild. Only they seemed to have strange power of understanding the human psyche.

Now this little kingfisher by the sea. It sat and looked at Somers, and cocked its head and listened. It *liked* to be talked to. When he came quite near, it sped with the straight low flight of kingfishers to another boulder, and waited for him. It was beautiful too: with a sheeny sea-green back and a pale breast touched with burnt yellow. A beautiful, dandy little fellow. And there he waited for Somers like a little penguin perching on a brown boulder. And Somers came softly near, talking quietly. Till he could almost touch the bird. Then away it sped a few yards, and waited. Sheeny greyish green, like the gum leaves become vivid: and yellowish breast, like the suave gum tree trunks. And listening, and waiting, and wanting to be talked to. Wanting the contact.

The other three had disappeared from the sea-side. Somers walked slowly on. Then suddenly he saw Jack running across the sand in a bathing-suit, and entering the shallow rim of a long, swift upwash. He went in gingerly—then threw himself into a little swell, and rolled in the water for a minute. Then he was rushing back, before the next big wave broke. He had gone again by the time Somers came to climb the cliff-bank to the house.

They had a cup of tea on the wooden veranda. The air had begun to waft icily from the inland, but in the sheltered place facing the sea it was still warm. This was only four o'clock—or to-day, five o'clock tea. Proper tea was at six or half-past, with meat and pies and fruit salad.

The women went indoors with the cups. Jack was smoking his pipe. There was something unnatural about his stillness.

"You had a dip after all," said Somers.

"Yes. A dip in and out."

Then silence again. Somers' thoughts wandered out to the gently darkening sea, and the bird, and the whole of vast Australia lying behind him flat and open to the sky.

"You like it down here?" said Jack.

"I do indeed."

"Let's go down to the rocks again, I like to be near the waves."

Somers rose and followed him. The house was already lit up. The sea was bluey. They went down the steps cut in the bank-top, and between the bushes to the sand. The tide was full, and swishing against a flat ledge of rocks. Jack went to the edge of this ledge, looking in at the surging water, white, hissing, heavy. Somers followed again. Jack turned his face to him.

"Funny thing it should go on doing this all the time, for no purpose," said Jack, amid all the noise.

"Yes."

Again they watched the heavy waves unfurl and fling the white challenge of foam on the shore.

"I say," Jack turned his face. "I shan't be making a mistake if I tell you a few things in confidence, shall I?"

"I hope not. But judge for yourself."

"Well, it's like this," shouted Jack—they had to shout at one another in unnaturally lifted voices, because of the huge noise of the sea. "There's a good many of us chaps as has been in

France, you know—and been through it all—in the army—we
jolly well know you can't keep a country going on the vote-
catching system—as you said the other day. We know it can't
be done."

"It can't," said Somers, with a shout, "for ever."

"If you've got to command, you don't have to ask your
men first if it's right, before you give the command."

"Of course not," yelled Somers.

But Jack was musing for the moment.

"What?" he shouted, as he woke up.

"No," yelled Somers.

A further muse, amid the roar of the waves.

"Do the men know better than the officers, or do the officers
know better than the men?" he barked.

"Of course," said Somers.

"These damned politicians—they invent a cry—and they
wait to see if the public will take it up. And if it won't
they drop it. And if it will, they make a mountain out of it,
if it's only an old flower-pot."

"They do," yelled Somers.

They stood close side by side, like two mariners in a storm,
amid the breathing spume of the foreshore, while darkness
slowly sank. Right at the tip of the flat, low rocks they stood,
like pilots.

"It's no good," barked Jack, with his hands in his pockets.
"Not a bit."

"If you're an officer, you study what is best, for the cause
and for the men. You study your men. But you don't ask
them what to do. If you do you're a wash-out."

"Quite."

"And that's where it is in politics. You see the papers howling and blubbering for a statesman. Why, if they'd got the
finest statesman the world ever saw, they'd chuck him on to
the scrap-heap the moment he really wanted his own way,
doing what he saw was the best. That's where they've got
anybody who's any good—on the scrap-heap."

"Same the world over."

"It's got to alter somewhere."

"It has."

"When you've been through the army, you know that what
you depend on is a *general*, and on *discipline*, and on *obedience*.
And nothing else is the slightest bit of good."

"But they say the civil world is *not* an army : it's the will of the people," cried Somers.

"Will of my grandmother's old tom-cat. They've got no will, except to stop anybody else from having any."

"I know."

"Look at Australia. Absolutely fermenting rotten with politicians and the will of the people. Look at the country—going rottener every day, like an old pear."

"All the democratic world the same."

"Of course it's the same. And you may well say Australian soil is waiting to be watered with blood. It's waiting to be watered with our blood, once England's got too soft to help herself, let alone us, and the Japs come down this way. They'd squash us like a soft pear."

"I think it's quite likely."

"What?"

"Likely."

"It's pretty well a certainty. And would you blame them? If you was thirsty, wouldn't you pick a ripe pear if it hung on nobody's tree? Why, of course you would. And who'd blame you."

"Blame myself if I didn't," said Somers.

"And then their coloured labour. I tell you, this country's too far from Europe to risk it. They'll swallow us. As sure as guns is guns, if we let in coloured labour, they'll swallow us. They hate us. All the other colours hate the white. And they're only waiting. And then what about poor little Australia?"

"Heaven knows."

"There'll be the Labour Party, the Socialists, uniting with the workers of the world. *They'll* be the workers, if ever it comes to it. Those black and yellow people'll make 'em work —not half. It isn't one side only that can keep slaves. Why, the fools, the coloured races don't have any *feeling* for liberty. They only think you're a fool when you give it to them, and if they got a chance, they'd drive you out to work in gangs, and fairly laugh at you. All this world's-worker business is simply playing their game."

"Of course," said Somers. "What is Indian Nationalism but a strong bid for power—for tyranny. The Brahmins want their old absolute caste-power—the most absolute tyranny—back again, and the Mahommedans want their military tyranny. That's what they are lusting for—to wield the rod again.

Slavery for millions. Japan the same. And China, in part, the same. The niggers the same. The real sense of liberty only goes with white blood. And the ideal of democratic liberty is an exploded ideal. You've got to have wisdom and authority somewhere, and you can't get it out of any further democracy."

"There!" said Jack. "That's what I mean. We s'll be wiped out, wiped out. And we know it. Look here, as man to man, you and me here: if you were an Australian, wouldn't you do something?"

"I would."

"Whether you got shot or whether you didn't! We went to France to get ourselves shot, for something that didn't touch us very close either. Then why shouldn't we run a bit of risk for what does touch us very close. Why, you know, with things as they are, I don't want Victoria and me to have any children. I'd a jolly sight rather not—and I'll watch it too."

"Same with me," yelled Somers.

Jack had come closer to him, and was now holding him by the arm.

"What's a man's life for, anyhow? Is it just to save up like rotten pears on a shelf, in the hopes that one day it'll rot into a pink canary or something of that?"

"No," said Somers.

"What we want in Australia," said Jack, "isn't a statesman, not yet. It's a set of chaps with some guts in them, who'll obey orders when they find a man who'll give the orders."

"Yes."

"And we've got such men—we've got them. But we want to see our way clear. We don't never feel quite *sure* enough over here. That's where it is. We sound as sure as a gas explosion. But it's all bang and no bump. We s'll never raise no lids. We shall only raise the roof—or our politicians will—with shouting. Because we're never quite sure. We know it when we meet you English people. You're a lot surer than we are. But you're mostly bigger fools as well. It takes a fool to be sure of himself, sometimes."

"Fact."

"And there's where it is. Most Englishmen are too big cocked-up fools for us. And there you are. Their sureness may help them along to the end of the road, but they haven't the wit to turn a corner: not a proper corner. And we can see it. They can only go back on themselves."

"Yes."

"You're the only man I've met who seems to me sure of himself and what he means. I may be mistaken, but that's how it seems to me. And William James knows it too. But it's my belief William James doesn't want you to come in, because it would spoil his little game."

"I don't understand."

"I know you don't. Now, look here. This is absolutely between ourselves, now, isn't it?"

"Yes."

"Certain?"

Jack was silent for a time. Then he looked round the almost dark shore. The stars were shining overhead.

"Give me your hand then," said Jack.

Somers gave him his hand, and Jack clasped it fast, drawing the smaller man to him and putting his arm round his shoulders and holding him near to him. It was a tense moment for Richard Lovat. He looked at the dark sea, and thought of his own everlasting gods, and felt the other man's body next to his.

"Well now," he said in Somers' ear, in a soothed tone. "There's quite a number of us in Sydney—and in the other towns as well—we're mostly diggers back from the war—we've joined up into a kind of club—and we're sworn in—and we're sworn to *obey* the leaders, no matter what the command, when the time is ready—and we're sworn to keep silent till then. We don't let out much, nothing of any consequence, to the general run of the members."

Richard listened with his soul. Jack's eager, conspirator voice seemed very close to his ear, and it had a kind of caress, a sort of embrace. Richard was absolutely motionless.

"But who are your leaders?" he asked, thinking of course that it was his own high destiny to be a leader.

"Why, the first club got fifty members to start with. Then we chose a leader and talked things over. And then we chose a secretary and a lieutenant. And every member quietly brought in more chaps. And as soon as we felt we could afford it, we separated, making the next thirty or so into a second club, with the lieutenant for a leader. Then we chose a new lieutenant—and the new club chose a secretary and a lieutenant."

Richard didn't follow all this lieutenant and club business very well. He was thinking of himself entering in with these

men in a dangerous, desperate cause. It seemed unreal. Yet
there he was, with Jack's arm round him. Jack would want
him to be his "mate". Could he? His cobber. Could he ever
be mate to any man?

"You sort of have a lot of leaders. What if one of them let
you down?" he asked.

"None of them have yet. But we've arranged for that."

"How?"

"I'll tell you later. But you get a bit of the hang of the
thing, do you?"

"I think so. But what do you call yourselves? How do you
appear to the public?"

"We call ourselves the diggers clubs, and we go in chiefly
for athletics. And we do spend most of the time in athletics.
But those that aren't diggers can join, if a pal brings them in
and vouches for them."

Richard was now feeling rather out of it. Returned soldiers,
and clubs, and athletics—all unnatural things to him. Was he
going to join in with this? How could he? He was so different
from it all.

"And how do you work—I mean together?" he faltered.

"We have a special lodge of the leaders and lieutenants and
secretaries from all the clubs, and again in every lodge they
choose a master, that's the highest; and then a Jack, he's like a
lieutenant; and a Teller, he's the sort of secretary and president.
We have lodges in all the biggish places. And then all the
masters of the lodges of the five states of Australia keep in
touch, and they choose five masters who are called the Five,
and these five agree among themselves which order shall stand
in: first, second, third, fourth, and fifth. When once they've
chosen the first, then he has two votes towards the placing of
the other four. And so they settle it. And then they grade the
five Jacks and the five Tellers. I tell it you just in rough, you
know."

"Yes. And what are you?"

"I'm a master."

Richard was still trying to see himself in connection with it
all. He tried to piece together all that Jack had been letting
off at him. Returned soldiers' clubs, chiefly athletics, with a
more or lesss secret core to each club, and all the secret cores
working together secretly in all the state under one chief head,
and apparently with military penalties for any transgression.

It was not a bad idea. And the aim, apparently, a sort of revolution and a seizing of political power.

"How long have you been started?" he asked.

"About eighteen months—nearly two years altogether."

Somers was silent, very much impressed, though his heart felt heavy. Why did his heart feel so heavy? Politics—conspiracy—political power: it was all so alien to him. Somehow, in his soul he always meant something quite different, when he thought of action along with other men. Yet Australia, the wonderful, lonely Australia, with her seven million people only —it might begin here. And the Australians, so queer, so abstract, as it were, leaving themselves out all the time—they might be capable of a beautiful unselfish and steadfastness of purpose. Only—his heart refused to respond.

"What is your aim, though? What do you want, finally?" he asked rather lamely.

Jack hesitated, and his grip on the other man's arm tightened.

"Well," he said. "It's like this. We don't talk a lot about what we intend: we fix nothing. But we start certain talks, and we listen, so we know more or less what most of the ordinary members feel like. Why, the plan is more or less this. The Labour people, the reds, are always talking about a revolution, and the Conservatives are always talking about a disaster. Well, we keep ourselves fit and ready for as soon as the revolution comes—or the disaster. Then we step in, you see, and we are the revolution. We've got most of the trained fighting men behind us, and we can *make* the will of the people, don't you see: if the members stand steady. We shall have 'Australia' for the word. We stand for Australia, not for any of your parties."

Somers at once felt the idea was a good one. Australia is not too big—seven millions or so, and the biggest part of the seven concentrated in the five or six cities. Get hold of your cities and you've got hold of Australia. The only thing he mistrusted was the dryness in Jack's voice: a sort of that's-how-it's-got-to be dryness, sharp and authoritative.

"What d'yer think of it?" said Jack.

"Good idea," said Somers.

"I know that—if we can bite on to it. Feel like joining in, d'yer think?"

Somers was silent. He was thinking of Jack even more than of the venture. Jack was trying to put something over him—

in some way, to get a hold over him. He felt like an animal that is being lassoed. Yet here was his chance, if he wanted to be a leader of men. He had only to give himself up to it and to the men.

"Let me think about it a bit, will you?" he replied, "and I'll tell you when I come up to Sydney."

"Right O!" said Jack, a twinge of disappointment in his acquiescence. "Look before you leap, you know."

"Yes—for both sides. You wouldn't want me to jump in, and then squirm because I didn't like it."

"Right you are, old man. You take your own time—I know you won't be wagging your jaw to anybody."

"No. Not even to Harriet."

"Oh, bless you, no. We're not having the women in, if we can help it. Don't believe in it, do you?"

"Not in real politics, I don't."

They stood a moment longer by the sea. Then Jack let go Somers' arm.

"Well," he said, "I'd rather die in a forlorn hope than drag my days out in a forlorn mope. Besides, damn it, I do want to have a shot at something, I do. These politicians absolutely get my wind up, running the country. If I can't do better than that, then let me be shot, and welcome."

"I agree," said Somers.

Jack put his hand on his shoulder, and pressed it hard.

"I knew you would," he said, in moved tones. "We want a man like you, you know—like a sort of queen bee to a hive."

Somers laughed, rather startled, by the metaphor. He had thought of himself as many things, but never as a queen bee to a hive of would-be revolutionaries. The two men went up to the house.

"Wherever have you been?" said Victoria.

"Talking politics and red-hot treason," said Jack, rubbing his hands.

"Till you're almost froze, I'm sure," said Victoria.

Harriet looked at the two men in curiosity and suspicion, but she said nothing. Only next morning when the Callcotts had gone she said to Lovat:

"What were you and Mr. Callcott talking about, really?"

"As he said, politics and hot treason. An idea that some of them have got for making a change in the constitution."

"What sort of change?" asked Harriet.

"Why—don't bother me yet. I don't know myself."

"Is it so important you mustn't tell me?" she asked sarcastically.

"Or else so vague," he answered.

But she saw by the shut look on his face that he was not going to tell her: that this was something he intended to keep apart from her: forever apart. A part of himself which he was not going to share with her. It seemed to her unnecessary, and a breach of faith on his part, wounding her. If their marriage was a real thing, then anything very serious was her matter as much as his, surely. Either her marriage with him was not very important, or else this Jack Callcott stuff wasn't very important. Which probably it wasn't. Yet she hated the hoity-toity way she was shut out.

"Pah!" she said. "A bit of little boy's silly showing off."

But he had this other cold side to his nature, that could keep a secret cold and isolated till Doomsday. And for two or three years now, since the war, he had talked like this about doing some work with men alone, sharing some activity with men. Turning away from the personal life to the hateful male impersonal activity, and shutting her out from this.

She continued bright through the day. Then at evening he found her sitting on her bed with tears in her eyes and her hands in her lap. At once his heart became very troubled: because after all she was all he had in the world, and he couldn't bear her to be really disappointed or wounded. He wanted to ask her what was the matter, and to try to comfort her. But he knew it would be false. He knew that her greatest grief was when he turned away from their personal human life of intimacy to this impersonal business of male activity for which he was always craving. So he felt miserable, but went away without saying anything. Because he was determined, if possible, to go forward in this matter with Jack. He was also determined that it was not a woman's matter. As soon as he could he would tell her about it: as much as it was necessary for her to know. But, once he had slowly and carefully weighed a course of action, he would not hold it subject to Harriet's approval of disapproval. It would be out of her sphere, outside the personal sphere of their two lives, and he would keep it there. She emphatically opposed this principle of her externality. She agreed with the necessity for impersonal activity, but oh, she insisted on being identified with the

D*

activity, impersonal or not. And he insisted that it could not and should not be: that the pure male activity should be womanless, beyond woman. No man was beyond woman. But in his one quality of ultimate maker and breaker, he was womanless. Harriet denied this bitterly. She wanted to share, to join in, not to be left out lonely. He looked at her in distress, and did not answer. It is a knot that can never be untied; it can only, like a navel string, be broken or cut.

For the moment, however, he said nothing. But Somers knew from his dreams what she was feeling: his dreams of a woman, a woman he loved, something like Harriet, something like his mother, and yet unlike her, a woman sullen and obstinate against him, repudiating him. Bitter the woman was grieved beyond words, grieved till her face was swollen and puffy and almost mad or imbecile, because she had loved him so much, and now she must see him betray her love. That was how the dream woman put it: he had betrayed her great love, and she must go down desolate into an everlasting hell, denied, and denying him absolutely in return, a sullen, awful soul. The face reminded him of Harriet, and of his mother, and of his sister, and of girls he had known when he was younger—strange glimpses of all of them, each glimpse excluding the last. And at the same time in the terrible face some of the look of that bloated face of a madwoman which hung over Jane Eyre in the night in Mr. Rochester's house.

The Somers of the dream was terribly upset. He cried tears from his very bowels, and laid his hand on the woman's arm saying:

"But I love you. Don't you *believe* in me? Don't you *believe* in me?" But the woman, she seemed almost old now—only shed a few bitter tears, bitter as vitriol, from her distorted face, and bitterly, hideously turned away, dragging her arm from the touch of his fingers; turned, as it seemed to the dream-Somers, away to the sullen and dreary, everlasting hell of repudiation.

He woke at this, and listened to the thunder of the sea with horror. With horror. Two women in his life he had loved down to the quick of life and death: his mother and Harriet. And the woman in the dream was so awfully his mother, risen from the dead, and at the same time Harriet, as it were, departing from this life, that he stared at the night paleness between the window-curtains in horror.

"They neither of them believed in me," he said to himself. Still in the spell of the dream, he put it in the past tense, though Harriet lay sleeping in the next bed. He could not get over it.

Then he tried to come right awake. In his full consciousness, he was a great enemy of dreams. For his own private life, he found his dreams were like devils. When he was asleep and off his guard, then his own weaknesses, especially his old weaknesses that he had overcome in his full, day-waking self, rose up again maliciously to take some picturesque form and torment and overcome his sleeping self. He always considered dreams as a kind of revenge which old weaknesses took on the victorious healthy consciousness, like past diseases come back for a phantom triumph. So he said to himself: "The dream is one of these larvæ of my past emotions. It means that the danger is passed, the evil is overcome, so it has to resort to dreams to terrify me. In dreams the diseases and evil weaknesses of the soul—and of our relations with other souls—take form to triumph falsely over the living, healthy, onward-struggling spirit. This dream means that the actual danger is gone." So he strengthened his spirit, and in the morning when he got up, and remembered, he was no longer afraid. A little uneasy still, maybe, especially as to what Harriet would do. But surely his mother was not hostile in death! And if she were a little bit hostile at this forsaking, it was not permanent, it was only the remains of a weakness, an unbelief which haunted the soul in life.

So he reasoned with himself. For he had an ingrained instinct or habit of thought which made him feel that he could never take the move into activity unless Harriet and his dead mother believed in him. They both loved him: that he knew. They both believed in him terribly, in personal being. In the individual man he was, and the son of man, they believed with all the intensity of undivided love. But in the impersonal man, the man that would go beyond them, with his back to them, away from them into an activity that excluded them, in this man they did not find it so easy to believe.

Harriet, however, said nothing for two days. She was happy in her new house, delighted with the sea and the being alone, she loved her *Coo-ee* bungalow, and loved making it look nice. She loved having Lovat alone with her, and all her desires, as it were, in the hollow of her hand. She was bright and affectionate with him. But underneath lurked this chagrin of his wanting to go away from her, for his activity.

"You don't take Callcott and his politics seriously, do you?" she said to him at evening.

"Yes," he said, rather hesitatingly.

"But what does he want?"

"To have another sort of government for the Commonwealth —with a sort of Dictator: not the democratic vote-cadging sort."

"But what does that matter to you?"

"It does matter. If you can start a new life-form."

"You know quite well you say yourself life doesn't *start* with a form. It starts with a new feeling, and ends with a form."

"I know. But I think there is a new feeling."

"In Callcott?" She had a very sceptical intonation.

"Yes."

"I very much doubt it. He's a returned war hero, and he wants a chance of keeping on being a hero—or something like that."

"But even that is a new feeling," he persisted.

"Yah!" she said, rather wearily sceptical. "I'd rather even believe in William James. There seems to me more real feeling even in him: deeper, at any rate. Your Jacks are shallow really."

"Nay, he seemed a man to me."

"I don't know what you mean by your *men*. Really, I give it up, I don't know what you do want. You change so. You've always said you despise politics, and yet here you are." She tailed off as if it were hopeless.

"It's not the politics. But it *is* a new life-form, a new social form. We're pot-bound inside democracy and the democratic feeling."

"But you know what you've said yourself. You didn't change the Roman Empire with a revolution. Christianity grew up for centuries without having anything at all to do with politics— just a *feeling*, and a belief."

This was indeed what he had said himself, often enough: that a new religious inspiration, and a new religious idea must gradually spring up and ripen before there could be any constructive change. And yet he felt that preaching and teaching were both no good at the world's present juncture. There must

be action, brave, faithful action : and in the action the new
spirit would arise.

"You see," he said, "Christianity is a religion which preaches
the despising of the material world. And I don't believe in that
part of it, at least, any longer. I believe that the men with the
real passion for life, for truth, for *living* and not for *having*, I
feel they now must seize control of the material possessions,
just to safeguard the world from all the masses who want to
seize material possessions for themselves, blindly, and nothing
else. The men with soul and with passionate truth in them
must control the world's material riches and supplies : absolutely put possessions out of the reach of the mass of mankind,
and let life begin to live again, in place of this struggle for
existence, or struggle for wealth."

"Yah, I don't believe it's so all-important who controls the
world's material riches and supplies. That'll always be the
same."

"It won't."

"It will. Conservatives or bolshevists or Labour Party—
they're all alike : they all want to grab and have things in
their clutches, and they're devilish with jealousy if they haven't
got them. That's politics. You've said thousands of times that
politics are a game for the base people with no human soul in
them. Thousands of times you've said it. And yet now——"

He was silent for a while.

"Now," he said slowly. "Now I see that you don't have only
to give all your possessions to the poor. You've got to *have* no
poor that can be saved just by possessions. You've got to put
the control of all supplies into the hands of sincere, sensible
men who are still men enough to know that manhood isn't the
same thing as goods. We don't want possessions. Nobody
wants possessions—more than just the immediate things : as
you say yourself, one trunk for you, one for me, and one for
the household goods. That's about all. We don't want anything else. And the world is ours—Australia or India, Coo-ee
or Ardnaree, or where you like. You have got to teach people
that, by withholding possessions and stopping the mere frenzy
for possession which runs the world to-day. You've got to do
that *first*, not last."

"And you think Jack Callcott will do it?"

"I did think so, as he talked to me."

"Well, then let him. Why do you want to interfere. In my

opinion he's chiefly jealous because other people run the show, and he doesn't have a look-in. Having once been a Captain with some power, he wants the same again, and more. I'd rather trust William James to be disinterested."

"Nay, Jack Callcott is generous by nature, and I believe he'd be disinterested."

"In his way, he's generous. But that isn't the same as being disinterested, for all that. He wants to have his finger in the pie, that's what he wants."

"To pull out plums? That's not true."

"Perhaps not to pull out money plums. But to be bossy. To be a Captain once more, feeling his feet and being a boss over something."

"Why shouldn't he be?"

"Why not? I don't care if he bosses all Australia and New Zealand and all the lot. But I don't see why you should call it disinterested. Because it isn't."

He paused, struck.

"Am I disinterested?" he asked.

"Not"—she hesitated—"not when you want just *power*."

"But I don't want just power. I only see that somebody must have power, so those should have it who don't want it selfishly, and who have some natural gift for it, and some reverence for the sacredness of it."

"Ha!—power! power! What does it all mean, after all! And especially in people like Jack Callcott. Where does he see any sacredness. He's a sentimentalist, and as you say yourself, nothing is sacred then."

This discussion ended in a draw. Harriet had struck home once or twice, and she knew it. That appeased her for the moment. But he stuck to his essential position, though he was not so sure of the circumstantial standing.

Harriet loved Coo-ee, and was determined to be happy there. She had at last gradually realised that Lovat was no longer lover to her or anybody, or even anything: and amidst the chagrin was a real relief. Because he was her husband, that was undeniable. And if, as her husband, he had to go on to other things, outside of marriage: well, that was his affair. It only angered her when he thought these other things—revolutions or governments or whatnot—higher than their essential marriage. But then he would come to himself and acknowledge that his marriage *was* the centre of his life, the core, the root

however he liked to put it : and this other business was the inevitable excursion into his future, into the unknown, onwards,
which man by his nature was condemned to make, even if he
lost his life a dozen times in it. Well, so be it. Let him make
the excursion : even without her. But she was not, if she could
help it, going to have him setting off on a trip that led nowhere.
No, if he was to excurse ahead, it must be ahead, and her
instinct must be convinced as the needle of a mariner's compass
is convinced. And regarding this Australian business of Callcott's, she had her doubts.

However, she had for the moment a home, where she felt for
the moment as rooted, as central as the tree of life itself. She
wasn't a bit of flotsam, and she wasn't a dog chained to a dog-
kennel. Coo-ee might be absurd—and she knew it was only a
camp. But then where she camped with Lovat Somers was now
the world's centre to her, and that was enough.

She loved to wake in the morning and open the bedroom
door—they had the north bedroom, on the veranda, the room
that had the sun all day long; then she liked to lie luxuriously
in bed and watch the lovely, broken colours of the Australian
dawn : always strange, mixed colours, never the primary reds
and yellows. The sun rose on the north-east—she could hardly
see it. But she watched the first yellow of morning, and then
the strange, strong, smoky red-purple of floating pieces of
cloud : then the rose and mist blue of the horizon, and the
sea all reddish, smoky flesh-colour, moving under a film of gold
like a glaze; then the sea gradually going yellow, going primrose, with the foam breaking blue as forget-me-nots or frost, in
front. And on the near swing of the bluey primrose, sticking
up through the marvellous liquid pale yellow glaze, the black
fins of sharks. The triangular, black fins of sharks, like small,
hard sails of hell-boats, amid the swimming luminousness.
Then she would run out on the veranda. Sharks! Four or five
sharks, skulking in the morning glow, and so near, she could
almost have thrown bread to them. Sharks, slinking along
quite near the coast, as if they were walking on the land. She
saw one caught in the heave of a breaker, and lifted. And then
she saw him start, saw the quick flurry of his tail as he flung
himself back. The land to him was horror—as to her the sea,
beyond that wall of ice-blue foam. She made Lovat come to
look. He watched them slowly, holding the brush in his hand.
He had made the fire, and was sweeping the hearth. Coffee was

ready by the time Harriet was dressed: and he was crouching making toast. They had breakfast together on the front veranda, facing the sea, eastwards. And the sun slanted warm, though it was mid-winter, and the much-washed red-and-white table-cloth that had been in so many lands with them and that they used outdoors, looked almost too strongly coloured in the tender seeming atmosphere. The coffee had a lot of chicory in it, but the butter and milk were good, and the brownish honey, that also, like the landscape, tasted queer, as if touched with unkindled smoke. It seemed to Somers as if the people of Australia *ought* to be dusky. Think of Sicilian honey—like the sound of birds singing: and now this with a dusky undertone to it. But good too—so good!

CHAPTER VI

KANGAROO

THEY went back to Sydney on the Thursday, for two days, to pack up and return to Coo-ee. All the time, they could hear the sea. It seemed strange that they felt the sea so far away, in Sydney. In Sydney itself, there is no sea. It might be Birmingham. Even in Mullimbimby, a queer raw little place, when Somers lifted his head and looked down Main Street and saw, a mile away, the high level of the solid sea, it was almost a shock to him. Half a mile inland, the influence of the sea has disappeared, and the land-sense is so heavy, buried, that it is hard to believe that the dull rumble in the air is the ocean. It sounds like a coal-mine or something.

"You'll let Mr. Somers and me have a little chat to ourselves, Mrs. Somers, won't you?" said Jack, appearing after tea.

"Willingly. I assure you *I* don't want to be bothered with your important affairs," said Harriet. None the less, she went over rather resentfully to Victoria, turned out of her own house. It wasn't that she wanted to listen. She would really have hated to attend to all their high-and-mighty revolution stuff. She didn't believe in revolutions—they were *vieux jeu,* out of date.

"Well," said Jack, settling down in a wooden arm-chair and starting his pipe. "You've thought it over, have you?"

"Over and over," laughed Somers.

"I knew you would."

He sucked his pipe and thought for a time.

"I've had a long talk with Kangaroo about you to-day," he said.

"Who's Kangaroo?"

"He's the First," replied Jack slowly. And again there was silence. Somers kept himself well in hand, and said nothing.

"A lawyer—well up—I knew him in the army, though. He was one of my lieutenants."

Still Somers waited, without speaking.

"He'd like to see you. Should you care to have lunch with him and me in town to-morrow?"

"Have you told him you've talked to me?"

"Oh yes—told him before I did it. He knows your writings—read all you've written, apparently. He'd heard about you too from a chap on the *Naldera*. That's the boat you came by, isn't it?"

"Yes," said Somers.

"Yes," echoed Jack. "He was all over me when I mentioned your name. You'd like Kangaroo. He's a great chap."

"What's his name?"

"Cooley—Ben—Benjamin Cooley."

"They like him on the *Bulletin*, don't they? Didn't I see something about Ben Cooley and his straight talk?"

"Yes. Oh, he can talk straight enough—and crooked enough as well, if it comes to that. You'll come to lunch then? We lunch in his chambers."

Somers agreed. Jack was silent, as if he had not much more to say. After a while he added reflectively:

"Yes, I'm glad to have brought you and Kangaroo together."

"Why do they call him Kangaroo?"

"Looks like one."

Again there was silence, each man thinking his own thoughts.

"You and Kangaroo will catch on like wax, as far as ideas go," Jack prognosticated. "But he's an unfeeling beggar, really. And that's where you *won't* cotton on to him. That's where *I* come in."

He looked at Somers with a faint smile.

"Come in to what?" laughed Somers.

Jack took his pipe from his mouth with a little flourish.

"In a job like this," he said, "a man wants a mate—yes, a mate—that he can say *anything* to, and be absolutely himself

with. Must have it. And as far as I go—for me—you don't
mind if I say it, do you?—Kangaroo could never have a mate.
He's as odd as any phœnix bird I've ever heard tell of. You
couldn't mate him to anything in the heavens above or in the
earth beneath or in the waters under the earth. No, there's no
female kangaroo of his species. Fine chap, for all that. But as
lonely as a nail in a post."

"Sounds something fatal and fixed," laughed Somers.

"It does. And he *is* fatal and fixed. Those eyeglasses of his,
you know—they alone make a man into a sort of eye of God,
rather glassy. But my idea is, in a job like this, every man
should have a mate—like most of us had in the war. Mine
was Victoria's brother—and still is, in a way. But he got
some sort of a sickness that seems to have taken all the fight
out of him. Fooling about with the wrong sort of women.
Can't get his pecker up again now, the fool. Poor devil an' all."

Jack sighed and resumed his pipe.

"Men fight better when they've got a mate. They'll stand
anything when they've got a mate," he went on again after a
while. "But a mate's not all that easy to strike. We're a lot
of decent chaps, stick at nothing once they wanted to put a
thing through, in our lodge—and in my club. But there's not
one of them I feel's quite up to me—if you know what I mean.
Rattling good fellows—but nary one of 'em quite my cut."

"That's usually so," laughed Somers.

"It is," said Jack. Then he narrowed and diminished his
voice. "Now I feel," he said cautiously and intensely, "that if
you and me was mates, we could put any damn mortal thing
through, if we had to knock the bottom out of the blanky show
to do it."

Somers dropped his head. He liked the man. But what about
the cause? What about the mistrust and reluctancy he felt?
And at the same time, the thrill of desire. What was offered?
He wanted so much. To be mates with Jack in this cause. Life
and death mates. And yet he felt he couldn't. Not quite. Something stopped him.

He looked up at Callcott. The other man's face was alert
and waiting: curiously naked a face too. Somers wished it had
had even a moustache, anything rather than this clean, all-
clean bare flesh. If Jack had only had a beard too—like a man
—and not one of these clean-shaven, too-much exposed faces.
Alert, waiting face—almost lurking, waiting for an answer.

"Could we ever be *quite* mates?" Somers asked gently.

Jack's dark eyes watched the other man fixedly. Jack himself wasn't unlike a kangaroo, thought Somers: a long-faced, smooth-faced, strangely watchful kangaroo with powerful hindquarters.

"Perhaps not as me and Fred Wilmot was. In a way you're higher up than I am. But that's what I like, you know—a mate that's better than I am, a mate who I *feel* is better than I am. That's what I feel about you: and that's what makes me feel, if we was mates, I'd stick to you through hell fire and back, and we'd clear some land between us. I *know* if you and me was mates, we could put any blooming thing through. There'd be nothing to stop us."

"Not even Kangaroo?"

"Oh, he'd be our way, and we'd be his. He's a sensible chap."

Somers was tempted to give Jack his hand there and then, and pledge himself to a friendship, or a comradeship, that nothing should ever alter. He wanted to do it. Yet something withheld him as if an invisible hand were upon him, preventing him.

"I'm not sure that I'm a mating man, either," he said slowly.

"You?" Jack eyed him. "You are and you aren't. If you'd once come over—why, man, do you think I wouldn't lay my life down for you!"

Somers went pale. He didn't want anybody laying down their lives for him. "Greater love than this——" But he didn't want this great love. He didn't *believe* in it: in that way of love.

"Let's leave it, Jack," he replied, laughing slowly and rising, giving his hand to the other man. "Don't let us make any pledges yet. We're friends, whatever else we are. As for being mates—wait till I feel sure. Wait till I've seen Kangaroo. Wait till I see my way clear. I feel I'm only six strides down the way yet, and you ask me to be at the end."

"At the start you mean," said Jack, gripping the other man's hand, and rising too. "But take your time, old man." He laid his hand on Somers' shoulder. "If you're slow and backward like a woman, it's because it's your nature. Not like me, I go at it in jumps like a kangaroo. I feel I could jump clean through the blooming tent canvas sometimes." As he spoke he was pale and tense with emotion, and his eyes were like black holes, almost wounds in the pallor of his face.

Somers was in a dilemma. Did he want to mix and make with this man? One part of him perhaps did. But not a very big part, since for his life he could not help resenting it when Jack put his hand on his shoulder, or called him "old man". It wasn't the commonness either. Jack's "common" speech and manner was largely assumed—part of the colonial bluff. He could be accurate enough if he chose—as Somers knew already, and would soon know more emphatically. No, it was not the commonness, the vulgar touch in the approach. Jack was sensitive enough, really. And the quiet, well-bred appeal of upper-class young Englishmen, who have the same yearning for intimate comradeship, combined with a sensitive delicacy really finer than a woman's, this made Somers shrink just the same. He half wanted to commit himself to this whole affection with a friend, a comrade, a mate. And then, in the last issue, he didn't want it at all. The affection would be deep and genuine enough: that he knew. But—when it came to the point, he didn't want any more affection. All his life he had cherished a beloved ideal of friendship—David and Jonathan. And now, when true and good friends offered, he found he simply could not commit himself, even to simple friendship. The whole trend of this affection, this mingling, this intimacy, this truly beautiful love, he found his soul just set against it. He couldn't go along with it. He didn't want a friend, he didn't want loving affection, he didn't want comradeship. No, his soul trembled when he tried to drive it along the way, trembled and stood still, like Balaam's Ass. It did not want friendship or comradeship, great or small, deep or shallow.

It took Lovat Somers some time before he would really admit and accept this new fact. Not till he had striven hard with his soul did he come to see the angel in the way; not till his soul, like Balaam's Ass, had spoken more than once. And then, when forced to admit, it was a revolution in his mind. He had all his life had this craving for an absolute friend, a David to his Jonathan, Pylades to his Orestes: a blood-brother. All his life he had secretly grieved over his friendlessness. And now at last, when it really offered—and it had offered twice before, since he had left Europe—he didn't want it, and he realised that in his innermost soul he had never wanted it.

Yet he wanted *some* living fellowship with other men; as it

was he was just isolated. Maybe a living fellowship!—but not
affection, not love, not comradeship. Not mates and equality
and mingling. Not blood-brotherhood. None of that.

What else? He didn't know. He only knew he was never
destined to be mate or comrade or even friend with any man.
Some other living relationship. But what? He did not know.
Perhaps the thing that the dark races know: that one can still
feel in India: the mystery of lordship. That which white men
have struggled so long against, and which is the clue to the
life of the Hindu. The mystery of lordship. The mystery of
innate, natural, sacred priority. The other mystic relationship
between men, which democracy and equality try to deny and
obliterate. Not any arbitrary caste or birth aristocracy. But
the mystic recognition of difference and innate priority, the
joy of obedience and the sacred responsibility of authority.

Before Somers went down to George Street to find Jack and
to be taken by him to luncheon with the Kangaroo, he had
come to the decision, or to the knowledge that mating or comradeship were contrary to his destiny. He would never pledge
himself to Jack, nor to this venture in which Jack was concerned.

They arrived at Mr. Cooley's chambers punctually. It was a
handsome apartment with handsome jarrah furniture, dark and
suave, and some very beautiful rugs. Mr. Cooley came at
once: and he *was* a kangaroo. His face was long and lean
and pendulous, with eyes set close together behind his pince-
nez: and his body was stout but firm. He was a man of forty
or so, hard to tell, swarthy, with short-cropped dark hair and
a smallish head carried rather forward on his large but sensitive, almost shy body. He leaned forward in his walk, and
seemed as if his hands didn't quite belong to him. But he shook
hands with a firm grip. He was really tall, but his way of dropping his head, and his sloping shoulders, took away from his
height. He seemed not much taller than Somers, towards
whom he seemed to lean the sensitive tip of his long nose,
hanging over him as he scrutinised him sharply through his eyeglasses, and approaching him with the front of his stomach.

"Very glad to see you," he said, in a voice half Australian,
half official.

The luncheon was almost impressive: a round table with a
huge bunch of violets in a queer old copper bowl, Queen Anne
silver, a table-cloth with heavy point edging, Venetian wine-

glasses, red and white wine in Venetian wine-jugs, a China-man waiting at table, offering first a silver dish of hors d'œuvres and a handsome crayfish with mayonnaise.

"Why," said Somers equivocally, "I might be anywhere."

Kangaroo looked at him sharply. Somers noticed that when he sat down, his thighs in his dark grey, striped trousers were very thick, making his shoulders seem almost slender; but though his stomach was stout, it was firm.

"Then I hope you feel at home," said Kangaroo. "Because I am sure you are at home anywhere." And he helped himself to olives, putting one in his queer, pursed, thick-lipped mouth.

"For which reason I'm never at home, presumably."

"That may easily be the case. Will you take red or white wine?"

"White," said Somers, oblivious of the poised Chinaman.

"You have come to a homely country," said the Kangaroo, without the ghost of a smile.

"Certainly to a very hospitable one."

"We rarely lock our doors," said Kangaroo.

"Or anything else," said Jack. "Though of course we may slay you in the scullery if you say a word against us."

"I'm not going to be so indiscreet," said Somers.

"Leave the indiscretion to us. We believe in it. Indiscretion is the better part of valour. You agree, Kangaroo?" said Jack, smiling over his plate directly at his host.

"I don't think I'd care to see you turn discreet, boy," returned the other. "Though your quotation isn't new."

"Even a crystal-gazer can't gaze to the bottom of a deep well, eh? Never mind, I'm as shallow as a pie-dish, and proud of it. Red, please." This to the Chink.

"That's why it's so nice knowing you," said Kangaroo.

"And you, of course, are a glass finger-bowl with a violet floating on it, you're so transparent," said Jack.

"I think that describes me beautifully. Mr. Somers, help yourself to wine, that's the most comfortable. I hope you are going to write something for us. Australia is waiting for her Homer—or her Theocritus."

"Or even her Ally Sloper," said Jack, "if I may be permitted to be so old-fashioned."

"If I were but blind," said Somers, "I might have a shot at Australian Homerics."

"His eyes hurt him still, with looking at Sydney," said Jack.

"There certainly is enough of it to look at," said Kangaroo.

"In acreage," said Jack.

"Pity it spreads over so much ground," said Somers.

"Oh, every man his little lot, and an extended tram service."

"In Rome," said Somers, "they piled up huge houses, vast, and stowed them away like grubs in a honeycomb."

"Who did the stowing?" asked Jack sarcastically.

"We don't like to have anybody overhead here," said Kangaroo. "We don't even care to go upstairs, because we are then one storey higher than our true, ground-floor selves."

"Prop us up on a dozen stumps, and we're cosy," said Jack. "Just a little above the earth level, and no higher, you know. Australians in their heart of hearts hate anything but a bungalow. They feel it's rock bottom, don't you see. None of your stair-climbing shams and upstairs importance."

"Good honest fellows," said Kangaroo, and it was impossible to know if he were joking or not.

"Till it comes to business," said Jack.

Kangaroo then started a discussion of tne much-mooted and at the moment fashionable Theory of Relativity.

"Of course it's popular," said Jack. "It absolutely takes the wind out of anybody's sails who wants to say 'I'm *It*.' Even the Lord Almighty is only relatively so and as it were."

"How nice for us all," laughed Somers. "It needed a Jew to lead us this last step in liberty."

"Now we're all little *Its*, chirping like so many molecules one with another," said Jack, eyeing the roast duck with a shrewd gaze.

The luncheon passed frivolously. Somers was bored, but he had a shrewd suspicion that the other two men really enjoyed it. They sauntered into the study for coffee. It was a smallish room, with big, deep leather chairs of a delicate brown colour, and a thick, bluey Oriental carpet. The walls even had an upper panelling of old embossed cordovan leather, a bluish colouring with gilt, old and tarnished away. It was evident that law pays, even in a new country.

Everybody waited for everybody to speak. Somers, of course, knew it was not his business to begin.

"The indiscreet Callcott told you about our Kangaroo clubs," said the host, smiling faintly. Somers thought that surely he had Jewish blood in him. He stirred his little gold coffee-cup slowly.

"He gave me a very sketchy outline."

"It interested you?"

"Exceedingly."

"I read your series of articles on Democracy," said Kangaroo. "In fact they helped me to this attempt now."

"I thought not a soul read them," said Somers, "in that absurd international paper published at The Hague, that they said was run absolutely by spies and shady people."

"It may have been. But I was a subscriber, and I read your essays here in Sydney. There was another man, too, writing on a new aristocracy. But it seemed to me there was too much fraternising in his scheme, too much reverence for the upper classes and passionate pity for the working classes. He wanted them all to be kind to one another, aristocrats of the spirit." Kangaroo smiled slowly. And when he smiled like that, there came an exceedingly sweet charm into his face, for a moment his face was like a flower. Yet he was quite ugly. And surely, thought Somers, it is Jewish blood. The very best that is in the Jewish blood: a faculty for pure disinterestedness, and warm, physically warm love, that seems to make the corpuscles of the blood glow. And after the smile his face went stupid and kangaroo-like, pendulous, with the eyes close together above the long, drooping nose. But the shape of the head was very beautiful, small, light, and fine. The man had surely Jewish blood. And he was almost purely *kind*, essential kindliness, embodied in an ancient, unscrupulous shrewdness. He was so shrewd, so clever. And with a rogue or a mean man, absolutely unscrupulous. But for any human being who showed himself sincere and vulnerable, his heart was pure in kindness. An extraordinary man. This pure kindliness had something Jehovah-like in it. And in every difficulty and every stress, he would remember it, his kindly love for real, vulnerable human beings. It had given his soul an absolute direction, whatever he said about relativity. Yet once he felt any man or woman was cold, mean, barren of this warmth which was in him, then he became at once utterly unscrupulous in defeating the creature. He was not angry or indignant. He was more like a real Jehovah. He had only to turn on all the levers and forces of his clever, almost fiendishly subtle will, and he could triumph. And he knew it. Somers had once had a Jewish friend with this wonderful, Jehovah-like kindliness, but also, without the shrewd fiendish subtlety of will. But it helped him to understand Cooley.

"Yes—I think the man sent me his book," said Somers. "I forget his name. I only remember there was a feverish adulation of Lord Something-or-other, and a terrible *cri du cœur* about the mother of the people, the poor elderly woman in a battered black bonnet and a shawl, going out with sixpence ha'penny to buy a shilling's-worth of necessaries for the home."

"Just so," said Kangaroo, smiling again. "No doubt her husband drank. If he did, who can wonder."

"The very sight of her makes one want to shove her out of the house—or out of the world, for that matter," said Somers.

"Nay," said Jack. "She's enjoying her misery, dear old soul. Don't envy her her bits of pleasures."

"Not envy," laughed Somers. "But I begrudge them her."

"What would you do with her?" asked Kangaroo.

"I wouldn't do anything. She mostly creeps in the East End, where one needn't bother about her. And she's as much at home there as an opossum is in the bush. So don't bother me about her."

"Just so," smiled Kangaroo. "I'd like to provide public kitchens where the children can get properly fed—and make the husband do a certain amount of state labour to pay for it. And for the rest, leave them to go their own way."

"But their minds, their souls, their spirits?" said Somers.

"They must more or less look after themselves. I want to keep *order*. I want to remove physical misery as far as possible. That I am sure of. And that you can only do by exerting strong, just *power* from above. There I agree with you."

"You don't believe in education?"

"Not much. That is to say, in ninety per cent of the people it is useless. But I do want those ninety per cent none the less to have full substantial lives: as even slaves have had under certain masters, and as our people hardly have at all. That again, I think, is one of your ideas."

"It is," said Somers. But his heart sank. "You want a kind of benevolent tyranny, then?"

"Not exactly. You see my tyrant would be so much circumscribed by the constitution I would establish. But in a sense, he would be a tyrant. Perhaps it would be nearer to say he would be a patriarch, or a pope: representing as near as possible the wise, subtle spirit of life. I should try to establish my state of Australia as a kind of Church, with the profound reverence for life, for life's deepest urges, as the motive power. Dostoevsky suggests this: and I believe it can be done."

"Perhaps it might be done here," blurted Somers. "Every continent has its own way, and its own needs."

"I agree," said Kangaroo. "I have the greatest admiration for the Roman Catholic Church, as an institution. But the creed and the theology are not natural to me, quite. Not quite. I think we need something more flexible, and a power less formal and dogmatic; more generous, shall I say. A *generous* power, that sees all the issue here, not in the after-life, and that does not concern itself with sin and repentance and redemption. I should try to teach my people what it is truly to be a *man*, and a woman. The salvation of souls seems too speculative a job. I think if a man is truly a man, true to his own being, his soul saves itself in that way. But no two people can save their souls alive, in the same way. As far as possible, we must leave it to them. *Fata volentem ducunt, nolentem trahunt.*"

"I believe that too."

"Yet there must be law, and there must be authority. But law more human, and authority much wiser. If a man loves life, and feels the sacredness and the mystery of life, then he knows that life is full of strange and subtle and even conflicting imperatives. And a wise man learns to recognise the imperatives as they arise—or nearly so—and to obey. But most men bruise themselves to death trying to fight and overcome their own new, life-born needs, life's ever-strange new imperatives. The secret of all life is in obedience: obedience to the urge that arises in the soul, the urge that is life itself, urging us on to new gestures, new embraces, new emotions, new combinations, new creations. It is a subtle and conflicting urge away from the thing we are. And there lies the pain. Because man builds himself in to his old house of life, builds his own blood into the roads he lays down, and to break from the old way, and to change his house of life, is almost like tearing him to pieces: a sacrilege. Life is cruel—and above all things man needs to be reassured and suggested into his new issues. And he needs to be relieved from this terrible responsibility of governing himself when he doesn't know what he wants, and has no aim towards which to govern himself. Man again needs a father—

not a friend or a brother sufferer, a suffering Saviour. Man needs a quiet, gentle father who uses his authority in the name of living life, and who is absolutely stern against anti-life. I offer no creed. I offer myself, my heart of wisdom, strange warm cavern where the voice of the oracle steams in from the unknown; I offer my consciousness, which hears the voice; and I offer my mind and my will, for the battle against every obstacle to respond to the voice of life, and to shelter mankind from the madness and the evil of anti-life."

"You believe in evil?"

"Ah, yes. Evil is the great principle that opposes life in its new urges. The principle of permanency, everlastingness is, in my opinion, the root of evil. The Ten Commandments which Moses heard were the very voice of life. But the tablets of stone he engraved them on are millstones round our necks. Commandments should fade as flowers do. They are no more divine than flowers are. But our divine flowers—look at those hibiscus—they don't want to immortalise themselves into stone. If they turned into stone on my table, my heart would almost stop beating, and lose its hope and its joy. But they won't. They will quietly, gently wither. And I love them for it. And so should all creeds, all gods, quietly and gently curl up and wither as their evening approaches. That is the only way of true holiness, in my opinion."

The man had a beautiful voice, when he was really talking. It was like a flute, a wood instrument. And his face, with that odd look of a sheep or a kangaroo, took on an extraordinary beauty of its own, a glow as if it were suffused with light. And the eyes shone with a queer, holy light, behind the eyeglasses. And yet it was still the kangaroo face.

Somers watched the face, and dropped his head. He sat feeling rebuked. He was so impatient and outrageous himself. And the steady loveliness of this man's warm, wise heart was too much for him. He was abashed before it.

"Ah, yes," Kangaroo re-echoed. "There is a principle of evil The principle of resistance. Malignant resistance to the life principle. And it uses the very life-force itself against life, and sometimes seems as if it were absolutely winning. Not only Jesus rose from the dead. Judas rose as well, and propagated himself on the face of the earth. He has many children now. The life opposers. The life-resisters. The life-enemies. But we will see who wins. We will see. In the name of life, and the love of life, a man is almost invincible. I have found it so."

"I believe it also," said Somers.

They were silent, and Kangaroo sat there with the rapt look on his face: a pondering, eternal look, like the eternity of the lamb of God grown into a sheep. This rather wicked idea came into Somers' mind: the lamb of God grown into a sheep. So the man sat there, with his wide-eyed, rapt face sunk forward to his breast, very beautiful, and as eternal as if it were a dream: so absolute.

A wonderful thing for a sculptor. For Kangaroo was really ugly: his pendulous Jewish face, his forward shoulders, his round stomach in its expensively tailored waistcoat and dark grey, striped trousers, his very big thighs. And yet even his body had become beautiful, to Somers—one might love it intensely, every one of its contours, its roundnesses and down-ward-drooping heaviness. Almost grotesque, like a Chinese Buddha. And yet not as grotesque. Beautiful, beautiful as some half-tropical, bulging flower from a tree.

Then Kangaroo looked with a teasing little smile at Somers.

"But you have your *own* idea of power, haven't you?" he said, getting up suddenly, with quick power in his bulk, and gripping the other man's shoulder.

"I thought I had," said Somers.

"Oh, you have, you have." There was a calm, easy tone in the voice, slightly fat, very agreeable. Somers thrilled to it as he had never thrilled.

"Why, the man is like a god, I love him," he said to his astonished self. And Kangaroo was hanging forward his face and smiling heavily and ambiguously to himself, knowing that Somers was with him.

> " 'Tiger, tiger, burning bright
>   In the forests of the night' "

he quoted in a queer, sonorous voice, like a priest. "The lion of your might would be a tiger, wouldn't it? The tiger and the unicorn were fighting for the crown. How about me for a unicorn?—if I tied a bayonet on my nose?" He rubbed his nose with a heavy playfulness.

"Is the tiger your principle of evil?"

"The tiger? Oh dear, no. The jackal, the hyena, and dear deadly humanity. No, no. The tiger stands on one side the shield, and the unicorn on the other, and they don't fight for the crown at all. They keep it up between them. The pillars of the world! The tiger and the kangaroo!" he boomed this out in a mock heroic voice, strutting with heavy playfulness. Then he laughed, looking winsomely at Somers. Heaven, what a beauty he had!

"Tiger, tiger, burning bright," he resumed, sing-song, abstract. "I knew you'd come. Ever since I heard your first book of poems—how many years is it ago?—ten?—eleven? I knew you'd come.

> 'Your hands are five-branded flames—
> *Noli me tangere*.'

Of course you had to come."

"Well, here I am, anyhow," said Somers.

"You are. You *are*!" shouted the other, and Somers was quite scared. Then Kangaroo laughed again. "Get up," he said. "Stand up and let me look at you."

The two men stood facing one another : Kangaroo large with his full stomach and his face hulking down, and his queer, glaring eyes; Somers slight and aloof-looking. Cooley eyed him up and down.

"A little bit of a fellow—too delicate for rough me," he said, then started quoting again :

> " 'Your hands are five-branded flames—
> *Noli me tangere*.'

I've got fat and bulky on all the poetry I never wrote. How do you do, Mr. Somers? How do you like Australia, and its national animal, the kangaroo?" Again he smiled with the sudden glow of warmth in his dark eyes, startling and wonderful.

"Australia is a weird country, and its national animal is beyond me," Somers said, smiling rather palely.

"Oh no, it isn't. You'll be patting it on the back as soon as you've taken your hands out of your pockets."

He stood silent a long while, with his feet apart, looking abstractedly at Somers through his *pince nez*.

"Ah, well," he sighed at last. "We shall see. We shall see. But I'm very glad you came. You understand what I mean, I know, when I say we are birds of the same feather. Aren't we?"

"In some ways I think we are."

"Yes. In the feathery line. When shall I see you again?"

"We are going back to the South Coast on Saturday."

"Then let me see you to-morrow. Let me call for you at your house—and bring you back into town for dinner in the evening. May I do that?"

"Thank you," said Somers.

"What does 'thank you' mean? *Danke!* No, thank you."

"Yes, thank you," said Somers.

"Don't thank *me*, man," suddenly shouted the other. "I'm the one to do the thanking."

Somers felt simple startled amazement at these sudden shouts —loud shouts, that you might almost hear in the street.

At last Jack and Somers left. Jack had felt it his business to keep quiet: he knew his chief. But now he opened his mouth.

"What do you think of Kangaroo?" he asked.

"I'm beyond thinking," said Somers.

"I know, that's how he leaves you when he makes a set at you. But he's a rattling fine sort, he is. He puts a heart into you when your chest's as hollow as an old mustard tin. He's a wonder, is Kangaroo: and he keeps on being a wonder."

"Yes, he's certainly a wonder."

"My, the brain the man has! I say, though, talking about tigers and kangaroos reminded me of a thing I once saw. It was up in the North. I was going along when I heard snarls out of some long buffalo grass that made my hair stand on end. I had to see what it was, though, so into the grass goes I. And there I saw a full-grown male kangaroo backed up against a tree, with the flesh of one leg torn clean from the bone. He was gasping, but he was still fighting. And the other was a great big cat, we call 'em tiger-cats, as big as a smallish leopard, a beauty—grey and black stripes, and straighter than a leopard. And before you could breathe, a streak of black and grey shot at that 'roo's throat, seemed to twist in mid air—and the 'roo slipped down to the ground with his entrails ripped right out. I was so dumbfounded I took a step in the grass, and the great hulking cat stopped and lifted his face from his warm food that he'd started on without ever looking up. He stood over that 'roo for ten seconds staring me in the eyes. Then the skin wrinkled back from his snout, and the fangs were so white and clean as death itself, and a low growl came out of his ugly throat. 'Come on, you swine,' it said as plain as words. I didn't you bet. I backed out of that beastly grass.

"The next one I saw was a dead one. And beside him lay the boss' best staghound, that had been trained to tackling wild boars since he was a pup: dead as well. The cat had come fossicking round our camp on the Madden River.

"My gad, though, but the size of the brute, and muscle like you couldn't find in any other beast. I looked at the claws on the pads. They're as sharp as a lancet, and they'd tear the guts out of a man before he could squeak. It was good-bye 'roo, that time.

"They put that yarn in the *Bulletin*. And some chap wrote and said it was a stiff 'un, and the wild cat must be descended from escaped tame cats, because this country has no pussy aboriginal of any sort. Couldn't say myself, except I saw that tiger-cat, and it didn't look much like the son of a homely tissey, either. Wonder what put the thing in my head. Perhaps Kangaroo's fat belly."

"He's not so very fat," said Somers.

"No, he's not got what you'd call a corporation and a whole urban council in front of him. Neither is he flat just there like you and me."

Kangaroo arrived the next day at Torestin with a large bunch of violets in his hand: pale, expensive, late winter violets. He took off his hat to Harriet and bowed quite deep, without shaking hands. He had been a student at Munich.

"Oh, how do you do!" cried Harriet. "Please don't look at the horrid room, we leave in the morning."

Kangaroo looked vacantly around. He was not interested, so he saw nothing: he might as well have been blind.

"It's a very nice room," he said. "May I give you the violets? The poet said you liked having them about."

She took them in her two hands, smelling their very faint fragrance.

"They're not like English violets—or those big dark fellows in Italy," he said. "But still we persuade ourselves that they are violets."

"They're lovely. I feel I could warm my hands over them," she said.

"And now they're quite happy violets," he replied, smiling his rare, sweet smile at her. "Why are you taking the poet away from Sydney?"

"Lovat? He wants to go."

"Lovat! What a good name to call him by!" He turned to Somers, looking at him closely. "May I call you Lovat?"

"Better that than *the poet*," said Somers, lifting his nose slightly with aversion.

The other man laughed, but softly and happily.

"His muse he's not in love with," he murmured to himself.

"No, he prefers his own name," said Somers.

"But supposing now," said Kangaroo, as if alert and interested, "your name was Cooley: Benjamin Cooley—Ben for short. You'd prefer even Kangaroo to that."

"In Australia the kangaroo is the king of beasts," said Somers.

> "*The kangaroo is the king of beasts,*
> *Inviting the other ones out to feasts,*"

sang the big man, continuing: "Won't you both come to dinner with the king of beasts? Won't you come too, Mrs. Somers?"

"You know you only want Lovat, to talk your *man's* stuff."

"I'm not a man, I'm a kangaroo. Besides, yesterday I hadn't seen you. If I had known, my dear Somers, that your wife, who is at this moment in her room hastily changing her dress, was such a beautiful person—I don't say woman merely—I'd have invited you for her sake, and not for your own."

"Then *I* wouldn't have come," said Somers.

"Hear them, what a haughty pair of individuals! I suppose you expect the king of beasts to go on his kness to you, like the rest of democratic kings to their constituents. Won't you get ready, Mrs. Somers?"

"You are quite sure you want me to come?" said Harriet suspiciously.

"Why, if you won't come, I shall ask Lovat—dear Lovat, by the happiest fluke in the world not Lovelace—to let me stay here to tea, dinner, or supper—that is, to the next meal, whatever name it may bear."

At this Harriet disappeared to put on a proper dress.

"We will go as soon as you are ready," called Kangaroo. "We can all squeeze into that automobile at your gate."

When Harriet reappeared the men rose. Kangaroo looked a her with admiration.

"What a remarkably beautiful person you are," he said. "Bu

mind, I don't say *woman*. *Dio liberi!*" he scuttled hurriedly to
the door.

They had a gay dinner. Kangaroo wasn't really witty. But
he had such an innocent charm, an extraordinary winsomeness, that it was much more delicious than wit. His presence
was so warm. You felt you were cuddled cosily, like a child,
on his breast, in the soft glow of his heart and that your feet
were nestling on his ample, beautiful "tummy".

"I wonder you were never married," said Harriet to him.

"I've been married several times," he replied.

"Really!" she cried.

"First to Benny Cooley—then to immortal verse—after that
to the law—once to a haughty lady—and now I'm wedded to
my ideals. This time it is final. I don't take another wife."

"I don't care about the rest. But were you ever married,
really?"

"To a woman? A mere woman? Why, yes indeed. A young
baroness too. And after seven months she told me she
couldn't stand me for another minute, and went off with Von
Rumpeldorf."

"Is it true?"

"Quite true."

"And is there still a Mrs. Kangaroo?"

"Alas, no! Like the unicorn, the family knows no female."

"But why couldn't she stand you?" cried Harriet.

"Think of it now. Could *any* woman stand me?" he asked
with a slight shrug.

"I should have thought they'd have *adored* you," she cried.

"Of course they do. They can't stand me, though. And I
thoroughly sympathise with them."

Harriet looked at him thoughtfully.

"Yes," she said slowly. "You're too much like Abraham's
bosom. One would feel nowhere."

Kangaroo threw down his napkin and pushed back his chair
and roared with laughter—roared and roared with laughter.
The Chinese man-servant stood back perturbed. Harriet went
very red—the dinner waited. Then suddenly he became quiet,
looking comically at Harriet, and still sitting back from table.
Then he opened his arms and held them outstretched, his head
on one side.

"The way to nowhere," he said, ironically.

She did not say any more, and he turned to the man-servant.

E

"My glass is empty, John," he said.

"Ah, well," he sighed, "if you please one woman you can't please all women."

"And you must please all women," said Harriet, thoughtfully. "Yes, perhaps you must. Perhaps it is your mission."

"Mission! Good God! Now I'm a fat missionary. Dear Mrs. Somers, eat my dinner, but don't swallow *me* in a mouthful. Eating your host for hors d'œuvres. You're a dangerous ogre, a Medusa with her hair under her hat. Let's talk of Peach Melba. Where have you had the very best Peach Melba you ever tasted?"

After this he became quiet, and a little constrained, and when they had withdrawn for coffee, the talk went subduedly, with a little difficulty.

"I suppose your husband will have told you, Mrs. Somers, of our heaven-inspired scheme of saving Australia from the dingoes, rabbits, rats and starlings, humanly speaking."

"No, he hasn't told me. He's only told me there was some political business going on."

"He may as well put it that way as any other. And you advised him not to have anything to do with it?"

"No," said Harriet, "I let him do as he likes."

"Wonderful woman! Even the wind bloweth where it listeth."

"So does he."

"With your permission."

"The wind has permission too," said Harriet. "Everything goes by permission of something else, in this world." But she went rather red.

"Bravo, a Daniel come to judgment!" Then his voice changed, became gentle and winning again. It was as if he had remembered to love her, in his way of love. "It's not quite a political thing," he said. "We want to take away the strain, the nervous tension out of life, and let folks be happy again unconsciously, instead of unhappy consciously. You wouldn't say that was wrong, would you?"

"No," she replied, rather unwilling.

"And if I have to be a fat old Kangaroo with—not an Abraham's bosom, but a pouch to carry young Australia in—why—do you really resent it?"

Harriet laughed, glancing involuntarily at his lowest waistcoat button. It seemed such a true figure.

"Why should I resent it? It's not my business."

"Let it be your business just a little bit. I want your sympathy."

"You mean you want Lovat?"

"Poor Lovat. Richard Lovat Somers! I do indeed want him. But just as much I want your symphathy."

Harriet smiled enigmatically. She was being her most annoying. A look of almost vicious anger came over the man's face as he leaned back in his chair, seeming to make his brows narrower, and a convulsion seemed to go through his belly. Then he recovered his calm, and seemed to forget. For a long time he lay silent, with a strange, hypnotic stillness, as if he were thinking far away, quite far away. Both Harriet and Somers felt spellbound. Then from the distance came his small voice:

"Man that is born of woman is sick of himself. Man that is born of woman is tired of his day after day. And woman is like a mother with a tiresome child: what is she to do with him? What is she to do with him?—man, that is born of woman.

"But the men that are born like ants, out of the cold interval, and are womanless, they are not sick of themselves. They are full of cold energy, and they seethe with cold fire in the ant-hill, making new corridors, new chambers—they alone know what for. And they have cold, formic-acid females, as restless as themselves, and as active about the ant-hill, and as identical with the dried clay of the building. And the active, important, so-called females, and the active, cold-blooded, energetic males, they shift twig after twig, and lay crumb of earth upon crumb of earth, and the females deposit cold white eggs of young. This is the world, and the people of the world. And with their cold, active bodies the ant men and the ant-women swarm over the face of the earth.

"And where then are the sons of men? Where are the sons of men, and man that is born of woman? Man that is born of woman is a slave in the cold, barren corridors of the ant-hill. Or if he goes out, the open spaces are but spaces between ant-hill and ant-hill. And as he goes he hears voices claiming him, saying: 'Hello, here comes a brother ant.' And they hail him as a brother ant. And from this there is no escape. None. Not even the lap of woman.

"But I am a son of man. I was once a man born of woman.

And by the warm heart of the mother that bore me, even if fifty wives denied me, I would still go on fighting with a warm heart to break down the ant-hill. I can fight them with their own weapons: the hard mandibles and the acid sting of the cold ant. But that is not how I fight them. I fight them with the warm heart. Deep calls to deep, and fire calls out fire. And for warmth, for the fire of sympathy, to burn out the ant-heap with the heat of fiery, living hearts: that is what I stand for.

"And if I can make no one single woman happy, I will make none unhappy either. But if I can let out the real fire of happiness from the heart and bowels of man that is born of woman and woman that is born of man." Then suddenly he broke off: "and whether I can or not, I *love* them," he shouted, in a voice suddenly become loud and passionate. "I love them. I *love* you, you woman born of man, I do, and I defy you to prevent me. Fiery you are, and fiery am I, and fire should be friends with fire. And when you make me angry, with your jealousy and mistrust like the ants, I remember, I remind myself: 'But see the beauty of the fire in her! And think how the ants have tortured her and filled her with fear and with horror! And then the rage goes down again, and I know I love you, and I know that fire loves fire, and that therefore you love me. And I chalk up another mark against the ants, who have tortured you with their cold energy and their conscious formic-acid that stings like fire. And I love you because you've suffered from them as I have. And I love you because you and your husband cherish the fire between you, sacred, apart from the ants. *A bas les fourmis.*

"I have been like a man buried up into his neck in an ant heap: so buried in the daily world, and stung and stung and stung again, because I wouldn't change and grow cold, till now their poison is innocuous, and the formic acid of social man has no effect on me. And I've kept my warmth. And I will keep it, till I give up to the unknown, out of my poor fat body. And it is my banner, and my wife and my children and my God— just the flicker that is in my heart like a fire, and that I live by. I *can't* speculate about God. I can't do it. It seems to me a cold, antish trick. But the fire that is in my heart is God, and I will not forswear it, no, not if you offer me all the world. And fire is full of seeds—full of seeds—and let them scatter. I won't cherish it on a domestic hearth. I say I won't. So don' bring that up against me. I won't cherish it on the domestic hearth. I will use it against the ants, while they swarm over everything. And I'll call fire to my fire, and set the ant-heap at last in a blaze. Like kerosene poured in. It shall be so. It shall be so. Don't oppose me. Believe the flame in your heart, once and for all, and don't oppose me. Believe the flame of your own heart, and be with me. Remember I am with you against the ants. Remember that. And if I am Abraham's bosom— isn't it better than no bosom, in a world that simmers with busy ants? And would you leave every young, warm naked thing on the ground for the ants to find. Would you?"

He looked at her searchingly. She was pale, and moved, but hostile. He swung round in his chair, swinging his heavy hips over and lying sideways.

"Shall I tell you a thing a man told me. He had it from the lady's own lips. It was when the Prince of Wales was in India just now. There had been a show—and then a dinner given by the governor of the town—some capital or other. The Prince sat next to the governor's lady, and he was glum, silent, tortured by them all a bit beyond bearance. And the governor's lady felt she ought to make conversation, ought to say some- thing to the poor devil, just for the show's sake and the occasion. So she *couldn't* think what to tell him that would interest him. Then she had a brilliant idea. 'Do you know what happened to me last week?' she said. 'You've seen my adorable little Pekinese, Chu? She had puppies—four darling queer little things—tiny little creepy-crawlies. Of course we loved them. But in the night I thought I heard them crying— I wasn't sure. But at last I went down. And what do you think! There was a swarm of white ants, and they were just eating up the last bits of them. Wasn't it awful.' The Prince went white as death. And just then an ant happened to come on the table-cloth. He took his glass and banged it over it, and never spoke another word all evening. Now that story was told by the woman herself. And this was what she did to a poor nerve-wracked lad she was supposed to honour. Now I ask you, where was the living heart in her? She was an ant, a white ant too."

He rolled over in his chair, bitterly, with massive bitterness, turning his back on Harriet. She sat with a pale, blenched face, and tears in her eyes.

"How cruel!" she said. "But she must have been a fool."

"Vile! Vile! No fool! Quite brilliant ant-tactics. There was warmth in the lad's heart, and she was out to do *her* bit of the quenching. Oh, she gave him her nip and sting. Ants, social ants. Social creatures! Cold—I'm as cold as they are when it comes to them. And as cunning, and *quite* as vicious. But that's not what I care for. I want to collect together all the fire in all the burning hearts in Australia : that's what I want. Collect the heart-fire, and the fire will be our fire. That's what I do want; apart from all antics and ant-tricks. *'We have lighted such a fire this day, Master Latimer.'* Yes, and we'll light another. You *needn't* be with me if you don't want to— if you're frightened of losing your monopoly over your precious husband. Take him home then—take him home."

And he rolled his back on her more than ever, finishing in a sudden gust of anger and weariness. He lay there rolled in his chair, a big, queer, heavy figure, with his face almost buried in the soft leather, and his big hips sticking out. Her face was quivering, wanting to cry. Then suddenly she broke into a laugh, saying rather shakily, venomously :

"Well, anyhow, you needn't turn the wrong end of you at me quite so undisguisedly."

"How do you know it *is* the wrong end of me?" he said, sitting up suddenly and letting his head hang, scowling.

"Façon de parler," she said, laughing rather stiffly.

Somers was silent, and kept silent till the end. He was thankful that Kangaroo was fighting the battle this time.

Their host sent them in his motor-car. Neither of them had anything to say. Then, as Harriet shut the door of Torestin, and they were quite alone, she said :

"Yes, he's right. I absolutely believe in him. I don't care *what* he does with you."

"I do, though," said Somers.

The next day they went to Mullumbimby. And the day after that, each of them wrote a letter to Kangaroo.

"Dear Kaiser Kangaroo," began Harriet, "I must thank you very much for the dinner and the violets, which are still quite fresh and blue in Coo-ee. I think you were very horrid to me, but also very nice, so I hope you don't think the worst of me. I want to tell you that I *do* sympathise, and that I am awfully glad if I can be of any use to you in any way. I have a holy terror of ants since I heard you, but I know what you mean by the fire. Lovat will hand over my portion when he comes to see you. But I shall make myself into a Fire Brigade, because I am sure you will be kindling fires all over everywhere, under the table and in the clothes-cupboard, and I, poor domestic wretch, shall have to be rushing to put them out. Being only a poor domestic female, I really don't feel safe with fires anywhere except in fire-places and in grates with hearths. But I do want you to know you have my sympathy—and my Lovat." She then signed herself Harriet Somers, and felt even more fluttered than when she had signed the marriage register.

She received for answer:

"Dear Mrs. Somers: I am much honoured and very grateful for the assurance of your sympathy. I have put a one-and-six-penny government stamp under your signature, to make your letter a legal document, and have further forged the signatures of two witnesses to your deed of gift to Lovat, so I am afraid there is no court of law in New South Wales in which you could now substantiate a further claim over him. I am sorry to take this mean advantage over you, but we lawyers know no scruples.

"I should be more than delighted if I could have the honour of entertaining once more in Sydney—say next Thursday—a beautiful person and remarkable woman (one and the same individual) who tells me to my nose that I am a Jew and that my name, instead of Benjamin, should be Abraham. Do please come again and call me Abraham's Bosom, but don't fail to bring your husband, for the simple look of the thing."

"The Kangaroo is a fighting beast, I believe," said Somers, looking at Harriet and laughing. He was not sorry when for once some other person gave her a dig.

"I think he's rather foolish," she said briefly.

These days Somers, too, was filled with fury. As for loving mankind, or having a fire of love in his heart, it was all rot. He felt almost fierily cold. He liked the sea, the pale sea of green glass that fell in such cold foam. Ice-fiery, fish-burning. He went out on to the low flat rocks at low tide, skirting the deep pock-holes that were full of brilliantly clear water and delicately-coloured shells and tiny, crimson anemones. Strangely sea-scooped sharp sea-bitter rock-floor, all wet and sea-savage. And standing at the edge looking at the waves rather terrifying rolling at him, where he stood low and exposed, far out from the sand-banks, and as he watched the gannets gleaming white, then falling with a splash like white sky-arrows into the waves, he wished as he had never wished before that he could be cold, as sea things are cold, and murderously fierce. To have oneself exultantly ice-cold, not one spark of this wretched warm flesh left, and to have all the terrific, icy energy of a fish. To surge with that cold exultance and passion of a sea thing! Now he understood the yearning in the seal-woman's croon, as she went back to the sea, leaving her husband and her children of warm flesh. No more cloying warmth. No more of this horrible stuffy heat of human beings. To be an isolated swift fish in the big seas, that are bigger than the earth; fierce with cold, cold life, in the watery twilight before sympathy was created to clog us.

These were his feelings now. Mankind? Ha, he turned his face to the centre of the seas, away from any land. The noise of waters, and dumbness like a fish. The cold, lovely silence, before crying and calling were invented. His tongue felt heavy in his mouth, as if it had relapsed away from speech altogether.

He did not care a straw what Kangaroo said or felt, or what anybody said or felt, even himself. He had no feelings, and speech had gone out of him. He wanted to be cold, cold, and alone like a single fish, with no feeling in his heart at all except a certain icy exultance and wild, fish-like rapacity. "Homo sum!" All right. Who sets a limit to what a man is? Man is also a fierce and fish-cold devil, in his hour, filled with cold fury of desire to get away from the cloy of human life altogether, not into death, but into that icily self-sufficient vigour of a fish.

CHAPTER VII

THE BATTLE OF TONGUES

As a rule the jetty on its poles straddling a little way into the sea was as deserted as if it were some relic left by an old invader. Then it had spurts of activity, when steamer after steamer came blorting and hanging miserably round, like cows to the cow-shed on a winter afternoon. Then a little engine would chuff along the pier, shoving a string of tip-up trucks and little men would saunter across the sky-line, and there would be a fine dimness of black dust round the low, red ship and the end of the jetty. Luckily it was far enough away, so that Harriet need not fear for her beautiful white washing. She washed her linen herself for the sheer joy of it, and loved nothing so much as thinking of it getting whiter and whiter, like the Spenserian maid, in the sun and sea, and visiting it on the grass every five minutes, and finding it every time really whiter, till Somers said it would reach a point of whiteness where the colours would break up, and she'd go out and find pieces of rainbow on the grass and bushes, instead of towels and shirts.

"Shouldn't I be startled!" she said, accepting it as quite a possible contingency, and adding thoughtfully: "No, not really."

One of these afternoons when Somers was walking down on the sands, looking at the different shells, their sea colours of pink and brown and rainbow and brilliant violet and shrimp-red, and when the boats were loading coal on the moderately quiet sea, he noticed the little engine standing steaming on the jetty, just overhead where he was going to pass under. Then his attention was drawn away to the men picking up the rounded, sea-smooth pebbles of coal in one little place where the beach was just a black slope of perfectly clean coal-pebbles: just like any other pebbles. There were usually some men, or women or children, picking here, putting the bigger pebbles of sea-coal into sacks. From the edge of the small waves Somers heard one man talking to another, and the English tones—unconsciously he expected a foreign language—and particularly the peculiar educated-artisan quality, almost a kind of uppishness that there is in the speech of Australian working men, struck him as incongruous with their picking up the coal-cobs from the shore. He watched them, in the chill of the shadow. Yes, they thought as much of themselves as anybody. But one was palpably a Welshman, and loved picking up something for nothing; and the other mixed his democratic uppishness with a queer lousy quality, like a bushranger. "They are ten times more foreign to me," said Somers, "than Italian scoundrels, or even Indians. They are so *foreign* to me. And yet their manner of life, their ordinary way of living is almost exactly what I was used to as a boy. Why are they so foreign to me?"

They silently objected to his looking, so he went on. He had come to the huge, high timbers of the tall jetty. There stood the little engine still overhead: and in the gloom among

E*

the timbers underneath water was dripping down from her, which gave Somers a distaste for passing just then. He looked up. There was the engine-driver in his dirty shirt and dirty bare arms, talking to another man. The other man saluted— and to Somers' surprise it was William James. He stood quite still, and a surprised smile of recognition greeted the other man, who saluted.

"Why, what are you doing here?" called Somers.

William James came to the edge of the jetty, but could not hear, because of the noise of the sea. His face had that small, subtle smile that was characteristic of him, and which Somers was never quite sure of, whether it was really jeering or in a cunning way friendly.

"Won't you come up a minute?" roared William James.

So Somers scrambled round up the banks, on to the railway track.

"I couldn't come down for the moment," said William James. "I'll have to see the manager, then I'm going off on this boat. We're ready to go. You heard her blowing."

"Where are you going? Back to Sydney?"

"Yes. I come down occasionally on this coal business, and if I like I go back on the collier. The sea is quiet, and I needn't wait for a train. Well, an' how're you gettin' on, like? Pleased with it down here all by yourselves?"

"Very."

"A bit lonely for you. I suppose you wouldn't like to know the manager here—Mr. Thomas? He's a decent chap—from South Wales originally."

"No. I like it best when I don't know anybody."

"That's a compliment for some of us. However—I know what you mean. I know what you mean. Jack tells me you saw Kangaroo. Made quite a fuss of you, I hear. I knew he would. Oh, Kangaroo knew all about you: all he wanted to know, anyhow. I say, if ye think of stoppin' down here, you might get in a ton of coal. It looks as if this strike might come off. That Arbitration Board's a fine failure, what?"

"As far as I gather."

"Oh, bound to be. Bound to be. They talk about scraps of paper, why, every agreement that's ever come to in this country, you could wrap your next red herring in it, for all it's worth."

"I suppose it's like Ireland, they don't want to agree."

"That's about it. The Labour people want this revolution of theirs. What?"—and he looked at Somers with a long, smiling, sardonic leer, like a wink. "There's a certain fact," he continued, "as far as any electioneering success goes, they're out of the running for a spell. What do you think of Trades Unions, one way and another?"

"I dislike them on the whole rather intensely. They're just the nastiest profiteering side of the working man—they make a fool of him too, in my opinion."

"Just my opinion. They make a fool of him. Wouldn't it be nice to have them for bosses of the whole country? They very nearly are. But I doubt very much if they'll ever cover the last lap—what?"

"Not if Kangaroo can help it," said Somers.

"No!" William James flashed a quick look at him from his queer grey eyes. "What did you make of him then? Could you make him out?"

"Not quite. I never met anyone like him. The wonder to me is, he seems to have as much spare time for entertaining and amusing his guests, as if he had no work at all on hand."

"Oh, that was just a special occasion. But he's a funny sort of Saviour, isn't he? Not much crown of thorns about him. Why, he'd look funny on a cross, what?"

"He's no intention of being put on one, I think," said Somers stiffly.

"Oh, I don't know. If the wrong party got hold of him. There's many mites in a pound of cheese, they say."

"Then I'll toast my cheese."

"Ha-ha! Oh yes, I like a bit of toasted cheese myself—or a Welsh rabbit, as well as any man."

"But you don't think they'd ever let him down, do you?—these Australians?"

"No-o," said William James. "I doubt if they'd ever let him down. But if he happened to *fall* down, you know, they'd soon forget him."

"You don't sound a very warm follower yourself."

"Oh, warm isn't my way, in anything. I like to see what I'm about. I can see that Kangaroo's a wonder. Oh yes, he's a world wonder. And I'd rather be in with him than anybody, if it was only for the sake of the spree, you know. Bound to be a spree some time—and before long, I should say, things going as they are. I wouldn't like to be left out of the fun."

"But you don't feel any strong devotion to your leader?"

"Why, no; I won't say it's exactly strong devotion. But I think he's a world wonder. He's not quite the *shape* of a man that I should throw away my eyes for, that's all I mean." Again William James looked at Somers with that long, perhaps mocking little smile in his grey eyes.

"I thought even his shape beautiful, when he talked to me."

"Oh yes, it's wonderful what a spell he can cast over you. But I'm a stuggy fellow myself, maybe that's how it is I can't ever quite see him in the same light as the thin chaps do. But that's just the looks of the thing. I can see there isn't another man in the world like him, and I'd cross the seas to join in with him, if only for the fun of the thing."

"But what about the end of the fun?" asked Somers.

"Oh, that I don't know. And nobody does, for that matter."

"But surely if one believes——"

"One believes a lot, and one believes very little, seems to me. Taking all in all, seems to me we live from hand to mouth, as far as beliefs go."

"You never *would* believe," said Somers, laughing.

"Not till I was made to," replied Jaz, twisting his face in his enigmatic smile.

Somers looked at the thick, stocky, silent figure in the well-made dark clothes that didn't in the least belong to him. There was something about him like a prisoner in prison uniform, in his town clothes—and something of that in his bearing. A stocky, silent, unconquerable prisoner. And in his imprisoned soul another kind of mystery, another sort of appeal.

The two men stood still in the cold wind that came up the sands to the south-west. To the left, as they faced the wind, went the black railway track on the pier, and the small engine stood dribbling. On the right the track ran curiously black past a little farm-place with a corrugated iron roof, and past a big field where the stubble of maize or beans stood ragged and sere, on into the little hollow of bush, where the mine was, beyond the stagnant creek. It was curious how intensely black, velvety and unnatural, the railway-track looked on this numb coast-front. The steamer hooted again.

"Cold it is up here," said Somers.

"It is cold. He's coming now, though," replied William James.

They stood together still another minute, looking down the

pale sands at the foam and the dark-blue sea, the sere grass scattered with bungalows.

It was a strange, different bond of sympathy united them, from that that subsisted between Somers and Jack, or Somers and Kangaroo. Hardly sympathy at all, but an ancient sort of root knowledge.

"Well, good-bye," said Somers, wanting to be gone before the manager came up with the papers. He shook hands with William James—but as usual, Jaz gave him a slack hand. Their eyes met—and the look, something like a taunt, in Trewhella's secretive grey eye, made Somers stiffen his back, and a kind of haughtiness flew into his soul.

"Different men, different ways, Mr. Trewhella," he said.

William James did not answer, but smiled rather stubbornly. It seemed to Somers the man would be smiling that stubborn, taunting smile till the crack of doom.

"I told Mrs. Somers what I think about it," said Jaz, with a very Cornish accent. "I doubt if she'll ever do much more believin' than I shall." And the taunt was forked this time.

"She says she believes entirely in Kangaroo."

"Does she now? Who did she tell it to?"

"Me."

Trewhella still stood with that faint grin on his face, short and stocky and erect like a little post left standing. Somers looked at him again, frowning, and turned abruptly down the bank. The smile left the face of the Cornishman, and he just looked obstinate, indifferent, and curiously alone, as if he stood there all alone in the world. He watched Somers emerge on the sands below, and go walking slowly among the sea-ragged flat shelves of the coast-bed rocks, his head dropping, looking in the pools, his hands in his pockets. And the obstinate light never changed in the eyes of the watcher, not even when he turned to the approaching manager.

Perhaps it was this meeting which made Somers want to see Kangaroo once more. Everything had suddenly become unreal to him. He went to Sydney and to Cooley's rooms. But during the first half-hour, the revulsion from the First persisted. Somers disliked his appearance, and the kangaroo look made him feel devilish. And then the queer, slow manner of approach. Kangaroo was not really ready for his visitor, and he seemed dense, heavy, absent, clownish. It was that kangarooish clownishness that made a vicious kind of hate spring into Somers' face. He talked in a hard, cutting voice. "Whom can you depend on in this world," he was saying. "Look at these Australians—they're awfully nice, but they've got no inside to them. They're hollow. How are you going to build on such hollow stalks. They may well call them corn-stalks. They're marvellous and manly and independent and all that, outside. But inside, they are not. When they're *quite* alone, they don't exist."

"Yet many of them have been alone a long time in the bush," said Kangaroo, watching his visitor with slow, dumb, unchanging eyes.

"Alone, what sort of alone. Physically alone. And they've just gone hollow. They're never alone in spirit: quite, quite alone in spirit. And the people who have are the only people you can depend on."

"Where shall I find them?"

"Not here. It seems to me, least of all here. The Colonies make for *outwardness*. Everything is outward—like hollow stalks of corn. The life makes this inevitable: all that struggle with bush and water and what-not, all the mad struggle with the material necessities and conveniences—the inside soul just withers and goes into the outside, and they're all just lusty robust hollow stalks of people."

"The corn-stalks bear the corn. I find them generous to reck-lessness—the greatest quality. The old world is cautious and for ever bargaining about its soul. Here they don't bother to bargain."

"They've no soul to bargain about. But they're even more full of conceit. What do you expect to do with such people. Build a straw castle?"

"You see, I believe in them—perhaps I know them a little better than you do."

"Perhaps you do. It'll be cornstalk castle, for all that. What *do* you expect to build on?"

"They're generous—generous to recklessness," shouted Kangaroo. "And I love them. I love them. Don't you come here carping to me about them. They are my children, I love them. If I'm not to believe in their generosity, am I to believe in your cautious, old-world carping, do you think? I *won't!*" he shouted fiercely. "I *won't*. Do you hear that!" And he sat hulked in his chair glowering like some queer dark god at bay. Somers paused, and his heart failed.

"Then make me believe in them and their generosity," he said dryly. "They're nice. But they haven't got the last everlasting central bit of soul, solitary soul, that makes a man himself. The central bit of himself. They all merge to the outside, away from the centre. And what can you do, *permanently*, with such people? You can have a fine corn-stalk blaze. But as for anything permanent——"

"I tell you I *hate* permanency," barked Kangaroo. "The phœnix rises out of the ashes." He rolled over angrily in his chair.

"Let her! Like Rider Haggard's *She*, I don't feel like risking it a second time," said Somers, like the venomous serpent he was.

"Generous, generous men!" Kangaroo muttered to himself. "At least you can get a blaze out of them. Not like European wet matches, that will never again strike alight—as you've said yourself."

"But a blaze for what? What's your blaze for?"

"I don't care," yelled Kangaroo, springing with sudden magnificent swiftness to his feet, and facing Somers, and seizing him by the shoulders and shaking him till his head nearly fell off, yelling all the time: "I don't care, I tell you, I don't care. Where there's fire there's change. And where the fire is love, there's creation. Seeds of fire. That's enough for me! Fire, and seeds of fire, and love. That's all I care about. Don't carp at me, I tell you. Don't carp at me with your old, European, damp spirit. If you can't take fire, *we can*. That's all. Generous, passionate men—and you dare to carp at them. You. What have you to show?" And he went back to his chair like a great sulky bear-god.

Somers sat rather stupefied than convinced. But he found himself again *wanting* to be convinced, wanting to be carried away. The desire hankered in his heart. Kangaroo had become again beautiful: huge and beautiful like some god that sways and seems clumsy, then suddenly flashes with all the agility of thunder and lightning. Huge and beautiful as he sat hulked in his chair. Somers *did* wish he would get up again and carry him quite away.

But where to? Where to? Where is one carried to when one is carried away? He had a bitter mistrust of seventh heavens and all heavens in general. But then the experience. If Kangaroo had got up at that moment Somers would have given him heart and soul and body, for the asking, and damn all consequences. He longed to do it. He knew that by just going over and laying a hand on the great figure of the sullen god he could achieve it. Kangaroo would leap like a thunder-cloud and catch him up—catch him up and away into a transport. A transport that should last for life. He knew it.

But alas, it was just too late. In some strange way Somers felt he had come to the end of transports: they had no more mystery for him; at least this kind: or perhaps no more charm. Some bubble or other had burst in his heart. All his body and fibres wanted to go over and touch the other great being into a storm of response. But his soul wouldn't. The coloured bubble had burst.

Kangaroo sat up and adjusted his eyeglasses.

"Don't you run away with the idea, though," he said, "that I am just an emotional fool." His voice was almost menacing, and with a strange cold, intellectual quality that Somers had never heard before.

"I believe in the one fire of love. I believe it is the one inspiration of all creative activity. I trust myself entirely to the fire of love. This I do with my reason also. I don't discard my reason. I use it at the service of love, like a sharp weapon. I try to keep it very sharp—and very dangerous. Where I don't love, I use only my will and my wits. Where I love, I trust to love alone." The voice came cold and static.

Somers sat rather blank. The change frightened him almost as something obscene. This was the reverse to the passionate thunder-god.

"But is love the only inspiration of creative activity?" he asked, rather feebly.

"This is the first time I have heard it questioned. Do you know of any other?"

Somers thought he did, but he was not going to give himself away to that sharp weapon of a voice, so he did not answer.

"*Is* there any other inspirational force than the force of love?" continued Kangaroo. "There is no other. Love makes the trees flower and shed their seed, love makes the animals mate and birds put on their best feather, and sing their best songs. And all that man has ever created on the face of the earth, or ever will create—if you will allow me the use of the word create, with regard to man's highest productive activities."

"It's the word I always use myself," said Somers.

"Naturally, since you know how to think inspiredly. Well then, all that man ever has created or ever will create, while he remains man, has been created in the inspiration and by the force of love. And not only man—all the living creatures are swayed to creation, to new creation, to the creation of song and beauty and lovely gesture, by love. I will go further. I believe the sun's attraction for the earth is a form of love."

"Then why doesn't the earth fly into the sun?" said Somers.

"For the same reason. Love is mutual. Each attracts the other. But in natural love each tries at the same time to withhold the other, to keep the other true to its own beloved nature. To any true lover, it would be the greatest disaster if the beloved broke down from her own nature and self and began to identify herself with him, with his nature and self. I say, to any genuine lover this is the greatest disaster, and he tries by every means in his power to prevent this. The earth and sun, on their plane, have discovered a perfect equilibrium. But man has not yet begun. His lesson is so much harder. His consciousness is at once so complicated and so cruelly limited. This is the lesson before us. Man has loved the beloved for the sake of love, so far, but rarely, rarely has he *consciously* known that he could only love her for her own separate, strange self: forever strange and a joyful mystery to him. Lovers henceforth have got to know one another. A terrible mistake, and a self delusion. True lovers only learn that as they know less, and less, and less of each other, the mystery of each grows more startling to the other. The tangible unknown: that is the magic, the mystery, and the grandeur of love, that it puts the tangible unknown in our arms, and against our breast: the beloved. We have made a fatal mistake. We have got to know so much *about* things, that we think we know the actuality, and contain it. The sun is as much outside us, and as eternally unknown, as ever it was. And the same with each man's beloved: like the sun. What do the facts we know *about* a man amount to? Only two things we can know of him, and this by pure soul-intuition: we can know if he is true to the flame of life and love which is inside his heart, or if he is false to it. If he is true, he is friend. If he is wilfully false, and inimical to the fire of life and love in his own heart, then he is my enemy as well as his own."

Somers listened. He seemed to see it all and hear it all with marvellous clarity. And he believed that it was all true.

"Yes," he said, "I believe that is all true."

"What is it then that you disbelieve?"

"I don't quite believe that love is the one and only exclusive force or mystery of living inspiration. I don't quite believe that. There is something else."

Kangaroo looked at him for once overbearingly and with a sort of contempt.

"Tell me what it is," he replied briefly.

"I am not very clear myself. And, you see, what I want to say, you don't want to hear."

"Yes, I do," snapped Kangaroo.

"With your ears and your critical mind only."

"Say it, anyhow, say it."

Richard sat feeling very stupid. The communicative soul is like the ass, you can lead him to the water, but you can't make him drink.

"Why," he said, "it means an end of us and what we are, in the first place. And then a re-entry into us of the great God, who enters us from below, not from above."

Kangaroo sat bunched up like some creature watching round-eyed out of a darker corner.

"How do you mean, enters us from below?" he barked.

"Not through the spirit. Enters us from the lower self, the dark self, the phallic self, if you like."

"Enters us from the phallic self?" snapped Kangaroo sharply.

"Sacredly. The god you can never see or visualise, who stands dark on the threshold of the phallic me."

"The phallic you, my dear young friend, what is that but love?"

Richard shook his head in silence.

"No," he said, in a slow, remote voice. "I know your love, Kangaroo. Working everything from the spirit, from the head. You work the lower self as an instrument of the spirit. Now it is time for the spirit to leave us again; it is time for the Son of Man to depart, and leave us dark, in front of the unspoken God: who is just beyond the dark threshold of the lower self, my lower self. There is a great God on the threshold of my lower self, whom I fear while he is my glory. And the spirit goes out like a spent candle."

Kangaroo watched with a heavy face like a mask.

"It is time for the spirit to leave us," he murmured in a somnambulist voice. "Time for the spirit to leave us."

Somers, who had dropped his face, hiding it as he spoke, watched the other man from under his brows. Kangaroo, who still sat impassive, like a frozen, antagonised Buddha, gave himself a jerk of recovery.

"Ah well!" he sighed, with a weary, impatient, condescending sigh. "I was never able to follow mysticism and metaphysics. One of my many limitations. I don't know what you mean."

"But what is your 'love' but a mystical thing?" asked Richard indignantly.

"My love? Why, that is something I *feel*, as plain as toothache."

"Well, so do I feel the other: and love has become like cardboard to me," said Richard, still indignant.

"Like cardboard? Well, I don't quite see love like cardboard, dear boy. For you *are* a dear boy, in spite of yourself. Oh yes, you are. There's some demon inside you makes you perverse, and won't let you be the dear, beautiful thing you are. But I'm going to exorcise that demon."

Somers gave a short laugh, the very voice of the demon speaking.

"Oh yes I am," said Kangaroo, in a steely voice. "I'm going to exorcise that demon, and release your beautiful Andromeda soul."

"Try," ejaculated Richard dryly, turning aside his face in distaste.

Kangaroo leaped to his feet and stood towering over the little enemy as if he would stoop over him and smother him in violent warmth and drive out the demon in that way. But Richard sat cold and withheld, and Kangaroo had not the power to touch him.

"I'm going to try," shouted the lawyer, in his slightly husky roar. "You've made it my prerogative by telling me to try. I'm going to love you, and you won't get away from that. I'm the hound of heaven after you, my boy, and I'm fatal to the hell hound that's leading you. Do you know I love you?—that I loved you long before I met you?"

Richard, curled narrow in his chair like a snake, glanced up at the big man projecting over him. A sort of magnetic effusion seemed to come out of Kangaroo's body, and Richard's hand was almost drawn in spite of himself to touch the other man's body. He had deliberately to refrain from laying his hand on the near, generous stomach of the Kangaroo, because automatically his hand would have lifted and sought that rest. But he prevented himself, and the eyes of the two men met. Kangaroo searched Lovat's eyes: but they seemed to be of cloudy blue like hell-smoke, impenetrable and devilish. Kangaroo watched a long time: but the other man was the unchangeable. Kangaroo turned aside suddenly.

"Ah well," he said. "I can see there is a beast in the way. There is a beast in your eyes, Lovat, and if I can't conquer him then—woe-betide you, my dear. But I love you, you see."

"Sounds like a threat," laughed Somers.

Kangaroo leaned and laid his hand gently on Lovat's shoulder.

"Don't say that;" his voice was small now, and very gentle. "I loved you before I knew you. My soul cries for you. And you hurt me with the demon that is in you."

Richard became very pale, and was silent for some moments. The hand sank heavier, nearer, on his shoulder.

"You see," said Somers, trying hard to be fair, "what you call my demon is what I identify myself with. It's my best me, and I stick to it. I think love, all this love of ours, is a devilish thing now: a slow poison. Really, I know the dark god at the lower threshold—even if I have to repeat it like a phrase. And in the sacred dark men meet and touch, and it is a great communion. But it isn't this love. There's no love in it. But something deeper. Love seems to me somehow trivial: and the spirit seems like something that belongs to paper. I can't help it—I know another God."

The pressure of the hand became inert.

"But aren't you merely inventing other terms for the same thing that I mean, and that I call love?" said Kangaroo, in a strange, toneless voice, looking aside.

"Does it seem to you that I am?" asked Lovat, gently and dispassionately.

The strange, great passionate cloud of Kangaroo still hung there, hovering over the pale, sharp isolation of Somers, who lay looking up. And then it seemed as if the glow and vibration left Kangaroo's body, the cloud became grey and heavy. He sighed, removed his hand, and turned away.

"Ah well!" he said. "Ah well!"

Somers rose, trembling now, and feeling frail.

"I'll go," he said.

"Yes, do go," said Kangaroo.

And without another word Somers went, leaving the other man sunk in a great heap in his chair, as if defeated. Somers did not even pity him. His heart felt queer and cave-like and devoid of emotion.

He was spending the night at the Callcotts. Harriet, too, was there. But he was in no hurry to get back there. It was a clear and very starry night. He took the tramcar away from the centre of the town, then walked. As was always the case with him, in this country, the land and the world disappeared as night fell, as if the day had been an illusion, and the sky came bending down. There was the Milky Way, in the clouds of star-fume, bending down right in front of him, right down till it seemed as if he would walk on to it, if he kept going. The pale, fumy drift of the Milky Way drooped down and seemed so near, straight in front, that it seemed the obvious road to take. And one would avoid the strange dark gaps, gulfs, in the way overhead. And one would look across to the floating isles of star-fume, to the south, across the gulfs where the sharp stars flashed like lighthouses, and one would be in a new way denizen of a new plane, walking by oneself. There would be a real new way to take. And the mechanical earth quite obliterated, sunk out.

Only he saw, on the sea's high black horizon, the various reddish sore-looking lights of a ship. There they were—the signs of the ways of men—hot-looking and weary. He turned quickly away from the marks of the far-off ship, to look again at the downward slope of the great hill of the Milky Way. He wanted so much to get out of this lit-up cloy of humanity, and the exhaust of love, and the fretfulness of desire. Why not swing away into cold separation? Why should desire always be fretting, fretting like a tugged chain? Why not break the bond and be single, take a fierce stoop and a swing back, as when a gannet plunges like a white, metallic arrow into the sea, raising a burst of spray, disappearing, completing the downward curve of the parabola in the invisible underwater where it seizes the object of desire, then away, away with success upwards, back flashing into the air and white space? Why not? Why want to urge, urge, urge oneself down the causeways of desirous love, hard pavements of love? Even like

Kangaroo. Why shouldn't meeting be a stoop as a gannet stoops into the sea, or a hawk, or a kite, in a swift rapacious parabola downwards, to touch at the lowermost turn of the curve, then up again?

It is a world of slaves: all love-professing. Why unite with them? Why pander to them? Why go with them at all? Why not strike at communion out of the unseen, as the gannet strikes into the unseen underwater, or the kite from above at a mouse? One seizure, and away again, back away into isolation. A touch, and away. Always back, away into isolation. Why be cloyed and clogged down like billions of fish in water, or billions of mice on land? It is a world of slaves. Then why not gannets in the upper air, having two worlds? Why only one element? If I am to have a meeting it shall be down, down in the invisible, and the moment I re-emerge it shall be alone. In the visible world I am alone, an isolate instance. My meeting is in the underworld, the dark. Beneath every gannet that jumps from the water ten thousand fish are swimming still. But they are swimming in a shudder of silver fear. That is the magic of the ocean. Let them shudder the huge ocean aglimmer.

He arrived at Wyewurk at last, and found a little party. William James was there, and Victoria had made, by coincidence, a Welsh rarebit. The beer was on the table.

"Just in time," said Jack. "As well you're not half an hour later, or there might 'a been no booze. How did you come—tram?"

"Yes—and walked part of the way."

"What kind of an evening did you have?" said Harriet.

He looked at her. A chill fell upon the little gathering, from his presence.

"We didn't agree," he replied.

"I know you wouldn't—not for long, anyhow," she replied. "I don't see you agreeing and playing second fiddle for long."

"Do you see me as a fiddler at all?"

"I've seen you fiddling away hard enough many times," retorted Harriet. "Why, what else do you do, all your life, but fiddle some tune or other?"

He did not reply, and there was a pause. His face was pale and very definite, as if it were some curious sea-shell.

"What did you get the wind up about, between you?" said Jack soothingly, pouring Somers a glass of beer.

"No wind. We're only not the same pair of shoes."

"I could have told you that before you went," said Jaz with quiet elation in his tones.

Victoria looked at Somers with dark, bright eyes. She was quite fascinated by him, as an Australian bird by some adder.

"Isn't Mr. Somers queer?" she said. "He doesn't seem to mind a bit."

Somers looked at her quickly, a smile round his eyes, and a curious, smiling devil inside them, cold as ice.

"Oh yes, he minds. Don't take any notice of his pretence. He's only in a bad temper," cried Harriet. "I know him by now. He's been in a temper for days."

"Oh, why?" cried Victoria. "I thought he was lovely this afternoon when he was here."

"Yes," said Harriet grimly. "Lovely! You should live with him."

But again Victoria looked at his clear, fixed face, with the false smile round the eyes, and her fascination did not diminish.

"What an excellent Welsh rarebit," he said. "If there were a little red pepper."

"Red pepper!" cried Victoria. "There is!" And she sprang up to get it for him. As she handed it to him he looked into her dilated, dark bright eyes, and thanked her courteously. When he was in this state his voice and tone in speaking were very melodious. Of course it set Harriet on edge. But Victoria stood fluttering with her hands over the table, bewildered.

"What are you feeling for?" asked Jack.

She only gave a little blind laugh, and remembered that she was going to sit down. So she sat down, and then wondered what it was she was going to do after that.

"So you don't cotton on to Kangaroo either?" said Jack easily.

"I have the greatest admiration for him."

"You're not alone there. But you don't fall over yourself, loving him."

"I only trip, and recover my balance for the moment."

Jaz gave a loud laugh, across his cheese.

"That's good!" he said.

"You trip, and recover your balance," said Jack. "You're a wary one. The rest of us falls right in, flop, and are never heard of again. And how did you part then?"

"We parted in mutual esteem. I said I would go, and he asked me please to do so as quickly as possible."

Jack made round eyes, and even Jaz left off eating.

"Did you *quarrel?*" cried Harriet.

"Oh yes, violently. But of course, not vulgarly. We parted, as I said, in mutual esteem, bowing each other out."

"You *are* awful. You only went on purpose to upset him. I knew that all along. Why must you be so spiteful?" said Harriet. "You're never happy unless you're upsetting somebody's apple-cart."

"Am I doomed to agree with everybody, then?"

"No. But you needn't *set out* to be disagreeable. And to Mr. Cooley especially, who likes you and is such a warm, big man. You ought to be flattered that he *cares* what you think. No, you have to go and try and undermine him. Ah—why was I ever pestered with such a viperish husband as you!" said Harriet.

Victoria made alert, frightened eyes. But Somers sat on with the same little smile and courteous bearing.

"I am, of course, immensely flattered at his noticing me," he replied. "Otherwise, naturally, I should have resented being told to leave. As it was I didn't resent it a bit."

"Didn't you!" cried Harriet. "I know you and your pretences. That is what has put you in such a temper."

"But you remember I've been in a temper for days," he replied calmly and gravely. "Therefore there could be no putting."

"Oh, it only made you worse. I'm tired of your temper, really."

"But Mr. Somers isn't in a temper at all!" cried Victoria. "He's nicer than any of us, really. Jack would be as angry as anything if I said all those things to him. Shouldn't you, Jack?" And she cuddled his arm.

"You'd be shut up in the coal-shed for the night before you got half-way through with it, if ever you started trying it on," he replied, with marital humour.

"No, I shouldn't, either: or it would be the last door you'd shut on *me*, so there. But anyhow you'd be in a waxy old temper."

And she smiled at Somers as she cuddled her husband's arm.

"If my hostess say I'm nice," said Somers, "I am not going to feel guilty, whatever my *wife* may say."

"Oh yes, you do feel guilty," said Harriet.

"Your hostess doesn't find any fault with you at all," cried Victoria. She was looking very pretty, in a brown chiffon dress. "She thinks you're the nicest of anybody here, there."

"What?" cried Jack. "When I'm here as well?"

"Whether you're here or not. You're not very nice to me to-night, and William James never is. But Mr. Somers is *awfully* nice." She blushed suddenly quite vividly, looking under her long lashes at him. He smiled a little more intensely to himself.

"I tell you what, Mrs. Somers," said Jack. "We'd better make a swap of it, till they alter their opinion. You and me had better strike up a match, and let them two elope with one another for a bit."

"And what about William James?" cried Victoria, with vivid excitement.

"Oh nobody need trouble themselves about William James," replied that individual. "It's about time he was rolling home."

"No," said Harriet, in answer to Jack. "I'm striking off no more matches, thank you. The game's not worth the candle."

"Why, maybe you've only struck on the rough side, you know," said Jack. "You might strike on the smooth next time."

"No," said Harriet. "I'm going to bed, and leave you all to your striking bad tempers. Good-night!"

She rose roughly. Victoria jumped up to accompany her to her room. The Somers had had a room each in Torestin, so Victoria had put them each separately into a nice little room in her house.

"Is it right," said Jack, "that you got the wind up to-night?"

"No," said Somers. "At least we only quite lovingly agreed to differ. Nothing else."

"I thought it would be like that," said Jack. "He thinks the world of you, I can see that."

William James stood ready to leave. He looked at Somers cunningly, as if reading into him with his light-grey, sceptical eyes.

"Mr. Somers doesn't care to commit himself so easily," he said.

"No," said Jack. "You blighters from the old country are so mighty careful of risking yourselves. That's what I'm not. When I feel a thing I jump up and go for it, and damn the consequences. There's always plenty of time to think about a thing after you've done it. And then if you're fool enough to wish you hadn't done it, why, that shows you *shouldn't* have. I don't go in for regrets, myself. I do what I want. And if I wanted to do a thing, then it's *all right* when it's done. All a man's got to do is to keep his mouth shut and his fists ready, and go down on his knees to *nothing*. Then he can damn well do as he pleases. And all he asks is that other folks shall do as they please, men or women. Damn all this careful stunt. I'll step along as far as the tram with you, Jaz, I feel like walking the Welsh rabbit down into his burrow. Vicky prefers Mr. Somers to me *pro tem*.—and I don't begrudge it her. Why should I?"

Victoria was putting away the dishes, and seemed not to hear. The two men went. Somers still sat in his chair. He was truely in a devil of a temper, with everybody and everything: a wicked, fiendish mood that made him *look* quite handsome, as fate would have it. He had heard Jack's hint. He knew Victoria was attracted to him: that she imagined no nonsense about love, she was too remote from the old world, and too momentary for that. The moment—that was all her feelings were to her. And at this moment she was fascinated, and when she said, in her slightly contralto voice:

"You're not in a temper with *me*, though, are you Mr. Somers?" she was so comely, like a maiden just ready for love, and like a comely, desirous virgin offering herself to the wayfarer, in the name of the god of bright desire, that Somers stretched out his hand and stroked her hot cheek very delicately with the tips of his fingers, replying:

"I could never be angry with you. You're much too winsone."

She looked at him with her dark eyes dilated into a glow, a glow of offering. He smiled faintly, rising to his feet, and desire in all his limbs like a power. The moment—and the power of the moment. Again he felt his limbs full of desire, like a power. And his days of anger seemed to culminate now in this moment, like bitter smouldering that at last leaps into flame. Not love—just weapon-like desire. He knew it. The god Bacchus. Iacchos! Iacchos! Bacchanals with weapon hands. She had the sacred glow in her eyes. Bacchus, the true Bacchus. Jack would not begrudge the god. And the fire was very clean and steely, after the smoke. And he felt the velvety fire from her face in his finger-tips.

And still his old stubborn self intervened. He decided almost involuntarily. Perhaps it was fear.

"Good-night," he said to her. "Jack will be back in a moment. You look bonnie to-night."

And he went to his room. When he had shut the door, he wondered if it was merely a sort of cowardice. Honour? No need as far as Jack was concerned, apparently. And Harriet? She was too honest a female. She would know that the dishonour, as far as she felt it, lay in the desire, not in the act. For her, too, honour did not consist in a pledged word kept according to the pledge, but in a genuine feeling faithfully followed. He had not to reckon with honour here.

What then? Why not follow the flame, the moment sacred to Bacchus? Why not, if it was the way of life? He did not know why not. Perhaps only old moral habit, or fear, as Jack said, of committing himself. Perhaps only that. It was Victoria's high moment; all her high moments would have this Bacchic, weapon-like momentaneity: since Victoria was Victoria. Why then deny it?

The pagan way, the many gods, the different service, the sacred moments of Bacchus. Other sacred moments: Zeus and Hera, for examples, Ares and Aphrodite, all the great moments of the gods. Why not know them all, all the great moments of the gods, from the major moments with Hera to the swift short moments of Io or Leda or Ganymede? Should not a man know the whole range? And especially the bright, swift, weapon-like Bacchic occasion, should not any man seize it when it offered?

But his heart of hearts was stubbornly puritanical. And his innermost soul was dark and sullen, black with a sort of scorn. These moments bred in the head and born in the eye: he had enough of them. These flashes of desire for a visual object would no longer carry him into action. He had no use for them. There was a downslope into Orcus, and a vast, phallic, sacred darkness, where one was enveloped into the greater god as in an Egyptian darkness. He would meet there or nowhere. To the visual travesty he would lend himself no more.

Pondering and turning recklessly he heard Jack come back. Then he began to doze. He did not sleep well in Australia, it seemed as if the aboriginal daimon entered his body as he slept, to destroy its old constitution. Sleep was almost pain, and too full of dreams. This night he woke almost at once from a vivid little dream. The fact of the soonness troubled him too, for at home he never dreamed till morning.

But the dream had been just this. He was standing in the living-room at Coo-ee, bending forward doing some little thing by the couch, perhaps folding the newspaper, making the room tidy at the last moment before going to bed, when suddenly a violent darkness came over him, he felt his arms pinned, and he heard a man's voice speaking mockingly behind him, with a laugh. It was as if he saw the man's face too—a stranger, a rough, strong sort of Australian. And he realised with horror: "Now they have put a sack over my head, and fastened my arms, and I am in the dark, and they are going to steal my little brown handbag from the bedroom, which contains all the money we have." The shock of intense reality made him fight his way out of the depths of the first sleep, but it was some time before he could really lay hold of facts, like: "I am not at Coo-ee. I am not at Mullumbimby. I am in Sydney at Wyewurk, and the Callcotts are in the next room." So he came really awake. But if the thing had really happened, it could hardly have happened to him more than in this dream.

In the morning they were returning to the South Coast. But Jack said to Somers, a little sarcastically:

"You aren't altogether pleased with us, then?"

Somers hesitated before replying:

"I'm not altogether pleased with myself, am I?"

"You don't have to be so particular, in this life," said Jack.

"I may have to be."

"You can't have it all perfect beforehand, you know. You've got to sink a few times before you can swim."

"Sink in what?"

"Why, it seems to me you want to have a thing all ready in your hand, know all about it, before you'll try it. And there's some things you can't do that with. You've just got to flop into them, like when you chuck a dog into water."

Somers received this rebuke rather sourly. This was the first wintry day they had really had. There was a cold fog in Sydney in the morning, and rain in the fog. In the hills it would be snow—away in the Blue Mountains. But the fog lifted, and the rain held off, and there was a wash of yellowish sunshine.

Harriet of course had to talk to a fellow-passenger in the train, because Lovat was his glummest. It was a red-moustached Welshman with a slightly injured look in his pale blue eyes, as if everything hadn't been as good to him as he thought it ought, considering his merit. He said his name was Evans, and he kept a store. He had been sixteen years in the country.

"And is it very hot in the summer?" said Harriet. "I suppose it is."

"Yes," he said, "it's very hot. I've known the days when I've had to lie down at two o'clock in the afternoon, and not been able to move. Overpowered, that's what it is, over-powered."

Harriet was suitably impressed, having tried heat in India.

"And do you think it takes one long to get used to this country?" she asked after a while.

"Well, I should say it takes about four or five years for your blood properly to thin down. You can't say you've begun, under two years."

"Four or five years!" re-echoed Harriet. But what she was really turning over in her mind was this phrase: "For your blood to thin down." To thin down! how queer! Lovat also heard the sentence, and realised that his blood took this thinning very badly, and still about four years of simmering ahead, apparently, if he stayed in this country. And when the blood had finished its thinning, what then? He looked at Mr. Evans, with the sharp pale nose and the reddish hair and the injured look in his pale blue eyes. Mr. Evans seemed to find it sweet still to talk to people from the "old country". "You're from the old country?"—the inevitable question. The thinning down had left him looking as if he felt he lacked something. Yet he wouldn't go back to South Wales. Oh no, he wouldn't go back.

"The blood is thinner out here than in the old country." The Australians seemed to accept this as a scientific fact. Richard felt he didn't want his blood thinned down to the Australian constituency. Yet no doubt in the night, in his sleep, the metabolic change was taking place fast and furious.

It was raining a little in the late afternoon when Somers and Harriet got back to Coo-ee. With infinite relief she stepped across her own threshold.

"Ah!" she said, taking a long breath. "Thank God to be back." She looked round, and went to rearrange on the sofa the cushions that they had whacked so hard to get the dust out.

Somers went to the edge of the grass to be near the sea. It was raving in long, rasping lines of hissing breakers—not very

high ones, but very long. The sky hung grey, with veils of
dark rain out to sea, and in the south a blackness of much rain
blowing nearer in the wind. At the end of the jetty, in the
mist of the sea-wind's spray, a long, heavy coal-steamer was
slowly toiling to cast loose and get away. The waves were so
long and the current so strong, they would hardly let her turn
and get clear of the misty-black jetty.

Under the dark-grey sky the sea looked bright, but coldly
bright, with its yellow-green waves and its ramparts of white
foam. There were usually three white ramparts, one behind
the other, of rasping surf: and sometimes four. Then the long
swish and surge of the shoreward wash. The coast was quite
deserted: the steep sand wet as the backwash slid away: the
rocks wet with rain: the low, long black steamer still laboured
in the fume of the wind, indistinctly.

Somers turned indoors, and suddenly began taking off his
clothes. In a minute he was running naked in the rain which
fell with lovely freshness on his skin. Ah, he felt so stuffy
after that sort of emotional heat in town. Harriet in amazement saw him whitely disappearing over the edge of the low
cliff-bank, and came to the edge to look.

He ran quickly over the sands, where the wind blew cold
but velvety, and the raindrops fell loosely. He walked straight
into the fore-wash, and fell into an advancing ripple. At least
it looked like a ripple, but was enough to roll him over so that
he went under and got a little taste of the Pacific. Ah, the fresh
cold wetness!—the fresh cold wetness! The water rushed in
the backwash and the sand melted under him, leaving him
stranded like a fish. He turned again to the water. The walls
of surf were some distance off, but near enough to look rather
awful as they raced in high white walls shattering towards
him. And above the ridge of the raving whiteness the dimness of the labouring steamer, as if it were perched on a
bough.

Of course he did not go near the surf. No, the last green
ripples of the broken swell were enough to catch him by the
scruff of the neck and tumble him rudely up the beach, in a
pell-mell. But even the blow did one good, as the sea struck
one heavily on the back, if one were fleeing; full on the chest,
if one were advancing.

It was raining quite heavily as he walked out, and the skies
hung low over the sea, dark over the green and white vigour

of the ocean. The shore was so foam-white it almost suggested sun. The rain felt almost warm.

Harriet came walking across the grass with a towel.

"What a good idea!" she said. "If I'd known I'd have come. I wish I had."

But he ignored the towel, and went into the little wash-place and under the shower, to wash off the sticky, strong Pacific. Harriet came along with the towel, and he put his hand to her face and nodded to her. She knew what he meant, and went wondering, and when he had rubbed the wet off himself he came to her.

To the end she was more wondering than anything. But when it was the end, and the night was falling outside, she laughed and said to him:

"That was done in style. That was *chic*. Straight from the sea, like another creature."

Style and *chic* seemed to him somewhat ill suited to the occasion, but he brought her a bowl of warm water and went and made the tea. The wind was getting noisier, and the sea was shut out but still calling outside the house. They had tea and toast and quince jam, and one of the seven brown tea-pots with a bit off the spout shone quite nicely and brightly at a corner of the little red-and-white check tea-cloth, which itself occupied a corner of the big, polished jarrah table. But, thank God, he felt cool and fresh and detached, not cosy and domestic. He was so thankful not to be feeling cosy and "homely". The room felt as penetrable to the outside influence as if it were a sea-shell lying on the beach, cool with the freshness and insistence of the sea, not a snug, cosy box to be secured inside.

And Jack Callcott's rebuke stuck in his throat. Perhaps after all he was just a Pommy, prescribing things with overmuch emphasis, and wanting to feel God-Almighty in the face of unborn events. A Pommy is a newcomer in Australia, from the Old Country.

Teacher: Why did you hit him, Georgie?

Georgie: Please, miss, he called me a Pommy.

Aussie (with a discoloured eye): Well, you're one, ain'cher? Can I help it that ch'are one?

Pommy is supposed to be short for pomegranate. Pomegranate, pronounced invariably pommygranate, is a near enough rhyme to immigrant, in a naturally rhyming country. Furthermore, immigrants are known in their first months, before their blood "thins down", by their round and ruddy cheeks. So we are told. Hence again, pomegranate, and hence Pommy. Let etymologists be appeased: it is the authorised derivation.

Perhaps, said Somers to himself, I am just a Pommy and a fool. If my blood had thinned down, I shouldn't make all this fuss over sharing in with Kangaroo or being mates with Jack Callcott. If I am not a ruddy Pommy, I am a green one. Of course they take the thing as it comes to them, and they expect me to do the same. Yet there I am hopping and hissing like a fish in a frying-pan. Putting too much "soul" into it. Far too much. When your blood has thinned down, out here, there's nothing but the merest sediment of a soul left, and your wits and your feelings are clear of it. You take things as they come, as Jack says. Isn't that the sanest way to take them, instead of trying to drive them through the exact hole in the hedge that you've managed to poke your head through? Oh, you unlearn a lot as your blood thins down. But there's an awful lot to be unlearnt. And when you've unlearnt it, you never say so. In the first place, because it's dead against the sane old British tradition. And in the second place, because you don't really care about telling what you feel, once your blood has thinned down and is clear of soul.

"Thin, you Australian burgundy," said Somers to his own body, when he caught a glimpse of it unawares, reflected in the glass as he was going to bed. "You're thin enough as a bottle, but the wine needs a lot of maturing. I've made a fool of myself latterly."

Yet he said to himself: "Do I want my blood to thin down like theirs?—that peculiar emptiness that is in them, because of the thinning that's gone out of them? Do I want this curious transparent blood of the antipodes, with its momentaneous feelings, and its sort of *absentness*? But of course till my blood has thinned down I shan't see with their eyes. And how in the name of heaven is this world-brotherhood mankind going to see with one eye, eye to eye, when the very blood is of different thickness on different continents, and with the difference in blood, the inevitable psychic difference? Different vision!"

CHAPTER VIII

VOLCANIC EVIDENCE

RICHARD LOVAT SOMERS registered a new vow: not to take things with too overwhelming an amount of emotional seriousness, but to accept everything that came along with a certain *sang froid*, and not to sit frenziedly in judgment before he had heard the case. He had come to the end of his own tether, so why should he go off into tantrums if other folks strayed about with the broken bits of their tethers trailing from their ankles. Is it better to be savagely tugging at the end of your rope, or to wander at random tetherless? Matter of choice!

But the day of the absolute is over, and we're in for the strange gods once more. "But when you get to the end of your tether you've nothing to do but die"—so sings an out-of-date vulgar song. But is it so? Why not all? When you come to the end of your tether you break the rope. When you come to the end of the lane you straggle on into the bush and beat about till you find a new way through, and no matter if you raise vipers or goannas or wallabies, or even only a stink. And if you see a man beating about for a new track you don't immediately shout, "Perverted wretch!" or "Villain!" or "Vicious creature!" or even merely "The fool", or mildly: "Poor dear!" You have to let him try. Anything is better than stewing in your own juice, or grinding at the end of your tether, or tread-milling away at a career. Better a "wicked creature" any day than a mechanical tread-miller of a careerist. Better anything on earth than the millions of human ants.

In this way Mr. Somers had to take himself to task, for his Pommy stupidity and his pommigrant superiority, and kick himself rather severely, looking at the ends of the tether he presumed he had just broken. Why should people who are tethered to a post be so God-Almighty puffed up about their posts? It seems queer. Yet there they are, going round and round at the ends of their tethers, and being immensely sniffy about the people who stray loose trailing the broken end of their old rope, and looking for a new way through the bush. Yet so men are. They will set up inquisitions and every manner of torture chamber to *compel* people to refrain from

F

breaking their tethers. But once man has broken any old particular hobble-line, not God Himself can safely knot it together again.

Somers now left off standing on his head in front of the word love, and looking at it calmly, decided he didn't care vastly either way. Harriet had on her dressing-table tray a painted wooden heart, painted red with dots round it, a Black Forest trifle which she had bought in Baden-Baden for a penny. On it was the motto:

"Dem Mutigen gehört die Welt."

That was the motto to have on one's red heart: not Love or Hope or any of those aspiring emotions: "The world belongs to the courageous." To be sure, it was a rather two-edged motto just now for Germany. And Somers was not quite sure that it was the "world" that he wanted.

Yes, it was. Not the tuppenny social world of present mankind: but the genuine world, full of life and eternal creative surprises, including of course destructive surprises: since destruction is part of creation. Somers did want the world. He did want to take it away from all the teeming human ants, human slaves, and all the successful, empty careerists. He wanted little that the present society can give. But the lovely other world that is in spite of the social man of to-day: that he wanted, to clear it, to free it. Freedom! Not for this subnormal slavish humanity of democratic antics. But for the world itself, and the *Mutigen*.

Mut! Muth! A good word. Better even than *courage*. Virtue, *virtus*, manliness. *Mut*—manliness. Not braggadoccio or insolence. *De l'audace, et de l'audace, et encore de l'audace!* Danton's word. But it was more than daring. It was *Mut*, profound manliness, that is not afraid of anything except of being cowardly or barren.

"Dem Mutigen gehört die Welt."
"To the manly brave belongs the world."

Somers wrote to Kangaroo, and enclosed the red wooden heart, which had a little loop of ribbon so that it could be hung on the wall.

"Dear Kangaroo—I send you my red heart (never mind that

it is wood, the wood once lived and was the tree of life) with its motto. I hope you will accept it, after all my annoying behaviour. It is not the love, but the *Mut* that I believe in, and join you in. Love may be an ingredient in *Muth*, so you have it all your own way. Anyhow, I send you my red motto-heart, and if you don't want it you can send it back—I will be your follower, in reverence for your virtue—*Virtus*. And you may command me."

The following day came the answer, in Kangaroo's difficult scrawl:

"Dear Lovat—Love is in your name, notwithstanding. I accept the red heart gladly, and when I win, I will wear it for my Order of Merit, pinned on my swelling chest.

"But you are the one person in the world I can never command. I knew it would be so. Yet I am unspeakably glad to have your approval, and perhaps your allegiance.

"Come and see me as soon as it is your wish to do so: I won't invite you, lest worse befall me. For you are either a terrible disappointment to me, or a great blessing in store. I wait for you."

Somers also wrote to Jack, to ask him to come down with Victoria for the week-end. But Jack replied that he couldn't get away this week-end, there was so much doing. Somers then invited him for the following one.

The newspapers were at this time full of the pending strike of coal-miners and shearers: that is, the Australian papers. The European papers were in a terrific stew about finance, and the German debt, and the more imposing Allied debt to America. Bolshevism, Communism, Labour, had all sunk into a sort of insignificance. The voice of mankind was against them for the time being, not now in hate and fear, as previously, but in a kind of bitter contempt: the kind of feeling one has when one has accepted a glib individual as a serious and remarkable man, only to find that he is a stupid vulgarian. Communism was a bubble that would never even float free and iridescent from the nasty pipe of the theorist.

What then? Nothing evident. There came dreary and fatuous letters from friends in England, refined young men of the upper middle-class writing with a guarded kind of friendliness, gentle and sweet, of course, but as dozy as ripe pears in their *laisser aller* heaviness. That was what it amounted to: they were over-ripe, they had been in the sun of prosperity too

long, and all their tissues were soft and sweetish. How could
they react with any sharpness to any appeal on earth? They
wanted just to hang against the warmest wall they could find,
as long as ever they could, till some last wind of death or disturbance shook them down into earth, mushy and over-ripe. A
sardonic letter from a Jewish friend in London, amusing but a
bit dreadful. Letters from women in London, friendly but
irritable. "I have decided I am a comfort-loving conventional
person, with just a dash of the other thing to keep me fidgetty"
—then accounts of buying old furniture, and gossip about
everybody: "Verden Grenfel in a restaurant with *two* bottles
of champagne, so he must be affluent just now." A girl taking
her honeymoon trip to Naples by one of the Orient boats, third
class: "There are 800 people on board, but room for another
400, so that on account of the missing 400 we have a six-berth
cabin to ourselves. It is a bit noisy and not luxurious, but clean
and comfortable, and you can imagine what it is to me, to be
on the glorious sea, and to go ashore at wonderful Gibraltar,
and to see the blue hills of Spain in the distance. Frederick
is struggling with a mass of Italian irregular verbs at the
moment." And in spite of all Somers' love of the Mediter-
ranean, the thought of sitting on a third-class deck with eight
hundred emigrants, including babies, made him almost sick.
"The glorious sea—wonderful Gibraltar." It takes quite a good
eyesight even to *see* the sea from the deck of a liner, let alone
out of the piled mass of humanity on the third-class deck. A
letter from Germany, about a wedding and a pending journey
into Austria and friends, written with a touch of philosophy
that comes to a man when he's fallen down and bumped himself, and strokes the bruise. A cheque for fifteen pounds seventeen shillings and fourpence, from a publisher: "Kindly
acknowledge." A letter from a farming friend who had
changed places: "A Major Ashworth has got the farm, and
has spent about £600 putting it into order. He has started as
a poultry farm, but has had bad luck in losing 400 chicks
straight away, with the cold weather. I hope our spell of bad
luck doesn't still hang over the place. I wish you would come
back to England for the summer. Viv. talks of getting a cara-
van, and then we might get two. Cold and wet weather for
weeks. All work and no play, not good enough." A letter from
Paris, artist friends: "I have sold one of the three pictures that
are in the last Salon." A letter from Somers' sister: "Louis has

been looking round everywhere to buy a little farm, but there doesn't seem to be a bit of land to be got anywhere. What do you think of our coming to Australia? I wish you would look for something for us, for we are terribly fed up with this place, nothing doing at all." A letter from Sicily: "I have had my father and stepmother over from New York. I had got them rooms here, but when I said so, the face of Anna, my step-mother, was a sight. She took me aside and told me that father was spoiling the trip entirely by his economies, and that she had set her heart on the Villa Igeia. Then Dad took me aside and said that he didn't wish to be reckless, but he didn't want to thwart Anna's wishes entirely, and was there nothing in the way of compromise? It ended by their staying two days here, and Anna said she thought it was very nice *for me*. Then they went to the Palmes, which is entirely up to Anna's ideas of luxury, and she is delighted."

Somers had fourteen letters by this mail. He read them with a sort of loathing, one after the other, piling them up on his left hand for Harriet, and throwing the envelopes in the fire. By the time he had done he wished that every mail-boat would go down that was bringing any letter to him, that a flood would rise and cover Europe entirely, that he could have a little opera-tion performed that would remove from him for ever his memory of Europe and everything in it—and so on. Then he went out and looked at the Pacific. He hadn't even the heart to bathe, and he felt so trite, with all those letters; he felt quite capable of saying "Good dog" to the sea: to quote one of the quips from the *Bulletin*. The sea that had been so full of potency, before the postman rode up on his pony and whistled with his policeman's whistle for Somers to come to the gate for that mass of letters. Never had Richard Lovat Somers felt so filled with spite against everybody he had ever known in the old life as now.

"And there was I, knave, fool, and ninny, whining to go back to Europe, and abusing Australia for not being like it. That horrible, horrible staleness of Europe, and all their trite con-sciousness, and their dreariness. The dreariness! The sterility of their feelings! And here was I carping at Kangaroo and at Jack Callcott, who are golden wonders compared with any-thing I have known in the old world. Australia has got some real, positive indifference to 'questions', but Europe is one big wriggling question and nothing else. A tangle of quibbles. I'd rather be shot here next week than quibble the rest of my life away in over-upholstered Europe."

He left off kicking himself, and went down to the shore to get away from himself. After all, he knew the endless water would soon make him forget. It had a language which spoke utterly without concern of him, and this utter unconcern gradually soothed him of himself and his world. He began to forget.

There had been a squall in the night. At the tip of the rock-shelves above the waves men and youths, with bare, reddish legs, were fishing with lines for blackfish. They looked like animal creatures perching there, and like creatures they were passive or darting in their movements. A big albatross swung slowly down the surf: albatross or mollyhawk, with wide, waving wings.

The sea had thrown up, all along the surf-line, queer glittery creatures that looked like thin blown glass. They were bright transparent bladders of the most delicate ink-blue, with a long crest of deeper blue, and blind ends of translucent purple. And they had bunches of blue, blue strings, and one long blue string that trailed almost a yard across the sand, straight and blue and translucent. They must have been some sort of little octopus, with the bright glass bladder, big as smallish narrow pears, with a blue frill along the top to float them, and the strings to feel with—and perhaps the long string to anchor by. Who knows? Yet there they were, soft, brilliant, like pouches of frailest sea-glass. It reminded Somers of the glass they blow at Murano, at Venice. But there they never get the lovely soft texture and the colour.

The sky was tufted with cloud, and in the afternoon veils of rain swept here and there across the sea, in a changing wind. But then it cleared again, and Somers and Harriet walked along the sands, watching the blue sky mirror purple and the white clouds mirror warm on the wet sand. The sea talked and talked all the time, in its disintegrative, elemental language. And at last it talked its way into Somers' soul, and he forgot the world again, the babel. The simplicity came back, and with it the inward peace. The world had left him again. He had been thinking, in his anger of the morning, that he would get Jack to teach him to shoot with a rifle and a revolver, so that he might take his part. He had never shot with a gun in his life, so he had thought it was high time to begin. But now he went back on his thoughts. What did he want with guns or revolvers? Nothing. He had nothing to do with them, as he had nothing to do with so much that is in the world of man. When he was truly himself he had a quiet stillness in his soul, an inward trust. Faith, undefined and undefinable. Then he was at peace with himself. Not content, but peace like a river, something flowing and full. A stillness at the very core.

But faith in what? In himself, in mankind, in the destiny of mankind? No, no. In Providence, in Almighty God? No, not even that. He tried to think of the dark God he declared he served. But he didn't want to. He shrank away from the effort. The fair morning seaward world, full of bubbles of life.

So again came back to him the ever-recurring warning that *some* men must of their own choice and will listen only to the living life that is a rising tide in their own being, and listen, listen, listen for the injunctions, and give heed and know and speak and obey all they can. Some men must live by this unremitting inwardness, no matter what the rest of the world does. They must not let the rush of the world's "outwardness" sweep them away: or if they are swept away, they must struggle back. Somers realised that he had had a fright against being swept away, because he half wanted to get swept away: but that now, thank God, he was flowing back. Not like the poor, weird "ink-bubbles", left high and dry on the sands.

Now he could remember the frenzied outward rushing of the vast masses of people, away from themselves, without being driven mad by it. But it seemed strange to him that they should rush like this in their vast herds, outwards, outwards, always frenziedly outwards, like souls with hydrophobia rushing away from the pool of water. He himself, when he was caught up in the rush, felt tortured and maddened, it was an agony of irritation to him till he could feel himself drifting back again like a creature into the sea. The sea of his own inward soul, his own unconscious faith, over which his will had no exercise. Why did the mass of people not want this stillness and this peace with their own being? Why did they want cinemas and excitements? Excitements are as nauseous as sea-sickness. Why does the world want them?

It is their problem. They must go their way. But some men, some women must stay by their own inmost being, in peace, and without envy. And there in the stillness listen, listen, and

try to know, and try to obey. From the innermost, not from
the outside. It is so lovely, the peace. But poor dear Richard,
he was only resting and basking in the old sunshine just now,
after his fray. The fight would come again, and only in the
fight would his soul burn its way once more to the knowledge,
the intense knowledge of his "dark god". The other was so
much sweeter and easier, while it lasted.

At tea-time it began to rain again. Somers sat on the veranda
looking at the dark green sea, with its films of floating yellow
light between the ruffled waves. Far back, in the east, was a
cloud that was a rainbow. It was a piece of rainbow, but not
sharp, in a band; it was a tall fume far back among the clouds
of the sea-wall.

"Who is there that you feel you are with, besides me—or
who feel themselves with you?" Harriet was asking.

"No one," he replied. And at the same moment he looked
up and saw the rainbow fume beyond the sea. But it was on a
dark background, like a coloured darkness. The rainbow was
always a symbol to him—a good symbol: of this peace. A
pledge of unbroken faith, between the universe and the innermost. And the very moment he said "No one" he saw the rainbow for an answer.

Many times in his life he had seen a rainbow. The last had
been on his arrival in Sydney. For some reason he felt absolutely wretched and dismal on that Saturday morning when
the ship came into Sydney Harbour. He had an unspeakable
desire not to get out of the ship, not to go down on to the
quay and into that town. The having to do it was a violation
of himself. When he came on deck after breakfast and the
ship had stopped, it was pouring with rain, the P. & O. wharf
looked black and dismal, empty. It might almost have been
an abandoned city. He walked round to the starboard side, to
look towards the unimposing hillock of the city and the
Circular Quay. Black, all black and unutterably dismal in the
pouring rain, even the green grass of the Botanical Gardens,
and the bits of battlement of the Conservatorium. Unspeakably forlorn. Yet over it all, spanning the harbour, the most
magnificent great rainbow. His mood was so miserable he
didn't want to see it. But it was unavoidable. A huge, brilliant,
supernatural rainbow, spanning all Sydney.

He was thinking of this, and still watching the dark-green,
yellow-reflecting sea, that was like a northern sea, a Whitby

sea, and watching the far-off fume of a dark rainbow appari-
tion, when Harriet heard somebody at the door. It was William
James, who had an hour to wait for his train, and thought they
wouldn't mind if he looked in. They were pleased, and Harriet
brought him a cup and plate.

Thank goodness he, too, came in a certain stillness of spirit,
saying very little, but being a quiet, grateful presence. When
the tea was finished he and Somers sat back on the veranda
out of the wind, and watched the yellow, cloudy evening sink.
They hardly spoke, but lay lying back in the deck-chairs.

"I was wondering," said Somers, "whom Kangaroo depends
on mostly for his following."

William James looked back at him, with quiet, steady eyes.

"On the diggers—the returned soldiers chiefly: and the
sailors."

"Of what class?"

"Of any class. But there aren't many rich ones. Mostly like
me and Jack, not quite simple working men. A few doctors
and architects and that sort."

"And do you think it means much to them?"

Jaz shifted his thick body uneasily in his chair.

"You never can tell," he said.

"That's true," said Somers. "I don't really know how much
Jack Callcott cares. I really can't make out."

"He cares as much as about anything," said Jaz. "Perhaps a
bit more. It's more exciting."

"Do you think it *is* the excitement they care about chiefly?"

"I should say so. You can die in Australia if you don't get a
bit of excitement." There was silence for a minute or two.

"In my opinion," said Somers, "it has to go deeper than
excitement." Again Jaz shifted uneasily in his chair.

"Oh, well—they don't set much store on deepness over here.
It's easy come, easy go, as a rule. Yet they're staunch chaps
while the job lasts, you know. They are true to their mates,
as a rule."

"I believe they are. It's the afterwards."

"Oh, well—afterwards is afterwards, as Jack always says."
And the two men were silent.

"If they cared deeply——" Somers began slowly—but he
did not continue, it seemed fatuous. Jaz did not answer for
some time.

"You see, it hasn't come to that with them," he said. "It

F*

might, perhaps, once they'd actually done the thing. It might come home to them then; they might *have* to care. It might be a force-put. *Then* they'd need a man."

"They've got Kangaroo," said Somers.

"You think Kangaroo would get them over the fence?" said Jaz carefully, looking up at Somers.

"He seems as if he would. He's a wonderful person. And there seems no alternative to him."

"Oh yes, he's a wonderful person. Perhaps a bit too much of a wonder. A hatchet doesn't look anything like so spanking as a lawn-mower, does it now, but it'll make a sight bigger clearing."

"That's true," said Somers, laughing. "But Kangaroo isn't a lawn-mower."

"Oh, I don't say so," smiled Jaz, fidgeting on his chair. "I should like to hear your rock-bottom opinion of him though."

"I should like to hear yours," said Somers. "You know him much better than I do. I haven't got a rock-bottom opinion of him yet."

"It's not a matter of the time you've known him," said Jaz. He was manifestly hedging, and trying to get at something. "You know I belong to his gang, don't you?"

"Yes," said Somers, wondering at the word "gang".

"And for that reason I oughtn't to criticise him, ought I?"

Somers reflected for some moments.

"There's no oughts, if you *feel* critical," he answered.

"I think you feel critical of him yourself at times," said Jaz, looking up with a slow, subtle smile of cunning: like a woman's disconcerting intuitive knowledge. It laid Somers' soul bare for the moment. He reflected. He had pledged no allegiance to Kangaroo.

"Yet," he said aloud to Jaz, "if I *had* joined him I wouldn't want to hinder him."

"No, we don't want to hinder him. But we need to know where we are. Supposing you were in my position—and you *didn't* feel sure of things! A man has to look things in the face. You yourself, now—you're holding back, aren't you?"

"I suppose I am," said Richard. "But then I hold back from everything."

Jaz looked at him searchingly.

"You don't like to commit yourself?" he said, with a sly smile.

"Not altogether that. I'd commit myself, if I could. It's just something inside me shakes its head and holds back."

Jaz studied his knuckles for some time.

"Yes," he said slowly. "Perhaps you can afford to stand out. You've got your life in other things. Some of us feel we haven't got any life if we're not—if we're not mixed up in something." He paused, and Richard waited. "But the point is this——" Jaz looked up again with his light-grey, serpent's eyes. "Do you yourself see Kangaroo pulling it off?" There was a subtle mockery in the question.

"What?"

"Why—you know. This revolution, and this new Australia. Do you see him figuring on the Australian postage stamps—and running the country like a new Jerusalem?"

The eyes watched Richard fixedly.

"If he's got a proper backing, why not?" Somers answered.

"I don't say why not. I ask you, *will he?* Won't you say how you feel?"

Richard sat quite still, not even thinking, but suspending himself. And in the suspense his heart went sad, oh so empty, inside him. He looked at Jaz, and the two men read the meaning in each other's eyes.

"You think he won't?" said Jaz, triumphing.

"No, I think he won't," said Richard.

"There now. I knew you felt like that."

"And yet," said Richard, "if men were men still—if they had any of that belief in love they pretend to have—if they were *fit* to follow Kangaroo," he added fiercely, feeling grief in his heart.

Jaz dropped his head and studied his knuckles, a queer, blank smile setting round his mouth.

"You have to take things as they are," he said in a small voice.

Richard sat silent, his heart for the moment broken again.

"And," added Jaz, looking up with a slow, subtle smile, "if men aren't what Kangaroo wants them to be, why should they be? If they don't want a new Jerusalem, why should they have it? It's another catch. They like to hear Kangaroo's sweet talk —and they'll probably follow him if he'll bring off a good big row, and they think he can make it all pretty afterwards." Again he smiled, but bitterly, mockingly. "I don't know why I say these things to you, I'm sure. But it's as well for a man to get to the bottom of what he thinks, isn't it? And I feel, you know, that you and me think alike, if we allow ourselves to think."

Richard looked at him, but never answered. He felt somehow treacherous.

"Kangaroo's clever," resumed Jaz. "He's a Jew, and he's damn clever. Maybe he's the cleverest. I'll tell you why. You're not offended now at what I say, are you?"

"What's the good of being offended by anything, if it's a genuine opinion."

"Well now, that's what I mean. And I say Kangaroo is cleverer than the Red people, because he can make it look as if it would be all rosy afterwards, you know, everything as good as apple-pie. I tell you what. All these Reds and I.W.W.s and all, why don't they make their revolution? Because they're frightened of it when they've made it. They're not frightened of hanging all the capitalists and such. But they're frightened to death of having to keep things going afterwards. They're frightened to death." Jaz smiled to himself with a chuckle. "Nothing frightens them so much as the thought of having to look after things when their revolution is made. It frightens them to death. And that's why they won't make their grand revolution. Never. Unless somebody shoves them into it. That's why they've got this new cry: Make the revolution by degrees, through winning in politics. But that's no revolution, you know. It's the same old thing with a bit of difference, such a small bit of difference that you'd never notice it if you weren't made to."

"I think that's true," said Richard. "Nobody's more frightened of a Red revolution than the Reds themselves. They just absolutely funk it."

"There now—that's the word—they funk it. Yet, you know, they're all ready for it. And if you got them started, if you could, they'd make a clearance, like they did in Russia. And we could do with that, don't you think?"

"I do," said Richard, sighing savagely.

"Well now, my idea's this. Couldn't we get Kangaroo to join the Reds—the I.W.W.s and all? Couldn't we get him to use all his men to back Red Labour in this country, and blow a cleavage through the old system. Because, you know he's got the trump cards in his hands. These Diggers' Clubs, they've got all the army men, dying for another scrap. And then a sort of secret organisation has ten times the hold over men than just a Labour Party, or a Trades Union. He's damned clever, he's got a wonderful scheme ready. But he'll spoil it, because he'll want it all to happen without hurting anybody. Won't he now?"

"Except a very few."

"Oh yes—maybe four of his enemies. But he wants to blow the house up without breaking the windows. He thinks he can turn the country upside-down without spilling milk, let alone blood. Now the Reds, let them loose, would make a hole in things. Only they'll never move on their own responsibility. They haven't got the guts, the stomach, the backbone."

"You're so clever, Jaz. I wonder you're not a leader yourself."

"Me?" A slow, ironical smile wreathed his face. "You're being sarcastic with me, Mr. Somers."

"Not at all. I think you're amazing."

Jaz only smiled sceptically still.

"You take what I mean, though, do you?"

"I do."

"And what do you think of it?"

"Very clever."

"But isn't it feasible? You get Kangaroo, with his Diggers— the cleverest idea in the country, really—to quietly came in with the Reds, and explode a revolution over here. You could soon do it, in the cities: and the country couldn't help itself. You let the Reds appear in the front, and take all the shine. You keep a bit of a brake on them. You let them call a Soviet, or whatever they want, and get into a real mess over it. And then Kangaroo steps in with the balm of Gilead and the New Jerusalem. But let them play Old Tommy Jenkins first with Capital and State Industries and the free press and religious sects. And then Kangaroo steps in like a redeeming angel, and reminds us that it's God's Own Country, so we're God's Own People, and makes us feel good again. Like Solomon, when David has done the dirty work."

"The only point," said Somers, smiling, "is that an Australian Lenin and an Australian Trotsky might pop up in the scrimmage, and then Kangaroo could take to the bush again."

Jaz shook his head.

"They wouldn't," he said. "There's nobody with any grip.

And you'd see, in this country, people would soon want to be
good again, because it costs them least effort."

"Perhaps Kangaroo is right, and they don't want to be anything *but* good."

Jaz shook his head.

"It's not goodness they're after just now," he said. "They
want to rip things up, or they want nothing. They aren't ready
to come under Kangaroo's loving wing just yet. They'd as leave
be under King George's thumb, they can peep out easier. It
seems to me, it's *spite* that's at the bottom, with most men.
And they've got to let it out before anything's any good."

Somers began to feel tired now.

"But after all, Jaz," he said, "what have I got to do with it?"

"You can put it to Kangaroo. You can make him see it. And
you can keep him to it, if you promise him you'll stick to
him."

"Me a power behind the throne?" protested the truly
sceptical Richard.

"I take it you don't want to sit on the throne yourself,'
smiled Jaz. "And Kangaroo's got more the figure. But what
do you think of it?"

Somers was silent. He now was smiling subtly and ironically,
and Jaz was watching him sharply, like a man who wants
something. Jaz waited.

"I'm afraid, Jaz," said Somers, "that, like Nietzsche, I no
longer believe in great events. The war was a great event—and
it made everything more pretty. I doubt if I care about the
mass of mankind, Jaz. You make them more than ever distaste-
ful to me."

"Oh, you know, you needn't commit yourself. You've only
to be friendly with Kangaroo, and work him into it. You know
you said yourself you'd give anything to have a clearance
made in the world."

"I know. Sometimes I feel I'd give anything, soul and body,
for a smash up in this social-industrial world we're in. And I
would. And then when I realise people—just people—the same
people after it as before—why, Jaz, then I don't care any more,
and feel it's time to turn to the gods."

"You feel there's any gods to turn to, do you?" asked Jaz,
with the sarcasm of disappointment.

"I feel it would probably be like Messina before and after
the earthquake. Before the earthquake it was what is called

a fine town, but commercial, low, and hateful. You felt you'd be glad if it was wiped out. After the earthquake it was horrible heaps of mortar and rubble, and now it's rows and rows of wood and tin shanties, streets of them, and more commercial, lower than ever, and infinitely more ugly. That would probably be the world after your revolution. No, Jaz, I leave mankind to its own contrivances, and turn to the gods."

"But you'll say a word to Kangaroo?" said Jaz, persistent.

"Yes, if I feel like it," said Richard.

Darkness had almost fallen, and Somers shivered as he rose to go indoors.

Next morning, when Somers had made the coffee, he and Harriet sat on the loggia at breakfast. It had rained in the night, and the sea was whitish, sluggish, with soft, furry waves that had no plunge. The last thin flush of foam behaved queerly, running along with a straight, swift splash, just as when a steel rope rips out of water, as a tug hauls suddenly, jerking up a white splash that runs along its length.

"What had William James so much to say about?" asked Harriet, on the warpath.

"Why don't you have the strength of mind not to ask?" he replied. "You know it's better you left it alone: that I'm not supposed to blab."

She gave him one fierce look, then went pale with anger. She was silent for some time. Then she burst out:

"Pah, as if I cared to know! What is all their revolution bosh to me! There have been revolutions enough, in my opinion, and each one more foolish than the last. And this will be the most foolish of the lot. And what have *you* got to do with revolutions, you petty and conceited creature? You and revolutions! You're not big enough, not grateful enough to do anything real. I give you my energy and my life, and you want to put me aside as if I was a charwoman. Acknowledge *me* first, before you can be any good." With which she swallowed her coffee and rose from the table.

He finished too, and got up to carry in the cups and do the few chores that remained for his share. He always got up in the morning, made the fire, swept the room, and tidied roughly. Then he brought in coal and wood, made the breakfast, and did any little outdoor job. After breakfast he helped to wash up, and settled the fire. Then he considered himself free to his own devices. Harriet could see to the rest.

His devices were not very many. He tried to write, that being his job. But usually, nowadays, when he tapped his unconscious, he found himself in a seethe of steady fury, general rage. He didn't hate anybody in particular, nor even any class or body of men. He loathed politicians, and the well-bred darling young men of the well-to-do middle classes made his bile stir. But he didn't fret himself about them specially. The off-hand self-assertive working people of Australia made him feel diabolic on their score sometimes. But as a rule the particulars were not in evidence, all the rocks were submerged, and his bile just swirled diabolically for no particular reason at all. He just felt generally diabolical, and tried merely to keep enough good sense not to turn his temper in any particular direction.

"You think that nothing but goodness and virtue and wonderfulness comes out of you," was one of Harriet's accusations against him. "You don't know how small and mean and ugly you are to other people."

"Which means I am small and ugly and mean in her eyes," he thought to himself. "All because of this precious gratitude which I am supposed to feel towards her, I suppose. Damn her and her gratitude. When she thwarts me and puts me in a temper I *don't* feel anything but spite. Damn her impudent gratitude."

But Harriet was not going to be ignored: no, she was not. She was not going to sink herself to the level of a convenience. She didn't really want protestations of gratitude or love. They only puzzled her and confused her. But she wanted him *inwardly* to keep a connection with her. Silently, he must maintain the flow between him and her, and safeguard it carefully. It is a thing which a man cannot do with his head: it isn't *remembering*. And it is a thing which a woman cannot explain or understand, because it is quite irrational. But it is one of the deepest realities in life. When a man and woman truly come together, when there is a marriage, then an unconscious, vital connection is established between them, like a throbbing blood-circuit. A man may forget a woman entirely with his head, and fling himself with energy and fervour into whatever job he is tackling, and all is well, all is good, if he does not break that inner vital connection which is the mystery of marriage. But let him once get out of unison, out of conjunction, let him inwardly break loose and come apart, let him fall into that worst of male vices, the vice of abstraction and mechanisation, and have a concert of working *alone* and of himself, then he commits the breach. He hurts the woman and he hurts himself, though neither may know why. The greatest hero that ever existed was heroic only whilst he kept the throbbing inner union with something, God, or Fatherland, or woman. The most immediate is woman, the wife. But the most grovelling wife-worshippers are the foulest of traitors and renegades to the inner unison. A man must strive onward, but from the root of marriage, marriage with God, with wife, with mankind. Like a tree that is rooted, always growing and flowering away from its root, so is a vitally active man. But let him take some false direction, and there is torture through the whole organism, roots and all. The woman suffers blindly from the man's mistaken direction, and reacts blindly.

Now in this revolution stunt, and his insistence on "male" activity, Somers had upturned the root flow, and Harriet was a devil to him—quite rightly—for he knew that inside himself he was devilish. She tried to keep her kindness and happiness. But no, it was false when the inner connection was betrayed. So her silent rage accumulated, and it was no good playing mental tricks of suppression with it. As for him, he was forced to recognise the devil in his own belly. He just felt devilish. While Harriet went about trying to be fair and happy, he realised that it was awful for him to be there, as black inside as an ink-bottle; however, he practised being nice. Theoretically he was grateful to her, and all that. But nothing conjured away that bellyful of black devilishness with which he was *enceinte*. He really felt like a woman who is with child by a corrosive fiend. In his lower man, just girning and demoniacal. No good pretending otherwise. No good playing tricks of being nice. Seven thousand devils!

When he saw a motor-car parked in the waste lot next to Coo-ee, and saw two women in twelve-guinea black coats and skirts hobbling across the grass to the bungalow farther down, perhaps wanting to hire it: then the devil came and sat black and naked in his eyes. They hobbled along the uneven place so commonly, they looked so crassly common in spite of their tailors' bills, so *low*, in spite of their motor-car, that the devil in him fairly lashed its tail like a cat. And yet, he knew, they were probably just two nice, kindly women, as the world goes.

And truly, even the devil in him did not want to do them any *personal* harm. If they had fallen, or got into difficulty, he would have gone out at once to help them all he could. And yet, at the sight of their backs in their tailored "costumes" hobbling past the bushes, the devil in him lashed its tail till he writhed.

So there you are. Or rather, there was Richard Lovat Somers. He tried to square accounts with himself. Surely, he said to himself, I am not just merely a sort of human bomb, all black inside, waiting to explode I don't know when or how or where. That's what I seem like to myself, nowadays. Yet surely it is not the only truth about me. When I feel at peace with myself, and, as it were, so quietly at the *centre* of things—like last evening, for example—surely that is also me. Harriet seems fairly to detest me for having this nice feeling all to myself. Well, it wasn't my fault if I had it. I did have it. What does she want? She won't leave a fellow alone. I felt fairly beatific last evening—I felt I could swim Australia into a future, and that Jaz was wonderful, and I was a sort of central angel. So now I must admit I am flabbergasted at finding my devil coiled up exultant like a black cat in my belly this morning, purring all the more loudly because of my "goodness" of last evening, and lashing his tail so venomously at the sight of the two women in the black "costumes". Is this devil after all my god? Do I stand with the debbil-debbil worshippers, in spite of all my efforts and protestations?

This morning I do, and I admit it. I can't help it: it is so, then let it be so. I shall change again, I know. I shall feel white again, and like a pearl, suave and quiet within the oyster of time. I shall feel again that, given but the *answer*, the black poisonous bud will burst into lovely new, unknown flower in me. The bud is deadly poison: the flower will be the flower of the tree of life. If Harriet let me alone, and people like Jaz really believed in me! Because they have a right to believe in me when I am at my best. Or perhaps he believes in me when I am my worst, and Kangaroo likes me when I am good. Yet I don't really like Kangaroo. The devil in me fairly hates him. Him and everybody. Well, all right then, if I *am* finally a sort of human bomb, black inside, and primed; I hope the hour and the place will come for my going off: for my exploding with the maximum amount of havoc. *Some* men have to be bombs, to explode and make breaches in the walls that shut life in. Blind, havoc-working bombs too. Then so be it.

That morning as luck would have it Somers read an article by A. Meston in an old *Sydney Daily Telegraph*, headed:

EARTHQUAKES

IS AUSTRALIA SAFE?

SLEEPING VOLCANOES

"The fact that Australia so far has had no trouble with volcanoes or earthquakes, and appears to be the most immune country in the world, accounts for our entire indifference to the whole subject. But there are phases of this problem entitled to some serious consideration by those in whom the thinking and observant faculties are not altogether dormant, and who have not a calm, cool disregard of very ominous inexorable facts. Australia is a very peaceful reposeful area, with the serious volcanoes of New Zealand on one side, and the still more serious volcanoes of Java on the other. We live in a soft flowery meadow between two jungles, a lion in one and a tiger in the other, but as neither animal has chased or bitten us, up to the present time, we go calmly to sleep quite satisfied they are harmless.

"Now the line of volcanic action on the east coast of Australia is very clearly defined, from the basalt of Illawarra, north to the basalt within three miles of Cape York. The chief areas over all that distance are the Big Scrup on the Richmond River, the Darling Downs, and the Atherton Tableland, behind Cairns.

"These are the largest basalt areas in Australia, the Darling Downs and Atherton containing each about 2,000,000 acres of basalt, the one chiefly black, and the other all red. The other conspicuous areas are the red basalt Isis and Woongarra scrubs, and north of Atherton the next basalt areas is on the M'Ivor and Morgan Rivers, 40 miles north of Cooktown. From there I saw no basalt on the coast of the Peninsula, until somewhat surprised to find great piles of black basaltic stone, like artificial quarry heaps, in the dense Seaforthia palm scrubs ten miles west of Somerset.

VOLCANIC EVIDENCE

"Here, then, is a clearly defined but very intermittent line of volcanic action along our entire east coast for over two thousand miles. Yet to-day there is not only not one active volcano on the whole of that area, but not even one clearly authentic dead one. There is nothing to show whence came the basalt of the Darling Downs, the Big Scrup, or the Atherton Tableland, unless in the last case the two deep freshwater lakes, Barrine and Eacham, the Barrang and Zeetcham of the aboriginals, represent the craters of extinct volcanoes.

"Whence, then, came the basalt spread along a narrow line of our east coast for two thousand miles, and all of it east of the Dividing Range? There is a lot of room for theories. . . .

"When the late Captain Audley Coote was laying the cable from New Caledonia to Sandy Cape, at the north end of Fraser Island, on the South Queensland coast, he passed a submerged mountain 6,000 feet in height, and found a tremendous chasm, so deep that they could find no bottom, and had to work the cable round the edge. When he reached the coast of Fraser Island he got the same soundings as Cook and Flinders and the Admiralty survey in the 'sixties, six to eight fathoms, but there came a break in the cable in after years, located in that six and eight fathom area, and they found the broken cable hanging over a submerged precipice of eight hundred feet!

"That I read in Captain Coote's own manuscript journal, and it was confirmed by Captain John Mackay, the Brisbane harbourmaster, who assured me that an 800 feet chasm had suddenly formed there in the bottom of the ocean.

"On the coast of Japan, the ocean bottoms sank in one place from four or five fathoms to 4,000 feet.

"The old Fraser Island aboriginals told me that the deep blue lake, two miles from the White Cliffs, was once a level plateau, on which their fathers held fights and corroborees, and that it sank in one night. On the North Queensland coast, there is fairly shallow water from the seashore out to the edge of the Barrier, and then the ocean goes down to depths up to two and three thousand feet, so if the sea were removed you would look down from the outer Barrier into a tremendous valley with a wall of granite cliffs.

"When the town of Port Royal in Jamaica was destroyed by an earthquake on June 7, 1692, the houses all disappeared into an ocean chasm 300 feet in depth; and in the terrible earthquake at Lisbon, 1755, destroying 2,000 houses and 5,000 people, the wharves and piers, and even the vessels lying beside them, disappeared into some tremendous gulf, leaving no trace whatever.

"It is a singular fact that the heights of the loftiest mountains correspond with the depths of the deepest seas, and that the 29,000 feet Mount Everest is equal with what is known as the 'Tuscarora Deep', fathomed by the U.S.A. vessel *Tuscarora*.

ISLANDS THAT VANISH

"From the days of Seneca there are records of islands suddenly appearing before astonished mariners, and others disappearing suddenly before mariners equally astonished. In the dreadful volcanic explosion of Krakatoa in August, 1883, one mountain peak was blown to pieces, while others were thrown up from the ocean. The tidal wave created by Krakatoa destroyed 40,000 people, and the air wave from the concussion pulsated three times round the world. And Krakatoa and the Javanese volcanoes are only a short distance from the coast of Australia!

"Doubtless many of the ships that have mysteriously disappeared, leaving no trace, have gone down in the vortex of a submarine earthquake, or a chasm created by a sudden shrinkage in the bottom of the ocean. From the facts above available it is reasonable to believe that the present continent of Australia is only a portion of the original, and that in some remote period it extended hundreds or thousands of miles to the eastward, probably including Lord Howe and Norfolk Islands and New Zealand, possibly New Caledonia. How came the ancient Cretaceous Ocean, which once covered all Central Australia, from the gulf to the Bight, to withdraw from the land, leaving nothing but marine fossils in the desert sandstone?

"Was the Cretaceous Ocean shallow all round this continent, and did it suddenly subside to fill some tremendous chasm caused by a sudden submarine shrinkage of the earth's crust, followed by the inland sea, which naturally rushed out into the vacancy?

"What seems the only real danger to Australia lies not in the eruptions of some suddenly created new volcano, or any ordinary earthquake, but in just such shrinkages in the sea bottom as occurred on the coast of Japan, off Fraser Island, and many other localities, including Lisbon and Port Royal.

"If such a subsidence were to come under Sydney, Melbourne, Adelaide or Brisbane, it might be of such a magnitude that the whole city would disappear into the gulf.

"We know nothing whatever of the awful forces at work beneath the crust of the earth, and nothing of the internal fires, or that awful subterranean abode where Shelley said 'the old earthquake Demon nurses her young Ruin.' The history of volcanoes and earthquakes is an appalling record of lost countless millions of lives and awful destruction.

"One Pekin earthquake destroyed 300,000 people, one in Naples 70,000, another at Naples 40,000; and we are not far from July, 1902, when the volcano of Mount Pelee, in the island of Martinique, wiped out the town of St. Pierre and 30,000 inhabitants.

"Still nearer is that 18th April, 1906, when the San Francisco earthquake killed over a thousand people, and did damage to the extent of sixty millions.

"And so far in Australian history we have not had an earthquake that would capsize a tumbler of hot punch."

Why hot punch, thought Somers, why not hop bitters or ice-cream soda, which are much more Austral and to the point? But he had read this almost thrilling bit of journalism with satisfaction. If the mother earth herself is so unstable, and upsets the apple-cart without caring a straw, why, what can a man say to himself if he *does* happen to have a devil in his belly!

And he looked at the ocean uneasily moving, and wondered when next it would thrust an angry shoulder out of the watery bed-covering, to give things a little jog. Or when his own devil would get a leg up into affairs.

CHAPTER IX

HARRIET AND LOVAT AT SEA IN MARRIAGE

WHEN a sincere man marries a wife, he has one or two courses open to him, which he can pursue with that wife. He can propose to himself to be (a) the lord and master who is honoured and obeyed (b) the perfect lover (c) the true friend and companion. Of these (a) is now rather out of date. The

lord and master has been proved, by most women quite satisfactorily, to be no more than a grown-up child, and his
arrogance is tolerated, because it is rather amusing, and up to
a certain point becoming. The case of (b), the perfect lover, is
the crux of all ideal marriage to-day. But alas, not even the
lord and master turns out such a fiasco as does the perfect
lover, ninety-nine times out of a hundred. The perfect-lover
marriage ends usually in a quite ghastly anti-climax, divorce
and horrors and the basest vituperation. Alas for the fact, as
compared with the ideal. A marriage of the perfect-lover type
is bound either to end in catastrophe, or to slide away towards
(a) or (c). It must either revert to a mild form of the lord-and-
master marriage, and a wise woman, who knows the sickeningness of catastrophes and the ridiculous futility of second shots
at the perfect-love paradise, often wisely pushes the marriage
back gradually into one of the little bays or creeks of this
Pacific Ocean of marriage, lord-and-masterdom. Not that either
party really believes in the lordship of man. But you've got to
get into still water some time or other. The perfect-love
business inevitably turns out to be a wildly stormy strait, like
the Straits of Magellan, where two fierce and opposing currents
meet and there is the devil of a business trying to keep the bark
of marriage, with the flag of perfect-love at the mast, from
dashing on a rock or floundering in the heavy seas. Two fierce
and opposing currents meet in the narrows of perfect love.
They may meet in blue and perfect weather, when the albatross
hovers in the great sky like a permanent benediction, and the
sea shimmers a second heaven. But you needn't wait long.
The seas will soon begin to rise, the ship to roll. And the waters
of perfect love—when once this love is consummated in
marriage—become inevitably a perfect hell of storms and
furies.

Then, as I say, the hymeneal bark either founders, or dashes
on a rock, or more wisely gets out of the clash of meeting
oceans and takes one tide or the other, where the flood has
things all its own way. The woman, being to-day the captain
of the marriage bark, either steers into the vast Pacific waters
of lord-and-masterdom, though never, of course, hauling down
the flag of perfect love; or else, much more frequently these
latter days, she steers into the rather grey Atlantic of true
friendship and companionship, still keeping the flag of perfect
love bravely afloat.

And now the bark is fairly safe. In the great Pacific, the woman can take the ease and warm repose of her new dependence, but she is usually laughing up her sleeve. She lets the lord and master manage the ship, but woe betide him if he seeks to haul down the flag of perfect love. There is mutiny in a moment. And his chief officers and his crew, namely, his children and his household servants, are up and ready to put him in irons at once, at a word from that wonderous goddess of the bark, the wife of his bosom. It is Aphrodite, mistress of the seas, in her grand capacity of motherhood and attendant wifehood. None the less, with a bit of managing the hymeneal bark sails on across the great waters into port. A lord and master is not much more than an upper servant while the flag of perfect love is flying and the sea-mother is on board. But a servant with the name of captain, and the pleasant job of sailing the ship and giving the necessary orders. He feels it is quite all right. He is supreme servant-in-command, while the mistress of mistresses smiles as she suckles his children. She is suckling him too.

Nevertheless, this is the course I would recommend young married women to *drift into*, after the first two years of "perfect love".

They won't often take my advice, I know that. Ha-ha! they will say. We see through your lord-and-master tricks. Course east-north-east, helmsman, into the safer and more populous waters of perfect companionship. If we can't have one thing perfect we'll have another. If it isn't exactly perfect love, it is perfect companionship, and the two are pretty nearly one and the same.

For women, even more than man, when once she gets an idea into her head, or worse, when once she gets *herself* into her head, will have nothing short of perfection. E.N.E., then into the democratic Atlantic of *perfect* companionship.

Well, they are grey waters, and the perfect companionship usually resolves, subtly, and always under the perfect-love flag into a very nearly perfect limited liability company, the bark steering nicely according to profit and loss, and usually "getting on" fabulously. The Golden Vanity. If this perfect love flag is a vanity, the perfect-companionship management is certainly Golden. I would recommend perfect-companionship to all those married couples who truly and sincerely want *to get on*.

Now the good bark *Harriet and Lovat* had risen from the

waves, like Aphrodite's shell as well as Aphrodite, in the extremest waters of perfect love. Love and love alone! Wild, wild lonely waters, with the great albatross like a sign of the cross, sloping in the immense heavens. At sea to themselves, the waters of perfect love. And the good ship *Harriet* and *Lovat*, with white sails spread, sailing with never a master, like the boat of Dionysus, which steered of its own accord across the waters, in the right direction mark you, to the sound of the music of the dolphins, while the mast of the ship put forth tendrils of vine and purple bunches of grapes, and the grapes of themselves dripped vinous down the throats of the true Dionysians. So sailed the fair ship *Harriet and Lovat* in the waters of perfect love.

I have not made up my mind whether she was a ship or a bark, or a schooner, technically speaking. Let us imagine her as any one of them. Or perhaps she was a clipper, or a frigate, or a brig. All I insist is that she was not a steamboat with a funnel, as most vessels are nowadays, sailing because they are stoked.

Fair weather and foul alternated. Sometimes the brig *Harriet and Lovat* skimmed along the path of the moon like a phantom: sometimes she lay becalmed, while sharks flicked her bottom: then she drove into the most awful hurricanes, and spun round in a typhoon: and yet behold her sailing out through the glowing arch of a rainbow into halcyon waters again. And so for years, till she began to look rather worn, but always attractive. Her paint had gone, so her timbers now were sea-silvery. Her sails were thin, but very white. The mainsail also was slit, and the stun-sails had been carried away in a blizzard. As for the flag of perfect love, the flag of the red-and-white rose upon the cross of thorns, all on a field of azure, it was woefully frayed and faded. The azure field was nearly tattered away, and the rose was fading into invisibility.

She had some awful weather, did the poor bark *Harriet and Lovat*. The seas opened great jaws to swallow her, the treacherous seas of perfect love, while cynical rocks gnashed their teeth at her, and unstable heavens opened chasms of wind on her, and fierce, full-blooded lusty bull-whales rushed at her and all but burst her timbers. Dazed and battered, she wandered hither and thither on the seas of perfect love, that she always had all to herself. Never another sail in sight, never another ship in hail. Only sometimes the smoke of a steamer skirting the horizon, making for one of the oceans.

And now the *Harriet and Lovat* began to feel the pull of the two opposing currents. It was as if she had a certain homesickness for one or other of the populous oceans: she was weary of the lone and wasteful waters of the sea of perfect love. Sometimes she drifted E.N.E. towards the Atlantic of true companionship. And then Lovat, seeing the long swell of that grey sea, and the funnels of ships like a city suburb, put the helm hard aport, and turned the ship about, and beat against a horrible sea and wind till they got into the opposite drift. Then things went a little easier, till Harriet saw before her the awful void opening of the other ocean, and the great dark-blue, dominant swell of the waters, and the loneliness and the vastness and the feeling of being overwhelmed. She looked at the mast and saw the flag of perfect love falling limp, the faded rose of all roses dying at last.

And in a moment when he was asleep, her almost lord-and master, she whipped the ship about and steered E.S.E. into the heart of the sea of perfect love, hoping to get into the current E.N.E. and so out into the open Atlantic. Then storms intolerable.

Then they took to cruising the far, lone, desert fringes of the sea of perfect love, utterly lonely and near the ice, the fringe of the seas of death. There they cruised, in the remote waters on the edge of extinction. And then they looked at one another

"We will be perfect companions: you know how I love you," said Harriet, of the good ship *Harriet and Lovat*.

"Never," said Lovat, of the same ship. "I will be lord and master, but ah, such a wonderful lord and master that it will be your bliss to belong to me. Look, I have been sewing a new flag."

She didn't even look at the flag.

"You!" she exclaimed. "You a lord and master! Why, don't you know that I love you as no man ever was loved? You a lord and master! Ph! you look it! Let me tell you I love you far, far more than ever you ought to be loved, and you should acknowledge it."

"I would rather," said he, "that you deferred your loving of me for a while, and considered the new propositions. We shall never sail any straight course at all, until you realise that I am lord and master, and you my blissful consort. Supposing now, you had the real Hermes for a husband, Trismegistus. Would you not hold your tongue for fear you lost him, and change from being a lover, and be a worshipper? Well, I am not Hermes or Dionysus, but I am a little nearer to it than you allow. And I want you to yield to my mystery and my divination, and let me put my flag of a phœnix rising from a nest in flames in place of that old rose on a field azure. The gules are almost faded out."

"It's a *lovely* design!" she cried, looking at the new flag. "I might make a cushion-embroidery of it. But as a flag it's absurd. Of course, you lonely phœnix, you are the bird and the ashes and the flames all by yourself! You would be. Nobody else enters in at all. I—I am just nowhere—I don't exist."

"Yes," he said, "you are the nest."

"I'll watch it!" she cried. "Then you shall sleep on thorns, Mister."

"But consider," he said.

"That's what I am doing," she replied. "Mr. Dionysus and Mr. Hermes and Mr. Thinks-himself-grand. I've got one thing to tell you. Without *me* you'd be nowhere, you'd be nothing, you'd not be *that*," and she snapped her fingers under his nose, a movement he particularly disliked.

"I agree," he replied, "that without the nest the phœnix would be—would be up a tree—would be in the air—would be nowhere, and couldn't find a stable spot to resurrect in. The nest is as the body to the soul: the cup that holds the fire, and in which the ashes fall to make form again. The cup is the container and the sustainer."

"Yes, I've done enough containing and sustaining of you, my gentleman, in the years I've known you. It's almost time you left off wanting so much mothering. You can't love a moment without me."

"I'll admit that the phœnix without a nest is a bird absolutely without a perch, he must dissipate in the air. But——"

"Then I'll make a cushion-cover of your flag, and you can rest on that."

"No, I'm going to haul down the flag of perfect love."

"Oh, are you! And sail without a flag? Just like you, destroy, destroy, and nothing to put in its place."

"Yes, I want to put in its place this crowned phœnix rising from the nest in flames. I want to set fire to our bark, *Harriet and Lovat*, and out of the ashes construct the frigate *Hermes*,

which name still contains the same reference, *her* and *me*, but
which has a higher total significance."

She looked at him speechless for some time. Then she merely
said:

"You're mad," and left him with his flag in his hands.

Nevertheless he was a determined little devil, as she knew
to her cost, and once he'd got an idea into his head not heaven
nor hell nor Harriet could ever batter it out. And now he'd
got into his head this idea of being lord and master, and
Harriet's acknowledging him as such. Not just verbally. No.
Not under the flag of perfect love. No. Obstinate and devilish
as he was, he wanted to haul down the flag of perfect love, to
set fire to the bark *Harriet and Lovat*, to seat himself in glory
on the ashes, like a resurrected phœnix, with an imaginary
crown on his head. And she was to be a comfortable nest for
his impertinence.

In short, he was to be the lord and master, and she the
humble slave. Thank you. Or at the very best, she was to be
a sort of domestic Mrs. Gladstone, the Mrs. Gladstone of that
old chestnut—who, when a female friend was lamenting over
the terrible state of affairs, in Ireland or somewhere, and wind-
ing up her lament with: "Terrible, terrible. But there is One
above"—replied: "Yes, he's just changing his socks. He'll be
down in a minute." Mr. Lovat was to be the One above, and she
was to be happy downstairs thinking that this lord, this master,
this Hermes-*cum*-Dionysus wonder, was comfortably changing
his socks. Thank you again. The man was mad.

Yet he stuck to his guns. She was to submit to the mystic
man and male in him, with reverence, and even a little awe,
like a woman before the altar of the great Hermes. She might
remember that he *was* only human, that he had to change his
socks if he got his feet wet, and that he would make a fool of
himself nine times out of ten. But—and the but was emphatic
as a thunderbolt—there was in him also the mystery and lordship of—of Hermes, if you like—but the mystery and the lordship of the forward-seeking male. That she must emphatically
realise and bow down to. Yes, bow down to. You can't have
two masters of one ship: neither can you have a ship without
a master. The *Harriet and Lovat* had been an experiment of
ten years' endurance. Now she was to be broken up, or burnt,
so he said, and the non-existent *Hermes* was to take her place.

You can't have two masters to one ship. And if it *is* a ship,

hat is, if it has a voyage to sail, a port to make, even a far
direction to take, into the unknown, then a master it must
have. Harriet said it wasn't a ship, it was a houseboat, and
they could lie so perfectly here by the Pacific for the rest of
time—or be towed away to some other lovely spot to house in.
She could imagine no fairer existence. It was a houseboat.

But he with his no, no, he almost drove her mad. The bark
of their marriage was a ship that must sail into uncharted seas,
and he must be the master, and she must be the crew, sworn
on. She was to believe in his adventure and deliver herself
over to it; she was to believe in his mystic vision of a land
beyond this charted world, where new life rose again.

And she just couldn't. His land beyond the land men knew,
where men were more than they are now: she couldn't believe
in it. "Then believe in *me*," he said desperately. "I know you
too well," she replied. And so, it was an impasse.

Him, a lord and master! Why, he was not really lord of his
own bread and butter; next year they might both be starving.
And he was not even master of himself, with his ungovernable
furies and his uncritical intimacies with people: even people
like Jack Callcott, whom Harriet quite liked, but whom she
would never have taken seriously. Yet there was Lovat pouring himself out to him. Pah—believe! How could one believe
in such a man! If he had been naturally a master of men,
general of an army, or manager of some great steel works, with
thousands of men under him—then, yes, she could have
acknowledged the *master* part of the bargain, if not the lord.
Whereas, as it was, he was the most forlorn and isolated
creature in the world, without even a dog to his command.
He was so isolated he was hardly a man at all, among men.
He had absolutely nothing but her. Among men he was like
some unbelievable creature—an emu, for example. Like an
emu in the streets or in a railway carriage. He might well
say phœnix.

All he could do was to try and come it over her with this
evolution rubbish and a stunt of "male" activity. If it were
even real!

He had nothing but her, absolutely. And that was why, presumably, he wanted to establish this ascendancy over her,
assume this arrogance. And so that he could refute her, deny
her, and imagine himself a unique male. He *wanted* to be
male and unique, like a freak of a phœnix. And then go

prancing off into connections with men like Jack Callcott an
Kangaroo, and saving the world. She could *not* stand the:
world saviours. And she, she must be safely there, as a ne:
for him, when he came home with his feathers pecked. Th:
was it. So that he could imagine himself absolutely an
arrogantly It, he would turn her into a nest, and sit on h
and overlook her, like the one and only phœnix in the dese:
of the world, gurgling hymns of salvation.

Poor Harriet! No wonder she resented it. Such a man, suc
a man to be tied to and tortured by!

And poor Richard! To be a man, and to have a man's u:
easy soul for his bed-fellow.

But he kicked against the pricks. He did not yet submit t
the fact which he *half* knew: that before mankind woul
accept any man for a king, and before Harriet would eve
accept him, Richard Lovat, as a lord and master, he, this sel
same Richard who was so strong on kingship, must open th
doors of his soul and let in a dark Lord and Master for hin
self, the dark god he had sensed outside the door. Let hi:
once truly submit to the dark majesty, break open his doo
to this fearful god who is master, and enters us from below
the lower doors; let himself once admit a Master, the unspea:
able god: and the rest would happen.

> "The fire began to burn the stick,
> The stick began to beat the dog,
> The dog began to bite the pig,
> The pig began to go over the bridge,
> And so the old woman got home that night . . ."

CHAPTER X

DIGGERS

THEY had another ferocious battle, Somers and Harriet; the
stood opposite to one another in such fury one against th
other that they nearly annihilated one another. He couldn
stay near her, so started walking off into the country. It w:
winter, but sunny, and hot walking. He climbed steadily u
and up the high-road between the dense, damp jungle th:
grew at the base and up the steep rise of the tor-face, whic

ιe wanted to get to the top of. Strange birds made weird, netallic noises. Tree-ferns rose on their notchy little trunks, ιnd great mosses tangled in with more ordinary bushes. Over-ιead rose the gum trees, sometimes with great stark, dead imbs thrown up, sometimes hands over like pine trees.

He sweated up the steep road till at last he came to the top. Γhere, on the farther side, the dip slope, the hills sank and ran n spurs, all fairly densely wooded, but not like the scarp slope ιp which he had toiled. The scarp slope was jungle, impene-rable, with tree ferns and bunchy cabbage-palms and mosses ike bushes, a thick matted undergrowth beneath the boles of he trees. But the dip slope was bush: gum trees rather scat-ered, and a low undergrowth like heath. The same lonely, ιnbreakable silence and loneliness that seemed to him the real ιush. Curiously unapproachable to him. The mystery of the ιush seems to recede from you as you advance, and then it is ιehind you if you look round. Lonely, and weird, and hoary.

He went on till he could look over the tor's edge at the land ιelow. There was the scalloped sea-shore, for miles, and the trip of flat coast-land, sometimes a mile wide, sprinkled as far s the eye could reach with the pale-grey zinc roofs of the ιungalows: all scattered like crystals in the loose cells of the ark tree-tissue of the shore. It was suggestive of Japanese ιndscape, dark trees and little, single, scattered toy houses. Γhen the bays of the shore, the coal-jetty, far off rocks down he coast, and long white lines of breakers.

But he was looking mostly straight below him, at the massed οliage of the cliff-slope. Down into the centre of the great, ιull-green whorls of the tree-ferns, and on to the shaggy mops f the cabbage-palms. In one place a long fall of creeper was ιellowish with damp flowers. Gum trees came up in tufts. he previous world!—the world of the coal age. The lonely, ιnely world that had waited, it seemed, since the coal age. hese ancient flat-topped tree-ferns, these towsled palms like ιops. What was the good of trying to be an alert conscious ιan here? You couldn't. Drift, drift into a sort of obscurity, ιackwards into a nameless past, hoary as the country is hoary. ιrange old feelings wake in the soul: old, non-human feelings. nd an old, old indifference, like a torpor invades the spirit. n old, saurian torpor. Who wins? There was the land ιrinkled with dwellings as with granulated sugar. There was black smoke of steamers on the high pale sea, and a white-

ness of steam from a colliery among the dull trees. Was the
land awake? Would the people waken this ancient land, or
would the land put them to sleep, drift them back into the
torpid semi-consciousness of the world of the twilight.

Somers felt the torpor coming over him. He hung there on
the parapet looking down, and he didn't care. How profoundly
darkly he didn't care. There are no problems for the soul in it
darkened, wide-eyed torpor. Neither Harriet nor Kangaroo nor
Jaz, nor even the world. Worlds come, and worlds go: ever
worlds. And when the old, old influence of the fern-world
comes over a man, how can he care? He breathes the fern
seed and drifts back, becomes darkly half vegetable, devoid of
pre-occupations. Even the never-slumbering urge of sex sink
down into something darker, more monotonous, incapable of
caring: like sex in trees. The dark world before conscious
responsibility was born.

A queer bird sat hunched on a bough a few yards away, just
below; a bird like a bunch of old rag, with a small rag of
dark tail, and a fluffy pale top like an owl, and a sort of frill
round his neck. He had a long, sharp, dangerous beak. But he
too was sunk in unutterable apathy. A kukooburra! Some
instinct made him know that Somers was watching, so he just
shuffled round on the bough and sat with his back to the man
and became utterly oblivious. Somers watched and wondered.
Then he whistled. No change. Then he clapped his hands. The
bird looked over its shoulder in surprise. What! it seemed to
say. Is there somebody alive? Is that a live somebody? It had
quite a handsome face, with the exquisite long, dagger beak.
It slowly took Somers in. Then he clapped again. Making an
effort the bird spread quite big wings and whirred in a queer
flickering flight to a bough a dozen yards farther off. And
there it clotted again.

Ah well, thought Somers, life is so big, and has such huge
ante-worlds of grey twilight. How can one care about any
thing in particular!

He went home again, and had forgotten the quarrel and for
gotten marriage or revolutions or anything: drifted away into
the grey pre-world where men didn't have emotions. Where
men didn't have emotions and personal consciousness, but
were shadowy like trees, and on the whole silent, with numb
brains and slow limbs and a great indifference.

But Harriet was waiting for him rather wistful, and loving

him rather quiveringly. And yet even in the quiver of her passion was some of this indifference, this twilight indifference of the fern world.

Jack and Victoria came for the week-end, and Somers and Callcott met in a much nearer sympathy than they had ever known before. Victoria was always thrilled and fascinated by both the Somers: they had an inexhaustible fascination for her, the tones of their voices, their manner, their way with each other. She could not understand the strange sureness they had in themselves, the sureness of what they were saying or going to say, the sureness of what they were feeling. For herself, her words fluttered out of her without her direct control, and her feelings fluttered in her the same. She was one perpetually agitated dovecot of words and emotions, always trying consciously to find *herself* amid the whirl, and never quite succeeding. She thought someone might *tell* her. Whereas the Somers had an unconscious sureness, something that seemed really royal to her. But she had in the last issue the twilight indifference of the fern-world. Only she still quivered for the light.

Poor Victoria! She clung to Jack's arm vibrating, always needing to vibrate outwards. And he seemed to become more Australian and apathetic every week. The great indifference, the darkness of the fern-world, upon his mind. Then spurts of energy, spurts of sudden violent desire, spurts of gambling excitement. But the mind in a kind of twilight sleep.

He made no more appeals. He was just static, and quite gentle. Even at table he was half oblivious of the presence of the other people. Then Victoria would poke him with her elbow, poke him hard, into consciousness, and bring back the lively Jack that the Somers had first known. Strange that the torpor had come on him so completely of late. Yet there was a queer light in his eyes, as if he might do something dangerous. And when he was once talking, he was perfectly logical and showed surprising calm common sense. When he was discussing or criticising, he seemed so unusually sane as to be peculiar. Like a man in his sleep.

Just outside the station was the football-field, and Mullumbimby was playing Wollondindy, Mullumbimby in royal blue, and Wollondindy in rather faded red. Along the roadside buggies and motor-cars were pulled up, the ponies were taken out of harness and left to feed on the roadside grass. Two riders

G

sat on horseback to survey the scene. And under the flowering
coral trees, with their sharp red cockatoo flowers, stood men
in their best clothes smoking pipes, or men in their best clothes
squatting on the fence, and lasses mingling in or strolling past
in white silk stockinette frocks, or pink crêpe-de-chine, or
muslin. Just like prostitutes, arm-in-arm, strolled the lasses,
airing themselves and their pronounced hips. And the men
apathetically took no notice, but watched the field.

This scene was too much for Jack Callcott. Somers or no
Somers, he must be there. So there he stood, in his best clothes
and a cream velour hat and a short pipe, staring with his long,
naked, Australian face, impassive. On the field the blues and
the reds darted madly about, like strange bird-creatures rather
than men. They were mostly blond, with hefty legs, and with
prominent round buttocks that worked madly inside the little
white cotton shorts. And Jack, with his dark eyes, watched as
if it was doomsday. Occasionally the tail-end of a smile would
cross his face, occasionally he would take his pipe-stem from
his mouth and gave a bright look into vacancy and say, "See
that!" Heaven knows what it was that he saw. The game,
the skill? Yes. But more, the motion, the wild combative
motion. And most of all, fate. Fate had a fascination for him
It was the only real point of curiosity left in him : how would
chance work things out. Chance! Now then, how would
chance settle it? Even the football-field, with its wildly scurry
ing blues and bits of red, was only a frenzied shuffling of fate
with men for the instruments. The living instruments of fate!
And how would it work out, how would it work out? He
could have stood there, static, with his little pipe, till Dooms
day, waiting for fate to settle it. The wild scurrying motion
and the jumps in the air, of course made his heart beat faster
Towards the close one of the chaps got a kick on the jaw, and
was knocked out. They couldn't finish the game. Hard lines

Jack was a queer sight to Somers, when he was in thi
brightly vacant mood, not a man at all, but a chance thing
gazing spellbound on the evolutions of chance. And in thi
state, this very Australian state, you could hardly get a wore
out of him. Or, when he broke into a little volley of speech
you listened with wonder to the noise of it, as if a weird anima
had suddenly given voice.

The indifference, the marvellous, bed-rock indifference. No
the static fatalism of the east. But an indifference based o

real recklessness, an indifference with a deep flow of loose
energy beneath it, ready to break out like a geyser. Ready to
break into a kind of frenzy, a berserk frenzy, running amok
in wild generosity, or still more wild smashing up. The wild
joy in letting loose, in a smash-up. But will he ever let loose?
Or will the static patience settle deeper, and the fern-twilight
altogether envelope him. The slow transmutation! What does
to-day matter, or this country? Time is so huge, and in
Australia the next step back is to the fern age.

The township looked its queerest as dusk fell. Then the odd
electric lights shone at rather wide intervals, the wide, unmade
roads of rutted earth seemed to belong again to the wild, in
the semi-dark, and the low bungalows with the doors open
and the light showing seemed like shacks in the wilderness, a
settlement in the fierce gloom of the wilderness. Then youths
dashed fiercely on horseback down the soft roads, standing in
the stirrups and crouching over the neck of the thin, queer
brown race-horses that sprinted along like ghosts. And the
young baker, in emulation, dashed through the village on his
cream pony. A collier who had been staying somewhere
cantered stiffly away into the dark on a pony like a rocking-
horse. Young maidens in cotton dresses stood at the little rail
gates of their bungalow homes talking to young men in a
buggy, or to a young man on foot, or to the last tradesman's
cart, or to youths who were strolling past. It was evening, and
the intense dusk of the far-off land, and white folks peering out
of the dusk almost like aborigines. The far-off land, just as far
off when you are in it: nay, then farthest off.

The evening came very dark, with lightning playing pallid
in the south-east, over the sea. There was nothing to be done
with Jack but to play draughts with him. He wasn't in a real
sporting mood, so he let himself be beaten even at draughts.
When he was in a sporting mood he could cast a spell of confusion over Somers, and win every time, with a sort of gloating. But when he wasn't in a sporting mood he would shove
up his men recklessly, and lose them. He didn't care. He just
leaned back and stretched himself in that intense physical way
which Somers thought just a trifle less than human. The man
was all body: a strong body full of energy like a machine that
has got steam up, but is inactive. He had no mind, no spirit,
no soul: just a tense, inactive body, and an eye rather glazed
and a trifle bloodshot. The old psyche slowly disintegrating.

Meanwhile Victoria in a trill of nervous excitement and exaltation was talking Europe with Harriet. Victoria was just the opposite of Jack: she was all a quiver of excited consciousness, to know, to see, to realise. She would almost have done anything to be able to *look* at life, look at the inside of it, see it in its intimacy. She had had wild ideas of being a stewardess on a boat, a chambermaid in an hotel, a waitress in a good restaurant, a hospital nurse—anything, so that she could *see* the intimacies, touch the private mysteries. To travel seemed to her the great desirable: to go to Europe and India, and *see* it all. She loved Australia, loved it far more quiveringly and excitedly than he. But it wasn't Australia that fascinated her: it was the secret intimacies of life, and what *other folks felt*. That strange and aboriginal indifference that was bottommost in him seemed like a dynamo in her. She fluttered in the air like a loose live nerve, a nerve of the sympathetic system. She was all sympathetic drive: and he was nearly all check. He sat there apathetic, nothing but body and solid, steady, physical indifference. He did not oppose her at all, or go counter to her. He was just the heavy opposite pole of her energy. And of course she belonged to him as one pole belongs to the other pole in a circuit.

And he, he would stretch his body continuously, but he would not go to bed, though Somers suggested it. No, there he sat. So Somers joined in the more exciting conversation of the women, and Jack sat solidly there. Whether he listened or whether he didn't, who knows? The aboriginal *sympathetic* apathy was upon him, he was like some creature that has lost its soul, and simply stares.

The morning was one of the loveliest Australian mornings, perfectly golden, all the air pure gold, the great gold effulgence to seaward, and the pure, cold, pale-blue inland, over the dark range. The wind was blowing from inland, the sea was quiet as a purring cat with white paws, becoming darkish green-blue flecked with innumerable white flecks like rain-spots splashing the surface of a pool. The horizon was a clear and hard and dark sea against an almost white sky, but from far behind the horizon showed the mirage-magic tops of hazed, gold-white clouds, that seemed as if they indicated the far Pacific isles.

Though it was cold, Jack was about sauntering in his shirt sleeves with his waistcoat open and his hands in his pockets: rather to the vexation of Victoria. "Pull yourself together, Jack dear, do. Put your collar and tie on," she coaxed, fondling him.

"In a minute," he said.

The indifference—the fern-dark indifference of this remote golden Australia. Not to care—from the bottom of one's soul, not to care. Overpowered in the twilight of fern odour. Just to keep enough grip to run the machinery of the day: and beyond that, to let yourself drift, not to think or strain or make any effort to consciousness whatsoever. That was Jack, sauntering down there in his shirt-sleeves, with his waistcoat open showing his white shirt, his strong neck bare: sauntering with his hands in his pockets beside Somers, at the water's edge. Somers wore a dark flannel jacket, and his neck-tie hung dark and broke the intimacy of the white shirt-breast.

The two women stood on the cliff, the low, bushy cliff, looking down. Harriet was in a plain dress of dark-coloured purplish-and-brown hand-woven stuff of cotton and silk mixture, with old silver lace round the collar; Victoria in a pale-green knitted dress. So they stood in the morning light, watching the men on the fawn-coloured sand by the sea-fringe, waiting to wave when they looked up.

Jack looked up first. The two women *coo-eed* and waved. He took his pipe from his mouth and held it high in his hand, in answer. A strange signal. The pale-green wisp of Victoria in the sky was part of his landscape. But the darker figure of Harriet had for some reason a menace to him, up there. He suddenly felt as if he were down below: he suddenly realised a need to bethink himself. He turned to Somers, looking down and saying in his peculiar Australian tone:

"Well, I suppose we'd better be going up."

The curious note of obedience in the manly twang!

Victoria made him put on coat and collar and tie for breakfast.

"Yes, dear, come on. I'll tie your tie for you."

"I suppose a man was born to give in," said he, with laconic good humour and obstinacy. But he was a little uneasy. He realised the need to gather himself together.

"You get like the rest of them," Victoria scolded him in a coaxing tone. "You used to be so smart. And you promised me you'd never go slack like they all are. Didn't you, you bad boy?"

"I forget," said he. But nevertheless the constraint of breakfast pulled him up. Because Harriet *really* disapproved, and he didn't know what was inside that rose-and-brown-purple cloud of her. The ancient judgment of the Old World. So he gathered himself somewhat together. But he was so far, fern-lost, from the Old World.

"My God!" thought Somers. "These are the men Kangaroo wants to build up a new state with."

After breakfast Somers got Jack to talk about Kangaroo and his plans. He heard again all about the Diggers' Clubs: nearly all soldiers and sailors who had been in the war, but not restricted to these. They had started like any other social club: games, athletics, lectures, readings, discussions, debates. No gambling, no drink, no class or party distinction. The clubs were still chiefly athletics, but not *sporting*. They went in for boxing, wrestling, fencing, and knife-throwing, and revolver practice. But they had swimming and rowing squads, and rifle-ranges for rifle practice, and they had regular military training. The colonel who planned out the military training was a clever chap. The men were grouped in little squads of twenty, each with sergeant and corporal. Each of these twenty was trained to act like a scout, independently, though the squad worked in absolute unison among themselves, and were pledged to absolute obedience of higher commands. These commands, however, left most of the devising and method of execution of the job in hand to the squad itself. In New South Wales the Maggies, as these private squads were called, numbered already about fourteen hundred, all perfectly trained and equipped. They had a distinctive badge of their own: a white, broad-brimmed felt hat, like the ordinary khaki military hat, but white, and with a tuft of white feathers. "Because," said Ennis, the colonel, "we're the only ones that can afford to show the white feather."

These Maggies, probably from Magpies, because Colonel Ennis used to wear white riding-breeches and black gaiters, and a black jacket and a white stock, with his white hat—were the core and heart of the Digger Movement. But Kangaroo had slaved at the other half of the business, the mental side. He *did* want his men to grip on to the problem of the future of Australia. He had insisted on attendance at debates and discussions: Australia and the World, Australia and the Future White Australia, Australia and the Reds, Class Feeling in Australia, Politics and Australia, Australians and Work, What is Democracy? What is an Australian? What do our Politicians

do for Australia? What our State Parliament does for us, What
our Federal Parliament does for us, What side of the Australian
does Parliament represent? Is Parliament necessary to Democracy? What is wrong with Soviet rule? Do we want a Statesman, or do we want a Leader? What kind of Leader do we
want? What aim have we in view? Are we Australians? Are
we Democratic? Do we believe in Ourselves?

So the debates had been going on, for a year and a half now.
These debates were for club members only. And each club
numbered only fifty members. Every member was asked to
take part in the debates, and a memorandum was kept of each
meeting. Then there were monthly united gatherings, of five
or six or more clubs together. And occasionally a mass meeting, at which Kangaroo spoke.

All this went on in the open, and roused some comment in
the press: at first a great deal of praise, later some suspicion
and considerable antagonism, both from Conservatives and
Labour. Ben Cooley was supposed to be working himself in
as a future Prime Minister, with a party behind him that would
make him absolute, a Dictator. As soon as one paper came out
with this alarm, an opponent sneered and pooh-poohed, and
spoke of the Reds lounging about, a fearful menace, in Sydney,
and recalled the Reigns of Terror in Paris and in Petrograd.
Was another Reign of Terror preparing for Sydney? Was a
bloodthirsty Robespierre or a ruthless Lenin awaiting his
moment? Would responsible citizens be lynched in Martin
Place, and dauntless citizenesses thrown into the harbour, when
the fatal hour struck? Whereupon a loud burst from the press:
were we to be alarmed by the knock-kneed, loutish socialist
gang that hung round Canberra House? These gentry could
hardly kill the vermin in their own clothing, not to speak of
lynching in Martin Place. Whereas the Maggies were a set of
efficient, well-armed, and no doubt unscrupulous tools of still
more designing and unscrupulous masters. If we had to choose
between Napoleon, in the shape of Ben Cooley, or Lenin, in the
lack-of-shape of Willie Struthers, we should be hard put to it
to know which was worse. Whereupon a fierce blast about
our returned heroes and the white-livered skulkers who had
got themselves soft jobs as coast-watchers, watching that the
sharks didn't nibble the rocks, and now dared lift their dis-
honourable croaks against the revered name of Digger. And a
ferocious rush-in from Labour, which didn't see much Napoleon

in Ben Cooley, except the belly and the knack of filling his pockets. Napoleon, though but a Dago and not a Jew, had filled one of the longest pockets Europe had ever emptied herself into, so where would poor little Australia be when the sham Kangaroo, with the help of the Magpies, which were indeed strictly Butcher Birds, started to coin her into shekels?

Then the boom died down, but the Digger Clubs had grown immensely on the strength of it. There were now more than a hundred clubs in New South Wales, and nearly as many in Victoria. The chief in Victoria was a smart chap, a mining expert. They called him the Emu, to match Kangaroo on the Australian coat of arms. He would be the Trotsky to the new Lenin, for he was a born handler of men. He had been a lieutenant-colonel in the war, a very smart soldier, and there had been a great cry to keep him on for the Defence Force. But he had got the shove from Government, so he cleared out and went back to his mining.

But every club had its own committee, and this committee was composed of five or six of the best, surest members, sworn in to secrecy and to absolute obedience to any decision. Each club committee handled every question of development, and the master and the teller went to section meetings. A section consisted of ten clubs. A decision at a section meeting was carried to the State meeting, where the chief of the State always had the ruling vote. Once a decision was passed, it became a law for all members, embodied in the person of the chief, and interpreted by him unquestioned save by his lieutenant, the chief of all the secretaries, or tellers.

The public members of the clubs were initiated into no secrets. The most important questions were discussed only among the chiefs. More general secrets were debated at the section meetings. That is, the great bulk of the members gave only their allegiance and their spirit of sympathy. The masters and chiefs carefully watched the response to all propositions at all open discussions. They carefully fostered the feeling they wished for, or which they were instructed to encourage. When the right feeling was arrived at, presumably, then the secret members started the discussion of propositions proposed from above. A secret member was allowed to make a proposition also, and the list was read over at the section meetings. But the Jack, the chief of the tellers, had right of absolute veto.

Somers could not get it very clear, from Jack Callcott's

description. But it seemed to him as if all the principal ideas originated with the chief, went round the circuit of the clubs, disguised as general topics for debate, and returned as confirmed principles, via the section meetings and the state meetings. All the debates had been a slow, deliberate crystallising of a few dominant ideas in all the members. In the actual putting into practice of any principle, the chief was an autocrat, though he might, if he chose, send his propositions through the section meetings and the state meetings for criticism and amendment.

"What I feel," said Somers to Jack, "is that the bulk of you just don't care what the chief does, so long as he does something."

"Oh, we don't lose our sleep at nights. If he likes to be the boss, let him do the thinking. We know he's our man, and so we'll follow him. We can't all be Peter and Paul and know all about it."

"You just feel he's your man?"

"Oh, we do."

"But supposing you go in and win—and he is the boss of Australia. Shall you still leave things to him?"

Jack thought lazily for a time.

"I should think so," he replied, with a queer, mistrustful tone.

And Somers felt again so distinctly they were doing it all just in order to have something to do, to put a spoke in the wheel of the present bosses, to make a change. Just temporary. There would be a change, and that was what they wanted. There was all the time the excitement. Damn the consequences.

"You don't think it would be as well to *have* a Soviet and Willie Struthers?"

"No, I don't," said Jack, in a thin, sharp voice. "I don't want to be bullied by any damned Red International Labour. I don't want to be kissing and hugging a lot of foreign labour tripe: niggers and what the hell. I'd rather have the British Empire ten thousand times over, and that bed's a bit too wide, and too many in it, for me. I don't like sleeping with a lot of neighbours. But when it comes to going to bed with a crowd of niggers and dagoes, in an International Labour Combine, with a pair of red sheets so that the dirt won't show, I'm absolutely sure I won't have it. That's why I like Kangaroo. We shall be just cosy and Australian, with a boss like a father who gets

G*

up first in the morning and locks up at night before you go to bed."

"And who will stop in the Empire?"

"Oh, I suppose so. But he won't be asking even the British to go to bed with him. He knows the difference between Australia and the rest of the Empire. The Empire's like a lot of lock-up shops that you do your trade in. But I know Kangaroo well enough to know he's not mixing his family in. He'll keep Australia close and cosy. That's what I want. And that's what we all want, when we're in our senses and aren't bitten into spots by the Red International bug."

Somers then mentioned Jaz's proposition, of a red revolution first.

"I know," said Jack. "It may be so. He's one of your sly, crawling devils, Jaz is, and that seems to be the road nowadays. I wouldn't mind egging the Reds in, and then slapping them clean out into nowhere. I wouldn't mind at all. But I'm bound to follow Kangaroo's orders, so I'm not bothering my chump over Jaz's boodle."

"You don't care which way it happens?"

Jack looked at him sideways, like the funny bird.

"No," he said, with an Australian drawl. "So long as it does happen. I don't like things as they are, and I don't feel safe about them. I don't mean I want to feel safe as if nothing would ever happen. There's some sorts of sport and risk that you enjoy, and there's others you hate the thought of. Now I hate the thought of being bossed and messed about by the Old Country, or by Jew capitalists and bankers, or by a lot of Labour bullies, or a Soviet. There's no fun in that sort of sport, to me, unless you can jolly well wipe the bleeders out afterwards. And I don't altogether want the mills of the British Empire to go grinding slowly on, and yourself compelled to do nothing but grind slowly with 'em. It's too much of a sameness altogether, and not as much sport as a tin Lizzie. We're too much mixed up with other folk's business, what's absolutely no fun for us. No, what I want is a cosy, lively little Australia away from all this blooming world-boost. I've no use for a lot of people across a lot of miles of sea nudging me while I handle my knife and fork. Leave us Australians to ourselves, we shall manage."

They were interrupted by Harriet calling for Somers to come and rescue the tea-towel from the horns of a cow who had

calmly scrambled through the fence on to their grass. Somers
was used to the cow: she had scrambled through the Coo-ee
fence long before the Somers had ever walked through the
gate, so she looked on them as mild intruders. He was quite
friendly with her, she ate the pumpkin rind and apple parings
from his hand. Now she looked at him half guiltily out of one
eye, the kitchen towel hanging over the other eye. She took it
quite calmly, but had a disreputable appearance.

"Come here," said he. "Come here and have it taken off.
Of course you had to poke your head into the bush if you
thought there was a towel on it."

She came mildly up and held her head while he disentangled
the towel from her horns. Then she went calmly on, snuffing
at the short, bitten grass for another mouthful, and twitching
leaves off the stunted bushes.

So they were, the cows, so unafraid. In Cornwall, Harriet
said, the cows had always sniffed in when she came near, and
then breathed out heavily, nnh! nnh! as if they did not like
the smell of human beings, breathing out against her, and backing. And that had scared her. But these cows didn't do that.
They seemed so calm. They fed over all the bush, the unoccupied grassy lots above the sea, among the unbuilt streets. And
they pushed in among the trees and bushes where the creek
came in. And then at dusk a boy would come on a cream-
coloured pony riding round and driving them in, scaring a sort
of crane or heron bird from the still waters of the marshy
creek-edge. Then the cows walked or trotted placidly home:
so unconcerned. And the bird with the great, arched grey
wings flapped in a low circle round, then settled again a yard
or two from where she was before.

So unconcerned. Somers had noticed a pair of fishing birds
by the creek, queer objects nearly as big as ducks, perched at
the extremity of a dead gum tree, above the water. They flew
away at his coming, but while he stood looking, they circled
with their longish necks stretched out and their wings sharply
flicking in the high air, then one returned and sat again on
the tree, and the other perched on another dead tree. The near
one looked sideways at him.

"Yes, I'm here," said he aloud.

Whereupon she did the inevitable, turned her back on him
and he no longer existed for her. These ostriches needed no
sand. She so far forgot him as to turn sideways to him again,

so he had her in profile, clutched grey like an old knot at the tip of the stark, dead grey tree. And there she performed queer corkscrew exercises with her neck in the air. Whether it was she was getting down a last fish-bone in her gizzard, or whether she was merely asserting herself in the upper air, he could not tell.

"What a fool you look," he said aloud to her.

Then away the birds rose. And he saw a seedy, elderly man in black, in a long-skirted black coat like a cast-off Methodist parson, spying at him furtively from behind the bushes on the other side of the creek. This parson-looking weed carried a gun, and was shooting heaven knows what. He thought Richard Lovat a very suspicious bird, and Richard Lovat thought him the last word in human weeds. So our young man turned away to the sands, where the afternoon sea had gone a very dark blue. Another human weed with a very thin neck and a very red face sat on the sand ridge up which the foam-edge swished, his feet wide apart, facing the ocean, and tending a line which he had in some way managed to cast out into the low surf. An urchin, barefoot, was pottering round in silence, like a sandpiper. The elderly one made unintelligible noises as Somers approached. The latter realised it meant he was not to catch with his foot the line, which reached out behind the thin fisherman, covered with sand. So he stepped over it. The brown, barefoot urchin pottered round unheeding. He did not even look up when the elder made more unintelligible sounds to him.

> "My father is a fisherman,
>   Oh a fisherman! Yes, a fisherman!
>   He catches all the fish-e-can."

Mondays, Wednesdays and Saturdays were the library nights. When you had crossed the iron footbridge over the railway, you came to a big wooden building with a corrugated iron roof, standing forlorn at an unmade corner, like the fag-end of the village. But the village was an agglomeration of fag-ends. This building might have been a temporary chapel, as you came at it from the back. But in front it was labelled "Pictoria", so it was the cinema. But there was also a black board with gilt letters, like a chapel notice-board, which said, "School of Arts Library." And the Pictoria had a sort of little wing, all wood, like a little school-room. And in one section of this wing was the School of Arts Library, which the Somers had joined. Four rows of novels: the top row a hundred or more thin books, all Nat Gould or Zane Grey. The young women came for Zane Grey. "Oh, *The Maid of Mudgee* is a lovely thing, lovely"—a young woman was pronouncing from the top of the broken chair which served as stool to give access to this top row. "Y'aven' got a new Zaine Greye, have yer?" She spoke in these tones or unmitigated intimacy to the white-moustached librarian. One would have thought he was her dear old dad. Then came a young railway man who had heard there was a new Nat Gould.

"But," said Somers, as he and Harriet went off with a Mary E. Mann and a George A. Birmingham, "I don't wonder they can't read English books, or only want Nat Gould. All the scruples and the emotions and the regrets in English novels do seem waste of time out here."

"I suppose," said Harriet, "if you don't have any inside life of your own it must seem a waste of time. But look at it— look!"

The object she bade him look at was a bone of contention between them. She wanted to give five pounds to have four posts and an iron chain put round it, and perhaps a bit of grass sowed inside the enclosure. He declared that they'd probably charge ten pounds for the chain alone, since it was Australia. And let it alone. It was of a piece with the rest. But Harriet said she couldn't leave the place till she'd had something done to it. He said she was an interfering female.

The object was the memorial to the fallen soldiers. It was really a quite attractive little monument: a statue in pale, fawnish stone, of a Tommy standing at ease, with his gun down at his side, wearing his puttees and his turned-up felt hat. The statue itself was about life size, but standing just overhead on a tall pedestal it looked small and stiff and rather touching. The pedestal was in very nice proportion, and had at eye level white inlet slabs between little columns of grey granite, bearing the names of the fallen on one slab, in small black letters, and on the other slabs the names of all the men who served: "God Bless Them." The fallen had "Lest we forget" for a motto. Carved on the bottom step it said, "Unveiled by Grannie Rhys." A real township monument, bearing the names of everybody possible: the fallen, all those who donned khaki, the people who presented it, and Grannie Rhys.

Wonderfully in keeping with the place and its people, naïve but quite attractive, with the stiff, pallid, delicate fawn-coloured soldier standing forever stiff and pathetic.

But there it stood, a few yards from the corner of the corrugated Pictoria, at the corner of the fag-end road to the station, like an old milk-can someone had set down and forgotten: or a brand-new milk-can. Old rags of paper littered the ground at the base, with an old tin or two. A little farther back was a German machine-gun, also looking as if it had been scrapped and forgotten. Standing there, with its big metal screen-flap, it looked exotic, a thing of some higher culture, demoniac and fallen.

Harriet was dying to rescue the forlorn monument that seemed as if it had been left there in the bustle of removal. She wanted to enclose it. But he said, "Leave it. Leave it. They don't like things enclosed."

She still had in her mind's eye an Australia with beautiful manorial farm-houses and dainty, perfect villages. She never acquiesced in the *uncreatedness* of the new country, the rawness, the slovenliness. It seemed to her comical, for instance, that no woman in Australia would carry a basket. Harriet went shopping as usual with her pretty straw basket in the village. But she felt that the women remarked on it. Only then did she notice that everybody carried a suitcase in this discreet country. The fat old woman who came to the door with a suitcase must, she thought, be a visitor coming to the wrong house. But no. "Did you want a cabbage?" In the suitcase two cabbages and half a pumpkin. A little girl goes to the dairy for six eggs and half a pound of butter with a small, elegant suitcase. Nay, a child of three toddled with a little six-inch suitcase, containing, as Harriet had occasion to see, two buns, because the suitcase flew open and the two buns rolled out. Australian suitcases were always flying open, and discharging groceries or a skinned rabbit or three bottles of beer. One had the impression that everybody was perpetually going away for the week-end: with a suitcase. Not so at all. Just a new-country bit of convention.

Ah, a new country! The cabbage, for example, cost tenpence in the normal course of things, and a cauliflower a shilling. And the tradesmen's carts flew round in the wilderness, delivering goods. There isn't much newness in *man*, whatever the country.

That old aeroplane that had lain broken-down in a field. It was nowadays always staggering in the low air just above the surf, past the front of Coo-ee, and lurching down on to the sands of the town "beach". There, in the cold wind, a forlorn group of men and boys round the aeroplane, the sea washing near, the marsh of the creek desolate behind. Then a "passenger" mounted, and men shoving the great insect of a thing along the sand to get it started. It buzzed venomously into the air, looking very unsafe and wanting to fall in the sea.

"Yes, he's carrying passengers. Oh, quite a fair trade. Thirty-five shillings a time. Yes, it seems a lot, but he has to make his money while he can. No, I've not been up myself, but my boy has. No, you see, there was four boys, and they had a sweepstake: eight-and-six apiece, and my boy won. He's just eleven. Yes, he liked it. But they was only up about four minutes: I timed them myself. Well, you know, it's hardly worth it. But he gets plenty to go. I heard he made over forty pound on Whit Monday, here on this beach. It seems to me, though, he favours some more than others. There's some he flies round with for ten minutes, and that last chap now, I'm sure he wasn't up a second more than three minutes. No, not quite fair. Yes, he's a man from Bulli: was a flying-man all through the war. Now he's got this machine of his own, he's quite right to make something for himself if he can. No, I don't know that he has any licence or anything. But a chap like that, who went through the war—why, who's going to interfere with his doing the best for himself?"

CHAPTER XI

WILLIE STRUTHERS AND KANGAROO

JAZ took Somers to the famous Canberra House, in Sydney, where the Socialists and Labour people had their premises: offices, meeting-rooms, club-rooms, quite an establishment. There was a lively feeling about the place, in spite of various down-at-heel malcontents who stood about in the passage and outside on the pavement. A business-like air.

The two men were conducted into an inner room where a man sat at a desk. He was very dark, red-faced, and thin, with deep lines in his face, a tight shut, receding mouth, and black, burning eyes. He reminded Somers of the portraits of Abraham Lincoln, the same sunken cheeks and deep, cadaverous lines and big black eyes. But this man, Willie Struthers, lacked that look of humour and almost of sweetness that one can find in Abraham Lincoln's portraits. Instead, he was suspicious, and seemed as if he were brooding an inner wrong.

He was a born Australian, had knocked about the continent, and spent many years on the goldfields. According to report, he was just comfortably well off—not rich. He looked rather shabby, seedy; his clothes had that look as if he had just thrown them on his back, after picking them off the floor. Also one of his thin shoulders was noticeably higher than the other. But he was a distinct Australian type, thin, hollow-cheeked, with a brightish, brittle, red skin on his face, and big, dark, incensed-looking eyes. He nodded to the two men as they entered, but did not speak nor rise from the desk.

"This is Mr. Somers," said Jaz. "You've read his book on democracy."

"Yes, I've read it," said Struthers. "Take a seat."

He spoke with a pronounced Australian accent—a bad cockney. He stared at Somers for a few seconds, then looked away.

He asked the usual question, how Richard liked Australia, how long he had been there, how long he thought of staying. The two didn't get into any easy harmony.

Then he began to put a few shrewd questions concerning the Fascisti and Socialisti in Italy, the appropriation of the land by the peasants, and so on; then about Germany, the actual temper of the working people, the quality of their patriotism since the war, and so on.

"You understand," said Somers, "I don't pretend to give any-thing but personal impressions. I have no claim to knowledge whatever."

"That's all right, Mr. Somers. I want your impressions. What they call knowledge is like any other currency, it's liable to depreciate. Sound valuable knowledge to-day may not be worth the paper it's printed on to-morrow—like the Austrian krone. We're no slaves to facts. Give us your impressions."

He spoke with a peculiar kind of bitterness, that showed passion too. They talked about Europe for some time. The man could listen : listen with his black eyes too. Watchful, always watchful, as if he expected some bird to fly suddenly out of the speaker's face. He was well-informed, and seemed to weigh and judge everything he heard as he heard it.

"Why, when I left Europe it seemed to me socialism was losing ground everywhere—in Italy especially. In 1920 it was quite a living, exciting thing, in Italy. It made people insolent, usually, but it lifted them up as well. Then it sort of fizzled down, and last year there was only the smoke of it: and a nasty sort of disappointment and disillusion, a grating sort of irritation. Florence, Siena—hateful! The Fascisti risen up and taking on airs, all just out of a sort of spite. The Dante festival at Florence, and the King there, for example. Just set your teeth on edge, ugh!—with their 'Savoia!' All false and out of spite."

"And what do you attribute that to, Mr. Somers?"

"Why, I think the Socialists didn't *quite* believe in their own socialism, so everybody felt let down. In Italy, particularly, it seemed to me they were on the brink of a revolution. And the King was ready to abdicate, and the Church was ready to make away with its possessions: I know that. Everything ready for a flight. And then the Socialists funked. They just funked. They daren't make a revolution, because then they'd be responsible for the country. And they *daren't*. And so the Fascisti, seeing the Socialists in a funk, got up and began to try to kick their behinds."

Mr. Struthers nodded his head slowly.

"I suppose that is so," he said. "I suppose that's what it amounts to, they didn't believe in what they were doing. But then they're a childish, excitable people, with no stability."

"But it seems to me socialism hasn't got the spark in it to make a revolution. Not in any country. It hasn't got the spunk, either. There's no spunk in it."

"What is there any spunk in?" asked the other man, a sort of bitter fire corroding in his eyes. "Where do you find any spunk?"

"Oh, nowhere," said Richard.

There was a silence. Struthers looked out of the window as if he didn't know what to say next, and he played irritably with a blotter on the desk with his right hand. Richard also sat uncomfortably silent.

"Nowhere any spunk?" said Struthers, in his flat, metallic voice.

"No," said Richard.

And again the uncomfortable silence.

"There was plenty of spunk in the war," said Struthers.

"Of a sort. And because they felt they *had* to, not from choice."

"And mayn't they feel they *have* to again?" said Struthers, smiling rather grimly.

The two men eyed one another.

"What'll make them?" asked Richard.

"Oh—circumstances."

"Ah well—if circumstances." Richard was almost rude. "I know if it was a question of *war* the majority of returned soldiers would join up in a month—in a week. You hear it over and over again from the Diggers here. The war was the only time they ever felt properly alive. But then they moved because they hated the Germans—self-righteously hated them. And they can't quite bring it off, to hate the capitalist with a self-righteous hate. They don't hate him. They know that if they themselves got a chance to make a pile of money and be capitalists, they'd *jump* at it. You can't work up a hate, except on fear. And they *don't* fear the capitalist, and you can't make them. The most they'll do is sneer about him."

Struthers still fidgetted with the blotter, with his thin, very red, hairy hand, and abstractedly stared at the desk in front of him.

"And what does all that mean, in your estimation, Mr. Somers?" he asked dryly, looking nervously up.

"That you'll never get them to act. You'll never get Labour, or any of the Socialists, to make a revolution. They just won't act. Only the Anarchists might—and they're too few."

"I'm afraid they are growing more."

"Are they? Of that I know nothing. I should have thought they were growing fewer."

Mr. Struthers did not seem to hear this. At least he did not answer. He sat with his head dropped, fingering the blotter, rather like a boy who is being told things he hates to hear, but which he doesn't deny.

At last he looked up, and the fighting look was in the front of his eyes.

"It may be as you say, Mr. Somers," he replied. "Men may not be ready yet for any great change. That does not make the change less inevitable. It's coming, and it's got to come.

If it isn't here to-day, it will be here next century, at least. Whatever you may say, the socialistic and communal ideal is a great ideal, which will be fulfilled when men are ready. We aren't impatient. If revolution seems a premature jump—and perhaps it does—then we can go on, step by step, towards where we intend to arrive at last. And that is, State Ownership, and International Labour Control. The General Confederation of Labour, as perhaps you know, does not aim at immediate revolutions. It wants to make the great revolution by degrees. Step by step, by winning political victories in each country, by having new laws passed by our insistence, we intend to advance more slowly, but more surely towards the goal we have in sight.

"Now, Mr. Somers, you are no believer in capitalism, and in this industrial system as we have it. If I judge you correctly from your writings, you are no lover of the great Washed Middle Classes. They are more than washed, they are washed out. And I think in your writings you say as much. You want a new spirit in society, a new bond between men. You want a new bond between men. Well, so do I, so do we. We realise that if we are going to go ahead we need first and foremost *solidarity*. Where we fail in our present position is in our lack of solidarity.

"And how are we to get it. You suggest us the answer in your writings. We must have a new bond between men, the bond of real brotherhood. And why don't we find that bond sufficiently among us? Because we have been brought up from childhood to mistrust ourselves and to mistrust each other. We have been brought up in a kind of fetish worship. We are like tribes of savages with their witch-doctors. And who are our witch-doctors, our medicine men? Why, they are professors of science and professors of medicine and professors of law and professors of religion, all of whom thump on their tom-tom drums and over-awe us and take us in. And they take us in with the clever cry, 'Listen to us, and you will get on, get on, get on, you will rise up into the middle classes and become one of the great washed.'

"The trick of this only educated men like yourself see through. The working man can't see through it. *He* can't see that, for every one that *gets on*, you must have five hundred fresh slavers and toilers to produce the graft. Tempt all men to get on, and it's like holding a carrot in front of five thousand asses all harnessed to your machine. One ass get the carrot, and all the others have done your pulling for you.

. "Now what we want is a new bond between fellow-men. We've got to knock down the middle-class fetish and the middle-class medicine-men. But you've got to build up as you knock down. You've got to build up the real fellow-feeling between fellow-men. You've got to teach us working men to trust one another, absolutely trust one another, and to take all our trust away from the Great Washed and their medicine men who bleed us like leeches. Let us mistrust them—but let us trust one another. First and foremost, let us trust one another, we working men.

"Now Mr. Somers, you are a working man's son. You know what I'm talking about. Isn't it right, what I say? And isn't it feasible?"

A strange glow had come into his large black eyes, something glistening and half sweet, fixing itself on you. You felt drawn towards a strange sweetness—perhaps poisonous. Yet it touched Richard on one of his quivering strings—the latent power that is in man to-day, to love his near mate with a passionate, absolutely trusting love. Whitman says the love of comrades. We say, the mate love. "He is my mate." A depth of unfathomed, unrealised love can go into that phrase! "My mate is waiting for me," a man says, and turns away from wife, children, mother and all. The love of a man for his mate.

Now Richard knew what Struthers wanted. He wanted this love, this mate-trust called into consciousness and highest honour. He wanted to set it where Whitman tried to set his Love of Comrades. It was to be the new tie between men, in the new democracy. It was to be the new passional bond in the new society. The trusting love of a man for his mate.

Our society is based on the family, the love of a man for his wife and his children, or for his mother and brothers. The family is our social bed-rock and limit. Whitman said the next, broader, more unselfish rock should be the Love of Comrades. The sacred relation of a man to his mate, his fellow-man.

If our society is going to develop a new great phase, developing from where we stand now, it must accept this new relationship as the new sacred social bond, beyond the family. You can't make bricks without straw. That is, you can't hold together the friable mixture of modern mankind without a new cohesive principle, a new unifying passion. And this will be the new passion of a man's absolute trust in his mate, his love for his mate.

Richard knew this. But he had learned something else as well. He had learned the great danger of the new passion, which as yet lay only half realised and half recognised, half effective.

Human love, human trust, are always perilous, because they break down. The greater the love, the greater the trust, and the greater the peril, the greater the disaster. Because to place absolute trust on another human being is in itself a disaster, both ways, since each human being is a ship that must sail its own course, even if it go in company with another ship. Two ships may sail together to the world's end. But lock them together in mid-ocean and try to steer both with one rudder, and they will smash one another to bits. So it is when one individual seeks absolutely to love, or trust, another. Absolute lovers always smash one another, absolute trusters the same. Since man has been trying absolutely to love women, and women to love man, the human species has almost wrecked itself. If now we start a still further campaign of men loving and absolutely trusting each other, comrades or mates, heaven knows the horror we are laying up.

And yet, love is the greatest thing between human beings, men and women, men and men, women and women, when it is love, when it happens. But when human love starts out to lock individuals together, it is just courting disaster.

Man-and-woman love is a disaster nowadays. What a holy horror man-and-man love would be: mates or comrades!

What is it then that is wrong? Why, human beings *can't* absolutely love one another. Each man *does* kill the thing he loves, by sheer dint of loving it. Is love then just a horror in life?

Ah no. This individuality which each of us has got and which makes him a wayward, wilful, dangerous, untrustworthy quantity to every other individual, because every individuality is bound to react at some time against every other individuality, without exception—or else lose its own integrity; because of the inevitable necessity of each individual to react away from any other individual, at certain times, human love is truly a relative thing, not an absolute. It *cannot* be absolute.

Yet the human heart must have an absolute. It is one of the

conditions of being human. The only thing is the God who is the source of all passion. Once go down before the God-passion and human passions take their right rhythm. But human love without the God-passion always kills the thing it loves. Man and woman virtually are killing each other with the love-will now. What would it be when mates, or comrades, broke down in their absolute love and trust? Because, without the polarised God-passion to hold them stable at the centre, break down they would. With no deep God who is source of all passion and life to hold them separate and yet sustained in accord, the loving comrades would smash one another, and smash all love, all feeling as well. It would be a rare gruesome sight.

Any more love is a hopeless thing, till we have found again, each of us for himself, the great dark God who alone will sustain us in our loving one another. Till then, best not play with more fire.

Richard knew this, and it came to him again powerfully, under the dark eyes of Mr. Struthers.

"Yes," he answered slowly. "I know what you mean, and you know I know. And it's probably your only chance of carrying Socialism through. I don't really know how much it is feasible. But——"

"'Wait a minute, Mr. Somers. You are the man I have been waiting for: all except the but. Listen to me a moment further. You know our situation here in Australia. You know that Labour is stronger here, perhaps, more unopposed than in any country in the world. We might do anything. Then why do we do nothing? You know as well as I do. Because there is no real unifying principle among us. We're not together, we aren't one. And probably you never *will* be able to unite Australians on the wage question and the State Ownership question alone. They don't care enough. It doesn't really touch them emotionally. And they need to be touched emotionally, brought together that way. Once that was done, we'd be a grand, solid working-class people; grand, unselfish: a real *People*. 'When wilt thou save the People, oh God of Israel, when?' It looks as if the God of Israel would never save them. We've got to save ourselves.

"Now you know quite well, Mr. Somers, we're an unstable, unreliable body to-day, the Labour Party here in Australia. And why? Because in the first place we haven't got any voice.

We want a voice. Think of it, we've got no real Labour newspaper in Sydney—or in Australia. How *can* we be united?
We've no voice to call us together. And why don't we have a
paper of our own? Well, why? Nobody has the initiative.
What would be the good, over here, of a grievance-airing rag
like your London *Daily Herald?* It wouldn't be taken any
more seriously than any other rag. It would have no real
effect. Australians are a good bit subtler and more disillusioned
than the English working classes. You can throw Australians
chaff, and they'll laugh at it. They may even pretend to peck
it up. But all the time they *know*, and they're not taken in.
The *Bulletin* would soon help them out, if they were. They've
got a natural sarcastic turn, have the Australians. They'll do
imbecile things: because one thing is pretty well as good as
another to them. They don't care.

"Then what's the good starting another Red rag, if the bull
won't run at it. And this Australian bull may play about with
a red rag, but it won't get his real dander up.

"No, you've got to give them something to appeal to the
deeper man in them. That deeper man is waiting to be appealed
to. And we're waiting for the right individual to come along
to put the appeal to them.

"Now, Mr. Somers, here's your chance. I'm in a position to
ask you, won't you help us to bring out a sincere, *constructive*
Social paper, not a grievance airer, but a paper that calls to the
constructive spirit in men? Deep calleth to deep. And the
trouble with us here, no one calls to our deeps, they lie there
stagnant. I can't do it, I'm too grimy. It wants a deep, fresh
nature, and I'm too stale.

"Now, Mr. Somers, you're the son of a working man. You
were born of the People. You haven't turned your back on
them, have you, now that you're a well-known gentleman?"

"No, no," said Richard, laughing at the irony.

"Then here is your work before you. Come and breathe the
breath of life into us, through the printed word. Come and
take charge of a true People's paper for us. We needn't make
it a daily. Make it a twice-weekly. And let it appeal to the
Australian, to his heart, for his heart is the right place to appeal
to. Let it breathe the new air of trust and comradeship into us.
We are ready for it: dying for it. Show us how to *believe* in
one another, with all our hearts. Show us that the issue isn't
just the wage issue, or who holds the money. It's brother-love

at last, on which Christ's Democracy is bound to rest. It's the living People. It is man to man at last."

The red face of Willie Struthers seemed to glow with fire, and his black eyes had a strange glisten as he watched Richard's face. Richard's pale, sombre face showed that he was moved. There was a strange excitement, a deep, exciting vibration in the air, as if something secret were taking place. Jaz in his corner sat silent as a mouse, his knees wide apart, his elbows on his knees, his head dropped. Richard's eyes at length met the black, excited, glistening eyes of the other man, and he felt that something in the glisten was bearing him down, as a snake bears down a bird. Himself the bird.

But his heart was big within him, swollen in his breast. Because in truth he did love the working people, he did know them capable of a great, generous love for one another. And he did also believe, in a way, that they were capable of building up this great Church of Christ, the great beauty of a People, upon the generous passion of mate-love. All this theoretical socialism started by Jews like Marx, and appealing only to the will-to-power in the masses, making money the whole crux, this has cruelly injured the working people of Europe. For the working people of Europe were generous by nature, and money was not their prime passion. All this political socialism—all politics, in fact—have conspired to make money the only god. It has been a great treacherous conspiracy against the generous heart of the people. And that heart is betrayed: and knows it.

Then can't the injury be remedied? Can't the working men be called back, man to man, to a generous opening of the heart to one another, money forgotten? Can't a new great inspiration of belief in the love of mates be breathed into the white Peoples of the world, and a new day be built on this belief?

It can be done. It could be done. Only, the terrible stress, the strain on the hearts of men, if as human beings the whole weight of the living world is to rest on them. Each man with the poles of the world resting on his heart. Men would go mad.

"You see," stammered Richard, "it needs more than a belief of men in each other."

"But what else is there to believe in? Quacks? Medicine-men? Scientists and politicians?"

"It *does* need some sort of religion."

"Well then—well then—the religious question is ticklish,

especially here in Australia. But all the churches are established on Christ. And Christ says Love one another."

Richard laughed suddenly.

"That makes Christ into another political agent," he said.

"Well then—I'm not deep enough for these matters. But surely you know how to square it with religion. Seems to me it *is* religion—love one another."

"Without a God."

"Well—as I say—it's Christ's teaching, and that ought to be God enough."

Richard was silent, his heart heavy. It all seemed so far from the dark God he wished to serve, the God from whom the dark, sensual passion of love emanates, not only the spiritual love of Christ. He wanted men once more to refer the sensual passion of love sacredly to the great dark God, the ithyphallic, of the first dark religions. And how could that be done, when each dry little individual ego was just mechanically set against any such dark flow, such ancient submission. As, for instance, Willie Struthers at this minute, Struthers didn't mind Christ. Christ could easily be made to subserve his egoistic purpose. But the first, dark, ithyphallic God whom men had once known so tremendous—Struthers had no use for Him.

"I don't think I can do it. I don't think I've the right touch," said Richard slowly.

"Nay, Mr. Somers, don't you be a funker, now. This is the work you were born for. Don't leave us in the lurch."

"I shouldn't be doing what you want me to do."

"Do what seems best to yourself. We'll risk it. Make your own conditions. I know as far as money goes you won't be hard. But take the job on now. It's been waiting for you, waiting for you to come out here. Don't funk at the last minute."

"I won't promise at this minute," said Richard, rising to escape. "I want to go now. I will tell you within a week. You might send me details of your scheme for the paper. Will you? And I'll think about it hard."

Mr. Struthers watched him as if he would read his soul. But Richard wasn't going to have his soul read by force.

"Very well. I'll see you have the whole scheme of the proposal to-morrow. I don't think you'll be able to run away from it."

Richard was thankful to get out of Canberra Hall. It was like escaping from one of the medical examination rooms in

the war. He and Jaz went in silence down the crowded, narrow
pavement of George Street, towards the Circular Quay. Richard
called at the General Post Office in Martin Place. As he came
out again, and stood on the steps, folding the stamps he had
bought, seeing the sun down Pitt Street, the people hurrying,
the flowers at the corner, the pink spread of *Bulletins* for sale
at the corner of George Street, the hansom cabs and taxis standing peacefully in the morning shadow of the post office, suddenly the whole thing switched right away from him. He
hailed a hansom.

"Jaz," he said, "I want to drive round the Botanical Gardens
and round the spit there—and I want to look at the peacocks
and cockatoos."

Jaz climbed in with him. "Right O!" said the cabby, hearing
the order, and they clock-clocked away up the hill to Macquarie
Street.

"You know, Jaz," said Richard, looking with joy at the blue
harbour inlet, where the Australian "fleet" lay rusting to bits,
with a few gay flags; "you know, Jaz, I shan't do it. I shan't
do anything. I just don't care about it."

"You don't?" said Jaz, with a sudden winsome smile.

"I try to kid myself that I care about mankind and its destiny.
And I have fits of wistful love for the working men. But at
the bottom I'm as hard as a mango nut. I don't care about
them all. I don't really care about anything, no, I don't. I just
don't care, so what's the good of fussing?"

"Why, no," said Jaz, again with a quick smile.

"I feel neither good nor bad. I feel like a fox that has gnawed
his tail off and so escaped out of a trap. It seems like a trap to
me, all this social business and this saving mankind. Why can't
mankind save itself? It can if it wants to. I'm a fool. I neither
want love nor power. I like the world. And I like to be alone
in it, by myself. What do you want, Jaz?"

Richard was like a child escaped from school, escaped from
his necessity to *be* something and to *do* something. They had
jogged past the palm trees and the grass of the gardens, and the
blue wrens had cocked their preposterous tails. They jogged to
the end of the promontory, under wild trees, and Richard
looked at the two lobes of the harbour, blue water on either
side, and another part of the town beyond.

"Now take us back to the cockatoos," he said to the
cabby.

Richard loved the look of Australia, that marvellous soft flower-blue of the air, and the sombre grey of the earth, the foliage, the brown of the low rocks: like the dull pelts of kangaroos. It had a wonder and a far-awayness, even here in the heart of Sydney. All the shibboleths of mankind are so trumpery. Australia is outside everything.

"I couldn't exactly say," Jaz answered. "You've got a bit of an Australian look this morning about you," he added with a smile.

"I feel Australian. I feel a new creature. But what's the outcome?"

"Oh, you'll come back to caring, I should think: for the sake of having something to care about. That's what most of them do. They want to turn bushrangers for six months, and then they get frightened of themselves, and come back and want to be good citizens."

"Bushranger? But Australia's like an open door with the blue beyond. You just walk out of the world and into Australia. And it's just somewhere else. All those nations left behind in their school-room, fussing. Let them fuss. This is Australia, where one can't care."

Jaz sat rather pale, and ten times more silent than ever.

"I expect you've got yourself to reckon with, no matter where you are. That's why most Australians have to fuss about something—politics, or horse-racing, or football. Though a man can go empty in Australia, if he likes: as you've said yourself," replied he.

"Then I'll go empty," said Richard. "What makes *you* fuss with Kangaroo and Struthers, Jaz?"

"Me?" The smile was slow and pale. "Go into the middle of Australia and see how empty it is. You can't face emptiness long. You have to come back and do something to keep from being frightened at your own emptiness, and everything else's emptiness. It may be empty. But it's wicked, and it'll kill you if it can. Something comes out of the emptiness, to kill you. You have to come back and do things with mankind, to forget."

"It's wonderful to be empty. It's wonderful to feel this blue globe of emptiness of the Australian air. It shuts everything out," protested Richard.

"You'll be an Aussie yet," smiled Jaz slowly.

"Shall I regret it?" asked Richard.

The eyes of the two men met. In the pale grey eyes of Jaz something lurking, like an old, experienced consciousness looking across at the childish consciousness of Somers, almost compassionately: and half in mockery.

"You'll change back before you regret it," he said.

"Are you wise, Jaz? And am I childish?" Richard's look suddenly changed also to mockery. "If you're wise, Jaz, why do you wander round like a lost soul? Because you do. And what takes you to Struthers, if you belong to Kangaroo?"

"I'm secretary for the coal and timber-merchants' union," said Jaz quietly.

They got out of the cab to look at the aviaries. Wonderful, brilliant-coloured little birds, the love-birds self-consciously smirking. "Hello!"—pronounced pure Australian cockney: "Helleow!" "Hello! Hello!" "Hello, Cocky! What yer want?" This in a more-than-human voice from a fine sulphur-crested cockatoo. "Hello, Cocky!" His thick black tongue worked in his narrow mouth. So absolutely human the sound, and yet a bird's. It was startling, and very funny. The two men talked to the cockatoos, fascinated and amused, for a quarter of an hour. The emu came prancing up, with his alert, large, sticking-out eyes and his whiskers. An alert gentleman, with the dark Australian eye. Very wide-awake, and yet far off in the past. And a remote, alert, sharp gentleness belonging to far past twilight ages, before enemies and iron weapons were perfected. A very remote, dirt-brown gentleman from the lost plains of time. The peacock rustling his blue fireworks seemed a sort of nouveau-riche in comparison.

Somers went in the evening of this memorable day to dine with Kangaroo. The other man was quiet, and seemed preoccupied.

"I went to Willie Struthers this morning," Somers said.

Kangaroo looked at him sharply through his pince-nez. On the subtle face of Somers a small, wicked smile hovered like a half-visible flame. But it was his alive, beautiful face. And his whole person seemed magnetic.

"Who took you there?" asked Kangaroo sharply.

"Jaz."

"Jaz is a meddlesome-Patty. Well, and what then?"

"I think Willie is rather a terror. I wouldn't like to have to spend my life with him. But he's shrewd. Only I don't like him physically—something thin and hairy and spiderish. I didn't want to touch him. But he's a force, he's *something*."

Kangaroo looked puzzled, and his face took a heavy, stupid look.

"He wouldn't want you to touch him," he barked. "He didn't offer to shake hands, did he?"

"No, thank goodness," said Somers, thinking of the red, dry, thin-skinned hand.

There was a hostile silence from Kangaroo. He knew that this subtle, attractive Somers with the faint glow about him, like an aura, was venomous. And yet he was helplessly attracted to him.

"And what do you mean about his being something? Some more Trewhella?"

"Perhaps. I couldn't help feeling that Struthers was shrewder than you are—in a way baser—but for that reason more likely to be effectual."

Kangaroo watched Richard for a long time in silence.

"I know why Trewhella took you there," he said sulkily.

"Why?"

"Oh, I know why. And what have you decided?"

"Nothing."

There was a long and obstinate silence. The two men were at loggerheads, and neither would make the first move.

"You seem very thick with Trewhella," said Kangaroo at last.

"Not thick," said Richard. "Celts—Cornish, Irish—they always interest me. What do you imagine is at the bottom of Jaz?"

"Treachery."

"Oh, not only," laughed Somers.

"Then why do you ask me, if you know better?"

"Because I don't really get to the bottom of him."

"There is no bottom to get to—he's the instinctive traitor, as they all are."

"Oh, surely not only that."

"I see nothing else. They would like the white civilisation to be trampled underfoot piecemeal. And at the same time they live on us like parasites." Kangaroo glowered fiercely.

"There's something more," replied Richard. "They don't believe in our gods, in our ideals. They remember older gods, older ideals, different gods: before the Jews invented a mental

Jehovah, and a spiritual Christ. They are nearer the magic of the animal world."

"Magic of the animal world!" roared Kangaroo. "What does that nonsense mean? Are you traitor to your own human intelligence?"

"All too human," smiled Richard.

Kangaroo sat up very straight, and looked at Somers. Somers still smiled faintly and luminously.

"Why are you so easily influenced?" said Kangaroo, with a certain cold reproof. "You are like a child. I know that is part of the charm of your nature, that you are naïve like a child, but sometimes you are childish rather than childlike. A perverse child."

"Let me be a perverse child then," laughed Somers, with a flash of attractive laughter at Kangaroo. It frightened the big man, this perverse mood. If only he could have got the wicked light out of Lovat's face, and brought back the fire of earnestness. And yet, as an individual, he was attracted to the little fellow now, like a moth to a candle: a great lumbering moth to a small, but dangerous flame of a candle.

"I'm sure it's Struthers' turn to set the world right, before it's yours," Somers said.

"Why are you sure?"

"I don't know. I thought so when I saw him. You're too human."

Kangaroo was silent, and offended.

"I don't think that is a final reason," he replied.

"For me it is. No, I want one of the olives that the man took away. You give one such good food, one forgets deep questions in your lovely salad. Why don't you do as Jaz says, and back up the Reds for the time being. Play your pawns and your bishops."

"You know that a bite from a hyena means blood-poisoning," said Kangaroo.

"Don't be solemn. You mean Willie Struthers? Yes, I wouldn't want to be bitten. But if you are so sure of love as an all-ruling influence, and so sure of the fidelity of the Diggers, through love, I should agree with Jaz. Push Struthers where he wants to go. Let him proclaim the rule of the People: let him nationalise all industries and resources, and confiscate property above a certain amount: and bring the world about his ears. Then you step in like a saviour. It's much easier to point to a wrecked house, if you want to build something new, than to persuade people to pull the house down and build it up in a better style."

Kangaroo was deeply offended, mortified. Yet he listened.

"You are hopelessly facile, Lovat," he said gently. "In the first place, the greatest danger to the world to-day is anarchy, not bolshevism. It is anarchy and unrule that are coming on us—and that is what I, as an order-loving Jew and one of the half-chosen people, do not want. I want one central principle in the world: the principle of love, the maximum of individual liberty, the minimum of human distress. Lovat, you know I am sincere, don't you?"

There was a certain dignity and pathos in the question.

"I do," replied Somers sincerely. "But I am tired of one central principle in the world."

"Anything else means chaos."

"There has to be chaos occasionally. And then, Roo, if you *do* want a benevolent fatherly autocracy, I'm sure you'd better step in after there's been a bit of chaos."

Kangaroo shook his head.

"Like a wayward child! Like a wayward child!" he murmured. "You are not such a fool, Lovat, that you can't see that once you break the last restraints on humanity to-day, it is the end. It is the end. Once burst the flood-gates, and you'll never get the water back into control. Never."

"Then let it distil up to heaven. I really don't care."

"But, man, you are *perverse*. What's the matter with you?" suddenly bellowed Kangaroo.

They had gone into the study for coffee. Kangaroo stood with his head dropped and his feet apart, his back to the fire. And suddenly he roared like a lion at Somers. Somers started, then laughed.

"Even perversity has its points," he said.

Kangaroo glowered like a massive cloud. Somers was standing staring at the Dürer etching of St. Jerome: he loved Dürer. Suddenly, with a great massive movement, Kangaroo caught the other man to his breast.

"Don't, Lovat," he said, in a much moved voice, pressing the slight body of the lesser man against his own big breast and body. "Don't!" he said, with a convulsive tightening of the arm.

Somers, squeezed so that he could hardly breathe, kept his

face from Kangaroo's jacket and managed to ejaculate:

"All right. Let me go and I won't."

"Don't thwart me," pleaded Kangaroo. "Don't—or I shall have to break all connection with you, and I love you so. I love you so. Don't be perverse, and put yourself against me."

He still kept Somers clasped against him, but not squeezed so hard. And Somers heard over his own head the voice speaking with a blind yearning. Not to himself. No. It was speaking over his head, to the void, to the infinite or something tiresome like that. Even the words: "I love you so. I love you so." They made the marrow in Lovat's bones melt, but they made his heart flicker even more devilishly.

"It is an impertinence, that he says he loves me," he thought to himself. But he did not speak, out of regard for Kangaroo's emotion, which was massive and genuine, even if Somers felt it missed his own particular self completely.

In those few moments when he was clasped to the warm passionate body of Kangaroo, Somers' mind flew with swift thought. "He doesn't love *me*," he thought to himself. "He just turns a great general emotion on me, like a tap. I feel as cold as steel, in his clasp—and as separate. It is presumption his loving me. If he was in any way really *aware* of me, he'd keep at the other end of the room, as if I was a dangerous little animal. He wouldn't be hugging me if I were a scorpion. And I *am* a scorpion. So why doesn't he know it. Damn his love. He wants to *force* me."

After a few minutes Kangaroo dropped his arm and turned his back. He stood there, a great, hulked, black back. Somers thought to himself: "If I were a kestrel I'd stoop and strike him straight in the back of the neck, and he'd die. He ought to die." Then he went and sat in his chair. Kangaroo left the room.

He did not come back for some time, and Lovat began to grow uncomfortable. But the devilishness in his heart continued, broken by moments of tenderness or pity or self-doubt. The gentleness was winning, when Kangaroo came in again. And one look at the big, gloomy figure set the devil alert like a flame again in the other man's heart.

Kangaroo took his place before the fire again, but looked aside.

"Of course you understand," he began in a muffled voice, "that it must be one thing or the other. Either you are with me, and I *feel* you with me: or you cease to exist for me."

Somers listened with wonder. He admired the man for his absoluteness, and his strange blind heroic obsession.

"I'm not really against you, am I?" said Somers. And his own heart answered, *Yes, you are!*

"You are not *with* me," said Kangaroo bitterly.

"No," said Somers slowly.

"Then why have you deceived me, played with me," suddenly roared Kangaroo. "I could have killed you."

"Don't do that," laughed Somers, rather coldly.

But the other did not answer. He was like a black cloud.

"I want to hear," said Kangaroo, "your case against me."

"It's not a case, Kangaroo," said Richard, "it's a sort of instinct."

"Against what?"

"Why, against your ponderousness. And against your insistence. And against the whole sticky stream of love, and the hateful will-to-love. It's the will-to-love that I hate, Kangaroo."

"In me?"

"In us all. I just hate it. It's a sort of syrup we *have* to stew in, and it's loathsome. Don't love me. Don't want to save mankind. You're so awfully *general*, and your love is so awfully general: as if one were only a cherry in the syrup. Don't love me. Don't want me to love you. Let's be hard, separate men. Let's understand one another deeper than love."

"Two human ants, in short," said Kangaroo, and his face was yellow.

"No, no. Two men. Let us go to the understanding that is deeper than love."

"Is any understanding deeper than love?" asked Kangaroo with a sneer.

"Why, yes, you know it is. At least between men."

"I'm afraid I don't know it. I know the understanding that is much *less* than love. If you want me to have a merely commonplace acquaintance with you, I refuse. That's all."

"We are neither of us capable of a quite commonplace acquaintance."

"Oh yes, I am," barked Kangaroo.

"I'm not. But you're such a Kangaroo, wanting to carry mankind in your belly-pouch, cosy, with its head and long ears peeping out. You sort of figure yourself a Kangaroo of Judah, instead of Lion of Judah: Jehovah with a great heavy

H

tail and a belly-pouch. Let's get off it, and be men, with the gods beyond us. I *don't* want to be godlike, Kangaroo. I like to know the gods beyond me. Let's start as men, with the great gods beyond us."

He looked up with a beautiful candour in his face, and a diabolic bit of mockery in his soul. For Kangaroo's face had gone like an angry wax mask, with mortification. An angry wax mask of mortification, haughty with a stiff, wooden haughtiness, and two little near-set holes for eyes, behind glass pince-nez. Richard had a moment of pure hate for him, in the silence. For Kangaroo refused to answer.

"What's the good, men trying to be gods?" said Richard. "You're a Jew, and you must be Jehovah or nothing. We're Christians, all little Christs walking without our crucifixes. Jaz is quite right to play us one against the other. Struthers is the anti-Christ, preaching love alone. I'm tired, tired. I want to be a man, with the gods beyond me, greater than me. I want the great gods, and my own mere manliness."

"It's that treacherous Trewhella," Kangaroo murmured to himself. Then he seemed to be thinking hard.

And then at last he lifted his head and looked at Somers. And now Somers openly hated him. His face was arrogant, insolent, righteous.

"I am sorry I have made a mistake in you," he said. "But we had better settle the matter finally here. I think the best thing you can do is to leave Australia. I don't think you can do me any serious damage with your talk. I would ask you—before I warn you—not to try. That is all. I should prefer now to be alone."

He had become again hideous, with a long yellowish face and black eyes close together, and a cold, mindless, dangerous hulk of his shoulders. For a moment Somers was afraid of him, as of some great ugly idol that might strike. He felt the intense hatred of the man coming at him in cold waves. He stood up in a kind of horror in front of the great, close-eyed, horrible thing that was now Kangaroo. Yes, a thing, not a whole man. A great Thing, a horror.

"I am sorry if I have been foolish," he said, backing away from the Thing. And as he went out of the door he made a quick movement, and his heart melted in horror lest the Thing Kangaroo should suddenly lurch forward and clutch him. If that happened, Kangaroo would have blood on his hands. But

Somers kept all his wits about him, and quickly, quietly got
his hat and walked to the hall door. It seemed like a dream,
as if it were miles to the outer door, as if his heart would burst
before he got there, as if he would never be able to undo the
fastening of the door.

But he kept all his wits about him, and as by inspiration
managed the three separate locks of the strong door. Kangaroo
had followed slowly, awfully, behind, like a madman. If he
came near enough to touch!

Somers had the door opened, and looked round. The huge
figure, the white face with the two eyes close together, like a
spider, approaching with awful stillness. If the stillness suddenly broke, and he struck out!

"Good-night!" said Somers, at the blind, horrible-looking
face. And he moved quickly down the stairs, though still not
apparently in flight, but going in that quick, controlled way
that acts as a check on an onlooker.

He was thankful for the streets, for the people. But by bad
luck, it was Saturday night, when Sydney is all shut up, and
the big streets seem dark and dreary, though thronging with
people. Dark streets, dark, streaming people. And fear. One
could feel such fear, in Australia.

CHAPTER XII

THE NIGHTMARE

HE had known such different deep fears. In Sicily, a sudden
fear, in the night of some single murderer, some single thing
hovering as it were out of the violent past, with the intent of
murder. Out of the old Greek past, that had been so vivid,
sometimes an unappeased spirit of murderous hate against the
usurping moderns. A sudden presence of murder in the air,
because of something which the modern psyche had excluded,
some old and vital thing which Christianity has cut out. An
old spirit, waiting for vengeance. But in England, during the
later years of the war, a true and deadly fear of the criminal
living spirit which arose in all the stay-at-home bullies who
governed the country during those years. From 1916 to 1919
a wave of criminal lust rose and possessed England, there was
a reign of terror, under a set of indecent bullies like Bottomley

of *John Bull* and other bottom-dog members of the House of Commons. Then Somers had known what it was to live in a perpetual state of semi-fear: the fear of the criminal public and the criminal government. The torture was steadily applied, during those years after Asquith fell, to break the independent soul in any man who would not hunt with the criminal mob. A man must identify himself with the criminal mob, sink his sense of truth, of justice, and of human honour, and bay like some horrible unclean hound, bay with a loud sound, from slavering, unclean jaws.

This Richard Lovat Somers had steadily refused to do. The deepest part of a man is his sense of essential truth, essential honour, essential justice. This deepest self makes him abide by his own feelings, come what may. It is not sentimentalism. It is just the male human creature, the thought-adventurer, driven to earth. Will he give in or won't he?

Many men, carried on a wave of patriotism and true belief in democracy, entered the war. Many men were driven in out of belief that it was necessary to save their property. Vast numbers of men were just bullied into the army. A few remained. Of these, many became conscientious objectors.

Somers tiresomely belonged to no group. He would not enter the army, because his profoundest instinct was against it. Yet he had no conscientious objection to war. It was the whole spirit of the war, the vast mob-spirit, which he could never acquiesce in. The terrible, terrible war, made so fearful because in every country practically every man lost his head, and lost his own centrality, his own manly isolation in his own integrity, which alone keeps life real. Practically every man being caught away from himself, as in some horrible flood, and swept away with the ghastly masses of other men, utterly unable to speak, or feel for himself, or to stand on his own feet, delivered over and swirling in the current, suffocated for the time being. Some of them to die for ever. Most to come back home victorious in circumstance, but with their inner pride gone: inwardly lost. To come back home, many of them, to wives who had egged them on to this downfall in themselves: black bitterness. Others to return to a bewildered wife who had in vain tried to keep her man true to himself, tried and tried, only to see him at last swept away. And oh, when he was swept away, how she loved him. But when he came back, when he crawled out like a dog out of a dirty stream, a stream that had suddenly gone slack and turbid: when he came back covered with outward glory and inward shame, then there was the price to pay.

And there *is* this bitter and sordid after-war price to pay because men lost their heads, and worse, lost their inward, individual integrity. And when a man loses his inward, isolated, manly integrity, it is a bad day for that man's true wife. A true man should not lose his head. The greater the crisis, the more intense should be his isolated reckoning with his own soul. And *then* let him act, of his own whole self. Not fling himself away: or much worse, let himself be *dragged* away, bit by bit.

Awful years—'16, '17, '18, '19—the years when the damage was done. The years when the world lost its real manhood. Not for lack of courage to face death. Plenty of superb courage to face death. But no courage in any man to face his own isolated soul, and abide by its decision. Easier to sacrifice oneself. So much easier!

Richard Lovat was one of those utterly unsatisfactory creatures who just would not. He had no conscientious objections. He knew that men *must* fight, some time in some way or other. He was no Quaker, to believe in perpetual peace. He had been in Germany times enough to know *how* much he detested the German military creatures: mechanical bullies they were. They had once threatened to arrest him as a spy, and had insulted him more than once. Oh, he would never forgive *them*, in his inward soul. But then the industrialism and commercialism of England, with which patriotism and democracy became identified: did not these insult a man and hit him pleasantly across the mouth? How much humiliation had Richard suffered, trying to earn his living! How had they tried, with their beastly industrial self-righteousness, to humiliate him as a separate, single man? They wanted to bring him to heel even more than the German militarist did. And if a man is to be brought to any heel, better a spurred heel than the heel of a Jewish financier. So Richard decided later, when the years let him think things over, and see where he was.

Therefore when the war came, his instinct was against it. When the Asquith government so softly foundered, he began to suffer agonies. But when the Asquith government went right under, and in its place came that *John Bull* government of '16, '17, '18, then agonies gave way to tortures. He was summoned to join the army: and went. Spent a night in barracks with forty other men, and not one of these other men but felt like a criminal condemned, bitter in dejection and humiliation. Was medically examined in the morning by two doctors, both gentlemen, who knew the sacredness of another naked man: and was rejected.

So, that was over. He went back home. And he made up his mind what he would do. He would never voluntarily make a martyr of himself. His feeling was private to himself, he didn't want to force it on any other man. He would just act alone. For the moment, he was rejected as medically unfit. If he was called up again, he would go again. But he would never serve.

"Once," he said to Harriet, "that they have really conscripted me, I will never obey another order, if they kill me."

Poor Harriet felt scared, and didn't know what else to say.

"If ever," he said, looking up from his own knees in their old grey flannel trousers, as he sat by the fire, "if ever I see my legs in khaki, I shall die. But they shall never put my legs into khaki."

That first time, at the barracks in the country town in the west, they had treated him with that instinctive regard and gentleness which he usually got from men who were not German militarist bullies, or worse, British commercial bullies. For instance, in the morning in that prison barracks room, these unexamined recruits were ordered to make their beds and sweep the room. In obedience, so far, Richard Lovat took one of the heavy brooms. He was pale, silent, isolated: a queer figure, a young man with a beard. The other soldiers— or must-be soldiers—had looked at him as a queer fish, but that he was used to.

"Say, Dad," said a fattish young fellow older than himself, the only blatherer, a loose fellow who had come from Canada to join up and was already cursing: he was a good deal older than Somers.

"Say, Dad," said this fellow, as they sat in the train coming up, "all that'll come off to-morrow—Qck, Qck!"—and he made two noises, and gave two long swipes with his finger round his chin, to intimate that Richard's beard would be cut off to-morrow.

"We'll see," said Richard, smiling with pale lips.

He said in his heart, the day his beard was shaven he was beaten, lost. He identified it with his isolate manhood. He never forgot that journey up to Bodmin, with the other men who were called up. They were all bitterly, desperately miserable, but still manly: mostly very quiet, yet neither sloppy nor frightened. Only the fat, loose fellow who had given up a damned good job in Canada to come and serve this bloody country, etc., etc., was a ranter and a bragger. Somers saw him afterwards naked: strange, fat, soft, like a woman. But in another carriage the men sang all the time, or howled like dogs in the night:

"I'll be your sweetheart, if you will be mine,
All my life I'll be you-o-o-ur Valentine.
Bluebells I'll gather, take them and be true,
When I'm a man, my plan will be to marry you."

Wailing down the lost corridors of hell, surely, those ghastly melancholy notes—

"All my li-i-i-ife—I'll be you-u-r Valentine."

Somers could never recall it without writhing. It is not death that matters, but the loss of the integral soul. And these men howled as if they were going to their doom, helplessly, ghastly. It was not the death in front. It was the surrender of all their old beliefs, and all their sacred liberty.

Those bluebells! They were worse than the earlier songs. In 1915, autumn, Hampstead Heath, leaves burning in heaps, in the blue air, London still almost pre-war London: but by the pond on the Spaniards Road, blue soldiers, wounded soldiers in their bright hospital blue and red, always there: and earth-coloured recruits with pale faces drilling near Parliament Hill. The pre-war world still lingering, and some vivid strangeness, glamour thrown in. At night all the great beams of the search-lights, in great straight bars, feeling across the London sky, feeling the clouds, feeling the body of the dark overhead. And then Zeppelin raids: the awful noise and the excitement. Somers was never afraid then. One evening he and Harriet walked from Platts Lane to the Spaniards Road, across the Heath: and there, in the sky, like some god vision, a Zeppelin, and the searchlights catching it, so that it gleamed like a mani-festation in the heavens, then losing it, so that only the strange drumming came down out of the sky where the searchlights tangled their feelers. There it was again, high, high, high, tiny, pale, as one might imagine the Holy Ghost, far, far above. And the crashes of guns, and the awful hoarseness of shells bursting in the city. Then gradually, quiet. And from Parliament Hill, a great red glare below, near St. Paul's. Something ablaze in the city. Harriet was horribly afraid. Yet as she looked up at the far-off Zeppelin, she said to Somers:

"Think, some of the boys I played with when I was a child are probably in it."

And he looked up at the far, luminous thing, like a moon. Were there men in it? Just men, with two vulnerable legs and warm mouths. The imagination could not go so far.

Those days, that autumn . . . people carried about chrysanthemums, yellow and brown chrysanthemums: and the smell of burning leaves: and the wounded, bright blue soldiers with their red cotton neck-ties, sitting together like macaws on the seats, pale and different from other people. And the star Jupiter very bright at nights over the cup hollow of the Vale, on Hampstead Heath. And the war news always coming, the war horror drifting in, drifting in, prices rising, excitement growing, people going mad about the Zeppelin raids. And always the one song:

> "Keep the home fires burning,
> Though your hearts be yearning."

It was in 1915 the old world ended. In the winter 1915-1916 the spirit of the old London collapsed; the city, in some way, perished, perished from being a heart of the world, and became a vortex of broken passions, lusts, hopes, fears, and horrors. The integrity of London collapsed, and the genuine debasement began, the unspeakable baseness of the press and the public voice, the reign of that bloated ignominy, *John Bull*.

No man who has really consciously lived through this can believe again absolutely in democracy. No man who has heard reiterated in thousands of tones from all the common people, during the crucial years of the war: "I believe in *John Bull*. Give me *John Bull*," can ever believe that in any crisis a people can govern itself, or is ever fit to govern itself. During the crucial years of the war, the people chose, and chose Bottom-leyism. Bottom enough.

The well-bred, really cultured classes were on the whole passive resisters. They shirked their duty. It is the business of people who really know better to fight tooth and nail to keep up a standard, to hold control of authority. Laisser-aller is as guilty as the actual, stinking mongrelism it gives place to.

It was in mid-winter 1915 that Somers and Harriet went down to Cornwall. The spirit of the war—the spirit of collapse and of human ignominy, had not travelled so far yet. It came in advancing waves.

We hear so much of the bravery and horrors at the front. Brave the men were, all honour to them. It was at home the world was lost. We hear too little of the collapse of the proud human spirit at home, the triumph of sordid, rampant, raging meanness. "The bite of a jackal is blood-poisoning and mortification." And at home stayed all the jackals, middle-aged, male and female jackals. And they bit us all. And blood-poisoning and mortification set in.

We should never have let the jackals loose, and patted them on the head. They were feeding on our death all the while.

Away in the west Richard and Harriet lived alone in their cottage by the savage Atlantic. He hardly wrote at all, and never any propaganda. But he hated the war, and said so to the few Cornish people around. He laughed at the palpable lies of the press, bitterly. And because of his isolation and his absolute separateness, he was marked out as a spy.

"I am not a spy," he said, "I leave it to dirtier people. I am myself, and I won't have popular lies."

So, there began the visits from the policeman. A large, blue, helmeted figure at the door.

"Excuse me, sir, I have just a few enquiries to make."

The police-sergeant always a decent, kindly fellow, driven by the military.

Somers and Harriet lived now with that suspense about them in the very air they breathed. They were suspects.

"Then let them suspect," said he. "I do nothing to them, so what can they do to me."

He still believed in the constitutional liberty of an Englishman.

"You know," said Harriet, "you *do* say things to these Cornish people."

"I only say, when they tell me newspaper lies, that they *are* lies."

But now the two began to be hated, hated far more than they knew.

"You want to be careful," warned one of the Cornish friends. "I've heard that the coast-watchers have got orders to keep very strict watch on you."

"Let them, they'll see nothing."

But it was not till afterwards that he learned that the watchers had lain behind the stone fence, to hear what he and Harriet talked about.

So, he was called up the first time and went. He was summoned to Penzance, and drove over with Harriet, expecting to return for the time at least. But he was ordered to proceed the same afternoon to Bodmin, along with sixteen or seventeen other fellows, farm hands and working men. He said good-bye to Harriet, who was to be driven back alone across the moors, to their lonely cottage on the other side.

"I shall be back to-morrow," he said.

England was still England, and he was not finally afraid.

The train-journey from Penzance to Bodmin with the other men : the fat, bragging other man : the tall man who felt as Somers did : the change at the roadside station, with the porters chaffing the men that the handcuffs were on them. Indeed, it was like being one of a gang of convicts. The great, prison-like barracks—the disgusting evening meal of which he could eat nothing—the little terrier-like sergeant of the regulars, who made them a little encouraging speech : not a bad chap. The lounging about that barracks yard, prisoners, till bed-time : the other men crowding to the canteen, himself mostly alone. The brief talks with men who were for a moment curious as to who and what he was. For a moment only. They were most of them miserable and bitter.

Gaol! It was like gaol. He thought of Oscar Wilde in prison. Night came, and the beds to be made.

"They're good beds, clean beds, you'll sleep quite comfortable in them," said the elderly little sergeant with a white moustache. Nine o'clock lights out. Somers had brought no night clothes, nothing. He slept in his woollen pants, and was ashamed because they had patches on the knees, for he and Harriet were very poor these years. In the next bed was a youth, a queer fellow, in a sloppy suit of black broadcloth, and down-at-heel boots. He had a degenerate sort of handsomeness too. He had never spoken a word. His face was long and

rather fine, but like an Apache, his straight black hair came
in a lock over his forehead. And there was an Apache sort of
sheepishness, stupidity, in everything he did. He was a long
time getting undressed. Then there he stood, and his white
cotton day-shirt was long below his knees, like a woman's
night-gown. A restless, bitter night, with one man cough,
cough, coughing, a hysterical cough, and others talking,
making noises in their sleep. Bugle at six, and a scramble to
wash themselves at the zinc trough in the wash-house. Somers
could not crowd in, did not get in till towards the end. Then
he had to borrow soap, and afterwards a piece of comb. The
men were all quiet and entirely inoffensive, common, but
gentle, by nature decent. A sickening breakfast, then wash-up
and sweep the floors. Somers took one of the heavy brooms,
as ordered, and began. He swept his own floors nearly every
day. But this was heavier work. The sergeant stopped him.
"Don't you do that. You go and help to wipe the pots, if you
like. Here, you boy, *you*—take that sweeping brush."

And Somers relinquished his broom to a bigger man.

They were kindly, and, in the essential sense, gentlemen, the
little terrier of a sergeant too. Englishmen, his own people.

When it came to Somers' turn to be examined, and he took
off his clothes and sat in his shirt in the cold lobby : the fat
fellow pointed to his thin, delicate legs with a jeer. But Somers
looked at him, and he was quiet again. The queer, soft, pale-
bodied fellow, against Somers' thin delicate whiteness. The
little sergeant kept saying :

"Don't you catch cold, you chaps."

In the warm room behind a screen, Richard took off his shirt
and was examined. The doctor asked him where he lived—
where was his home—asked as a gentleman asks, treated him
with that gentle consideration Somers usually met with, save
from business people or official people.

"We shall reject you, leave you free," said the doctor, after
consulting with the more elderly, officious little man, "but we
leave it to you to do what you can for your country."

"Thank you," said Richard, looking at him.

"Every man must do what he can," put in the other doctor,
who was elderly and officious, but a gentleman. "The country
needs the help of every man, and though we leave you free,
we expect you to apply yourself to *some* service."

"Yes," said Somers, looking at him, and speaking in an abso-

lutely neutral voice. Things said like that to him were never
real to him, more like the noise of a cart passing, just a noise.

The two doctors looked from his face down his thin nakedness again.

"Put your shirt on," said the younger one.

And Somers could hear the mental comment, "Rum sort of
a fellow," as he did so.

There was still a wait for the card. It was one of those cards:
A—Called up for military service. B—Called up for service
at the front, but not in the lines. C—Called up for non-military
service. R—Rejected. A, B, and C were ruled out in red ink,
leaving the Rejected. He still had to go to another office for his
pay—two shillings and fourpence, or something like that. He
signed for this and was free. Free—with two shillings and
fourpence, and pass for a railway ticket—and God's air. The
moment he stepped out with his card, he realised that it was
Saturday morning, that the sun was shining, filling the big
stone yard of the barracks, from which he could look to the
station and the hill with its grass beyond. That hill beyond—
he had seemed to look at it through darkened glass before.
Till now, the morning had been a timeless greyness. Indeed,
it had rained at seven o'clock, as they stood lounging miserably about in the barracks yard with its high wall, cold and
bitter. And the tall man had talked to him bitterly.

But now the sun shone, the dark-green, Cornish hill, hard-
looking, was just a near hill. He walked through the great
gates. Ah God, he was out, he was free. The road with trees
went down-hill to the town. He hastened down, a free human
being, on Saturday morning, the grey glaze gone from his eyes.

He telegraphed the ignominious word Rejected, and the time
of his arrival, to Harriet. Then he went and had dinner. Some
of the other men came in. They were reserved now—there
was a distance between him and them—he was not of their
social class.

"What are you?" they asked him.

"Rejected," he said.

And they looked at him grudgingly, thinking it was because
he was not a working man he had got special favour. He
knew what they thought, and he tried not to look so glad.
But glad he was, and in some mysterious way, triumphant.

It was a wonderful journey on the Saturday afternoon home
—sunny, busy, lovely. He changed at Truro and went into

town. On the road he met some of the other fellows, who were called up, but not summoned for service immediately. They had some weeks, or months, of torment and suspense before them. They looked at Somers, and grinned rather jeeringly at him. They envied him—no wonder. And already he was a stranger, in another walk of life.

Rejected as unfit. One of the unfit. What did he care? The Cornish are always horrified of any ailment or physical disablement. "What's amiss then?" they would ask. They would *say* that you might as well be shot outright as labelled unfit. But most of them tried hard to find constitutional weaknesses in themselves, that would get them rejected also, notwithstanding. And at the same time they felt they must be horribly ashamed of their physical ignominy if they were *labelled* unfit.

Somers did not care. Let them label me unfit, he said to himself. I know my own body is fragile, in its way, but also it is very strong, and it's the only body that would carry my particular self. Let the fools peer at it and put me down undeveloped chest and what they like, so long as they leave me to my own way.

Then the kindly doctor's exhortation that he should find some way for himself of serving his country. He thought about that many times. But always, as he came near to the fact of committing himself, he knew that he simply could not commit himself to any service whatsoever. In no shape or form could he serve the war, either indirectly or directly. Yet it would have been so easy. He had quite enough influential friends in London to put him into some job, even some quite congenial, literary job, with a sufficient salary. They would be only too glad to do it, for there in his remoteness, writing occasionally an essay that only bothered them, he was a thorn in their flesh. And men and women with sons, brothers, husbands away fighting, it was small pleasure for them to read Mr. Somers and his pronunciation. "This trench and machine warfare is a blasphemy against life itself, a blasphemy which we are all committing." All very well, they said, but we are in for a war, and what are we to do? We hate it as much as he does. But we can't all sit safely in Cornwall.

That was true too, and he knew it, and he felt the most a dreary misery, knowing how many brave, generous men were being put through this slaughter-machine of human devilishness. They were doing their best, and there was nothing else to do. But even that was no reason why he should go and do likewise.

If men had kept their souls firm and integral through the years, the war would never have come on. If, in the beginning, there had been enough strong, proud souls in England to concentrate the English feeling into stern, fierce, honourable fighting, the war would never have gone as it went. But England slopped and wobbled, and the tide of horror accumulated.

And now, if circumstances had roped nearly all men into the horror, and it was a case of adding horror to horror, or dying well, on the other hand, the irremediable circumstance of his own separate soul made Richard Lovat's inevitable standing out. If there is an outward, circumstantial unreason and fatality, there is inward unreason and inward fate. He would have to dare to follow his inward fate. He must remain alone, outside of everything, everything, conscious of what was going on, conscious of what he was doing and not doing. Conscious he must be and consciously he must stick to it. To be forced into nothing.

For, above all things, man is a land animal and a thought-adventurer. Once the human consciousness really sinks and is swamped under the tide of events—as the best English consciousness was swamped, pacifist and patriotic alike—then the adventure is doomed. The English soul went under in the war, and, as a conscious, proud, adventurous, self-responsible soul, it was lost. We all lost the war: perhaps Germany least. Lost all the lot. The adventure is always lost when the human conscious soul gives way under the stress, fails to keep control, and is submerged. Then out swarm the rats and the Bottomleys and crew, and the ship of human adventure is a horrible piratic affair, a dirty sort of freebooting.

Richard Lovat had nothing to hang on to but his own soul. So he hung on to it, and tried to keep his wits. If no man was with him, he was hardly aware of it, he had to grip on so desperately, like a man on a plank in a shipwreck. The plank was his own individual self.

Followed that period of suspense which changed his life for ever. If the postman was coming plunging downhill through the bushes over the moor, the first thought was: What is he bringing now? The postman was over military age, and had a chuckle of pleasure in handing out those accursed *On His Majesty's Service* envelopes which meant that a man was

summoned for torture. The postman was a great Wesleyan
and a chapel preacher, and the thought of hell for other men
was sweet in him : he had a religious zest added to his natural
Cornish zest in other people's disasters.

Again, if there was the glint of a bicycle on the moor road,
and if it turned down the by-path towards the cottage, then
Somers strained his eyes to see if the rider were fat and blue,
or tall and blue. Was it the police sergeant, or the police con-
stable, coming for more identification proofs?

"We want your birth certificate," said the sergeant. "They've
written from Bodmin asking you to produce your birth
certificate."

"Then tell them to get it. No, I haven't got it. You've had
my marriage certificate. You know who I am and where I was
born and all the rest. Now let them get the birth certificate
themselves."

Richard Lovat was at the end of all patience. They persisted
he was a foreigner—poor Somers, just because he had a beard.
One of the most intensely English little men England ever
produced, with a passion for his country, even if it were often
a passion of hatred. But no, they persisted he was a foreigner.
Pah!

He and Harriet did all their own work, their own shopping.
One wintry afternoon they were coming home with a knap-
sack, along the field path above the sea, when two khaki
individuals, officers of some sort, strode after them.

"Excuse me," said one, in a damnatory officious voice. "What
have you got in that sack?"

"A few groceries," said Lovat.

"I would like to look."

Somers put the sack down on the path. The tall and lofty
officer stooped and groped nobly among a pound of rice and a
piece of soap and a dozen candles.

"Ha!" he cried, exultant. "What's this? A camera!"

Richard peeped in the bag at the groping red military hands.
For a moment he almost believed that a camera had spirited
itself in among his few goods, the implication of his guilt was
so powerful. He saw a block in brown paper.

"A penn'orth of salt," he said quietly, though pale to the
lips with anger and insult.

But the gentlemanly officer—a captain—tore open the paper.
Yes, a common block of salt. He pushed the bag aside.

"We have to be careful," said the other, lesser man.

"Good afternoon!" said Harriet.

The fellows half saluted, and turned hastening away. Richard and Harriet had the advantage of sauntering behind them and looking at their noble backs. Oh, they were gentlemen, true English gentlemen: perhaps Cornish.

Harriet gave a pouf of laughter.

"The poor innocent salt!" she exclaimed.

And no doubt that also was chalked up against her.

It was Christmas time, and two friends came down to stay at the cottage with the Somers. Those were the days before America joined the Allies. The man friend arrived with a whole parcel of American dainties, buckwheat meal and sweet potatoes and maple sugar: the woman friend brought a good basket of fruit. They were to have a Christmas in the lonely cottage in spite of everything.

It was Christmas Eve, and a pouring black wet night outside. Nowhere can it be so black as on the edge of a Cornish moor, above the western sea, near the rocks where the ancient worshippers used to sacrifice. The darkness of menhirs. The American woman friend was crouching at the fire making fudge, the man was away in his room, when a thundering knock at the door. Ah Lord!

The burly police sergeant, and his bicycle.

"Sorry to trouble you, sir, but an American, a Mr. Monsell, stopping here with you? He is. Can I have a word with him?"

"Yes. Won't you come in?"

Into the cosy cottage room, with the American girl at the fire, her face flushed with the fudge-making, entered the big, burly ruddy police sergeant, his black mackintosh-cape streaming wet.

"We give you a terrible lot of trouble, I'm sorry to say," said Harriet ironically. "What an awful night for you to have to come all these miles. I'm sure it isn't *our* doing."

"No, ma'm, I know that. It's the doing of people who like to meddle. These military orders, they take some keeping pace with."

"I'm sure they do."

Harriet was all sympathy. So he, too, was goaded by these military canaille.

Somers fetched the American friend, and he was asked to produce papers, and give information. He gave it, being an honourable citizen and a well-bred American, with complete *sang froid*. At that moment Somers would have given a lot to be American too, and not English. But wait—those were early days, when America was still being jeered at for standing out and filling her pockets. She was not yet the intensely loved ally. The police sergeant was pleasant as ever. He apologised again, and went out into the black and pouring night. So much for Christmas Eve.

"But that's not the end of the horrid affair," as the song says. When Monsell got back to Londin he was arrested, and conveyed to Scotland Yard: there examined stripped naked, his clothes taken away. Then he was kept for a night in a cell—next evening liberated and advised to return to America.

Poor Monsell, and he was so very anti-German, so very pro-British. It was a blow for him. He did not leave off being anti-German, but he was much less pro-British. And after all, it was wartime, when these things must happen, we are told. Such a wartime that let loose the foulest feelings of a mob, particularly of "gentlemen", to torture any single, independent man as a mob always tortures the isolated and independent.

In despair, Somers thought he would go to America. He had passports, he was Rejected. They had no use for him, and he had no use for them. So he posted his passports to the Foreign Office, for the military permit to depart.

It was January, and there was a thin film of half-melted snow, like silver, on the fields and the path. A white, static, arrested morning, away there in the west of Cornwall, with the moors looking primeval, and the huge granite boulders bulging out of the earth like presences. So easy to realise men worshipping stones. It is not the stone. It is the mystery of the powerful, pre-human earth, showing its might. And all, this morning, static, arrested in a cold, milky whiteness, like death, the west lost in the sea.

A man culminates in intense moments. This was one of Somers' white, death-like moments, as he walked home from the tiny post office in the hamlet, on the wintry morning, after he had posted his passports asking for visas to go to New York. It was like walking in death: a strange, arrested land of death. Never had he known that feeling before: as if he were a ghost in the after-death, walking a strange, pale, static, cold world. It almost frightened him. "Have I done wrong?" he asked himself. "Am I wrong, to leave my country and go to America?"

It was then as if he *had* left his country : and that was like
death, a still, static, corporate death. America was the death
of his own country in him, he realised that.

But he need not have bothered. The Foreign Office kept his
passports, and did not so much as answer him. He waited
in vain.

Spring came—and one morning the news that Asquith was
out of the Government, that Lloyd George was in. And this
was another of Somers' crises. He felt he must go away from
the house, away from everywhere. And as he walked, clear
as a voice out of the moors, came a voice saying: "It is the
end of England. It is the end of the old England. It is finished.
England will never be England any more."

Cornwall is a country that makes a man psyche. The longer
he stayed, the more intensely it had that effect on Somers. It
was as if he were developing second sight, and second hearing.
He would go out into the blackness of night and listen to the
blackness, and call, call softly, for the spirits, the presences
he felt coming downhill from the moors in the night.
"Tuatha De Danaan!" he would call softly. "Tuatha De
Danaan! Be with me. Be with me." And it was as if he felt
them come.

And so this morning the voice struck into his consciousness.
"It is the end of England." So he walked along blindly, up the
valley and on the moors. He loved the country intensely. It
seemed to answer him. But his consciousness was all confused.
In his mind, he did not at all see why it should be the end of
England. Mr. Asquith was called Old Wait-and-See. And truly,
English Liberalism had proved a slobbery affair, all sad
sympathy with everybody, and no iron backbone, these years.
Repulsively humble, too, on its own account. It was no time
for Christian humility. And yet, it was true to its great
creed.

Whereas Lloyd George! Somers knew nothing about Lloyd
George. A little Welsh lawyer, not an Englishman at all. He
had no real significance in Richard Lovat's soul. Only, Somers
gradually came to believe that all Jews, and all Celts, even
whilst they espoused the cause of England, subtly lived to
bring about the last humiliation of the great old England. They
could never do so if England *would not be* humiliated. But
with an England fairly offering herself to ignominy, where
was the help? Let the Celts work out their subtlety. If England

wanted to be betrayed, in the deeper issues. Perhaps Jesus wanted to be betrayed. He did. He chose Judas.

Well, the story could have no other ending.

The war-wave had broken right over England, now: right over Cornwall. Probably throughout the ages Cornwall had not been finally swept, submerged by any English spirit. Now it happened—the accursed later war spirit. Now the tales began to go round full-tilt against Somers. A chimney of his house was tarred to keep out the damp: that was a signal to the Germans. He and his wife carried food to supply German submarines. They had secret stores of petrol in the cliff. They were watched and listened to, spied on, by men lying behind the low stone fences. It was a job the Cornish loved. They didn't even mind being caught at it: lying behind a fence with field-glasses, watching through a hole in the drystone wall a man with a lass, on the edge of the moors. Perhaps they were proud of it. If a man wanted to hear what was said about him—or anything—he lay behind a wall at the field-corners, where the youths talked before they parted and went indoors, late of a Saturday night. A whole intense life of spying going on all the time.

Harriet could not hang out a towel on a bush, or carry out the slops, in the empty landscape of moors and sea, without her every movement being followed by invisible eyes. And at evening, when the doors were shut, valiant men lay under the windows to listen to the conversation in the cosy little room. And bitter enough were the things they said: and damnatory, the two Somers. Richard did not hold himself in. And he talked too with the men on the farm: openly. For they had had exactly the same anti-military feeling as himself, and they simply loathed the thought of being compelled to serve. Most men in the west, Somers thought, would have committed murder to escape, if murder would have helped them. It wouldn't. He loved the people at the farms, and the men kindled their rage together. And again Somers' farmer friend warned him, how he was being watched. But Somers *would* not heed. "What can they do to me!" he said. "I am not a spy in any way whatsoever. There is nothing they can do to me. I make no public appearance at all. I am just by myself. What can they do to me? Let them go to hell."

He refused to be watchful, guarded, furtive, like the people around, saying double things as occasion arose, and hiding their

secret thoughts and secret malignancy. He still believed in the
freedom of the individual.—Yes, freedom of the individual!

He was aware of the mass of secret feeling against him. Yet
the people he came into daily contact with liked him—almost
loved him. So he kept on defying the rest, and went along
blithe and open as ever, saying what he really felt, or holding
his tongue. Enemies! How could he have any *personal*
enemies? He had never done harm to any of these people,
had never even felt any harm. He did not believe in personal
enemies. It was just the military.

Enemies he had, however, people he didn't know and hadn't
even spoken to. Enemies who hated him like poison. They
hated him because he was free, because of his different, unafraid face. They hated him because he wasn't cowed as they
were all cowed. They hated him for his intimacy at the farm,
in the hamlet. For each farm was bitter jealous of each
other.

Yet he never believed he had any *personal* enemies. And he
had all the west hating him like poison. He realised once, when
two men came down the moorland by-road—officers in khaki
—on a motor-bicycle, and went trying the door of the next
cottage, which was shut up. Somers went to the door, in all
simplicity.

"Did you want me?" he asked.

"No, we didn't want *you*," replied one of the fellows, in a
genteel voice and a tone like a slap in the face. Somers spoken
to as if he were the lowest of the low. He shut his cottage
door. Was it so? Had they wilfully spoken to him like that?
He would not believe it.

But inwardly, he knew it was so. That was what they
intended to convey to him: that he was the lowest of the low.
He began even to feel guilty, under this mass of poisonous condemnation. And he realised that they had come, on their own,
to get into the other cottage and see if there were some wireless
installation or something else criminal. But it was fastened
tight, and apparently they gave up their design of breaking in,
for they turned the motor-cycle and went away.

Day followed day in this tension of suspense. Submarines
were off the coast; Harriet saw a ship sunk, away to sea.
Horrible excitement, and the postman asking sly questions to
try to catch Somers out. Increased rigour of coast watching,
and *no* light must be shown. Yet along the highroad on the

hillside above, plainer than any house-light, danced the lights of a cart, moving, or slowly sped the light of a bicycle, on the blackness. Then a Spanish coal vessel, three thousand tons, ran on the rocks in a fog, straight under the cottage. She was completely wrecked. Somers watched the waves break over her. Her coal washed ashore, and the farmers carried it up the cliffs in sacks.

There was to be a calling-up now and a re-examination of every man—Somers felt the crisis approaching. The ordeal was to go through, once more. The first rejection meant nothing. There were certain reservations. He had himself examined again by a doctor. The strain told on his heart as well as his breathing. He sent in this note to the authorities. A reply: "You must present yourself for examination, as ordered."

He knew that if he was really ever summoned to any service, and finally violated, he would be broken, and die. But patience. In the meanwhile he went to see his people: the long journey up the west, changing at Plymouth and Bristol and Birmingham, up to Derby. Glamorous west of England: if a man were free. He sat through the whole day, very still, looking at the world. Very still, gone very far inside himself, travelling through this England in spring. He loved it so much. But it was in the grip of something monstrous, not English, and he was almost gripped too. As it was, by making himself far away inside himself, he contained himself, and was still.

He arrived late in Derby: Saturday night, and no train for the next ten miles. But luckily, there was a motor-bus going out to the outlying villages. Derby was very dark, like a savage town, a feeling of savagery. And at last the bus was ready: full of young miners, more or less intoxicated. The bus was crammed, a solid jam of men, sitting on each other's knees, standing blocked and wedged. There was no outside accommodation. And inside were jammed eighteen more men than was allowed. It was like being pressed into one block of corned beef.

The bus ran six miles without stopping, through an absolutely dark country, Zeppelin black, and having one feeble light of its own. The roads were unmended, and very bad. But the bus charged on, madly, at full speed, like a dim consciousness madly charging through the night. And the mass of colliers swayed with the bus, intoxicated into a living block, and with high, loud, wailing voices they sang:

> "There's a long, long trail a-winding
> Into the land of my dreams—
> Where the nightingales are singing and the——"

This ghastly trailing song, like death itself. The colliers seemed to tear it out of their bowels, in a long, wild chant. They, too, all loathed the war: loathed it. And this awful song! They subsided, and somebody started "Tipperary".

> "It's a long, long way to Tipperary,
> It's a long way to go——"

But Tipperary was already felt as something of a Jonah: a bad-luck song, so it did not last long. The miserable songs—with their long, long ways that ended in sheer lugubriousness: real death-wails! These for battle songs. The wail of dying humanity.

Somebody started:

> "Good-bye—eeee
> Don't cry—eee
> Wipe the tear, baby dear, from your eye—eee—
> For it's hard to part I know.
> I'll—be—tickled-to-death to go,
> Good-bye—eeee
> Don't cry—eee——"

But the others didn't know this ragtime, and they weren't yet in the mood. They drifted drunkenly back to the ineffable howl of:

> "There's a long, long trail——"

A black, wild Saturday night. These were the collier youths Somers has been to school with—approximately. As they tore their bowels with their singing, they tore his. But as he sat squashed far back among all that coated flesh, in the dimmest glim of a light, that only made darkness more substantial, he felt like some strange isolated cell in some tensely packed organism that was hurling through chaos into oblivion. The colliers. He was more at one with them. But they were blind, ventral. Once they broke loose heaven knowns what it would be.

The Midlands—the theatre in Nottingham—the pretence of amusement, and the feeling of murder in the dark, dreadful city. In the daytime these songs—this horrible long trail, and "Good-byeeee" and "Way down in Tennessee". They tried to keep up their spirits with this ragtime Tennessee. But there was murder in the air in the Midlands, among the colliers. In the theatre particularly, a shut-in, awful feeling of souls fit for murder.

London—mid-war London, nothing but war, war. Lovely sunny weather, and bombs at midday in the Strand. Summery weather. Berkshire—aeroplanes—springtime. He was as if blind; he must hurry the long journey back to Harriet and Cornwall.

Yes—he had his papers—he must present himself again at Bodmin barracks. He was just simply summoned as if he were already conscripted. But he knew he must be medically examined. He went—left home at seven in the morning to catch the train. Harriet watched him go across the field. She was left alone, in a strange country.

"I shall be back to-night," he said.

It was a still morning, remote, as if one were not in the world. On the hill down to the station he lingered. "Shall I not go! Shall I not go!" he said to himself. He wanted to break away. But what good? He would only be arrested and lost. Yet he had dawdled this time, he had to run hard to catch the train in the end.

This time things went much more quickly. He was only two hours in the barracks. He was examined. He could tell they knew about him and disliked him. He was put in class C 3—unfit for military service, but conscripted for light non-military duties. There were no rejections now. Still, it was good enough. There were thousands of C men, men who wanted to have jobs as C men, so they were not very likely to fetch him up. He would only be a nuisance anyhow. That was clear all round.

Through the little window at the back of their ancient granite cottage, Harriet, peeping wistfully out to sea—poor Harriet, she was always frightened now—saw Richard coming across the fields, home, walking fast, and with that intent look about him that she half feared. She ran out in a sort of fear, then waited. She would wait.

He saw her face very bright with fear and joy at seeing him

back: very beautiful in his eyes. The only real thing, perhaps, left in his world.

"Here you are! So early!" she cried. "I didn't expect you. The dinner isn't ready yet. Well?"

"C 3," he replied. "It's all right."

"I *knew* it would be," she cried, seizing his arm and hugging it to her. They went in the cottage to finish cooking the evening meal. And immediately one of the farm girls came running up to see what it was.

"Oh, C 3—so you're all right, Mr. Somers. Glad, I'm glad."

Harriet never forgot the straight, intent bee-line for home which he was making when she peeped out of that window unaware.

So, another respite. They were not going to touch him. They knew he would be a firebrand in their army, a dangerous man to put with any group of men. They would leave him alone. C 3.

He had almost entirely left off writing now, and spent most of his days working on the farm. Again the neighbours were jealous.

"Buryan gets his labour cheap. He'd never have got his hay in but for Mr. Somers," they said. And that was another reason for wishing to remove Richard Lovat. Work went like steam when he was on Trendrinnan farm, and he was too thick with the Buryans. Much too thick. And John Thomas Buryan rather bragged of Mr. Somers at market, and how he, Richard Lovat, wasn't afraid of any of them, etc., etc.—that he wasn't going to serve anybody, etc.—and that nobody could make him —etc., etc.

But Richard drifted away this summer, on the land, into the weather, into Cornwall. He worked out of doors all the time—he ceased to care inwardly—he began to drift away from himself. He was very thick with John Thomas, and nearly always at the farm. Harriet was a great deal alone. And he seemed to be drifting away, drifting back to the common people, becoming a working man, of the lower classes. It had its charm for Harriet, this aspect of him—careless, rather reckless, in old clothes and an old battered hat. He kept his sharp wits, but his *spirit* became careless, lost it concentration.

"I declare!" said John Thomas, as Somers appeared in the cornfield, "you look more like one of us every day." And he looked with a bright Cornish eye at Somers' careless, belted figure and old jacket. The speech struck Richard: it sounded half triumphant, half mocking. "He thinks I'm coming down in the world—it is half a rebuke," thought Somers to himself. But he was half pleased: and half he *was* rebuked.

Corn harvest lasted long, and was a happy time for them all. It went well, well. Also from London occasionally a young man came down and stayed at the inn in the church town, some young friend of Somers who hated the army and the Government and was generally discontented, and so fitfully came as an adherent to Richard Lovat. One of these was James Sharpe, a young Edinburgh man with a moderate income of his own, interested in music. Sharpe was hardly more than a lad—but he was the type of lowland Scotsman who is half an artist, not more, and so can never get on in the ordinary respectable life, rebels against it all the time, and yet can never get away from it or free himself from its dictates.

Sharp had taken a house farther along the coast, brought his piano down from London and sufficient furniture and a house-keeper, and insisted, like a morose bird, that he wanted to be alone. But he wasn't really morose, and he didn't want really to be alone. His old house, rather ramshackle, stood back a little way from the cliffs, where the moor came down savagely to the sea, past a deserted tin-mine. It was lonely, wild, and in a savage way, poetic enough. Here Sharpe installed himself for the moment: to be alone with his music and his general discontent.

Of course he excited the wildest comments. He had window curtains of different colours, so of course, *here* was plain signal-ing to the German submarines. Spies, the lot of them. When still another young man of the same set came and took a bungalow on the moor, West Cornwall decided that it was being delivered straight into German hands. Not that West Cornwall would really have minded that so terribly. No; it wasn't that it feared the Germans. It was that it hated the sight of these recalcitrant young men. And Somers the instigator, the arch-spy, the responsible little swine with his beard.

Somers, meanwhile, began to chuckle a bit to himself. After all he was getting the better of the military *canaille. Canaille! Canaglia! Schweinerei!* He loathed them in all the languages he could lay his tongue to.

So Somers and Harriet went to stay a week-end with Sharpe

at Trevenna, as the house was called. Sharpe was a C 2 man, on perpetual tenterhooks. He had decided that if ever *he* were summoned to serve, he would just disappear. The Somers drove over, only three or four miles, on the Saturday afternoon, and the three wandered on the moor and down the cliff. No one was in sight. But how many pairs of eyes were watching, who knows? Sharpe lighting a cigarette for Harriet was an indication of untold immorality.

Evening came, the lamps were lit, and the incriminating curtains carefully drawn. The three sat before the fire in the long music-room, and tried to be cosy and jolly. But there was something wrong with the mood. After dinner it was even worse. Harriet curled herself up on the sofa with a cigarette, Sharpe spread himself in profound melancholy in his big chair, Somers sat back, nearer the window. They talked in occasional snatches, in mockery of the enemy that surrounded them. Then Somers sang to himself, in an irritating way, one German folksong after another, not in a songful, but in a defiant way.

"Annchen von Tharau"—"Schatz, mein Schatz, reite nicht so weit von mir." Zu Strasburg auf der Schanz, da fiel mein Unglück ein." This went on till Sharpe asked him to stop.

And in the silence, the tense and irritable silence that followed, came a loud bang. All got up in alarm, and followed Sharpe through the dining-room to the small entrance-room where a dim light was burning. A lieutenant and three sordid men in the dark behind him, one with a lantern.

"Mr. Sharpe?" the authoritative, and absolutely-in-the-right voice of the puppy lieutenant.

Sharpe took his pipe from his mouth and said laconically "Yes."

"You've a light burning in your window facing the sea."

"I think not. There is only one window, and that's on the passage where I never go, upstairs."

"A light was showing from that window ten minutes ago."

"I don't think it can have been."

"It was." And the stern, puppy lieutenant turned to his followers, who clustered there in the dark.

"Yes, there was a light there ten minutes since," chimed the followers.

"I don't see how it's possible," persisted Sharpe.

"Oh, well— there is sufficient evidence that it was. What other persons have you in the house——" and this officer an gentleman stepped into the room, followed by his three Cornish weeds, one of whom had fallen into a ditch in his assiduous serving of his country, and was a sorry sight. Of course Harriet saw chiefly him, and had to laugh.

"There's Mrs. Waugh, the housekeeper—but she's in bed."

The party now stood and eyed one another—the lieutenant with his three sorry braves on one hand, Sharpe, Somers, and Harriet in an old dress of soft silk on the other.

"Well, Mr. Sharpe, the light was seen."

"I don't see how it was possible. We've none of us been upstairs, and Mrs. Waugh has been in bed for half an hour."

"Is there a curtain to the passage window?" put in Somers quietly. He had helped Sharpe in setting up house.

"I don't believe there is," said Sharpe. "I forgot all about it, as it wasn't in a room, and I never go to that side of the house. Even Mrs. Waugh is supposed to go up the kitchen stairs, and so she doesn't have to pass it."

"She must have gone across with a candle as she went to bed," said Somers.

But the lieutenant didn't like being pushed into unimportance while these young men so quietly and naturally spoke together, excluding him as if he were an inferior: which they meant to do.

"You have an uncurtained window overlooking the sea, Mr. Sharpe?" he said, in his military counter-jumping voice.

"You'll have to put a curtain to it to-morrow," said Somers to Sharpe.

"What is your name?" chimed the lieutenant.

"Somers—I wasn't speaking to you," said Richard coldly. And then to Sharpe, with a note of contempt: "That's what it is. Mrs. Waugh must just have passed with a candle."

There was a silence. The wonderful watchers did not contradict.

"Yes, I suppose that's it," said Sharpe, fretfully.

"We'll put a curtain up to-morrow," said Somers.

The lieutenant would have liked to search the house. He would have liked to destroy its privacy. He glanced down to the music-room. But Harriet, so obviously a lady, even if a hateful one; and Somers with his pale look of derision; and Sharpe so impassive with his pipe; and the weedy watchers in the background, knowing just how it all was, and *almost* ready to take sides with the "gentleman" against the officer: they were too much for the lieutenant.

"Well, the light was there, Mr. Sharpe. Distinctly visible from the sea," and he turned to his followers for confirmation.

"Oh, yes, a light plain enough," said the one who had fallen into a ditch, and wanted a bit of his own back.

"A candle!" said Sharpe, with his queer, musical note of derision and fretfulness. "A candle just passing——"

"You have an uncurtained window to the sea, and lights were showing. I shall have to report this to headquarters. Perhaps if you write and apologise to Major Caerlyon it may be passed over, if nothing of the like occurs again——"

So they departed, and the three went back to their room, fuming with rage and mockery. They mocked the appearance and voice of the lieutenant, the appearance of the weeds, and Harriet rejoiced over the one who had fallen into a ditch. This regardless of the fact that they knew that some of the watchers were lying listening in the gorse bushes under the windows, and had been lying there all the evening.

"Shall you write and apologise?" said Somers.

"Apologise! No!" replied Sharpe, with peevish contempt.

Harriet and Somers went back home on the Monday. On the Tuesday appeared Sharpe, the police had been and left him a summons to appear at the market town, charged under the Defence of the Realm Act.

"I suppose you'll have to go," said Somers.

"Oh, I shall go," said he.

They waited for the day. In the afternoon Sharpe came with a white face and tears of rage and mortification in his eyes. The magistrate had told him he ought to be serving his country and not causing mischief and skulking in an out-of-the-way corner. And had fined him twenty pounds.

"*I* shan't pay it," cried Sharpe.

"Your mother will," said Somers.

And so it was. What was the good of putting oneself in their power in *any* way, if it could be avoided?

So the lower fields were cleared of corn, and they started on the two big fields above on the moors. Sharpe cycled over to say a farmer had asked *him* to go and help at Westyr; and for once he had gone; but he felt spiteful to Somers for letting him in for this.

But Somers was very fond of the family at Buryan Farm, and

he loved working with John Thomas and the girls. John
Thomas was a year or two older than Somers, and at this
time his dearest friend. And so he loved working all day
among the corn beyond the high-road, with the savage moors
all round, and the hill with its pre-Christian granite rocks rising
like a great dark pyramid on the left, the sea in front. Sometimes a great airship hung over the sea, watching for submarines. The work stopped in the field, and the men watched.
Then it went on again, and the wagon rocked slowly down
the wild, granite road, rocked like a ship past Harriet's sunken
cottage. But Somers stayed above all day, loading or picking,
or resting, talking in the intervals with John Thomas, who
loved a half-philosophical, mystical talking about the sun, and
the moon, the mysterious powers of the moon at night, and
the mysterious change in man with the change of season, and
the mysterious effects of sex on a man. So they talked, lying
in the bracken or on the heather as they waited for a wain.
Or one of the girls came with dinner in a huge basket, and
they ate all together, so happy with the moors and sky and
touch of autumn. Somers loved these people. He loved the
sensitiveness of their intelligence. They were not educated.
But they had an endless curiosity about the world, and an endless interest in what was *right*.

"Now do you think it's right, Mr. Somers?" The times that
Somers heard that question, from the girls, from Arthur, from
John Thomas. They spoke in the quick Cornish way, with the
West Cornish accent. Sometimes it was:

"Now do'ee think it right?"

And with their black eyes they watched the ethical issue in
his face. Queer it was. Right and wrong was not fixed for them
as for the English. There was still a mystery for them in what
was right and what was wrong. Only one thing was wrong—
any sort of *physical* compulsion or hurt. That they were sure
of. But as for the rest of behaviour—it was all a flux. They
had none of the ethics of chivalry or of love.

Sometimes Harriet came also to tea: but not often. They
loved her to come: and yet they were a little uneasy when
she was there. Harriet was so definitely a lady. She liked them
all. But it was a bit *noli me tangere*, with her. Somers was so
very intimate with them. She couldn't be. And the girls said,
"Mrs. Somers don't mix in wi' the likes o' we like Mr. Somers
do." Yet they were always very pleased when Harriet came.

Poor Harriet spent many lonely days in the cottage. Richard was not interested in her now. He was only interested in John Thomas and the farm people, and he was growing more like a labourer every day. And the farm people didn't mind how long *she* was left alone, at night too, in that lonely little cottage, and with all the tension of fear upon her. Because she felt that it was *she* whom these authorities, these English, hated even more than Somers. Because she made them feel she despised them. And as they were really rather despicable, they hated her at sight, her beauty, her reckless pride, her touch of derision. But Richard—even he neglected her and hated her. She was driven back on herself like a fury. And many a bitter fight they had, he and she.

The days grew shorter before the corn was all down from the moors. Sometimes Somers alone lay on the sheaves, waiting for the last wain to come to be loaded, while the others were down milking. And then the Cornish night would gradually come down upon the dark, shaggy moors, that were like the fur of some beast, and upon the pale-grey granite masses, so ancient and Druidical, suggesting blood-sacrifice. And as Somers sat there on the sheaves in the under-dark, seeing the light swim above the sea, he felt he was over the border, in another world. Over the border, in that twilight awesome world of the previous Celts. The spirit of the ancient pre-Christian world, which lingers still in the truly Celtic places, he could feel it invade him in the savage dusk, making him savage too, and at the same time, strangely sensitive and subtle, understanding the mystery of blood-sacrifice: to sacrifice one's victim, and let the blood run to the fire, there beyond the gorse upon the old grey granite: and at the same time to understand most sensitively the dark flicker of animal life about him, even in a bat, even in the writhing of a maggot in a dead rabbit. Writhe then, Life, he seemed to say to the things—and he no longer saw its sickeningness.

The old Celtic countries have never had our Latin–Teutonic consciousness, never will have. They have never been Christian in the blue-eyed, or even in the truly Roman, Latin sense of the word. But they have been overlaid by our consciousness and our civilisation, smouldering underneath in a slow, eternal fire that you can never put out till it burns itself out.

And this autumn Richard Lovat seemed to drift back. He had a passion, a profound nostalgia for the place. He could feel himself metamorphosing. He no longer wanted to struggle consciously along, a thought adventurer. He preferred to drift into a sort of blood-darkness, to take up in his veins again the savage vibrations that still lingered round the secret rocks, the place of the pre-Christian human sacrifice. Human sacrifice! He could feel his dark, blood-consciousness tingle to it again, the desire of it, the mystery of it. Old presences, old awful presences round the black moor-edge, in the thick dusk, as the sky of light was pushed pulsing upwards, away. Then an owl would fly and hoot, and Richard lay with his soul departed back, back into the blood-sacrificial pre-world, and the sun-mystery, and the moon-power, and the mistletoe on the tree, away from his own white world, his own white, conscious day. Away from the burden of intensive mental consciousness. Back, back into semi-dark, the half-conscious, the *clair-obscur*, where consciousness pulsed as a passional vibration, not as mind-knowledge.

Then would come John Thomas with the wain, and the two men would linger putting up the sheaves, linger, talking, till the dark, talking of the half-mystical things with which they both were filled. John Thomas, with his nervous ways and his quick brown eyes, was full of fear: fear of the unseen, fear of the unknown malevolencies, above all, fear of death. So they would talk of death, and the powers of death. And the farmer, in a non-mental way, understood, understood even more than Somers.

And then in the first dark they went down the hill with the wain, to part at the cottage door. And to Harriet, with her pure Teutonic consciousness, John Thomas' greeting would sound like a jeer, as he called to her. And Somers seemed to come home like an enemy, like an enemy, with that look on his face, and that pregnant malevolency of Cornwall investing him. It was a bitter time, to Harriet. Yet glamorous too.

Autumn drew on, corn-harvest was over, it was October. John Thomas drove every Thursday over the moors to market—a two-hours' drive. To-day Somers would go with him—and Ann the sister also, to do some shopping. It was a lovely October morning. They passed the stony little huddle of the church town, and on up the hill, where the great granite boulders shoved out of the land, and the barrenness was ancient and inviolable. They could see the gulls under the big cliffs beyond—and there was a buzzard circling over the

marshy place below church town. A Cornish, magic morning.
John Thomas and Somers were walking up the hill, leaving the
reins to Ann, seated high in the trap.

"One day, when the war ends, before long," said Somers as
they climbed behind the trap in the sun, past the still-flickering
gorse-bushes, "we will go far across the sea—to Mexico, to
Australia—and try living there. You must come too, and we
will have a farm."

"Me!" said John Thomas. "Why, however should I come?"

"Why not?"

But the Cornishman smiled with that peculiar sceptical
smile.

They reached town at length, over the moors and down the
long hill. John Thomas was always late. Somers went about
doing his shopping—and then met Ann at an eating-house
John Thomas was to have been there too. But he failed them
Somers walked about the Cornish seaport—he knew it now—
and by sight he too was known, and execrated. Yet the trades
people were always so pleasant and courteous to him. And it
was such a sunny day.

The town was buzzing with a story. Two German submarine
officers had come into the town, dressed in clothes they had
taken from an English ship they had sunk. They had stayed a
night at the Mounts Bay Hotel. And two days later they had
told the story to some fisherman whose fishing-boat they
stopped. They had shown the incredulous fisherman the hotel
bill. Then they had sunk the fishing-boat, sending the three
fishermen ashore in the row-boat.

John Thomas, the chatterbox, should have been at the stable
at five. He was an endless gossip, never by any chance
punctual. Somers and Ann waited till six—all the farmers
drove out home, theirs was the last trap.

"Buryan's trap—always the last," said the ostler.

It became dark—the shops were all closing—it was night
And now the town, so busy at noon and all the afternoon
seemed cold, stony, deserted, with the wind blowing down it
steep street. Nearly seven, and still no John Thomas. Ann was
furious, but she knew him. Somers was more quiet: but he
knew that this was a sort of deliberate insult on John Thomas
part, and that he must never trust him again.

It was well after seven when the fellow came—smiling with
subtle malevolence and excusing himself so easily.

"I shall never come with you again," said Somers quietly.

"I should think not, Mr. Somers," cried Ann.

It was a two-hours' drive home—a long climb to the dark stretch of the moors—then across the moors in the cold of the night, to the steep, cliff-like descent on the north, where church-town lay, and the sea beyond. As they drew near to the north descent, the home face, and the darkness was below them, Somers suddenly said:

"I don't think I shall ever drive this way again."

"Don't you? Why, what makes you say that?" cried the facile John Thomas.

Past nine o'clock as they came down the rocky road and saw the yellow curtain of the cottage glowing. Poor Harriet. Somers was stiff with cold as he rose to jump down.

"I'll come down for my parcels later," he said. Easier to take them out at the farm, and he must fetch the milk.

Harriet opened the door.

"At last you've come," she said. "Something has happened, Lovat!" One of John Thomas' sisters came out too—she had come up with Mr. Somers out of sympathy.

"What?" he said. And up came all the fear.

It was evident Harriet had had a bad shock. She had walked in the afternoon across to Sharpe's place, three miles away: and had got back just at nightfall, expecting Somers home by even. She had left the doors unlocked, as they usually did. The moment she came in, in the dusk, she knew something had happened. She made a light, and looked round. Things were disturbed. She looked in her little treasure-boxes—everything there, but moved. She looked in the drawers—everything turned upside down. The whole house ransacked, searched.

A terrible fear came over her. She knew she was antagonistic to the government people: in her soul she hated the fixed society with its barrenness and its barren laws. She had always been afraid—always shrunk from the sight of a policeman, as if she were guilty of heaven knows what. And now the horror had happened: all the black animosity of authority was encompassing her. The unknown of it: and the horror.

She fled down to the farm. Yes, three men had come, asking for Mr. and Mrs. Somers. They had told the one who came to the farm that Mr. Somers had driven to town, and Mrs. Somers they had seen going across the fields to church-town. Then the men had gone up to the cottage again, and gone inside.

I

"And they've searched everything—everything," said Harriet, shocked right through with awful fear.

"Well, there was nothing to find. They must have been disappointed," said Richard.

But it was a shock to him also: great consternation at the farm.

"It must have been something connected with Sharpe—it must have been that," said Somers, trying to reassure himself.

"Thank goodness the house was so clean and tidy," said Harriet. But it was a last blow to her.

What had they taken? They had not touched Somers' papers. But they had been through his pockets—they had taken the few loose letters from the pocket of his day-jacket—they had taken a book—and a sort of note-book with scraps of notes for essays in it—and his address-book—yes, a few things like that.

"But it'll be nothing. It'll be something to do with Sharpe's bother."

But he felt sick and sullen, and wouldn't get up early in the morning. Harriet was more prepared. She was down, dressed and tidy, making the breakfast. It was eight o'clock in the morning. Suddenly Somers heard her call:

"Lovat, they're here. Get up."

He heard the dread in her voice, and sprang into his clothes and came downstairs: a young officer, the burly police sergeant, and two other loutish-looking men. Somers came down without a collar.

"I have here a warrant to search your house," said the young officer.

"But you searched it yesterday, didn't you?" cried Harriet.

The young officer looked at her coldly, without replying. He read the search-warrant, and the two lout detectives, in civilian clothes, began to nose round.

"And the police-sergeant will read this order to you."

Somers, white and very still, spoke no word, but waited. Then the police-sergeant, in rather stumbling fashion, began to read an order from the military authorities that Richard Lovat Somers, and Harriet Emma Marianna Johanna Somers, of Trevetham Cottage, etc., should leave the county of Cornwall within the space of three days. And further, within the space of twenty-four hours of their arrival in any place they must report themselves at the police station of the said place, giving their address. And they were forbidden to enter any part of the area of Cornwall, etc., etc., etc.

Somers listened in silence.

"But why?" cried Harriet. "Why. What have we done?"

"I can't say what you have done," said the young officer in a cold tone, "but it must be something sufficiently serious. They don't send out these orders for nothing."

"But what is it then? What is it? *I* don't know what we've done. Have we no right to know what you accuse us of?"

"No, you have no right to know anything further than what is said in the order." And he folded up the said official foolscap, and handed it officially to Somers. Richard silently took it and read it again.

"But it's monstrous! What have they against us? We live here simply—we do nothing at all that they can charge us with. What have we done?" cried Harriet.

"I don't know what you've done. But we can take no risks in these times—and evidently there is a risk in leaving you here."

"But I should like to know *what?*" cried Harriet.

"That I cannot tell you."

"But do you *know?*" woman-like, she persisted.

"No, I don't even know," he replied coldly.

Harriet broke into a few tears of fright, fear, and chagrin.

"Have we no rights at all?" she cried, furious.

"Be quiet," said Richard to her.

"Yes. It is your duty to serve your country, if it is your country, by every means in your power. If you choose to put yourself under suspicion——"

"Suspicion of what?"

"I tell you, I do not know, and could not tell you even if I did know."

The foul, loutish detectives meanwhile were fumbling around, taking the books off the shelves and looking inside the clock. Somers watched them with a cold eye.

"Is this yours?" said one of the louts, producing a book with queer diagrams.

"Yes, it's a botany notebook," said Somers coldly.

The man secured it.

"He can learn the structure of moulds and parasites," said Richard bitterly to Harriet.

"The house is all open, the men can search everything?" asked the officer coldly.

"You know it is," said Somers. "You tried yesterday while we were out." Then he asked, "Who is responsible for this? Whom can I write to?"

"You can write to Major Witham, Headquarters, Southern Division, Salisbury, if it will do any good," was the answer.

There was a pause. Somers wrote it down: not in his address book because that was gone.

"And one is treated like this for nothing," cried Harriet, again in tears. "For nothing, but just because I wasn't born English. Yet one has married an Englishman, and they don't let one live anywhere but in England."

"It is more than that. It is more than the fact that you are not English born," said the officer.

"Then what? What?" she cried.

He refused to answer this time. The police-sergeant looked on with troubled blue eyes.

"Nothing. It's nothing but that, because it *can't* be," wept Harriet. "It can't be anything else, because we've never done anything else. Just because one wasn't born in England—as if one could help that. And to be persecuted like this, for nothing, for nothing else. And not even openly accused! Not even that." She wiped her tears, half enjoying it now. The police-sergeant looked into the road. One of the louts clumped downstairs and began to look once more among the books.

"That'll do here!" said the officer quietly to the detective lout. But the detective lout wasn't going to be ordered, and persisted.

"This your sketch-book, Mr. Somers?" said the lout.

"No, those are Lady Hermione Rogers' sketches," said Somers, with derision. And the lout stuffed the book back.

"And why don't they let us go away?" cried Harriet. "Why don't they let us go to America? We don't *want* to be here if we are a nuisance. We want to go right away. Why won't they even let us do that!" She was all tear-marked now.

"They must have their reasons," said the young officer, who was getting more and more uncomfortable. He again tried to hurry up the detective lout. But they were enjoying nosing round among other people's privacies.

"And what'll happen to us if we don't go, if we just stay?" said Harriet, being altogether a female.

"You'd better not try," said the young man grimly, so utterly confident in the absoluteness of the powers and the rightness he represented. And Somers would have liked to hit him across the mouth for that.

"Hold your tongue, Harriet," he said, turning on her fiercely. "You've said enough now. Be still, and let them do what they like, since they've the power to do it."

And Harriet was silent. And in the silence only the louts rummaging among the linen, and one looking into the bread-tin and into the tea-caddy. Somers watched them with a cold eye, and that queer slight lifting of his nose, rather like a dog when it shows disgust. And the officer again tried to hurry the louts, in his low tone of command, which had so little effect.

"Where do you intend to go?" said the officer to Somers.

"Oh, just to London," said Somers, who did not feel communicative.

"I suppose they will send the things back that they take?" he said, indicating the louts.

"I should think so—anything that is not evidence."

The louts were drawing to an end: it was nearly over.

"Of course this has nothing to do with me: I have to obey orders, no matter what they are," said the young officer, half apologising.

Somers just looked at him, but did not answer. His face was pale and still and distant, unconscious that the other people were real human beings. To him they were not: they were just *things*, obeying orders. And his eyes showed that. The young officer wanted to get out.

At last it was over: the louts had collected a very few trifles. The officer saw them on to the road, bade them good-morning, and got out of the house as quick as he could.

"Good-morning, sir! Good-morning, mam!" said the police-sergeant in tones of sympathy.

Yes, it was over. Harriet and Lovat looked at one another in silent consternation.

"Well, we must just go," she said.

"Oh yes," he replied.

And she studied the insolent notice to quit the area of Corn-wall. In her heart of hearts she was not sorry to quit it. It had become too painful.

In a minute up came one of the farm girls to hear the news: then later Somers went down. Arthur, the boy, had heard the

officer say to the police-sergeant as he went up the hill:
"Well, that's a job I'd rather not have had to do."

Harriet was alternately bitter and mocking: but badly shocked. Somers had had in his pocket the words of one of the Hebridean folk songs which Sharpe had brought down, and which they all thought so wonderful. On a bit of paper in his jacket pocket, the words which have no meaning in any language apparently, but are just vocal, almost animal sounds: the Seal Woman's Song—this they had taken.

> "Ver mi hiu—ravo na la vo—
> Ver mi hiu—ravo hovo i—
> Ver mi hiu—ravo na la vo—an catal—
> Traum—san jechar——"

What would the investigation make of this? What, oh, what? Harriet loved to think of it. Somers really expected to be examined under torture, to make him confess. The only obvious word—Traum—pure German.

The day was Friday: they must leave on Monday by the Great Western express. Started a bitter rush of packing. Somers, so sick of things, had a great fire of all his old manuscripts. They decided to leave the house as it was, the books on the shelves, to take only their personal belongings. For Somers was determined to come back. Until he had made up his mind to this, he felt paralysed. He loved the place so much. Ever since the conscription suspense began he had said to himself, when he walked up the wild, little road from his cottage to the moor: shall I see the foxgloves come out? If only I can stay till the foxgloves come. And he had seen the foxgloves come. Then it was the heather—would he see the heather? And then the primroses in the hollow down to the sea: the tufts and tufts of primroses, where the fox stood and looked at him.

Lately, however, he had begun to feel secure, as if he had sunk some of himself into the earth there, and were rooted for ever. His very soul seemed to have sunk into that Cornwall, that wild place under the moors. And now he must tear himself out. He was quite paralysed, could scarcely move. And at the farm they all looked at him with blank faces. He went back to the cottage to burn more manuscripts and pack up.

And then, like a revelation, he decided he would come back

He would use all his strength, put himself against all the authorities, and in a month or two he would come back. Before the snowdrops came in the farm garden.

"I shall be back in a month or two—three months," he said to everybody, and they looked at him.

But John Thomas said to him:

"You remember you said you would never drive to town again. Eh?" And in the black, bright eyes Somers saw that it was so. Yet he persisted.

"It only meant not yet awhile."

On the Monday morning he went down to say good-bye at the farm. It was a bitter moment, he was so much attached to them. And they to him. He could not bear to go. Only one was not there—the Uncle James. Many a time Somers wondered why Uncle James had gone down the fields, so as not to say good-bye.

John Thomas was driving them down in the trap—Arthur had taken the gig luggage in the cart. The family at the farm did everything they could. Somers never forgot that while he and Harriet were slaving, on the Sunday, to get things packed, John Thomas came up with their dinners, from the farm Sunday dinner.

It was a lovely, lovely morning as they drove across the hill-slopes above the sea: Harriet and Somers and John Thomas. In spite of themselves they felt cheerful. It seemed like an adventure.

"I don't know," said John Thomas, "but I feel in myself as if it was all going to turn out for the best." And he smiled in his bright, wondering way.

"So do I," cried Harriet. "As if we were going to be more free."

"As if we were setting out on a long adventure," said Somers.

They drove through the town, where, of course, they were marked people. But it was curious how little they cared, how indifferent they felt to everybody.

At the station Somers bade good-bye to John Thomas, with whom he had been such friends.

"Well, I wonder when we shall see each other again," said the young farmer.

"Soon. We will *make* it soon," said Somers. "We will *make* it soon. And you can come to London to see us."

"Well—if I can manage it—there's nothing would please me better," replied the other. But even as he said it, Somers was thinking of the evening in town, when he and Ann had been kept waiting so long. And he knew he would not see John Thomas again soon.

During the long journey up to London, Somers sat facing Harriet, quite still. The train was full: soldiers and sailors from Plymouth. One naval man talked to Harriet: bitter like all the rest. As soon as a man began to talk seriously, it was in bitterness. But many were beginning to make a mock of their own feelings even. Songs like "Good-byeeee" had taken the place of "Bluebells", and marked the change.

But Somers sat there feeling he had been killed: perfectly still, and pale, in a kind of after death, feeling he had been killed. He had always *believed* so in everything—society, love, friends. This was one of his serious deaths in belief. So he sat with his immobile face of a crucified Christ who makes no complaint, only broods silently and alone, remote. This face distressed Harriet horribly. It made her feel lost and shipwrecked, as if her heart was destined to break also. And she was in rather good spirits really. Her horror had been that she would be interned in one of the horrible camps, away from Somers. She had far less belief than he in the goodness of mankind. And she was rather relieved to get out of Cornwall. She had felt herself under a pressure there, long suffering. That very pressure he had loved so much. And so, while his still, fixed, crucified face distressed her horribly, at the same time it made her angry. What did he want to look like that for? Why didn't he show fight?

They came to London, and he tried taxi after taxi before he could get one to take them up to Hampstead. He had written to a staunch friend, and asked her to wire if she would receive them for a day or two. She wired that she would. So they went to her house. She was a little delicate lady who reminded Somers of his mother, though she was younger than his mother would have been. She and her husband had been friends of William Morris in those busy days of incipient Fabianism. Now her husband was sick, and she lived with him and a nurse and her grown-up daughter in a little old house in Hampstead.

Mrs. Redburn was frightened, receiving the tainted Somers But she had pluck. Everybody in London was frightened at this time, everybody who was not a rabid and disgusting so-called patriot. It was a reign of terror. Mrs. Redburn was a staunch little soul, but she was bewildered: and she was frightened. They did such horrible things to you, the authorities. Poor tiny Hattie, with her cameo face, like a wise child, and her grey, bobbed hair. Such a frail little thing to have gone sailing these seas of ideas, and to suffer the awful breakdown of her husband. A tiny little woman with grey, bobbed hair and wide, unyielding eyes. She had three great children. It all seemed a joke and a tragedy mixed to her. And now the war. She was just bewildered, and would not live long. Poor, frail, tiny Hattie, receiving the Somers into her still, tiny old house. Both Richard and Harriet loved her. He had pledged himself, in some queer way, to keep a place in his heart for her for ever, even when she was dead. Which he did.

But he suffered from London. It was cold, heavy, foggy weather, and he pined for his cottage, the granite-strewn, gorse-grown slope from the moors to the sea. He could not bear Hampstead Heath now. In his eyes he saw the farm below—grey, naked, stony, with the big, pale-roofed new barn—and the network of dark green fields with the pale-grey walls—and the gorse and the sea. Torture of nostalgia. He craved to be back, his soul was there. He wrote passionately to John Thomas.

Richard and Harriet went to a police station for the first time in their lives. They went and reported themselves. The police at the station knew nothing about them and said they needn't have come. But next day a great policeman thumping at Hattie's door, and were some people called Somers staying there? It was explained to the policeman that they had already reported—but he knew nothing of it.

Somers wanted as quickly as possible to find rooms, to take the burden from Hattie. The American wife of an English friend, a poet serving in the army, offered her rooms in Mecklenburgh Square, and the third day after their arrival in London Somers and Harriet moved there: very grateful indeed to the American girl. They had no money. But the young woman tossed the rooms to them, and food and fuel, with a wild free hand. She was beautiful, reckless, one of the poetesses whose poetry Richard feared and wondered over.

Started a new life: anguish of nostalgia for Cornwall, from Somers. Wandering in the King's Cross Road or Theobald's

Road, seeing his cottage and the road going up to the moors. He wrote twice to the headquarters at Salisbury insisting on being allowed to return. Came a reply, this could not be permitted. Then one day a man called and left a book and the little bundle of papers—a handful only—which the detectives had confiscated. A poor little show. Even the scrap of paper with *Ver mi hiu*. Again Somers wrote—but to no effect. Came a letter from John Thomas describing events in the west —the last Somers ever had from his friend.

Then Sharpe came up to London: it was too lonely down there. And they had some gay evenings. Many people came to see Somers. But Sharpe said to him:

"They're watching you still. There were two policemen near the door watching who came in."

There was an atmosphere of terror all through London, as under the Czar when no man dared open his mouth. Only this time it was the lowest orders of mankind spying on the upper orders, to drag them down.

One evening there was a gorgeous commotion in Somers' rooms, four poets and three non-poets, all fighting out poetry: a splendid time. Somers ran down the stairs in the black dark —no lights in the hall—to open the door. He opened quickly— three policemen in the porch. They slipped out before they could be spoken to.

Harriet and Somers had reported at Bow Street—wonderful how little heed the police took of them. Somers could tell how the civil police loathed being under the military orders.

But watched and followed he knew he was. After two months the American friend needed her rooms. The Somers transferred to Kensington, to a flat belonging to Sharpe's mother. Again many friends came. One evening Sharpe was called out from the drawing-room: detectives in the hall enquiring about Somers, where he got his money from, etc., etc., such clowns, louts, mongrels of detectives. Even Sharpe laughed in their faces: such *canaille*. At the same time detectives inquiring for them at the old address: though they had reported the change. Such a confusion in the official mind!

It was becoming impossible. Somers wrote bitterly to friends who had been all-influential till lately, but whom the *canaille* were now trying to taint also. And then he and Harriet moved to a little cottage he rented from his dear Hattie, in Oxfordshire. Once more they reported to the police in the market-town: once more the police sympathetic.

"I will report no more," said Somers.

But still he knew he was being watched all the time. Strange men questioning the cottage woman next door, as to all his doings. He began to *feel* a criminal. A sense of guilt, of self-horror began to grow up in him. He saw himself set apart from mankind, a Cain, or worse. Though of course he had committed no murder. But what might he not have done? A leper, a criminal! The foul, dense, carrion-eating mob were trying to set their teeth in him. Which meant mortification and death.

It was Christmas—winter—very cold. He and Harriet were very poor. Then he became ill. He lay in the tiny bedroom looking at the wintry sky and the deep, thatched roof of the cottage beyond. Sick. But then his soul revived. "No," he said to himself. "No. Whatever I do or have done, I am not wrong. Even if I commit what they call a crime, why should I accept *their* condemnation or verdict. Whatever I do, I do of my own responsible self. I refuse their imputations. I despise them. They are *canaille*, carrion-eating, filthy-mouthed *canaille*, like dead-men-devouring jackals. I wish to God I could kill them. I wish I had power to blight them, to slay them with a blight, slay them in thousands and thousands. I wish to God I could kill them off, the masses of *canaille*. Would they make me feel in the wrong? Would they? They shall not. Never. I will watch that they never set their unclean teeth in me, for a bite is blood-poisoning. But fear them! Feel in the wrong because of them? Never. Not if I were Cain several times over, and had killed several brothers and sisters as well. Not if I had committed all the crimes in their calendar. I will not be put in the wrong by them, God knows I will not. And I will report myself no more at their police-stations."

So, whenever the feeling of terror came over him, the feeling of being marked out, branded, a criminal marked out by society, marked out for annihilation, he pulled himself together, saying to himself:

"I am letting them make me feel in the wrong. I am degrading myself by feeling guilty, marked out, and I have convulsions of fear. But I am *not* wrong. I have done no wrong, whatever I have done. That is, no wrong that society has to do with. Whatever wrongs I have done are my own, and private between myself and the other person. One may be wrong, yes, one is often wrong. But not for *them* to judge. For my own soul only to judge. Let me know them for human filth, all these pullers-down, and let me watch them, as I would watch a reeking hyena, but never fear them. Let me watch them, to keep them at bay. But let me never admit for one single moment that *they* may be *my* judges. That, never. I have judged them: they are *canaille*. I am a man, and I abide by my own soul. Never shall they have a chance of judging me."

So he discovered the great secret: to stand alone as his own judge of himself absolutely. He took his stand absolutely on his own judgment of himself. Then, the mongrel-mouthed world would say and do what it liked. This is the greatest secret of behaviour: to stand alone, and judge oneself from the deeps of one's own soul. And then, to know, to hear what the others say and think: to refer their judgment to the touch-stone of one's own soul-judgment. To fear one's own inward soul, and never to fear the outside world, nay, not even one single person, nor even fifty million persons.

To learn to be afraid of nothing but one's own deepest soul: but to keep a sharp eye on the millions of the others. Somers would say to himself: "There are fifty million people in Great Britain, and they would nearly all be against me. Let them."

So a period of quiet followed. Somers got no answers to his letters to John Thomas: it was like the evening when he had been kept waiting. The man was scared. It was an end.

And the authorities still would allow of no return to Corn-wall. So let that be an end too. He wrote for his books and household linen to be sent up, the rest could be sold.

Bitter, in Oxfordshire, to unpack the things he had loved so dearly in Cornwall. Life would never be quite the same again. Then let it be otherwise. He hardened his heart and his soul.

It was a lovely spring: and here, in the heart of England— Shakespeare's England—there was a sweetness and a human-ness that he had never known before. The people were friendly and unsuspicious, though they knew all about the trouble. The police too were delicate and kindly. It was a human world once more, human and lovely: though the gangs of wood-men were cutting down the trees, baring the beautiful spring woods, making logs for trench-props.

And there was always the suspense of being once more called

up for military service. "But surely," thought Somers, "if I am
so vile they will be glad to leave me alone."

Spring passed on. Somers' sisters were alone, their husbands
at the war. His younger sister took a cottage for him in their
own bleak Derbyshire. And so he returned, after six years, to
his own country. A bitter stranger too, he felt. It was northern,
and the industrial spirit was permeated through everything:
the alien spirit of coal and iron. People living for coal and
iron, nothing else. What good was it all?

This time he would not go to the police-station to report. So
one day a police-inspector called. But he was a kindly man,
and a little bitter too. Strange that among the civil police,
everyone that Somers met was kindly and understanding. But
the so-called, brand-new military, they were insolent jacka-
napes, especially the stay-at-home military who had all the
authority in England.

In September, on his birthday, came the third summons:
On His Majesty's Service. His Majesty's Service, God help us!
Somers was bidden present himself at Derby on a certain date,
to join the colours. He replied, "If I am turned out of my
home, and forbidden to enter the area of Cornwall: if I am
forced to report myself to the police wherever I go, and am
treated like a criminal, you surely cannot wish me to present
myself to join the colours."

There was an interval: much correspondence with Bodmin,
where they seemed to have forgotten him again. Then he
received a notice that he was to present himself as ordered.

What else was there to do? But he was growing devilish inside himself. However, he went: and Harriet accompanied
him to the town. The recruiting place was a sort of big Sunday School—you went down a little flight of steps from the
road. In a smallish ante-room like a basement he sat on a form
and waited while all his papers were filed. Beside him sat a
big collier, about as old as himself. And the man's face was a
study of anger and devilishness growing under humiliation.
After an hour's waiting Somers was called. He stripped as
usual, but this time was told to put on his jacket over his complete nakedness.

And so—he was shown into a high, long school-room with
various sections down one side—bits of screens where various
doctor-fellows were performing—and opposite, a long writing-
table where clerks and old military buffers in uniform sat in

power: the clerks dutifully scribbling, glad to be in a safe job, no doubt, the old military buffers staring about. Near this Judgment-Day table a fire was burning, and there was a bench where two naked men sat ignominiously waiting, trying to cover their nakedness a little with their jackets, but too much upset to care really.

"Good God!" thought Somers. "Naked civilised men in their Sunday jackets and nothing else make the most heaven-forsaken sight I have ever seen."

The big stark-naked collier was being measured: a big, gaunt, naked figure, with a gruesome sort of nudity. "Oh, God, oh God," thought Somers, "why do the animals none of them look like this? It doesn't look like life, like a living creature's figure. It is gruesome, with no life-meaning."

In another section a youth of about twenty-five, stark naked too, was throwing out his chest while a chit of a doctor-fellow felt him between the legs. This naked young fellow evidently thought himself an athlete, and that he must make a good impression, so he threw his head up in a would-be noble attitude, and coughed bravely when the doctor-buffoon said cough! Like a piece of furniture waiting to be sat on, the athletic young man looked.

Across the room the military buffers looked on at the operette; occasionally a joke, incomprehensible, at the expense of the naked, was called across from the military papas to the fellows who may have been doctors. The place was full of an indescribable tone of jeering, gibing shamelessness. Somers stood in his street jacket and thin legs and beard—a sight enough for any gods—and waited his turn. Then he took off the jacket and was cleanly naked, and stood to be measured and weighed—being moved about like a block of meat, in the atmosphere of corrosive derision.

Then he was sent to the next section for eye-tests, and jokes were called across the room. Then after a time to the next section, where he was made to hop on one foot—then on the other foot—bend over—and so on: apparently to see if he had any physical deformity.

In due course to the next section where a fool of a little fellow, surely no doctor, eyed him up and down and said:

"Anything to complain of?"

"Yes," said Somers. "I've had pneumonia three times and been threatened with consumption."

"Oh. Go over there then."

So in his stalky, ignominious nakedness he was sent over to another section, where an elderly fool turned his back on him for ten minutes, before looking round and saying:

"Yes. What have you to say?"

Somers repeated.

"When did you have pneumonia?"

Somers answered—he could hardly speak, he was in such a fury of rage and humiliation.

"What doctor said you were threatened with consumption? Give his name." This in a tone of sneering scepticism.

The whole room was watching and listening. Somers knew his appearance had been anticipated, and they wanted to count him out. But he kept his head. The elderly fellow then proceeded to listen to his heart and lungs with a stethoscope, jabbing the end of the instrument against the flesh as if he wished to make a pattern on it. Somers kept a set face. He knew what he was out against, and he just hated and despised them all.

The fellow at length threw the stethoscope aside as if he were throwing Somers aside, and went to write. Somers stood still, with a set face, and waited.

Then he was sent to the next section, and the stethoscoping doctor strolled over to the great judgment table. In the final section was a young puppy, like a chemist's assistant, who made most of the jokes. Jokes were all the time passing across the room—but Somers had the faculty of becoming quite deaf to anything that might disturb his equanimity.

The chemist-assistant puppy looked him up and down with a small grin as if to say, "Law-lummy, what a sight of a human scarecrow!" Somers looked him back again, under lowered lids, and the puppy left off joking for the moment. He told Somers to take up other attitudes. Then he came forward close to him, right till their bodies almost touched, the one in a navy blue serge, holding back a little as if from the contagion of the naked one. He put his hand between Somers' legs, and pressed it upwards, under the genitals. Somers felt his eyes going black.

"Cough," said the puppy. He coughed.

"Again," said the puppy. He made a noise in his throat, then turned aside in disgust.

"Turn round," said the puppy. "Face the other way."

Somers turned and faced the shameful monkey-faces at the

long table. So, he had his back to the tall window: and the puppy stood plumb behind him.

"Put your feet apart."

He put his feet apart.

"Bend forward—further—further——"

Somers bent forward, lower, and realised that the puppy was standing aloof behind him to look into his anus. And that this was the source of the wonderful jesting that went on all the time.

"That will do. Get your jacket and go over there."

Somers put on his jacket and went and sat on the form that was placed endwise at the side of the fire, facing the side of the judgment table. The big, gaunt collier was still being fooled. He apparently was not very intelligent, and didn't know what they meant when they told him to bend forward. Instead of bending with stiff knees—not knowing at all what they wanted—he crouched down, squatting on his heels as colliers do. And the doctor puppy, amid the hugest amusement, had to start him over again. So the game went on, and Somers watched them all.

The collier was terrible to him. He had a sort of Irish face with a short nose and a thin black head. This snub-nose face had gone quite blank with a ghastly voidness, void of intelligence, bewildered and blind. It was as if the big, ugly, powerful body could not *obey* words any more. Oh God, such an ugly body—not as if it belonged to a living creature.

Somers kept himself hard and in command, face set, eyes watchful. He felt his cup had been filled now. He watched these buffoons in this great room, as he sat there naked save for his jacket, and he felt that from his heart, from his spine went out vibrations that should annihilate them—blot them out, the *canaille*, stamp them into the mud they belonged to.

He was called at length to the table.

"What is your name?" asked one of the old parties. Somers looked at him.

"Somers," he said, in a very low tone.

"Somers—Richard Lovat?" with an indescribable sneer.

Richard Lovat realised that they had got their knife into him. So! He had his knife in them, and it would strike deeper at last.

"You describe yourself as a writer."

He did not answer.

"A writer of what?"—with a perfect sneer.

"Books—essays."

The old buffer went on writing. Oh, yes, they intended to make him feel they had got their knife into him. They would have his beard off, too! But would they! He stood there with his ridiculous thin legs, in his ridiculous jacket, but he did not feel a fool. Oh, God, no. The white composure of his face, the slight lifting of his nose, like a dog's disgust, the heavy un-shakeable watchfulness of his eyes brought even the judgment table to silence: even the puppy doctors. It was not till he was walking out of the room, with his jacket about his thin legs, and his beard in front of him, that they lifted their heads for a final jeer.

He dressed and waited for his card. It was Saturday morn-ing, and he was almost the last man to be examined. He wondered what instructions they had had about him. Oh, foul dogs. But they were very close on him now, very close. They were grinning very close behind him, like hyenas just going to bite. Yes, they were running him to earth. They had exposed all his nakedness to gibes. And they were pining, almost whimpering to give the last grab at him, and haul him to earth, a victim. Finished!

But not yet! Oh, no, not yet. Not yet, not now, nor ever. Not while life was life, should they lay hold of him. Never again. Never would he be touched again. And because they had handled his private parts, and looked into them, their eyes should burst and their hands should wither and their hearts should rot. So he cursed them in his blood, with an unremitting curse, as he waited.

They gave him his card: C 2. Fit for non-military service. He knew what they would like to make him do. They would like to seize him and compel him to empty latrines in some camp. They had that in mind for him. But he had other things in mind.

He went out into accursed Derby, to Harriet. She was re-assured again. But he was not. He hated the Midlands now, he hated the North. They were viler than the South, even than Cornwall. They had a universal desire to take life and down it: these horrible machine people, these iron and coal people. They wanted to set their foot absolutely on life, grind it down, and be masters. Masters, as they were of the foul machines. Masters of life, as they were masters of steam-power and electric-power and above all, of money-power. Masters of money-power, with an obscene hatred of life, true spontaneous life.

Another flight. He was determined not to stop in the Derby Military Area. He would move one stage out of their grip, at least. So he and Harriet prepared to go back with their trunks to the Oxfordshire cottage, which they loved. He would not report, nor give any sign of himself. Fortunately in the village everybody was slack and friendly.

Derby had been a crisis. He would obey no more : not one more stride. If they summoned him he would disappear : or find some means of fighting them. But no more obedience : no more presenting himself when called up. By God, no! Never while he lived, again, would he be at the disposal of society.

So they moved south—to be one step removed. They had been living in this remote cottage in the Derbyshire hills : and they must leave at half-past seven in the morning, to complete their journey in a day. It was a black morning, with a slow dawn. Somers had the trunks ready. He stood looking at the dark gulf of the valley below. Meanwhile heavy clouds sank over the bare, Derbyshire hills, and the dawn was blotted out before it came. Then broke a terrific thunderstorm, and hail lashed down with a noise like insanity. He stood at the big window over the valley, and watched. Come hail, come rain, he would go : for ever.

This was his home district—but from the deepest soul he now hated it, mistrusted it even more than he hated it. As far as *life* went, he mistrusted it utterly, with a black soul. Mistrusted it and hated it, with its smoke and its money-power and its squirming millions who aren't human any more.

Ah, how lovely the South-West seemed, after it all. There was hardly any food, but neither he nor Harriet minded. They could pick up and be wonderfully happy again, gathering the little chestnuts in the woods, and the few last bilberries. Men were working harder than ever felling trees for trench-timber, denuding the land. But their brush-fires were burning in the woods, and when they had gone, in the cold dusk, Somers went with a sack to pick up the unburnt faggots and the great chips of wood the axes had left golden against the felled logs. Flakes of sweet, pale gold oak. He gathered them in the dusk, in a sack, along with the other poor villagers. For he was poorer even than they. Still, it made him very happy to do these things —to see a big, glowing pile of wood-flakes in his shed—and to dig the garden, and set the rubbish burning in the late, wistful autumn—or to wander through the hazel copses, away to the real old English hamlets, that are still like Shakespeare—and like Hardy's *Woodlanders*.

Then, in November, the Armistice. It was almost too much to believe. The war was over! It *was* too much to believe. He and Harriet sat and sang German songs, in the cottage, that strange night of the Armistice, away there in the country : and she cried—and he wondered what now, now the walls would come no nearer. It had been like Edgar Allen Poe's story of the Pit and the Pendulum—where the walls come in, in, in, till the prisoner is almost squeezed. So the black walls of the war—and he had been trapped, and very nearly squeezed into the pit where the rats were. So nearly! So very nearly. And now the black walls had stopped, and he was *not* pushed into the pit, and the rats. And he knew it in his soul. What next then?

He insisted on going back to Derbyshire. Harriet, who hated him for the move, refused to go. So he went alone : back to his sisters, and to finish the year in the house which they had paid for him. Harriet refused to go. She stayed with Hattie in London.

At St. Pancras, as Somers left the taxi and went across the pavement to the station, he fell down, fell smack down on the pavement. He did not hurt himself. But he got up rather dazed, saying to himself, "Is that a bad omen? Ought I not to be going back?" But again he thought of Scipio Africanus, and went on.

The cold, black December days, alone in the cottage on the cold hills—Adam Bede country, Snowfields, Dinah Morris' home. Such heavy, cold, savage, frustrated blackness. He had known it when he was a boy. Then Harriet came—and they spent Christmas with his sister. And when January came he fell ill with the influenza, and was ill for a long time. In March the snow was up to the window-sills of their house.

"Will the winter never end?" he asked his soul.

May brought the year's house-rent of the Derbyshire cottage to an end : and back they went to Oxfordshire. But now the place seemed weary to him, tame, after the black iron of the North. The walls had gone—and now he felt nowhere.

So they applied for passports—Harriet to go to Germany, himself to Italy. A lovely summer went by, a lovely autumn came. But the meaning had gone out of everything for him. He had lost his meaning. England had lost its meaning for him. The free England had died, this England of the peace was like a corpse. It was the corpse of a country to him.

In October came the passports. He saw Harriet off to Germany—said good-bye at the Great Eastern Station, while she she sat in the Harwich–Hook of Holland express. She had a look of almost vindictive triumph, and almost malignant love, as the train drew out. So he went back to his meaninglessness at the cottage.

Then, finding the meaninglessness too much, he gathered his pounds together and in November left for Italy. Left England, England which he had loved so bitterly, bitterly—and now was leaving, alone, and with a feeling of expressionlessness in his soul. It was a cold day. There was snow on the Downs like a shroud. And as he looked back from the boat, when they had left Folkestone behind and only England was there, England looked like a grey, dreary-grey coffin sinking in the sea behind, with her dead grey cliffs and the white, worn-out cloth of snow above.

Memory of all this came on him so violently, now in the Australian night, that he trembled helplessly under the shock of it. He ought to have gone up to Jack's place for the night. But no, he could not speak to anybody. Of all the black throng in the dark Sydney streets, he was the most remote. He strayed round in a torture of fear, and then at last suddenly went to the Carlton Hotel, got a room, and went to bed, to be alone and think.

Detail for detail he thought out his experiences with the authorities, during the war, lying perfectly still and tense. Till now, he had always kept the memory at bay, afraid of it. Now it all came back, in a rush. It was like a volcanic eruption in his consciousness. For some weeks he had felt the great uneasiness in his unconscious. For some time he had known spasms of that same fear that he had known during the war: the fear of the base and malignant power of the mob-like authorities. Since he had been in Italy the fear had left him entirely. He had not even remembered it, in India. Only in the quiet of Coo-ee, strangely enough, it had come back in spasms: dread, almost the horror, of democratic society, the mob. Harriet had been feeling it too. Why? Why, in this free Australia? Why? Why should they both have been feeling this same terror and pressure that they had known during the war, why should it have come on again in Mullumbimby? Perhaps in Mullumbimby they were suspect again, two strangers, so much alone. Perhaps the secret service was making investigations about them. Ah, *canaille*!

Richard faced out all his memories like a nightmare in the night, and cut clear. He felt broken off from his fellow-men. He felt broken off from the England he had belonged to. The ties were gone. He was loose like a single timber of some wrecked ship, drifting over the face of the earth. Without a people, without a land. So be it. He was broken apart, apart he would remain.

CHAPTER XIII

"REVENGE!" TIMOTHEUS CRIES

AT last he had it all out with himself, right to the bitter end. And then he realised that all the time, since the year 1918, whether he was in Sicily or Switzerland or Venice or Germany or in the Austrian Tyrol, deep in his unconsciousness had lain this accumulation of black fury and fear, like frenzied lava quiescent in his soul. And now it had burst up: the fear, then the acute remembrance. So he faced it out, trembling with shock and bitterness, every detail. And then he tried to reckon it all up.

But first, why had it all come back on him? It had seemed so past, so gone. Why should it suddenly erupt like white-hot lava, to set in hot black rock round the wound of his soul? Who knows? Perhaps there is periodicity even in volcanic eruption. Or perhaps it was this contact with Kangaroo and Willie Struthers, contact with the accumulating forces of social violence. Or perhaps it was being again in a purely English-speaking country, and feeling again that queer revulsion from the English form of democracy. He realised that the oh-so-pleasant democracy of the English lower classes frightened him. Yet everybody was so very pleasant and easy-going down in Mullumbimby. It *really* seemed so free.

Free! Free! What did it mean? It was this very ultra-freedom that frightened him, like a still pause before a thunderstorm. "Let him that thinketh he stand take heed lest he fall."

Or perhaps it was just the inversion of the season, the climate. His blood, his whole corporeal being, expected summer, and long days and short nights. And here he had wilfully come into the Southern hemisphere, with long starry nights of winter, and the late sun rising north-east behind the sea, and travelling northwards up the sky, as if running away, and setting in a cold glare north-west, behind the bluey-black range. It should have been bird-nesting time, and leaves and flowers and tall corn and full summer with cherry blossom fallen and cherries beginning to change colour. Whereas the grass was sere and brown, the earth had gone winter-numb, the few deciduous trees were bare, and only the uncanny coral tree flared its flowers of red-hot iron.

Perhaps it was just this: the inversion of the seasons, the shock to his blood and his system. For, of course, the body has its own rhythm, with the sun and with the moon. The great nerve ganglia and the subtle glands have their regular times and motions, in correspondence with the outer universe. And these times and motions had suddenly received a check from the outer universe: a distinct check. He had had an inkling of what it would be when, from the ship in the Indian Ocean he had seen the great and beloved constellation Orion standing on its head as if pitching head foremost into the sea, and the bright dog Sirius coursing high above his heels in the outer air. Then he had realised the inversion in the heavens.

And perhaps it was this inversion which had brought up all that corrosive and bitter fire from the bowels of his unconscious, up again into his full consciousness. If so, then let it be so.

One thing he realised, however: that if the fire had suddenly erupted in his own belly, it would erupt one day in the bellies of all men. Because there it had accumulated, like a great horrible lava-pool, deep in the unconscious bowels of all men. All who were not dead. And even the dead were many of them raging in the invisible, with gnashing of teeth. But the living dead, these he could not reckon with: they with poisonous teeth like hyenas.

Rage! Rage! Rage! The awful accumulations that lie quiescent and pregnant in the bowels of men. He thought of the big gaunt collier with the blunt, seal-like face shorn of its intelligence, squatting naked and ghastly on his heels. It passes, it passes for the time being. But in those moments there is an inward disruption, and the death-hot lava pours loose into the deepest reservoirs of the soul. One day to erupt: or else to go hard and rocky, dead.

Even the athletic young man who wanted to be approved of. Even he. He had not much true spunk. But what was he feeling now? Unless, of course, he had got into business and was successfully coining money. That seemed to be the only safety-valve: success in money-making. But how many men were successful, now?

Of course it was all necessary, the conscription, the medical examinations. Of course, of course. We all know it. But when it comes to the deepest things, men are as entirely irrational as women. You can reason with a sex-angry woman till you are black in the face. And if for a time you *do* overcome her with reason, the sex-anger only arises more hideously and furiously, later. Perhaps in another guise.

There is no arguing with the instinctive passional self. Not the least use in the world. Yes, you are quite right, quite right in all your contentions. *But!* And the But just explodes everything like a bomb.

The conscription, all the whole performance of the war was absolutely circumstantially necessary. It was necessary to investigate even the secret parts of a man. Agreed! Agreed! But——

It was *necessary* to put Richard Lovat and the ugly collier through that business at Derby. Many men were put through things a thousand times worse. Agreed! Oh, entirely agreed! The war couldn't be lost, at that hour. Quite, quite, quite! Even Richard, even now, agreed fully to all these contentions. *But——!*

And there you are. *But——.* He was full of a lava fire of rage and hate, at the bottom of his soul. And he knew it was the same with most men. He felt desecrated. And he knew it was the same with most men. He felt sold. And he knew most men felt the same.

He cared for nothing now, but to let loose the hell-rage that was in him. Get rid of it by letting it out. For there was no digesting it. He had been trying that for three years, and roaming the face of the earth trying to soothe himself with the sops of travel and new experience and scenery. He knew now the worth of all sops. Once that disruption had taken place in a man's soul, and in a stress of humiliation, under the presence of *compulsion*, something has broken in his tissue and the liquid fire has run out loose into his blood, then no sops will be of any avail. The lava-fire at the bottom of a man's belly breeds more lava-fire, and more, and more—till there is an eruption. As the lava-fire accumulates, the man becomes more and more reckless. Till he reaches a pitch of dehumanised recklessness, and then the lid is blown off, as the top is blown off a hill to make a new volcano. Or else it all sets into rocky deadness.

Richard felt himself reaching the volcanic pitch. He had as good as reached it. And he realised that the Russians must have reached it during the war: that the Irish had got there: that the Indians in India were approaching the point: that the whole world was gradually working up to the pitch. The whole world. It was as inevitable as the coming of summer. It might be soon—it might be slow. But inevitable it was. Or else the alternative, the dead-rock barrenness.

But why? Why, oh why? Is human life just opposed to human reason? The Allies *did* have to win the war. For it would certainly not have been any better letting Germany win. Unless a very great disaster might have shocked men to their deeper senses. But doubtful. Things *had* to go as they went.

So, it was just Thomas Hardy's Blind Fate? No, said Lovat to himself, no. *Fata volentem ducunt, nolentem trahunt.* The Fates lead on the willing man, the unwilling man they drag.

The Fates? What Fates? It takes a willing man to answer. Man is not a creature of circumstance, neither is he the result of cause-and-effect throughout the ages, neither is he a product of evolution, neither is he a living *Mind*, part of the Universal Mind. Neither is he a complicated make-up of forces and chemicals and organs. Neither is he a term of love. Neither is he the mere instrument of God's will. None of these things.

Man lives according to his own idea of himself. When circumstances begin really to run counter to his idea of himself, he damns circumstances. When the running-counter persists, he damns the nature of things. And when it *still* persists, he becomes a fatalist. A fatalist or an opportunist—anything of that sort.

Whose fault is it? Fate's? Not at all. It is man's fault for persisting in some fixed idea of himself.

Yet, being an animal saddled with a mental consciousness, which means ideas, a man *must* have some idea of himself. He just must, and those that deny it have got a more fixed idea than anybody.

Man must have some idea of himself. He must live *hard, hard,* up to this idea of himself.

But the idea is perishable. Say what you like, every idea is perishable: even the idea of God or Love or Humanity or Liberty—even the greatest idea has its day and perishes. Each formulated religion is in the end only a great idea. Once the idea becomes explicit, it is dead. Yet we must *have* ideas.

When a man follows the true inspiration of a new, living idea, he then is the willing man whom the Fates lead onwards: like St. Paul or Pope Hildebrand or Martin Luther or Cromwell or Abraham Lincoln. But when the idea is really dead, and *still* man persists in following it, then he is the unwilling man whom the Fates destroy, like Kaiser Wilhelm or President Wilson, or, to-day, the world at large.

For the idea, or ideal of Love, Self-sacrifice, Humanity united in love, in brotherhood, in peace—all this is dead. There is no arguing about it. It is dead. The great ideal is dead.

How do we know? By putting off our conscious conceit and listening to our own soul.

So then, why will men not forgive the war, and their humiliations at the hands of these war-like authorities? Because men were *compelled* into the service of a dead ideal. And perhaps nothing but this compulsion made them realise it *was a dead* ideal. But all those filthy little stay-at-home officers and coast-watchers and dirty-minded doctors who tortured men during the *first* stages of the torture, did these men *in their souls* believe in what they were doing? They didn't. They *had* no souls. They had only their beastly little *wills*, which they used to bully all men with. With their wills they determined to fight for a dead ideal, and to bully every other man into compliance. The inspiring motive was the bullying. And every other man complied. Or else, by admitting a conscientious objection to war, he admitted the dead ideal, but took refuge in one of its side-tracks.

All men alike, and all women, admitted and still admit the face value of the ideal of Love, Self-sacrifice, and Humanity united in love, brotherhood, and peace. So, they persist in the dead ideal. *Fata nolunt.* Fata nolunt. Then see how the Fates betray them. In their service of the defunct ideals they find themselves utterly humiliated, *sold.* In England, Italy,

Germany, India, Australia, that had been the one word men
had used to describe their feeling. They had been sold. But
not before they had sold themselves. Now then. The moment
a man feels he has been sold, sold in the deepest things, something goes wrong with his whole mechanism. Something breaks,
in his tissue, and the black poison is emitted into his blood.
And then he follows a natural course, and becomes a creature
of slow, or of quick, revenge. Revenge on all that the old ideal
is and stands for. Revenge on the whole system. Just revenge.
Even further revenge on himself.

Men revenged themselves on Athens, when they felt sold.
When Rome, persisting in an old, defunct ideal, gradually made
her subjects feel sold, they were revenged on her, no matter
how. Constantinople and the Byzantine Empire the same. And
now our turn. "Revenge," Timotheus cries. And Timotheus is
just everybody, except those that have got hold of the money
or the power.

There is nothing for it but revenge. If you sow the dragon's
teeth, you musn't expect lilies of the valley to spring up in
sweet meekness.

And Kangaroo? Kangaroo insisted on the old idea as hard as
ever, though on the Power of Love rather than on the Submission and Sacrifice of Love. He wanted to take his revenge
in an odour of sanctification and Lily of the Valley essence.
But he was the mob, really. See his face in a rage. He was
the mob: *vengeful* mob. Oh, God, the most terrifying of all
things.

And Willie Struthers? The vengeful mob also. But if the
old ideal had still a logical leaf to put forth, it was this last
leaf of communism—before the lily tree of humanity rooted
in love and died its final death. Perhaps better Struthers than
Kangaroo.

"But what about myself?" said Richard Lovat to himself,
as he lay in the darkness of Sydney, his brain afire. For the
horrible bitter fire seemed really to have got into his brain,
burst up from his deepest bowels. "What about me? Am I too
Timotheus crying *Revenge?*"

Oh, revenge, yes, he wanted to be avenged. He wanted to
be avenged. Especially when he felt tangled up in the horrible
human affair, the ideal become like an octopus with a ghastly
eye in the centre, and white arms enwreathing the world. Oh,
then he wanted to be avenged.

But now, for the moment he felt he had cut himself clear. He exhausted and almost wrecked—but he felt clear again. If no other ghastly arm of the octopus should flash out and encircle him.

For the moment he felt himself lying inert, but clear, the dragon dead. The ever-renewed dragon of a great old ideal, with its foul poison-breath. It seemed as if, for himself, he had killed it.

That was now all he wanted: to get clear. Not to save humanity or to help humanity or to have anything to do with humanity. No—no. Kangaroo had been his last embrace with humanity. Now, all he wanted was to cut himself clear. To be clear of humanity altogether, to be alone. To be clear of love, and pity, and hate. To be alone from it all. To cut himself finally clear from the last encircling arm of the octopus humanity. To turn to the old dark gods, who had waited so long in the outer dark.

Humanity could do as it liked: he did not care. So long as he could get his own soul clear. For he believed in the inward soul, in the profound unconscious of man. Not an ideal God. The ideal God is a proposition of the mental consciousness, all-too-limitedly human. "No," he said to himself. "There *is* God. But forever dark, forever unrealisable: forever and forever. The unutterable name, because it can never have a name. The great living darkness which we represent by the glyph, God."

There is this ever-present, living darkness inexhaustible and unknowable. It *is*. And it is all the God and the gods.

And every *living* human soul in a well-head to this darkness of the living unutterable. Into every living soul wells up the darkness, the unutterable. And then there is travail of the visible with the invisible. Man is in travail with his own soul, while ever his soul lives. Into his unconscious surges a new flood of the God-darkness, the living unutterable. And this unutterable is like a germ, a fœtus with which he must travail, bringing it at last into utterance, into action, into *being*.

But in most people the soul is withered at the source, like a woman whose ovaries withered before she became a woman, or a man whose sex-glands died at the moment when they should have come into life. Like unsexed people, the mass of mankind is soulless. Because to persist in resistance of the sensitive influx of the dark gradually withers the soul, makes it die, and leaves a human idealist and an automaton. Most people are dead, and scurrying and talking in the sleep of death. Life has its automatic side, sometimes in direct conflict with the spontaneous soul. Then there is a fight. And the spontaneous soul must extricate itself from the meshes of the *almost* automatic white octopus of the human ideal, the octopus of humanity. It must struggle clear, knowing what it is doing: not waste itself in revenge. The revenge is inevitable enough, for each denial of the spontaneous dark soul creates the reflex of its own revenge. But the greatest revenge on the lie is to get clear of the lie.

The long travail. The long gestation of the soul within a man, and the final parturition, the birth of a new way of knowing, a new God-influx. A new idea, true enough. But at the centre, the old anti-idea: the dark, the unutterable God. This time not a God scribbling on tablets of stone or bronze. No everlasting decalogues. No sermons on mounts, either. The dark God, the forever unrevealed. The God who is many gods to many men: all things to all men. The source of passions and strange motives. It is a frightening thought, but very liberating.

"Ah, my soul," said Richard to himself, "you have to look more ways than one. First to the unutterable dark of God: first and foremost. Then to the utterable and sometimes very loud dark of that woman Harriet. I must admit that only the dark god in her fighting with my white idealism has got me so clear: and that only the dark god in her answering the dark god in me has got my soul heavy and fecund with a new sort of infant. But even now I can't bring it forth. I can't bring it forth. I need something else. Some other answer."

Life makes no absolute statement: the true life makes no absolute statement. "Thou shalt have no other God before me." The very Commandment suggests that it is possible to have other gods, and to put them before Jehovah. "Thou shalt love thy neighbour as thyself." But, oh deepest of perplexing questions, *how* do I love myself? Am I to love my neighbour as if he *were* myself? But my very love makes me know that he *isn't* myself, and that therein lies his lovableness, unless I am a conceited prig. Am I to love my neighbour as *much* as myself? And how much do I love myself? It is a wildly problematic Commandment. Suppose I love my neighbour more than myself. That again is a catastrophe.

Since every man must love himself in a different way—

unless he is a materialist or a prig—he must love his neigh-bour in a different way. So Christ's Commandment is as large as life, and its meaning can never be fixed. I sometimes hate myself: and my neighbour as myself.

Life makes no absolute statement. It is all Call and Answer. As soon as the Call ceases, the Answer is invalid. And till the Answer comes, a Call is but a crying in the wilderness. And every Answer must wait until it hears the Call. Till the Call comes, the Answer is but an unborn fœtus.

And so it is. Life is so wonderful and complex, and *always* relative. A man's soul is a perpetual call and answer. He can never be the call and the answer in one: between the dark God and the incarnate man: between the dark soul of woman, and the opposite dark soul of man: and finally, between the souls of man and man, strangers to one another, but answerers. So it is for ever, the eternal weaving of calls and answers, and the fabric of life woven and perishing again. But the calls never cease, and the answers never fail for long. And when the fabric becomes grey and machine-made, some strange clarion-call makes men start to smash it up. So it is.

Blessed are the pure in heart. That is absolute truth, a state-ment of living relativity, because the pure in heart are those who quiver to the dark God, to the call of woman, and to the call of men. The pure in heart are the listeners and the answerers. But Ramescs II was no doubt as pure in heart as John the Evangel. Indeed perhaps purer, since John was an *insister*. To be pure in heart, man must listen to the dark gods as well as to the white gods, to the call to blood-sacrifice as well as to the eucharist.

Blessed are the poor in spirit. It depends. If it means *listen-ing*. Not if it means taking up a permanent attitude.

Blessed are the peace-makers. It depends. If it means *answer-ing*. Not if it means enforcing the peace, like policemen.

Blessed are the meek. It depends on the occasion.

Blessed are they that mourn. It depends altogether.

Blessed are they that do hunger and thirst after righteous-ness. Ah, yes, but the righteousness of the profound listener, and of the answerer who will answer come what may. Not any other righteousness of the commandment sort.

Blessed are ye when men shall despise you. Nay, nay, it is rather: *unblessed* are the despisers——

After all his terrific upheaval, Richard Lovat at last gave it up, and went to sleep. A man must even know how to give up his own earnestness, when its hour is over, and not to bother about anything any more, when he's bothered enough.

CHAPTER XIV

BITS

THE following day Somers felt savage with himself again. "Fool that I am, fool!" he said, mentally kicking himself. And he looked at the big pink spread of his Sydney *Bulletin* viciously. The *Bulletin* was the only periodical in the world that really amused him. The horrible stuffiness of English newspapers he could not stand: they had the same effect on him as fish-balls in a restaurant, loathsome, stuffy fare. English magazines were too piffling, too imbecile. But the "Bully", even if it was made up all of bits, and had neither head nor tail nor feet nor wings, was still a lively creature. He liked its straightforwardness and the kick in some of its tantrums. It beat no solemn drums. It had no deadly earnestness. It was just stoical, and spitefully humorous. Yes, at the moment he liked the *Bulletin* better than any paper he knew, though even the *Bulletin* tried a dowdy bit of swagger sometimes, especially on the pink page. But then the pink page was just "literary", and who cares?

Who cares, anyhow? Perhaps a bit sad, after all. But more fool you for being sad.

So he rushed to read the "bits". They would make Bishop Latimer forget himself and his martyrdom at the stake.

"1085: The casual Digger of war-days has carried it into civvies. Sighted one of the original Tenth at the Outer Harbour (Adelaide) wharf last week fishing. His sinker was his 1914 Star."

Yes, couldn't Somers just see that forlorn Outer Harbour at Adelaide, and the Digger, like some rag of seaweed dripping over the edge of the wharf, fishing, and using his medal for a weight?

"Wilfrido: A recent advertisement for the Wellington (New Zealand) Art Gallery attracted 72 applicants. Among them were two solicitors (one an Oxford M.A.); five sheep-farmers on whose lands the mortgage had foreclosed; and a multitude of clerks. The post is not exactly a sinecure, either: it demands attendance on seven days a week at £150 p.a."

Then a little cartoon of Ivan, the Russian workman, going for a tram-drive, and taking huge bundles of money with him, sackfuls of roubles, to pay the fare. The "Bully" was sardonic about Bolshevism.

"Ned Kelly: Hearing the deuce of a racket in the abo (aborigines) camp near our place, we strolled over to see what was wrong, and saw a young Binghi giving his gin a father of a hiding for making eyes at another buck. Every respectable Binghi has the right to wallop his missis, but this one laid it on so much that he knocked her senseless. This enraged her relatives, and they went for him *en masse*, while two or three gins applied restoratives to the battered wife. She soon came round, and, seeing how things were, grabbed a waddy and went to the assistance of her lord and master. In the end the twain routed the phalanxed relations. Same old woman, whatever her line!"

Bits about bullock-drivers and the biggest loads on record, about the biggest piece of land ploughed by a man in a day, recipes for mange in horses, twins, turnips, accidents to reverend clergymen, and so on.

"Pick: In the arid parts out back the wild birds infallibly indicate to the wayfarer when the water in his bag must be vigorously conserved. If in the early morning they descend in flocks to the plain, and there collect the globules of dew among the dry stalks of grass, it means that every tank, gilgal and puddle-hole within a bird's drinking flight has gone dry."

"Cellu Lloyd: Before you close down on mangey horses here's a cure I've never known to fail. To one bullock's gall add kerosene to make up a full pint. Heat sufficiently to enable it to mix well, not forgetting, of course, that half of it is kerosene. When well mixed add one teaspoonful of chrysophanic acid. Bottle and shake well. Before applying take a hard scrubbing-brush and thoroughly scrub the part with carbolic soap and hot water, and when applying the mixture use the brush again. In one case I struck a pair of buggy ponies that had actually bitten pieces from each other, and rubbed down a hundred yards or so of fence in trying to allay the burning itch. Two months afterwards they were growing hair and gaining condition, and not a trace of mange remained. It is wonderful, however, how lightly some horse-owners treat

the matter. When a horse works hard all day, and spends the
night rubbing a fence flat in his itch frenzy, he at once loses
condition and usefulness; but in most cases the owners builds
the fence stronger instead of giving the unfortunate animal
the necessary attention."

This recipe brought many biting comments in later issues.

Somers liked the concise, laconic style. It seemed to him
manly and without trimmings. Put ship-shape in the office, no
doubt. Sometimes the drawings were good, and sometimes they
weren't.

"Lady (who has just opened door to country girl carrying
suitcase): 'I am suited. A country girl has been engaged, and
I'm getting her to-morrow.'

"Girl: 'I'm her; and you're not. The 'ouse is too big.' "

There, thought Somers, you have the whole spirit of
Australian labour.

"K. Sped: A week or two back a Mildura (Vic.) motor-cyclist
ran over a tiger-snake while travelling at 35 m.p.h. Ten minutes
later the leg became itchy, and shortly afterwards, feeling
giddy, he started back to the local hospital. He made a wobbly
passage and collapsed at the hospital gates. He was bad for a
week, and was told that if the reptile had not struck him on
the bone he would never have reached the ward. The snake
must have doubled up when the wheel struck it, and by the
merest fluke struck the rider's leg in mid-air."

"Fraoch: I knew another case of a white girl marrying an
aboriginal about 20 years ago on the Northern Rivers (N.S.W.).
She was rather pretty, a descendant of an English family.
Binghi was a landed proprietor, having acquired a very decent
estate on the death of a former spinster employer. (Binghi
must have had 'a way wid 'im'). He owned a large, well-
furnished house, did himself well, and had a fair education,
and was a good rough-rider. But every year the 'call of the
wild' came to him, and he would leave his wife and kids (they
had three) and take himself to an old tumble-down hut in the
bush, and there for a month or two live in solitude on his
natural tucker. Under the will of the aforesaid spinster, upon
Binghi's demise the estate was to revert to her relatives. With
an optimism that was not without a pathos of its own, they
used to trot out every outlaw in the district for their dusky
friend to ride; but his neck was still intact when I left."

"Sucre: Peering through her drawing-room window shortly

before lunch, the benevolent old suburban lady saw a shivering man in a ruined overcoat. Not all the members of the capitalist classes are iron-souled creatures bent on grinding the faces of the afflicted, yet virtuous poor. Taking a ten-shilling note from a heavy-beaded bag, she scribbled on a piece of paper the words, *Cheer Up*, put both in an envelope, and told the maid to give it to the outcast from her. While the family was at dinner that evening a ring sounded at the front door. Argument followed in the hall between a hoarse male voice and that of the maid. 'You can't come in. They're at dinner.' 'I'd *rather* come in, miss. Always like for to fix these things up in person.' 'You can't come.' Another moment and the needy wayfarer was in the dining-room. He carefully laid five filthy £1 notes on the table before his benefactress. 'There you are, mum,' he said, with a rough salute. 'Cheer Up won all right. I'm mostly on the corner, race days, as your cook will tell you; an' I'd like to say that if any uv your *friends*——' "

Bits, bits, bits. Yet Richard Lovat read on. It was not mere anecdotage. It was the sheer momentaneous life of the continent. There was no consecutive thread. Only the laconic courage of experience.

All the better. He could have kicked himself for wanting to help mankind, join in revolutions or reforms or any of that stuff. And he kicked himself still harder thinking of his frantic struggles with the "soul" and the "dark god" and the "listener" and the "answerer". Blarney—blarney—blarney! He was a preacher and a blatherer, and he hated himself for it. Damn the "soul", damn the "dark god", damn the "listener" and the "answerer", and above all, damn his own interfering, nosy self.

What right had he to go nosing round Kangaroo, and making up to Jaz or to Jack? Why couldn't he keep off it all? Let the whole show go its own gay course to hell, without Mr. Richard Lovat Somers trying to show it the way it should go.

A very strong wind had got up from the west. It blew down from the dark hills in a fury, and was cold as flat ice. It blew the sea back until the great water looked like dark, ruffled mole-fur. It blew it back till the waves got littler and littler, and could hardly uncurl the least swish of a rat-tail of foam.

On such a day his restlessness had driven them on a trip along the coast to Wolloona. They got to the lost little town just before midday, and looked at the shops. The sales were on, and prices were "smashed to bits", "Prices Smashed to Bits", in big labels. Harriet, of course, fascinated in the Main Street, that ran towards the sea, with the steep hill at the back. "Hitch your motor to a star.—Star Motor Company." "Your piano is the most important article of furniture in your drawing-room. You will not be proud of your drawing-room unless your piano has a HANDSOME APPEARANCE and a BEAUTIFUL TONE. Both these requisites——"

It was a wonderful Main Street, and, thank heaven, out of the wind. There were several large but rather scaring brown hotels, with balconies all round: there was a yellow stucco church with a red-painted tin steeple, like a weird toy: there were high roofs and low roofs, all corrugated iron: and you came to an opening, and there, behold, were one or two forlorn bungalows inside their wooden palings, and then the void. The naked bush, sinking in a hollow to a sort of marsh, and then down the coast some sort of "works", brick-works or something, smoking. All as if it had tumbled haphazard off the pantechnicon of civilisation as it dragged round the edges of this wild land, and there lay, busy but not rooted in. As if none of the houses had any foundations.

Bright the sun, the air of marvellous clarity, tall stalks of cabbage palms rising in the hollow, and far off, tufted gum trees against a perfectly new sky, the tufts at the end of wire branches. And farther off, blue, blue hills. In the Main Street large and expensive motor-cars and women in fuzzy fur coats, long, quiescent Australian men in tired-out-looking navy blue suits trotting on brown ponies, with a carpet-bag in one hand doing the shopping; girls in very much-made hats, also flirtily shopping; three boys with big, magnificent bare legs, lying in a sunny corner in the dust; a lonely white pony hitched as if forever to a post at a street-corner.

"I like it," said Harriet. "It doesn't feel *finished*."

"Not even begun," he laughed.

But he liked it too: even the slummyness of some of the bungalows inside their wooden palings, drab-wood, decrepit houses, old tins, broken pots, a greeny-white pony reminding one of a mildewed old shoe, two half-naked babies sitting like bits of live refuse in the dirt, but with bonny, healthy bare legs: the awful place called "The Travellers' Rest—Mr Coddy's Boarding House"—a sort of blind, squalid, corner building made of wood and tin, with flat pieces of old lace

curtain nailed inside the windows, and the green blinds
hermetically drawn. What must it have been like inside?
Then an open space, and coral trees bristling with red crest-
flowers on their bare, cold boughs: and the hollow space
of the open country, and the marvellous blue hills of the
distance.

The wind was cold enough to make you die. Harriet was
disgusted at having been dragged away from home. They trailed
to the sea to try and get out of it, for it blew from the land,
and the sun was hot. On the bay one lone man flinging a line
into the water, on the edge of the conch-shaped, sloping sands.
Dark-blue water, ruffled like mole-fur, and flicked all over with
froth as with bits of feather-fluff. And many white gannets
turning in the air like a snow-storm and plunging down into
the water like bombs. And fish leaped in the furry water, as if
the wind had turned them upside-down. And the gannets dropping and exploding into the wave, and disappearing. On the
sea's horizon, so perfectly clear, a steamer like a beetle walking
slowly along. Clear, with a non-earthly clarity.

Harriet and Somers sat and ate sandwiches with a little sand,
she dazed but still expostulating. Then they went to walk on
the sea's edge, where the sands might be firm. But the beach
sloped too much, and they were not firm. The lonely fisherman held up his thin silvery line for them to pass under.

"Don't bother," said Somers.

"Right O!" said he.

He had a sad, beery moustache, a very cold-looking face,
and, of course, a little boy, his son, no doubt, for a satellite.

There were little, exquisite pink shells, like Venetian pink
glass with white veins or black veins round their sharp little
steeples. Harriet loved them, among her grumbles, and they
began to gather them: "for trimmings," said Harriet. So, in
the flat-icy wind, that no life had ever softened and no god
ever tempered, they crouched on the sea's edge picking these
marvellous little shells.

Suddenly, with a cry, to find the water rushing round their
ankles and surging up their legs, they dragged their way wildly
forward with the wave, and out and up the sand. Where
immediately a stronger blast seized Lovat's hat and sent it spin-
ning to the sea again, and he after it like a bird. He caught it
as the water lifted it, and then the waste of water enveloped
him. Above his knees swirled the green flood, there was water

all around him swaying, he looked down at it in amazement, reeling and clutching his hat.

Then once more he clambered out. Harriet had fallen on her knees on the sand in a paroxysm of laughter, and there she was doubled up like a sack, shrieking between her gasps:

"His hat! His hat! He wouldn't let it go"—shrieks, and her head like a sand-bag flops to the sand—"no—not if he had to swim"—shrieks—"swim to Samoa."

He was looking at his wet legs and chuckling with his inward laughter. Vivid, the blue sky: intensely clear, the dark sea, the yellow sands, the swoop of the bay, the low headlands: clear like a miracle. And the water bubbling in his shoes as he walked rolling up the sands.

At last she recovered enough to crawl after him. They sat in a sand-hollow under a big bush with odd red berries, and he wrung out his socks, and all he could of his under-pants and trousers. Then he put on his socks and shoes again, and they set off for the station.

"The Pacific water," he said, "is so very seaey, it is almost warm."

At which, looking at his wet legs and wet hat, she went off into shrieks again. But she made him be quick, because there was a train they could catch.

However, in the Main Street they thought they would buy another pair of socks. So he bought them, and changed in the shop. And they missed the train, and Harriet expostulated louder.

They went home in a motor-bus and a cloud of dust, with the heaven bluer than blue above, the hills dark and fascinating, and the land so remote seeming. Everything so clear, so very distinct, and yet so marvellously aloof.

All the miles alongside the road tin bungalows in their paling fences: and a man on a pony, in a long black overcoat and a cold nose, driving three happy, fleecy cows: long men in jerseys and white kerchiefs round their necks, à la Buffalo Bill, riding nice slim horses; a woman riding astride top speed on the roadside grass. A motor-car at the palings of one of the bungalows. A few carts coming.

And the occupants of the bus bouncing and bobbing like a circus, because of the very bumpy road.

"Shakes your dinner down," said the old woman with the terribly home-made hat—oh, such difficult, awful hats.

"It does, if you've had any," laughed Harriet.

"Why, you've 'ad your dinner, 'aven't you?"

As concerned as if Harriet was her own stomach, such a nice old woman. And a lovely little boy with the bright, wide, gentle eyes of these Australians. So alert and alive and with that lovableness that almost hurts one. Absolute trust in the "niceness" of the world. A tall, stalky, ginger man with the same bright eyes and a turned-up nose and long stalky legs. An elderly man with bright, friendly, elderly eyes and careless hair and careless clothing. He was Joe, and the other was Alf. Real careless Australians, careless of their appearance, careless of their speech, of their money, of everything—except of their happy-go-lucky, democratic friendliness. Really nice, with bright, quick, willing eyes. Then a young man, perhaps a commercial traveller, with a suitcase. He was quite smartly dressed, and had fancy socks. He was one of those with the big, heavy legs, heavy thighs and calves that showed even in his trousers. And he was physically very self-conscious, very self-conscious of Lovat and Harriet. The driver's face was long and deep red. He was absolutely laconic. And yet, absolutely willing, as if life held no other possibility than that of being an absolutely willing citizen. A fat man with a fat little girl waiting at one of the corners.

"Up she goes!" he said as he lifted her in.

A perpetual, unchanging willingness, and an absolute equality. The same good-humoured, right-you-are approach from everybody to everybody. "Right-you-are! Right-O!" Somers had been told so many hundreds of times, Right-he-was, Right-O!, that he almost had dropped into the way of it. It was like sleeping between blankets—so cosy. So cosy.

They were really awfully nice. There was a winsome charm about them. They none of them seemed mean, or tight, or petty.

The young man with the fine suit and the great legs put down his money, gently and shyly as a girl, beside the driver on the little window-ledge. Then he got out and strode off, shy and quick, with his suitcase.

"Hey!"

The young man turned at the driver's summons, and came back.

"Did yer pay me?"

The question was put briskly, good-humouredly, with a touch even of tenderness. The young man pointed to the money. The driver glanced round and saw it.

"Oh! Right you are! Right-O!"

A faint little smile of almost tender understanding, and the young man turned again. And the driver bustled to carry out some goods. The way he stooped to pick up the heavy wooden box in his arms; so *willing* to stoop to burdens. So long, of course, as his Rights of Man were fully recognised. You mustn't try any superior tricks with him.

Well, it was really awfully nice. It was touching. And it made life so easy, so easy.

Of course these were not government servants. Government servants have another sort of feeling. They feel their office, even in N.S.W.—even a railway-clerk. Oh yes.

So nice, so nice, so gentle. The strange, bright-eyed gentleness. Of course, really rub him the wrong way, and you've got a Tartar. But not before you've asked for one. Gentle as a Kangaroo, or a wallaby, with that wide-eyed, bright-eyed, alert, *responsible* gentleness Somers had never known in Europe. It had a great beauty. And at the same time it made his spirits sink.

It made him feel so sad underneath, or uneasy, like an impending disaster. Such a charm. He was so tempted to commit himself to this strange continent and its strange people. It was so fascinating. It seemed so free, an absence of any form of stress whatsoever. No strain in any way, once you could accept it.

He was so tempted, save for a sense of impending disaster at the bottom of his soul. And there a voice kept saying, "No, no. No, no. It won't do. You've got to have a reversion. You can't carry this mode any further. You've got to have a recognition of the innate, sacred separateness."

So when they were walking home in a whirl of the coldest, most flat-edged wind they had ever known, he stopped in front of her to remark:

"Of course you can't go on with a soft, oh-so-friendly life like this here. You've got to have an awakening of the old recognition of the aristocratic principle, the *innate* difference between people."

"Aristocratic principle!" she shrieked on the wind. "You should have seen yourself, flying like a feather into the sea after your hat. Aristocratic *principle!*" She shrieked again with laughter.

"There you are, you see," he said to himself. "I'm at it again." And he laughed too.

The wind blew them home. He made a big fire, and changed, and they drank coffee made with milk, and ate buns.

"Thank heaven for a home," he said, as they sat in the dark, big rooms at Coo-ee, and ate their buns, and looked out of the windows and saw here as well a whirl of gannets like a snowstorm, and a dark sea littered with white fluffs. The wind roared in the chimney, and for the first time the sea was inaudible.

"You see," she said, "how thankful you are for a home."

"Chilled to the bone!" she said. "I'm chilled to the bone with my day's pleasure-outing."

So they drew up the couch before the fire, and he piled rugs on her and jarrah chunks on the fire, and at last it was toastingly warm. He sat on a little barrel which he had discovered in the shed, and in which he kept the coal for the fire. He had been at a loss for a lid to this barrel, till he had found a big tin-lid thrown out on the waste lot. And now the wee barrel with the slightly rusty tin-lid was his perch when he wanted to get quite near the fire. Harriet hated it, and had moments when she even carried the lid to the cliff to throw it in the sea. But she brought it back, because she knew he would be so indignant. She reviled him, however.

"Shameful! Hideous! Old tin-lids! How you can *sit* on it. How you can bring yourself to sit on such a thing, and not feel humiliated. Is that your aristocratic principle?"

"I put a cushion on it," he said.

As he squatted on his tub this evening in the fire-corner, she suddenly turned from her book and cried:

"There he is, on his throne! Sitting on his aristocratic principle!" And again she roared with laughter.

He, however, shook some coal out of the little tub on to the fire, replaced the tin lid and the cushions, and resumed his thoughts. The fire was very warm. She lay stretched in front of it on the sofa, covered with an eiderdown, and reading a Nat Gould novel, to get the real tang of Australia.

"Of course," he said, "this land always gives me the feeling that it doesn't *want* to be touched, it doesn't *want* men to get hold of it."

She looked up from her Nat Gould.

"Yes," she admitted slowly. "And my ideal has always been a farm. But I know now. The farms don't really belong to the land. They only scratch it and irritate it, and are never at one with it."

Whereupon she returned to her Nat Gould, and there was silence save for the hollow of the wind. When she had finished her paper-backed book, she said:

"It's just like them—just like they *think* they are."

"Yes," he said vaguely.

"But, bah!" she added, "they make me sick. So absolutely dull—worse than an 'At Home' in the middle classes."

And after a silence, another shriek of laughter suddenly.

"Like a flying-fish! Like a flying-fish dashing into the waves! Dashing into the waves after his hat——"

He giggled on his tub.

"Fancy, that I'm here in Coo-ee after my day's outing! I can't believe it. I shall call you the flying-fish. It's hard to believe that one was so many things in one day. Suddenly the water! Won't you go now and do the tailor? Twenty to eight! The bold buccaneer!"

The tailor was a fish that had cost a shilling, and which he was to prepare for supper.

"Globe: There can't be much telepathy about bullocks, anyhow. In Gippsland (Vic.) last season a score of them were put into a strange paddock, and the whole 20 were found drowned in a hole next morning. Tracks showed that they had gone each on his own along a path, overbalanced one after the other, and were unable to clamber up the rocky banks."

That, thought Richard at the close of the day, is a sufficient comment on herd-unity, equality, domestication, and civilisation. He felt he would have liked to climb down into that hole in which the bullocks were drowning and beat them all hard before they expired, for being such mechanical logs of life.

Telepathy! Think of the marvellous vivid communication of the huge sperm whales. Huge, grand, phallic beasts! Bullocks! Geldings! Men! R. L. wished he could take to the sea and be a whale, a great surge of living blood: away from these all-too-white people, who ought *all* to be called Cellu Lloyd, not only the horse-mange man.

Man is a thought-adventurer. Man is more, he is a life-adventurer. Which means he is a thought-adventurer, an emotion-adventurer, and a discoverer of himself and of the outer universe. A discoverer.

"I am a fool," said Richard Lovat, which was the most frequent discovery he made. It came, moreover, every time with a new shock of surprise and chagrin. Every time he climbed a new mountain range and looked over, he saw, not only a new world, but a big anticipatory fool on this side of it, namely, himself.

Now a novel is supposed to be a mere record of emotion-adventures, floundering in feelings. We insist that a novel is, or should be, also a thought-adventure, if it is to be anything at all complete.

"I am a fool," thought Richard to himself, "to imagine that I can flounder in a sympathetic universe like a fly in the ointment." We think of ourselves, we think of the ointment, but we do not consider the fly. It fell into the ointment, crying, "Ah, here is a pure and balmy element in which all is unalloyed goodness. Here is attar of roses without a thorn." Hence the fly in the ointment: embalmed in balm. And our repugnance.

"I am a fool," said Richard to himself, "to be floundering round in this easy, cosy, all-so-friendly world. I feel like a fly in the ointment. For heaven's sake let me get out. I suffocate."

Where to? If you're going to get out you must have something to get out on to. Stifling in unctuous sympathy of a harmless humanity.

"Oh," cried the stifling R. "Where is my Rock of Ages?"

He knew well enough. It was where it always has been: in the middle of him.

"Let me get back to my own self," he panted, "hard and central in the centre of myself. I am drowning in this merge of harmlessness, this sympathetic humanity. Oh, for heaven's sake let me crawl out of the sympathetic smear, and get myself clean again."

Back to his own centre—back—back. The inevitable recoil.

"Everything," said R. to himself, in one of those endless conversations with himself which were his chief delight, "everything is relative".

And flop he went into the pot of spikenard.

"Not quite," he gasped, as he crawled out. "Let me drag my isolate and absolute individual self out of this mess."

Which is the history of relativity in man. All is relative as

K*

we go flop into the ointment: or the treacle or the flame. But as we crawl out, or flutter out with a smell of burning, the *absolute* holds us spellbound. Oh to be isolate and absolute, and breathe clear.

So that even relativity is only relative. Relative to the absolute.

I am sorry to have to stand, a sorry sight, preening my wings on the brink of the ointment-pot, thought Richard. But from this vantage ground let me preach to myself. He preached, and the record was taken down for this gramophone of a novel.

No, the self is absolute. It may be relative to everything else in the universe. But to itself it is an absolute.

Back to the central self, the isolate, absolute self.

"Now," thought Richard to himself, waving his front paws with gratification: "I must sound the muezzin and summon all men back to their central, isolate selves."

So he drew himself up, when—*urch!!* He was sluthering over the brim of the ointment-pot into the balm of humanity once more.

"Oh, Lord, I nearly did it again," he thought as he clambered out with a sick heart. "I shall do it once too often. The bulk of mankind haven't got any central selves: haven't got any. They're all bits."

Nothing but his fright would have struck this truth out of him. So he crouched still, like a fly very tired with crawling out of the ointment, to think about it.

"The bulk of people haven't got any central selves. They're all bits."

He knew it was true, and he felt rather sick of the sweet odour of the balm of human beatitudes, in which he had been so nearly lost.

"It takes how many thousand facets to make the eye of a fly—or a spider?" he asked himself, being rather lazy scientifically. "Well, all these people are just facets: just bits, that fitted together make a whole. But you can fit the bits together time after time, yet it won't bring the bug to life."

The people of this terrestial sphere are all bits. Isolate one of them, and he is still only a bit. Isolate your man in the street, and he is just a rudimentary fragment. Supposing you have the misfortune to have your little toe cut off. That little toe won't at once rear on its hind legs and begin to announce,

"I'm an isolated individual with an immortal soul." It won't. But your man in the street will. And he is a liar. He's only a bit, and he's only got a minute share of the collective soul. Soul of his own he has none: and never will have. Just a share in the collective soul, no more. Never a thing by himself.

Damn the man in the street, said Richard to himself. Damn the collective soul, it's a dead rat in a hole. Let humanity scratch its own lice.

Now I'll sound my muezzin again. *The man by himself*. "Allah bismallah! God is God and man is man and has a soul of his own. Each man to himself! Each man back to his own soul! Alone, alone, with his own soul alone. God is God and man is man and the man in the street is a louse."

Whatever your relativity, that's the starting point and the finishing point: a man alone with his own soul: and the dark God beyond him.

A man by himself.

Begin then.

Let the men in the street—ugh, horrid millions, crawl the face of the earth like lice or ants or some other ignominy.

The man by himself.

That was one of the names of Erasmus of Rotterdam.

The man by himself.

That is the beginning and end, the alpha and the omega, the one absolute: the man alone by himself, alone with his own soul, alone with his eyes on the darkness which is the dark god of life. Alone like a pythoness on her tripod, like the oracle alone above the fissure into the unknown. The oracle, the fissure down into the unknown, the strange exhalations from the dark, the strange words that the oracle must utter. Strange, cruel, pregnant words: the new term of consciousness.

This is the innermost symbol of man: alone in the darkness of the cavern of himself, listening to soundlessness of inflowing fate. Inflowing fate, inflowing doom, what does it matter? The man by himself—that is the absolute—listening—that is the relativity—for the influx of his fate, or doom.

The man by himself. The listener.

But most men can't listen any more. The fissure is closed up. There is no soundless voice. They are deaf and dumb, ants, scurrying ants.

That is their doom. It is a new kind of absolute. Like riff-raff, which has fallen out of living relativity, on the teeming absolute of the dust-heap, or the ant-heap. Sometimes the dust-heap becomes huge, huge, huge, and covers nearly all the world. Then it turns into a volcano, and all starts again.

"It has nothing to do with me," said Richard to himself. I hope, dear reader, you like plenty of *conversation* in a novel: it makes it so much lighter and brisker.

"It has nothing to do with me," said Richard to himself. "They do as they like. But since, after all, I *am* a kind-hearted dear creature, I will just climb the minaret of myself and sound my muezzin."

So behold the poor dear on his pinnacle lifting his hands.

"God is God and man is man; and every man by himself. Every man by himself, alone with his own soul. Alone as if he were dead. Dead to himself. He is dead and alone. He is dead; alone. His soul is alone. Alone with God, with the dark God. God is God."

But if he likes to shout muezzins, instead of hawking fried fish or newspapers or lottery tickets, let him.

Poor dear, it was rather an anomalous call: "Listen to me, and be alone." Yet he felt called upon to call it.

To be alone, to be alone, and to rest on the unknown God alone.

The God must be unknown. Once you have defined him or described him, he is the most chummy of pals, as you'll know if you listen to preachers. And once you've chummed up with your God, you'll never be alone again, poor you. For that's the end of you. You and your God chumming it through time and eternity.

Poor Richard saw himself in funny situations.

"My dear young lady, let me entreat you, be alone, only be alone."

"Oh, Mr. Somers, I should love to, if you'd hold my hand."

"There is a gulf," growing sterner, "surrounds each solitary soul. A gulf surrounds you—a gulf surrounds me——"

"*I'm falling!*" shrieks and flings her arms around his neck. Or Kangaroo.

"Why am I so beastly to Kangaroo?" said Richard to himself. "For beastly I am. I am a detestable little brat to them all round."

A detestable little brat he felt.

But Kangaroo wanted to be queen bee of another hive, with all the other bees clustering on him like some huge mulberry

Sickening! Why couldn't he be alone? At least for *once*. For once withdraw entirely.

And a queen bee buzzing with beatitudes. Beatitudes, beatitudes. Bee attitudes or any other attitudes, it made Richard feel tired. More benevolence, more nauseating benevolence. "Charity suffereth long."

Yet one cannot live a life of entire loneliness, like a monkey on a stick, up and down one's own obstacle. There's got to be meeting: even communion. Well, then, let us have the other communion. "This is thy body which I take from thee and eat," as the priest, also the God, says in the ritual of blood sacrifice. The ritual of supreme responsibility, and offering. Sacrifice to the dark God, and to the men in whom the dark God is manifest. Sacrifice to the strong, not to the weak. In awe, not in dribbling love. The communion in power, the assumption into glory. *La gloire.*

CHAPTER XV

JACK SLAPS BACK

CHAPTER follows chapter, and nothing doing. But man is a thought-adventurer, and he falls into the Charybdis of ointment, and his shipwrecks on the rocks of ages, and his kisses across chasms, and his silhouette on a minaret: surely these are as thrilling as most things.

To be brief, there was a Harriet, a Kangaroo, a Jack and a Jaz and a Vicky, let alone a number of mere Australians. But you know as well as I do that Harriet is quite happy rubbing her hair with hair-wash and brushing it over her forehead in the sun and looking at the threads of gold and gun-metal, and the few threads, alas, of silver and tin, with admiration. And Kangaroo has just got a very serious brief, with thousands and thousands of pounds at stake in it. Of course he is fully occupied keeping them at stake, till some of them wander into his pocket. And Jack and Vicky have gone down to her father's for the week-end, and he's out fishing, and has already landed a rock-cod, a leather-jacket, a large schnapper, a rainbow-fish, seven black-fish, and a cuttlefish. So what's wrong with him? While she is trotting over on a pony to have a look at an old sweetheart who is much too young to be neglected. And Jaz is arguing with a man about the freight rates. And all the scattered Australians are just having a bet on something or other. So what's wrong with Richard's climbing a mental minaret or two in the interim? Of course there isn't any interim. But you *know* that Harriet is brushing her hair in the sun, and Kangaroo looking at huge sums of money on paper, and Jack fishing, and Vicky flirting, and Jaz bargaining, so what more do you want to know? We can't be at a stretch of tension *all* the time, like the E string on a fiddle. If you don't like the novel, don't read it. If the pudding doesn't please you, leave it, *I* don't mind your saucy plate. I know too well that you can bring an ass to water, etc.

As for gods, thought Richard, there are gods of vengeance. "For I, the Lord thy God, am a jealous God." So true. A jealous God, and a vengeful—"Visiting the sins of the fathers upon the children, unto the third and fourth generation of them that hate me." Of course. The fathers get off. You don't begin to pay the penalty till the second and third generation. That is something for *us* to put in our pipes and smoke. Because *we* are the second generation, and it was our fathers who had a nice rosy time among the flesh-pots, cooking themselves the tit-bits of this newly-gutted globe of ours. They cooked the tit-bits, we are left with the carrion.

"The Lord thy God am a jealous God."

So He is. The Lord thy God is the invisible stranger at the gate in the night, knocking. He is the mysterious life-suggestion, tapping for admission. And the wondrous Victorian Age managed to fasten the door so tight, and light up the compound so brilliantly with electric light, that really, there *was* no outside, it was all in. The unknown became a joke: is still a joke.

Yet there it is, outside the gate, getting angry. "Behold I stand at the gate and knock." "Knock away," said complacent benevolent humanity, which had just discovered its own monkey origin to account for its own monkey tricks. "Knock away, nobody will hinder you from knocking."

And Holman Hunt paints a pretty picture of a man with a Stars-and-Stripes lantern and a red beard, knocking. But whoever it is that's knocking had been knocking for three generations now, and he's got sick of it. He'll be kicking the door in just now.

"For I the Lord thy God am a jealous God."

It is not that He is jealous of Thor or Zeus or Bacchus o

Venus. The great dark God outside the gate is all these gods. You open the gate, and sometimes in rushes Thor and gives you a bang on the head with a hammer; or Bacchus comes mysteriously through, and your mind goes dark and your knees and thighs begin to glow; or it is Venus, and you close your eyes and open your nostrils to a perfume, like a bull. All the gods. When they come through the gate they are personified. But outside the gate it is one dark God, the Unknown. And the Unknown is a terribly jealous God, and vengeful. A fearfully vengeful god: Moloch, Astarte, Ashtaroth, and Baal. That is why we dare not open now. It would be a hell-god, and we know it. We are the second generation. Our children are the third. And our children's children are the fourth. Eheu! Eheu! Who knocks?

Jack trotted over to Coo-ee on the Sunday afternoon, when he was staying with his wife's people. He knew Richard and Harriet would most probably be at home: they didn't like going out on Sundays, when all the world and his wife, in their exceedingly Sunday clothes, swarmed on the face of the earth.

Yes, they were at home: sitting on the veranda, a bit of rain spitting from the grey sky, and the sea gone colourless and small. Suddenly, there stood Jack. He had come round the corner on to the grass. Somers started as if an enemy were upon him. Jack looked very tall and wiry, in an old grey suit. He hesitated before coming forward, as if measuring the pair of unsuspecting turtle doves on the loggia, and on his face was a faint grin. His eyes were dark and grinning too, as he hung back there. Somers watched him quickly. Harriet looked over her shoulder.

"Oh, Mr. Callcott—why—how do you do?" And she got up, startled, and went across the loggia holding out her hand, to shake hands. So Jack had to come forward. Richard, very silent, shook hands also, and went indoors to fetch a chair and a cup and a plate, while Jack made his explanation to Harriet.

"Such a long time since we saw you," she was saying. "Why didn't Mrs. Callcott come, I should have liked so much to see her?"

"Ah—you see I came over on the pony. Doesn't look very promising weather." And he looked away across the sea, averting his face.

"No—and the *terrible* cold winds! I'm so glad if it will rain. simply love the smell of rain in the air: especially here in

Australia. It makes the air seem so much *kinder*, not so dry
and savage——"

"Ah—yes—it does," he said vaguely, still averting his face
from her. He seemed strange to her. And his face looked
different—as if he had been drinking, or as if he had
indigestion.

The two men were aloof like two strange tom-cats.

"Were you disgusted with Lovat when he didn't turn up the
other Saturday?" said Harriet. "I do hope you weren't sitting
waiting for him."

"Well—er—yes, we did wait up a while for him."

"Oh, but what a shame! But you know by now he's the
most undependable creature on earth. I wish you'd be angry
with him. It's no good what *I* say."

"No," said he—the peculiar slow Cockney no—"I'm not
angry with him."

"But you should be," cried Harriet. "It would be good for
him."

"Would it?" smiled Jack. His eyes were dark and inchoate,
and there seemed a devil in his long, wiry body. He did not
look at Somers.

"You know of course what happened?" said Harriet.

"Er—when?"

"When Lovat went to see Mr. Cooley."

"Er—no."

Again that peculiar Australian no, like a scorpion that stings
with its tail.

"Didn't Mr. Cooley tell you?" cried Harriet.

"No." There was indescribable malice in the monosyllable

"Didn't he——!" cried Harriet, and she hesitated.

"You be quiet," said Lovat crossly, to her. "Of course *you'c
have to rush in."

"You think angels would fear to tread in such a delicate
mess?" said Harriet, with a flash of mocking wit that sent a
faint smile up Jack's face, like a red flame. His nose, hi
mouth were curiously reddened. He liked Harriet's attacks
He looked at her with dark, attentive eyes. Then he turnec
vaguely to Somers.

"What was it?" he asked

"Nothing at all new," said Somers. "You know he and
start to quarrel the moment we set eyes on one another."

"They might be man and wife," mocked Harriet, and agai

Jack turned to her a look of black, smiling, malicious recognition.

"Another quarrel?" he said quietly.

But Somers was almost *sure* he knew all about it, and had only come like a spy to take soundings.

"Another quarrel," he replied, smiling, fencing. "And once more shown the door."

"I should think," said Harriet, "you'd soon know that door when you see it."

"Oh, yes," said Richard. He had not told her the worst of the encounter. He never told her the worst, nor her nor anybody.

Jack was looking from one to the other to see how much each knew.

"Was it a specially bad blow-up?" he said, in his quiet voice, that had a lurking tone of watchfulness in it.

"Oh, yes, final," laughed Richard. "I am even going to leave Australia."

"When?"

"I think in six weeks."

There was a silence for some moments.

"You've not booked your berths yet?" asked Jack.

"No. I must go up to Sydney."

Again Jack waited before he spoke. Then he said:

"What made you settle on going?"

"I don't know. I feel it's my fate to go now."

"Ha, your fate!" said Harriet. "It's always your fate with you. If it was me it would be my foolish restlessness."

Jack looked at her with another quick smile, and a curious glance of dark recognition in his eyes, almost like a caress. Strangely apart, too, as if he and she were in an inner dark circle, and Somers was away outside.

"Don't you want to go, Mrs. Somers?" he asked.

"Of course I don't. I love Australia," she protested.

"Then don't you go," said Jack. "You stop behind."

When he lowered his voice it took on a faint, indescribable huskiness. It made Harriet a little uneasy. She watched Lovat. She did not like Jack's new turn of husky intimacy. She wanted Richard to rescue her.

"Ha!" she said. "He'd never be able to get through the world without me."

"Does it matter?" said Jack, grinning faintly at her and keep-

ing the husky note in his voice. "He knows his own mind—
or his fate. You stop here. We'll look after you."

But she watched Richard. He was hardly listening. He was
thinking again that Jack was feeling malevolent towards him,
wanting to destroy him, as in those early days when they used
to play chess together.

"No," said Harriet, watching Lovat's face. "I suppose I shall
have to trail myself along, poor woman, till I see the end
of him."

"He'll lead you many a dance before that happens," grinned
Richard. He rather enjoyed Jack's malevolence this time.

"Ha, you've led me all your dances that you know," she
retorted. "I know there'll be nothing new, unfortunately."

"Why don't you stay in Australia?" Jack said to her, with
the same quiet, husky note of intimacy, insistency, and the
reddish light on his face.

She was somewhat startled and offended. Wasn't the man
sober, or what?

"Oh, he wouldn't give me any money, and I haven't a *sou*
of my own," she said lightly, laughing it off.

"You wouldn't be short of money," said Jack. "Plenty of
money."

"You see I couldn't just live on charity, could I?" she replied
delicately.

"It wouldn't be charity."

"What then?"

There was a very awkward pause. Then a wicked redness
came into Jack's face, and a flicker into his voice.

"Appreciation. You'd be appreciated." He seemed to speak
with muted lips. There was a cold silence. Harriet was
offended now.

"I'll just clear the table," she said, rising briskly.

Jack sat rather slack in his chair, his long, malevolent body
half sunk, and his chin dropped.

"What boat do you think you'll catch?" he asked.

"The *Manganui*. Why?"

But Jack did not speak. He sat there with his head sunk on
his chin, his body half-turgid, as if he were really not quite
sober.

"You won't be honouring Australia long with your presence," he said ironically.

"Nor dishonouring it," said Richard. He was like a creature

that is going to escape. Some of the fear he had felt for
Kangaroo he now felt for Jack. Jack was really very malevolent. There was hell in his reddened face, and in his black,
inchoate eyes, and in his long, pent-up body. But he kept an
air of quiescence, of resignation, as if he were still really
benevolent.

"Oh, I don't say that," he remarked in answer to Richard's
last, but in a tone which said so plainly what he felt: an
insulting tone.

Said Richard to himself: "I wouldn't like to fall into your
clutches, my friend, altogether: or to give your benevolence a
chance to condemn me."

Aloud, he said to Jack:

"If I can't join in with what you're doing here, heart and
soul, I'd better take myself off, hadn't I? You've all been good
to me, and in a measure, trusted me. I shall always owe you
a debt of gratitude, and keep your trust inviolable. You know
that. But I am one of those who must stand and wait—though
I don't pretend that by so doing I also serve."

"You take no risks," said Jack quietly.

Another home-thrust.

"Why—I would take risks—if only I felt it was any good."

"What does it matter about it's being any good? You can't
tell what good a thing will be or won't be. All you can do is
to take a bet on it."

"You see it isn't my nature to bet."

"Not a sporting nature, you mean?"

"No, not a sporting nature."

"Like a woman—you like to feel safe all round," said Jack,
slowly raising his dark eyes to Somers in a faint smile of contempt and malevolence. And Richard had to acknowledge to
himself that he was cutting a poor figure: nosing in, like a
Mr. Nosy Parker, then drawing back quickly if he saw two
sparks fly.

"Do you think I've let you down? I never pledged myself,"
he said coldly.

"Oh, no, you never pledged yourself," said Jack laconically.

"You see I don't *believe* in these things," said Somers,
flushing.

"What's that you don't believe in?"

And Jack watched him with two black, round eyes, with a
spark dancing slowly in each, in a slow gaze putting forth all

his power. But Somers now looked back into the two dark, malevolent pools.

"In revolutions—and public love and benevolence and feeling righteous," he said.

"What love, what benevolence and righteousness?" asked Jack, vaguely, still watching with those black, sardonic eyes. "I never said anything about them."

"You know you want to be the saviours of Australia," said Richard.

"I didn't know. But what's wrong with it?"

"I'm no good at saving."

"We don't pretend to be saviours. We want to do our best for Australia, it being our own country. And the Pommies come out from England to try to upset us. But they won't. They may as well stop in their dead-and-rotten old country."

"I'm sorry it looks to you like that," said Richard.

"Oh, don't apologise," said Jack, with a faint, but even more malevolent smile. "It's pretty well always the same. You come out from the old countries very cocksure, with a lot of criticism to you. But when it comes to doing anything, you sort of fade out, you're nowhere. We're used to it, we don't mind."

There was a silence of hate.

"No, we don't mind," Jack continued. "It's quite right, you haven't let us down, because we haven't given you a chance. That's all. In so far as you've had any chance to, you've let us down, and we know it."

Richard was silent. Perhaps it was true. And he hated such a truth.

"All right," he said. "I've let you down. I suppose I shall have to admit it. I'm sorry—but I can't help myself."

Jack took not the slightest notice of this admission, sat as if he had not heard it.

"I'm sorry I've sort of fizzled out so quickly," said Richard. "But you wouldn't have me pretend, would you? I'd better be honest at the beginning."

Jack looked at him slowly, with slow, inchoate eyes, and a look of contempt on his face. The contempt on Jack's face, the contempt of the confident he-man for the shifty she-man, made Richard flush with anger, and drove him back on his deeper self once more.

"What do you call honest?" said Jack, sneering.

Richard became very silent, very still. He realised that Jack would like to give him a thrashing. The thought was horrible to Richard Lovat, who could never bear to be touched physically. And the other man sitting there as if he were drunk was very repugnant to him. It was a bad moment.

"Why," he replied, in answer to the question, while Jack's eyes fixed him with a sort of jeering malevolence: "I can't honestly say I feel at one with you, you and Kangaroo, so I say so, and stand aside."

"You've found out all you wanted to know, I suppose?" said Jack.

"I didn't *want* to know anything. I didn't come asking or seeking. It was you who chose to tell me."

"You didn't try drawing us out, in your own way?"

"Why, no, I don't think so."

Again Jack looked up at him with a faint contemptuous smile of derision.

"I should have said myself you did. And you got what you wanted, and now you are clearing out with it. Exactly like a spy, in my opinion."

Richard opened wide eyes, and went pale.

"A spy!" he exclaimed. "But it's just absurd."

Jack did not vouchsafe any answer, but sat there as if he had come for some definite purpose, something menacing, and was going to have it out with the other man.

"Kangaroo doesn't think I came spying, does he?" asked Richard, aghast. "It's too impossible."

"I don't know what he thinks," said Jack. "But it isn't 'too impossible' at all. It looks as if it had happened."

Richard was now dumb. He realised the depth of the other man's malevolence, and was aghast. Just aghast. Some fear too—and a certain horror, as if human beings had suddenly become horrible to him. Another gulf opened in front of him.

"Then what do you want of me now?" he asked, very coldly.

"Some sort of security, I suppose," said Jack, looking away at the sea.

Richard was silent with rage and cold disgust, and a sort of police-fear.

"Pray what sort of security?" he replied, coldly.

"That's for you to say, maybe. But we want some sort of security that you'll keep quiet, before we let you leave Australia."

Richard's heart blazed in him with anger and disgust.

"You need not be afraid," he said. "You've made it all too repulsive to me now, for me ever to want to open my mouth about it all. You can be quite assured: nothing will ever come out through me."

Jack looked up with a faint, sneering smile.

"And you think we shall be satisfied with your bare word?" he said uglily.

But now Richard looked him square in the eyes.

"Either that or nothing," he replied.

And unconscious of what he was doing, he sat looking direct down into the dark, shifting malice of Jack's eyes, till Jack turned aside. Richard was now so angry and insulted he felt only pure indignation.

"We'll see," said Jack.

Somers did not even heed him. He was too indignant to think of him any more. He only retreated into his own soul, and turned aside, invoking his own soul: "Oh, dark God, smite him over the mouth for insulting me. Be with me, gods of the other world, and strike down these liars."

Harriet came out on to the veranda.

"What are you two men talking about?" she said. "I hear two very cross and snarling voices, though I can't tell what they say."

"I was just saying Mr. Somers can't expect to have it all his own way," said Jack in his low, intense, slightly husky voice, that was now jeering viciously.

"He'll try his best to," said Harriet. "But whatever have you both got so furious about. Just look at Lovat, green with fury. It's really shameful. Men are like impish children—you daren't leave them together for a minute."

"It was about time you came to throw cold water over us," smiled Jack sardonically. Ah, how sardonic he could be: deep, deep and devilish. He too must have a very big devil in his soul. But he never let it out. Or did he? Harriet looked at him, and shuddered slightly. He scared her, she had a revulsion from him. He was a bit repulsive to her. And she knew he had always been so.

"Ah, well!" said Jack. "Cheery-o! We aren't such fools as we seem. The milk's spilt, we won't sulk over it."

"No, don't," cried Harriet. "I hate sulky people."

"So do I, Mrs. Somers, worse than water in my beer," said

Jack genially. "You and me, we're not going to fall out, are we?"

"No," said Harriet. "I don't fall out with people—and I don't let them fall out with me."

"Quite right. Don't give 'em a chance, eh? You're right of it. You and me are pals, aren't we?"

"Yes," said Harriet easily, as if she were talking to some child she must soothe. "We're pals. But why didn't you bring your wife? I'm so fond of her."

"Oh, Vicky's all right. She's A 1 stuff. She thinks the world of you, you know. By golly, she does; she thinks the world of you."

"Then why didn't you bring her to see me?"

"Eh? Why didn't I? Oh—well—let me see—why she'd got her married sister and so forth come to see her, so she couldn't leave them. But she sent her love, and all that sort of sweet nothing, you know. I told her I should never have the face to repeat it, you know. I was to give you *heaps* of love. 'Heaps of love to Mrs. Somers!' Damn it, I said, how do I know she wants me dumping down heaps of love on her. But that was the message—heaps of love to Mrs. Somers, and don't you forget it. I'm not likely to forget it, by gee! There aren't two Mrs. Somers in the universe: I'm ready to bet all I've got on that. Ay, and a bit over. Now, look here, Mrs. Somers, between you and me and the bed-post——"

"Do you mean Lovat is the bed-post?" put in Harriet. "He's silent enough for one."

Jack glanced at Somers, and also relapsed into silence.

CHAPTER XVI

A ROW IN TOWN

THE thing that Kangaroo had to reckon with, and would not reckon with, was the mass-spirit. A collection of men—an accidental gathering—may be just a gathering, drawn by a moment's curiosity, or it may be an audience drawn to hear something, or it may be a congregation, gathered together in some spirit of earnest desire: or it may be just a crowd, inspired by no one motive. The mass-spirit is complex. At its lowest it is a mob. And what is a mob?

To put it as briefly as possible, it is a collection of all the weak souls, sickeningly conscious of their weakness, into a heavy mob, that lusts to glut itself with blind destructive power. Not even vengeance. The spirit of vengeance belongs to a mass which is higher than a mob.

The study of collective psychology to-day is absurd in its inadequacy. Man is supposed to be an automaton working in certain automatic ways when you touch certain springs. These springs are all labelled: they form a keyboard to the human psyche, according to modern psychology. And the chief labels are herd instinct, collective interest, hunger, fear, collective prestige, and so on.

But the only way to make any study of collective psychology is to study the isolated individual. Upon your conception of the single individual, all your descriptions will be based, all your science established. For this reason, the human sciences, philosophy, ethics, psychology, politics, economics, can never be sciences at all. There can never be an exact science dealing with individual life. *L'anatomia presuppone il cadavere:* anatomy presupposes a corpse, says D'Annunzio. You can establish an exact science on a corpse, supposing you start with the corpse, and don't try to derive it from a living creature. But upon life itself, or any instance of life, you cannot establish a science.

Because even science must start from definition, or from precise description. And you can never define or precisely describe any living creature. Iron must remain iron, or cease to exist. But a rabbit might evolve into something which is still rabbit, and yet different from that which a rabbit now is. So how can you define or precisely describe a rabbit? There is always the unstable *creative* element present in life, and this science can never tackle. Science is cause-and-effect.

Before we can begin any of the so-called humane sciences we must take on trust a purely unscientific fact: namely, that every living creature has an individual soul, however trivial or rudimentary, which connects it individually with the source of all life, as man, in the religious terminology, is connected with God, and inseparable from God. So is every creature, even an ant or a louse, individually in contact with the great life-urge which we call God. To call this connection the will-to-live is not quite sufficient. It is more than a will-to-persist. It is a will-to-live in the further sense, a will-to-change, a will-to-evolve, a will towards further creation of the self. The urge towards evolution if you like. But it is more than evolution. There is no simple cause-and-effect sequence. The change from caterpillar to butterfly is not cause and effect. It is a new gesture in creation. Science can wriggle as hard as it likes, but the change from caterpillar to butterfly is utterly unscientific, illogical, and *unnatural*, if we take science's definition of nature. It is an answer to the strange creative urge, the God-whisper, which is the one and only everlasting motive for everything.

So then man. He is said to be a creature of cause-and-effect, or a creature of free-will. The two are the same. Free-will means acting according to reasoned choice, which is a purest instance of cause-and-effect. Logic is the quintessence of cause-and-effect. And idealism, the ruling of life by the instrumentality of the idea, is precisely the mechanical, even automatic cause-and-effect process. The idea, or ideal, becomes a fixed principle, and life, like any other force, is driven into mechanical repetition of given motions—millions of times over and over again—according to the fixed ideal. So, the Christian-democratic world prescribes certain motions, and men proceed to repeat these motions, till they conceive that there *are* no other motions but these. And that is pure automatism. When scientists describe savages, or ancient Egyptians, or Aztecs, they assume that these far-off peoples acted, but in a crude, clumsy way, from the same motives which move us. "Too much ego in his cosmos." Men have had strange, inconceivable motives and impulses, which were just as "right" as ours are. And our "right" motives will cease to activate, even as the lost motives of the Assyrians have ceased. Our "right" and our righteousness will go pop, and there will be another sort of right and righteousness.

The mob, then. Now, the vast bulk of mankind has always been, and always will be, helpless. By which we mean, helpless to interpret the new prompting of the God-urge. The highest function of *mind* is its function of messenger. The curious throbs and pulses of the God-urge in man would go on for ever ignored, if it were not for some few exquisitely sensitive and fearless souls who struggle with all their might to make that strange translation of the low, dark throbbing into open act or speech. Like a wireless message the new suggestion enters the soul, throb-throb, throb-throb-throb. And it beats and beats for years, before the mind, frightened of this new knocking in the dark, can be brought to listen and attend.

For the mind is busy in a house of its own, which house it calls the universe. And how can there be anything outside the universe?

There is though. There is always something outside our universe. And it is always at the doors of the innermost, sentient soul. And there throb-throb, throb-throb-throb, throb-throb. It is like the almost inaudible beating of a wireless machine. Nine hundred and ninety-nine men out of a thousand hear nothing at all. Absolutely nothing. They racket away in their nice, complete, homely universe, running their trains and making their wars and saving the world for democracy. They hear not a thing. A tiny minority of sensitive souls feel the throb, and are frightened, and cry for more virtue, more goodness, more righteousness à la mode. But all the righteousness and goodness in all the world won't answer the throb, or interpret the faint but painful thresh of the message.

There is no Morse code. There never will be. Every new code supersedes the current code. Nowadays, when we feel the throb, vaguely, we cry, "More love, more peace, more charity, more freedom, more self-sacrifice." Which makes matters all the worse, because the new throb interpreted mechanically according to the old code breeds madness and insanity. It may be that there is an insufficient activity of the thyroid glands, or the adrenalin cortex isn't making its secretions, or the pituitary or the pineal body is not working adequately. But this is result, not cause, of our neurasthenia and complexes. The neurasthenia comes from the inattention to the suggestion, or from a false interpretation. The best souls in the world make some of the worst interpretations—like President Wilson—and this is the bitterest tragedy of righteousness. The heroic effort to carry out the old righteousness becomes at last sheer wrongeousness. Men in the past have chosen to be martyred for an unborn truth. But life itself inflicts something worse than martyrdom on them if they will persist too long in the old truth.

Alas, there is no Morse code for interpreting the new life prompting, the new God-urge. And there never will be. It needs a new term of speech invented each time. A whole new concept of the universe gradually born, shedding the old concept.

Well now. There is the dark god knocking afresh at the door. The vast mass hear nothing, but say, "We know all about the universe. Our job is to make a real smart place of it." So they make more aeroplanes and old-age pensions and are furious when Kaiser William interrupts them. The more sensitive hear something, feel a new urge and are uneasy. They cry, "We are not pure in heart. We are too selfish. Let us educate the poor. Let us remove the slums. Let us save the children. Let us spend all we have on the noble work of education." So they spend a bit more than before, but by no means all they have, with the result that now everybody reads the newspapers and discusses world-politics and feel himself most one-sidedly a bit of the great Godhead of the sacred People.

And still the knocking goes on, on, on, till some soul that dares as well as can, listens, and struggles to interpret. Every new word is anathema—bound to be. Jargon, rant, mystical tosh, and so on. Evil, and anti-civilisation. Naturally. For the machine of the human psyche, once wound up to a certain ideal, doesn't want to stop.

And still, all the time, even in the vulgar uneducated—perhaps more in them than in the hearty money-makers of the lower middle-classes—throb-throb-throb goes the god-urge deep in their souls, driving them almost mad. They are quite stone-deaf to any new meaning. They would jeer an attempt at a new interpretation, jeer it to death. So there they are, between the rocky Scylla of the fixed, established ideal, and the whirling Charybdis of the conservative opposition to this ideal. Between these two perils they must pass. For behind them drives the unknown current of the god-urge, on, on through the straits.

They will never get through the straits. They do not know that there *is* any getting through. Scylla must beat Charybdis, and Charybdis must beat Scylla. So the monster of humanity, with a Scylla of an ideal of equality for the head, and a Charybdis of industrialism and possessive conservatism for the tail, howls with frenzy, and lashes the straits till every boat goes down, that tried to make a passage.

Well, Scylla must have it out with Charybdis, that's all, and we must wait outside the straits till the storm is over.

It won't be over yet, though.

Now this is the state of the mass. It is driven, goaded mad at length by the pricking of the God-urge which it will not,

cannot attend to or interpret. It is so goaded that it is mad
with its own wrongs. It is wronged, so wronged that it is mad.

And what is the wrong, pray? The mass doesn't know.
There is no connection at all between the burning, throbbing
unconscious soul and the clear-as-daylight conscious mind.
The whole of Labour, to-day, sees the situation clear as daylight. So does the whole of Capital. And yet the whole of the
daylight situation has really nothing to do with it. It is the
god-urge which drives them mad, the unacknowledged, un-
admitted, non-existent god-urge.

They may become a mob. A mob is like a mass of bullocks
driven to frenzy by some bott-fly, and charging frantically
against the tents of some herdsman, imagining that all the evil
comes out of these tents. There is a gulf between the quivering hurt in the unconscious soul, and the round, flat world of
the visible existence. A sense of weakness and injury, at last
an intolerable sense of wrong, turning to a fiendish madness.
A mad necessity to wreck something, cost what it may. For
only the flat, round, visible world exists.

And yet it is the bott-fly of the Holy Ghost, unlistened to,
that is the real cause of everything.

But the mob has no direction even in its destructive lust. The
vengeful masses *have* direction. And it is no good trying to
reason with them. The mass does not act by reason. A mass
is not even formed by reason. The more intense or extended
the *collective* consciousness, the more does the truly reasonable, individual consciousness sink into abeyance.

The herd instinct, for example, is of many sorts. It has two
main divisions, the fear-instinct, and the aggressive instinct
But the vengeance instinct is not part of the herd instinct.

But consider the mode of communication of herd instinct.
The communication between the individuals in a herd is not
through the *mind*. It is not through anything said or known
It is sub-mental. It is telepathic.

Why does a flock of birds rise suddenly from the tree-tops
all at once, in one spring, and swirl round in one cloud towards
the water? There was no visible sign or communication given
It was a telepathic communication. They sat and waited, and
waited, and let the individual mind merge into a kind of col
lective trance. Then click!—the unison was complete, the
knowledge or suggestion was one suggestion all through, the
action was one action.

This so-called telepathy is the clue to all herd instinct. It is not instinct. It is a vertebral-telegraphy, like radio-telegraphy. It is a complex interplay of vibrations from the big nerve-centres of the vertebral system in all the individuals of the flock, till, click!—there is a unanimity. They have one mind. And this one-mindedness of the many-in-one will last while ever the peculiar pitch of vertebral nerve-vibrations continues unbroken through them all. As the vibration slacks off, the flock falls apart.

This vertebral telepathy is the true means of communication between animals. It is perhaps most highly developed where the brain, the mental consciousness, is smallest. Indeed the two forms of consciousness, mental and vertebral, are mutually exclusive. The highest form of vertebral telepathy seems to exist in the great sperm whales. Communication between these herds of roving monsters is of marvellous rapidity and perection. They are lounging, feeding lazily, individually, in mid-ocean, with no cohesion. Suddenly, a quick thought-wave from the leader-bull, and as quick as answering thoughts the cows and young bulls are ranged, the herd is taking its direction with a precision little short of miraculous. Perhaps water acts as a most perfect transmitter of vertebral telepathy.

This is the famous wisdom of the serpent, this vertebral consciousness and telepathy. This is what makes the magic of a leader like Napoleon—his powers of sending out intense vibrations, messages to his men, without the exact intermediation of mental correspondence. It is not brain-power. In fact, it is, in some ways, the very *reverse* of brain-power: it might be called the acme of stupidity. It is the stupendous wits of brainless intelligence. A marvellous reversion to the pre-mental form of consciousness.

This pre-mental form of consciousness seems most perfect in the great whales: more even in them than in the flocks of migrating birds. After the whales, the herds of wolves and deer and buffaloes. But it is most *absolute* in the cold fishes and serpents, reptiles. The fishes have no other correspondence save this cold, vertebral vibration. And this is, as it were, blind. The fish is absolutely stone-wall limited in its consciousness, to itself. It knows none other. Stony, abstract, cold, alone, the fish has still the power of radio-communication. It is a form of telepathy, like a radium-effluence, vibrating fear principally. Fear is the first of the actuating gods.

Then come the reptiles. They have sex, and dimly, darkly discern the bulk of the answerer. They are drawn to contact. It's the new motive. The fishes are never drawn to contact. Only food and fear. So in the reptiles the second telepathic vibration, the sympathetic, is set up. The primary consciousness is cold, the wisdom is isolated, cold, moon-like, knowing none other: the self alone in knowledge, utterly subtle. But then sex comes upon them, and the isolation is broken. Another flow sets up. They must seek the answerer. It is love.

So, telepathy, communication in the vertebrates. Ants and bees too have a one-conscious vibration. Even they have perfect ganglia-communication. But it is enough to consider the vertebrates.

In the sperm whale, intense is the passion of amorous love, intense is the cold exultance in power, isolate kingship. With the most intense enveloping vibration of possessive and protective love, the great bull encloses his herd into a oneness. And with the intensest vibration of power he keeps it subdued in awe, in fear. These are the two great telepathic vibrations which rule all the vertebrates, man as well as beast. Man, whether in a savage tribe or in a complex modern society, is held in unison by these two great vibrations emitted unconsciously from the leader, the leaders, the governing classes, the authorities. First, the great influence of shadow of power, causing trust, fear and obedience: second, the great influence of protective love, causing productivity and the sense of safety. Those two powerful influences are emitted by men like Gladstone or Abraham Lincoln, against their knowledge, but none the less emitted. Only Gladstone and Lincoln justify themselves in speech. And both insist on the single influence of love, and denounce the influence of fear.

A mob occurs when men turn upon *all* leadership. For true, living activity the mental and the vertebral consciousness should be in harmony. In Cæsar and Napoleon the vertebral influence of power prevailed—and there was a break of balance, and a fall. In Lincoln and President Wilson the vertebral influence of love got out of balance, and there was a fall. There was no balance between the two modes of influence: the mind ran on, as it were, without a brake, towards absurdity. So it ran to absurdity in Napoleon.

Break the balance of the two great controlling influences and you get, not a simple preponderance of the one influence

but a third state, the mob-state. This is the state when the
society tribe or herd degenerates into a mob. In man, the mind
runs on with a sort of terrible automatism, which has no true
connection with the *vertebral* consciousness. The vertebral
inter-communication gradually gathers force, apart from all
mental expression. Its vibration steadily increases till there
comes a sudden click! And then you have the strange pheno-
menon of revolution, like the Russian and the French revolutions. It is a great disruptive outburst. It is a great eruption
against the classes in authority. And it is, finally, a passionate,
mindless vengeance taken by the collective, vertebral psyche
upon the authority of orthodox *mind*. In the Russian revolution it was the *educated* classes that were the enemy really:
the deepest inspiration the hatred of the conscious classes. But
revolution is not a mob-movement. Revolution has direction,
and leadership, however temporary. There is point to its
destructive frenzy.

In the end, it is a question with us to-day whether the masses
will degenerate into mobs, or whether they will still keep a
spark of direction. All great mass uprisings are really acts of
vengeance against the dominant consciousness of the day. It
is the dynamic, vertebral consciousness in man bursting up
and smashing through the fixed, superimposed mental consciousness of mankind, which mental consciousness has de-
generated and become automatic.

The masses are always, strictly, non-mental. Their consciousness is preponderantly vertebral. And from time to time, as
some great life-idea cools down and sets upon them like a cold
crust of lava, the vertebral powers will work below the crust,
apart from the mental consciousness, till they have come to
such a heat of unison and unanimity, such a pitch of vibration
that men are reduced to a great, non-mental oneness as in the
hot-blooded whales, and then, like whales which suddenly
charge upon the ship which tortures them, so they burst upon
the vessel of civilisation. Or like whales that burst up through
the ice that suffocates them, so they will burst up through the
fixed consciousness, the congealed idea which they can now
only blindly react against. At the right moment, a certain cry,
like a war-cry, a catchword, suddenly sounds, and the movement begins.

The purest lesson our era has taught is that man, at his
highest, is an individual, single, isolate, alone, in direct soul-

communication with the unknown God, which prompts within him.

This lesson, however, puts us in danger of conceit, especially spiritual conceit.

In his supreme being, man is alone, isolate, nakedly himself, in contact only with the unknown God.

This is our way of expressing Nirvana.

But just as a tree is only perfect in blossom because it has groping roots, so is man only perfected in his individual being by his groping, pulsing unison with mankind. The unknown God is within, at the quick. But this quick must send down roots into the great flesh of mankind.

In short, the "spirit" has got a lesson to learn: the lesson of its own limitation. This is for the individual. And the infinite, which is Man writ large, or Humanity, has a still bitterer lesson to learn. It is the individual alone who can save humanity alive. But the greatest of great individuals must have deep, throbbing roots down in the dark red soil of the living flesh of humanity. Which is the bitter pill which Buddhists and all advocates of pure *Spirit* must swallow.

In short, man, even the greatest man, does not live only by his spirit and his pure contact with the Godhead—for example, Nirvana. Blessed are the pure in heart, Blessed are the poor in spirit. He is *forced* to live in vivid rapport with the mass of men. If he denies this, he cuts his roots. He intermingles as the roots of a tree interpenetrate the fat, rock-ribbed earth.

How? In this same vertebral correspondence. The mystic may stare at his own navel and try to abstract himself for ever towards Nirvana: it is half at least illusion. There is all the time a powerful, unconscious interplay going on between the vertebral centres of consciousness in all men, a deep, mindless current flashing and quivering through the family, the community, the nation, the continent, and even the world. No man can *really* isolate himself. And this vertebral interplay is the root of our living: must always be so.

And this vertebral interplay is subject to the laws of polarity since it is an inter-communion of active, polarised conscience force. There is a dual polarity, and a dual direction. There is the outward, or downward pulse, in the great motion of sympathy or love, the love that goes out to the weaker, to the poor, to the humble. The vast, prostrate mass now become the positive pole of attraction: woman, the working-classes.

The whole of the great current of vertebral consciousness in mankind is supposed, now, to run in this direction. But the whole movement is but a polarised circuit. Insist on one direction overmuch, derange the circuit, and you have a terrible débâcle. Which brings us to another aspect of relativity: relativity in dynamic living.

When the flow is sympathetic, or love, then the weak, the woman, the masses, assume the positivity. But the balance even is only kept by stern *authority*, the unflinching obstinacy of the return-force, of power.

When the flow is power, might, majesty, glory, then it is a culminating flow towards one individual, through circles of aristocracy towards one grand centre. Emperor, Pope, Tyrant, King: whatever may be. It is the grand obeisance before a master.

In the balance of these two flows lies the secret of human stability. In the absolute triumph of either flow lies the immediate surety of collapse.

We have gone very far in the first direction. Democracy has *almost* triumphed. The only real master left is the boss in industry. And he is to be dethroned. Labour is to wear the absolute crown of the everyday hat. Even the top hat is doomed. Labour shall be its own boss, and possess its own means and ends. The serpent shall swallow itself in a last gulp.

Mastership is based on possessions. To kill mastership you must have communal ownership. Then have it, for this superiority based on possession of money is worse than any of the pretensions of Labour or Bolshevism, strictly. Let the serpent swallow itself. Then we can have a new snake.

The moment Labour takes upon itself to be its own boss, the whole show is up, the end has begun. While ever the existing boss succeeds in hanging on to his money-capital, we get the present conditions of nullity and nagging. We're between the devil and a deep sea.

What Richard wanted was some sort of a new show: a new recognition of the life-mystery, a departure from the dreariness of money-making, money-having, and money-spending. It meant a new recognition of difference, of highness and of lowness, of one man meet for service and another man clean with glory, having majesty in himself, the innate majesty of the purest *individual*, not the strongest instrument, like Napoleon. Not the tuppenny trick-majesty of Kaisers. But the true majesty of the single soul which has all its own weaknesses, but its strength in spite of them, its own lovableness, as well as its might and dread. The single soul that stands naked between the dark God and the dark-blooded masses of men. "Now, Kangaroo," said Richard, "is in a false position. He wants to save property for the property owners, and he wants to save Labour from itself and from the capitalist and the politician and all. In fact, he wants to save everything as we have it, and it can't be done. You can't eat your cake and have it, and I prefer Willie Struthers. Bolshevism is at least not sentimental. It's a last step towards an end, a hopeless end. But better disaster from an equivocal nothingness, like the present. Kangaroo wants to be God Himself, and save everybody, which is just irritating, at last. Kangaroo as God Himself, with a kind marsupial belly, is worse than Struthers' absolute of the People. Though it's a choice of evils, and I choose neither. I choose the Lord Almighty."

Having made up his mind so far, Richard came up to the big mass meeting of Labour in the great Canberra Hall in Sydney. The Labour leaders had lost much ground. Labour was slipping into disorganisation : the property-owning Conservatives and Liberals were just beginning to rejoice again. The reduction of the basic wage had been brought about, a further reduction was announced. At the same time the Government was aiming a strong blow at the Unions. It had pronounced the right of every man to work as he himself chose, and the right of employers to agree with non-union workers as to rate of wages. It had further announced its determination to protect the non-union worker, by holding the union responsible for any attacks on non-union men. The leaders of a union were to be arrested and held responsible for attacks on non-workers. In case of bloodshed and death, they were to be tried for manslaughter or for murder. The first to be arrested should be the chief of the union concerned. After him, his immediate subordinates

Now the sword was drawn, and Labour was up in arms Meetings were held every day. A special meeting wa announced at Canberra Hall, admission by ticket. Somers had asked Jaz if he could get him a ticket, and Jaz had succeeded There were two meetings : one, a small gathering for discussion, at half-past eight in the morning; the other, the mass meeting, at seven at night.

Richard got up in the dark to catch the six o'clock train to

Sydney. It was a dark, cloudy morning—night still—and a few frogs still were rattling away in a hollow towards the sea, like a weird little factory of machines whirring and trilling and screeching in the dark. At the station some miners were filling their tin bottles at the water-tap: pale and extinguished-looking men.

Dawn began to break over the sea, in a bluey-green rift between clouds. There seemed to be rain. The journey was endless.

In Sydney it was raining, but Richard did not notice. He hurried to the hall to the meeting. It lasted only half an hour, but it was straightforward and sensible. When Richard heard the men among themselves, he realised how *logical* their position was, in pure philosophy.

He came out with Jaz, whom he had not seen for a long time. Jaz looked rather pale, and he was very silent, brooding.

"Your sympathy is with Labour, Jaz?"

"My sympathy is with various people, Mr. Somers," replied Jaz, non-communicative.

It was no use talking to him: he was too much immersed.

The morning was very rainy, and Sydney, big city as it is, a real metropolis in Pitt Street and George Street, seemed again like a settlement in the wilderness, without any core. One of the great cities of the world. But without a core: unless, perhaps, Canberra Hall were its real centre. Everybody very friendly and nice. The friendliest country in the world: in some ways, the gentlest. But without a core. There was no heart in it all, it seemed hollow.

With midday came the sun and the clear sky: a wonderful clear sky and a hot, hot sun. Richard bought sandwiches and a piece of apple-turnover, and went into the Palace Gardens to eat them, so that he need not sit in a restaurant. He loathed the promiscuity and publicity of even the good restaurants. The promiscuous feeding gave him a feeling of disgust. So he walked down the beautiful slope to the water again, and sat on a seat by himself, near a clump of strange palm trees that made a weird noise in the breeze. The water was blue and dancing: and again he felt as if the harbour were wild, lost and undiscovered, as it was in Captain Cook's time. The city wasn't real.

In front in the small blue bay lay two little warships, pale grey, with the white flag having the Union Jack in one corner floating behind. And one boat had the Australian flag, with the five stars on a red field. They lay quite still, and seemed as lost as everything else, rustling into the water. Nothing seemed to keep its positive reality, this morning in the strong sun after the rain. The two ships were like bits of palpable memory, that persisted, but were only memory images.

Two tiny birds, one brown, one with a sky-blue patch on his head, like a dab of sky, fluttered and strutted, hoisting their long tails at an absurd angle. They were real: the absurd, sharp, unafraid creatures. They seemed to have no deep natural fear, as creatures in Europe have. Again and again Somers had felt this in Australia: the creatures had no sense of fear as in Europe. There was no animal fear in the air, as there is so deeply in India. Only sometimes a grey metaphysical dread.

"Perhaps," thought he to himself, "this is really the country where men might live in a sort of harmless Eden, once they have settled the old Adam in themselves."

He wandered the hot streets, walked round the circular quay and saw the women going to the ferries. So many women, *almost* elegant. Yet their elegance provincial, without pride, awful. So many *almost* beautiful women. When they were in repose, quite beautiful, with pure, wistful faces, and some nobility of expression. Then, see them change countenance, and it seemed almost always a grimace of ugliness. Hear them speak, and it was startling, so ugly. Once in motion they were not beautiful. Still, when their features were immobile, they were lovely.

Richard had noticed this in many cases. And they were like the birds, quite without fear, impudent, perky, with a strange spasmodic self-satisfaction. Almost every one of the younger women walked as if she thought she was sexually trailing every man in the street after her. And that was absurd, too, because the men seemed more often than not to hurry away and leave a blank space between them and these women. But it made no matter: like madwomen the females, in their quasi-elegance, pranced with that prance of crazy triumph in their own sexual powers which left little Richard flabbergasted.

Hot, big, free-and-easy streets of Sydney: without any sense of an imposition of *control*. No control, everybody going his own ways with alert harmlessness. On the pavement the foot-passengers walked in two divided streams, keeping to the left,

and by their unanimity made it impossible for you to wander
and look at the shops, if the shops happened to be on your
right. The stream of foot passengers flowed over you.

And so it was: far more regulated than London, yet all with
a curious exhilaration of voluntariness that oppressed Richard
like a madness. No control, and no opposition to control.
Policemen were cyphers, not noticeable. Every man his own
policeman. The terrible lift of the *harmless* crowd. The strange
relief from all super-imposed control. One feels the police, for
example, in London, and their civic majesty of authority. But
in Sydney no majesty of authority at all. Absolute freedom
from all that. Great freedom in the air. Yet, if you got into
the wrong stream on the pavement you felt they'd tread you
down, almost unseeing. You just *mustn't* get in the wrong
stream—Liberty!

Yes—the strange unanimity of *harmlessness* in the crowd
had a half-paralysing effect on Richard. "Can it be?" he said
to himself, as he drifted in the strong sun-warmth of the world
after rain, in the afternoon of this strange, antipodal city. "Can
it be that there is any harm in these people at all?"

They were quick, and their manners were, in a free way,
natural and kindly. They might say Right-O, Right you are!—
they did say it, even in the most handsome and palatial banks
and shipping offices. But they were patient and unaffected in
their response. That was the beauty of the men: their absolute lack of affectation, their naïve simplicity, which was at
the same time sensitive and gentle. The gentlest country in the
world. Really, a high pitch of breeding. Good breeding at a
very high pitch, innate, and in its shirt-sleeves.

A strange country. A wonderful country. Who knows what
future it may have? Can a great continent breed a people of
this magic harmlessness without becoming a sacrifice of some
other, external power? The land that invites parasites now—
where parasites breed like nightmares—what would happen if
the power-lust came that way?

Richard bought himself a big, knobbly, green, soft-crusted
apple, at a Chinese shop, and a pretty mother-of-pearl spoon
to eat it with. The queer Chinese, with their gabbling-gobbling
way of speaking—were they parasites too? A strange, strange
world. He took himself off to the gardens to eat his custard
apple—a pudding inside a knobbly green skin—and to relax
into the magic ease of the afternoon. The warm sun, the big,

blue harbour with its hidden bays, the palm trees, the ferry-
steamers sliding flatly, the perky birds, the inevitable shabby-
looking, loafing sort of men strolling across the green slopes,
past the red poinsetta bush, under the big flame tree, under
the blue, blue sky—Australian Sydney, with a magic like sleep,
like sweet, soft sleep—a vast, endless, sun-hot, afternoon sleep
with the world a mirage. He could taste it all in the soft,
sweet, creamy custard apple. A wonderful sweet place to drift
in. But surely a place that will some day wake terribly from
this sleep.

Yet why should it? Why should it not drift marvellously
for ever, with its sun and its marsupials?

The meeting in the evening, none the less, was a wild one.
And Richard could not believe there was any *real* vindictiveness. He couldn't believe that anybody *really* hated anybody.
There was a touch of sardonic tolerance in it all. Oh, that
sardonic tolerance! And at the same time that overwhelming obstinacy and power of endurance. The strange, Australian power of enduring—enduring suffering or opposition or
difficulty—just black enduring. In the long run, just endure.

Richard sat next to Jaz. Jaz was very still, very still indeed,
seated with his hands in his lap.

"Will there be many diggers here?" Lovat asked.

"Oh yes. There's quite a crowd over there, with Jack."

And Richard looked quickly, and saw Jack. He knew Jack
had seen him. But now he was looking the other way. And
again, Richard felt afraid of something.

It was a packed hall, tense. There was plenty of noise and
interruption, plenty of home-thrusts at the speakers from the
audience. But still, that sense of sardonic tolerance, endurance.
"What's the odds, boys?"

Willie Struthers gave the main speech: on the solidarity of
Labour. He sketched the industrial situation, and elaborated
the charge that Labour was cutting its own throat by wrecking
industry and commerce.

"But will anything get us away from this fact, mates," he
said: "that there's never a shop shuts down because it can't
pay the weekly wage-bill. If a shop shuts down, it is because it
can't pay a high enough *dividend*, and there you've got it.

"Australian Labour has set out from the first on the principle
that huge fortunes should not be made out of its efforts. We
have had the obvious example of America before us, and we

have been determined from the start that Australia should not
fall into the hands of a small number of millionaires and a
larger number of semi-millionaires. It has been our idea that
a just proportion of all profits should circulate among the
workers in the form of wages. Supposing the worker *does* get
his pound a day. It is enormous, isn't it! It is preposterous.
Of course it is. But it isn't preposterous for a small bunch
of owners or shareholders to get their ten pounds a day *for
doing nothing.* Sundays included. That isn't preposterous,
is it?

"They raise the plea that their fathers and their forefathers
accumulated the capital by their labours. Well, haven't *our*
fathers and forefathers laboured? Haven't they? And what
have they accumulated? The right to labour on, and be paid
for it what the others like to give 'em.

"We don't want to wreck industry. But, we say, wages shall
go up so that profits shall go down. Why should there be any
profits, after all? Forefathers! Why, we've all had forefathers,
and I'm sure mine worked. Why should there be any profits
at all, I should like to know. And if profits there *must* be, well
then, the profit grabber isn't going to get ten times as much as
the wage-earner, just because he had a few screwing forefathers. We, who work for what we get, are going to see that
the man who doesn't work shall not receive a large income for
not working. If he's *got* to have an income for doing nothing,
let him have no more than what we call wages. The labourer
is worthy of his hire, and the hire is worthy of his labourer.
But I can *not* see that any man is worthy of an unearned income. Let there be no unearned incomes. So much for the
basic wage. We know it is not the basic wage that wrecks
industry. It's big profits. When the profits are not forthcoming
the directors would rather close down. A criminal proceeding.
Because, after all, any big works is run, first, to supply the
community with goods, and second, to give a certain proportion of the community a satisfactory occupation. Whatever
net profits are made are made by cheating the worker and the
consumer, filching a bit from every one of them, no matter
how small a bit. And we will not see wages reduced one
ha'penny, to help to fill the pockets of shareholders——"

"What about your own shares in Nestlés Milk, Willie?"
asked a voice.

"I'll throw them in the fire the minute they're out of

date," said Willie promptly, "they're pretty well waste paper already."

He went on to answer the charges of corruption and "Tammany", with which the Labour Party in Australia had been accused. This led to the point of class hatred.

"It is we who are supposed to foster class hatred," he said. "Now I put it to you. Does the so-called upper class hate us, or do we hate them more? If you'll let me answer, I tell you it's they who do the hating. We don't wear the flesh off our bones hating them. They aren't worth it. They're far beneath hatred.

"We do not want one class only—not your various shades of upper and lower. We want The People—and The People means the worker. I don't mind what a man works at. He can be a doctor or a lawyer even, if men are such fools they must have doctors and lawyers. But look here, mates, what do we all work *for?* For a living? Then why won't a working-man's living wage do for a lawyer? Why not? Perhaps a lawyer makes an ideal of his job. Perhaps he is inspired in his efforts to right the wrongs of his client. Very well: virtue is its own reward. If he wants to be paid for it, it isn't virtue any more. It's dirty trading in justice, or whatever law means.

"Look at your upper classes, mates. Look at your lawyer charging you two guineas for half an hour's work. Look at your doctor scrambling for his guinea a visit. Look at your experts with their five thousand a year. Call these *upper* classes? Upper in what? In the make-and-grab faculties, that's all.

"To hell with their 'upper'. If a working man thinks he'll be in the running, and demand, say, half of what these gentry get, then he's the assassin of his trade and country. It's his business to grovel before these 'upper' gents, is it?

"No, mates, it's his business to rise up and give 'em a good kick in the seats of their pants, to remind them of their bedrock bottoms. You'd think, to hear all the fairy-tales they let off, that their pants didn't have such a region as seats. Like the blooming little angels, all fluttery tops and no bottoms. Don't you be sucked in any more, mates. Look at 'em, and you'll see they've got good, heavy-weight sit-upons, and big, deep trouser pockets next door. That's them. Up-end 'em for once, and look at 'em upside down. Greedy fat-arses, mates, if you'll pardon the vulgarity for once. Greedy fat-arses.

"And that's what we've got to knuckle under to, is it?
They're the upper classes? Them and a few derelict lords and
cuttlefish capitalists. Upper classes? I'm damned if I see much
upper about it, mates. Drop 'em in the sea and they'll float
butt-end uppermost, you see if they don't. For that's where
they keep their fat, like the camel his hump. Upper classes!

"But I wish them no special harm. A bit of a kick in the
rear, to remind them that they've got a rear, a largely kick-
able rear. And then, let them pick themselves up and mingle
with the rest. Give them a living wage, like any other working man. But it's hell on earth to see them floating their fat
bottoms through the upper regions, and just stooping low
enough to lick the cream off things, as it were, and to squeal
if a working man asks for more than a gill of the skilly.

"Work? What is one man's job more than another. Your
Andrew Carnegies and your Rothschilds may be very smart at
their jobs. All right—give 'em the maximum wage. Give 'em
a pound a day. They won't starve on it. And what do they
want with more? A job is nothing but a job, when all's said
and done. And if Mr. Hebrew Rothchild is smart on the
finance job, so am I a smart sheepshearer, hold my own with
any man. And what's the odds? Wherein is Mr. Hebrew, or
Lord Benjamin Israelite any better man than I am? Why does
he want so damned much for his dirty financing, and begrudges
me my bit for shearing ten score o' sheep?

"No, mates, we're not sucked in. It may be Mr. Steeltrust
Carnegie, it may even be Mr. Very-clever Marconi, it may be
Marquis Tribes von Israel; and it certainly *is* Willie Struthers.
Now, mates, I, Willie Struthers, a big fortune I *do not want*.
But I'm damned if I am going to let a few other brainy
vampires suck big fortunes out of me. Not I. I wouldn't be
a man if I did. Upper classes? They've got more greedy brains
in the seats of their pants than in their top storeys.

"We're having no more of their classes and masses. We'll
just put a hook in their trouser-bottoms and hook 'em gently
to earth. That's all. And put 'em on a basic wage like all the
rest: one job, one wage. Isn't that fair? No man can do more
than his best. And why should one poor devil get ten bob for
his level best, and another fat-arse get ten thousand for some
blooming trick? No, no, if a man's a sincere citizen he does
his *best* for the community he belongs to. And his simple wage
is enough for him to live on.

"That's why we'll have a Soviet. Water finds its own level, and so shall money. It shall not be dammed up by a few sly fat-arses much longer. I don't pretend it will be paradise. But there'll be fewer lies about it, and less fat-arsed hypocrisy, and less dirty injustice than there is now. If a man works, he shall not have less than the basic wage, be he even a lying lawyer. There shall be no politicians, thank God. But more than the basic wage also he shall not have. Let us bring things down to a rock-bottom.

"Upper? Why, all their uppishness amounts to is extra special greedy guts, ten-thousand-a-year minimum. Upper classes! Upper classes! Upper arses.

"We'll have a Soviet, mates, and then we shall feel better about it. We s'll be getting nasty tempered if we put it off much longer. Let's know our own mind. We'll unite with the World's Workers. Which doesn't mean we'll take the hearts out of our chests to give it Brother Brown to eat. No, Brother Brown and Brother Yellow had, on the whole, best stop at home and sweep their own streets, rather than come and sweep ours. But that doesn't mean we can't come to more or less of an understanding with them. We don't want to get too much mixed up with them or anybody. But a proper understanding we can have. I don't say, Open the gates of Australia to all the waiting workers of India and China, let alone Japan. But, mates, you can be quite friendly with your neighbour over the fence without giving him the run of your house. And that is International Labour. You have a genuine understanding with your neighbours down the street. You know they won't shy stones through your windows or break into your house at night or kill your children in a dark corner. Why not? Because they're your neighbours and you all have a certain amount of trust in one another. And that is International Labour. That is the World's Workers.

"After all, mates, the biggest part of our waking lives belongs to our work. And certainly the biggest part of our importance is our importance as workers. Mates we are, and we are bound to be, workers, first and foremost. So were our fathers before us, so will our children be after us. Workers first. And as workers, mates. On this everything else depends. On our being workers depends our being husbands and fathers and playmates: nay, our being men. If we are not workers we are not even men, for we can't exist.

"Workers we are, mates, workers we must be, and workers we will be, and there's the end of it. We take our stand on it. Workers first, and whatever soul we have, it must go first into our work. Workers, mates, we are workers. A man is a man because he works. He must work and he does work. Call it a curse, call it a blessing, call it what you like. But the Garden of Eden is gone for ever, and while the ages roll, we must work.

"Let us take our stand on that fact, mates, and trim our lives accordingly. While time lasts, whatever ages come or go, we must work, day in, day out, year in, year out, so for ever. Then, mates, let us abide by it. Let us abide by it, and shape things to fit. No use shuffling, mates. Though you or I may make a little fortune, enough for the moment to keep us in idleness, yet, mates, as sure as ever the sun rises, as long as ever time lasts, the children of men must rise up to their daily toil.

"Is it a curse?—is it a blessing? I prefer to think it is a blessing, so long as, like everything else, it is in just proportion. My happiest days have been shearing sheep, or away in the gold-mines——"

"What, not talking on a platform?" asked a voice.

"No, not talking on a platform. Working along with my mates, in the bush, in the mines, wherever it was. That's where I put my manhood into my work. There I had my mates—my fellow workers. I've had playmates as well. Wife, children, friends—playmates all of them. My fellow workers were my mates.

"So, since workers we are and shall be, till the end of time, let us shape the world accordingly. The world is shaped now for the idlers and the play-babies, and we work to keep *that* going. No, no, mates, it won't do.

"Join hands with the workers of the world: just a fistgrip, as a token and a pledge. Take nobody to your bosom—a worker hasn't got a bosom. He's got a fist, to work with, to hit with, and lastly, to give the tight grip of fellowship to his fellow workers and fellow mates, no matter what colour or country he belongs to. The World's Workers—and since they *are* the world, let them take their own, and not leave it all to a set of silly playboys and Hebrews who are not only silly but worse. The World's Workers—we, who are the world's millions, the world is our world. Let it be so, then. And let us so arrange it.

"What's the scare about being mixed up with Brother Brown

and Chinky and all the rest: the Indians in India, the niggers in the Transvaal, for instance? Aren't we tight mixed up with them as it is? Aren't we in one box with them, in this Empire business? Aren't we all children of the same noble Empire, brown, black, white, green, or whatever colour we may be? We may not, of course, be reposing on the bosom of Brother Brown and Brother Black. But we are pretty well chained at his side in a sort of slavery, slaving to keep this marvellous Empire going, with its out-of-date Lords and its fat-arsed, hypocritical upper classes. I don't know whether you prefer working in the same imperial slave-gang with Brother Brown of India, or whether you'd prefer to shake hands with him as a free worker, one of the world's workers—but——"

"*One!*" came a loud, distinct voice, as if from nowhere, like a gun going off.

"But one or the other——"

"*Two!*" a solid block of men's voices, like a bell.

"One or the other you'll——"

"*Three!*" The voice, like a tolling bell, of men counting the speaker out. It was the Diggers.

A thrill went through the audience. The Diggers sat mostly together, in the middle of the hall, around Jack. Their faces were lit up with a new light. And like a bell they tolled the numbers against the speaker, counting him out, by their moral unison annihilating him.

Willie Struthers, his dark-yellow face gone demonic, stood and faced them. His eyes too had suddenly leaped with a new look: big, dark, glancing eyes, like an aboriginal's, glancing strangely. Was it fear, was it a glancing, gulf-like menace? He stood there, a shabby figure of a man, with undignified legs, facing the tolling enemy.

"*Four!*" came the sonorous, perfect rhythm. It was a strange sound, heavy, hypnotic, trance-like. Willie Struthers stood as if he were fascinated, glaring spell-bound.

"*Five!*" The sound was unbearable, a madness, tolling out of a certain devilish cavern in the back of the men's unconscious mind, in terrible malignancy. The Socialists began to leap to their feet in fury, turning towards the block of Diggers. But the lean, naked faces of the ex-soldiers gleamed with a smiling, demonish light, and from their narrow mouth simultaneously:

"*Six!*"

Struthers, looking as if he were crouching to spring, glared back at them from the platform. They did not even look at him.

"*Seven!*" In two syllables, *Sev-en!*

The sonorous gloating in the sound was unbearable. It was like hammer-strokes on the back of the brain. Everybody had started up save the Diggers. Even Somers was wildly on his feet, feeling as if he could fly, swoop like some enraged bird. But his feeling wavered. At one moment he gloated with the Diggers against the black and devilish figure of the isolated man on the platform, who half-crouched as if he were going to jump, his face black and satanic. And then, as the numbers came, unbearable in its ghastly striking:

"*Eight!*" like some hammer-stroke on the back of his brain it sent him clean mad, and he jumped up into the air like a lunatic, at the same moment as Struthers sprang with a clear leap, like a cat, towards the group of static, grinning ex-soldiers.

There was a crash, and the hall was like a bomb that has exploded. Somers tried to spring forward. In the blind moment he wanted to kill—to kill the soldiers. Jaz held him back, saying something. There was a most fearful roar, and a mad whirl of men, broken chairs, pieces of chairs brandished, men fighting madly with fists, claws, pieces of wood—any weapon they could lay hold of. The red flag suddenly flashing like blood, and bellowing rage at the sight of it. A Union Jack torn to fragments, stamped upon. A mob with many different centres, some fighting frenziedly round a red flag, some clutching fragments of the Union Jack, as if it were God incarnate. But the central heap a mass struggling with the Diggers, in real blood-murder passion, a tense mass with long, naked faces gashed with blood, and hair all wild, and eyes demented, and collars bursted, and arms frantically waving over the dense bunch of horrific life, hands in the air with weapons, hands clawing to drag them down, wrists bleeding, hands bleeding, arms with the sleeves ripped back, white, naked arms with brownish hands, and thud! as the white flesh was struck with a chair leg.

The doors had been flung open—many men had gone out, but more rushed in. The police in blue uniforms and in blue clothes wielding their batons, the whole place gone mad. Richard, small as he was, felt a great frenzy on him, a great longing to let go. But since he didn't *really* know whom he wanted to let go at, he was not quite carried away. And Jaz, quiet, persistent, drew him gradually out into the street. Though not before he had lost his hat and had had his collar torn open, and had received a bang over the forehead that helped to bring him to his senses.

Smash went the lights of the hall—somebody smashing the electric lamps. The place was almost in darkness. It was unthinkable.

Jaz drew Somers into the street, which was already a wide mass of a crowd, and mounted police urging their way to the door, laying about them. The crowd too was waiting to catch fire. Almost beside himself Richard struggled out of the crowd, to get out of the crowd. Then there were shots in the night, and a great howl from the crowd. Among the police on horseback he saw a white hat—a white felt hat looped up at the side—and he seemed to hear the bellowing of a big husky voice. Surely that was Kangaroo, that was Kangaroo shouting. Then there was a loud explosion and a crash—a bomb of some sort.

And Richard suddenly was faint—Jaz was leading him by the arm—leading him away—in the city night that roared from the direction of the hall, while men and women were running thither madly, and running as madly away, and motor-cars came rushing: and even the fire brigade with bright brass helmets—a great rush towards the centre of conflict—and a rush away, outwards. While hats—white hats—Somers, in his dazed condition saw three or four, and they occupied his consciousness as if they were thousands.

"We must go back," he cried. "We must go back to them!"

"What for?" said Jaz. "We're best away."

And he led him sturdily down a side-street, while Somers was conscious only of the scene he had left, and the sound of shots.

They went to one of the smaller, more remote Digger's Clubs. It consisted only of one large room, meeting-room and gymnastics hall in turn, and a couple of small rooms, one belonging to the secretary and the head, and the other a sort of little kitchen with a sink and a stove. The one-armed caretaker was in attendance, but nobody else was there. Jaz and Somers went into the secretary's room, and Jaz made Richard lie down on the sofa.

"Stay here," he said, "while I go and have a look round."

Richard looked at him. He was feeling very sick: perhaps the bang over the head. Yet he wanted to go back into the town, into the mêlée. He felt he would even die if he did so.

But then why not die? Why stay outside the row? He had always been outside the world's affairs.

"I'll come with you again," he said.

"No, I don't want you," snapped Jaz. "I have a few of my own things to attend to."

"Then I'll go by myself," said Richard.

"If I were you I wouldn't," said Jaz.

And Richard sat back feeling very sick, and confused. But such a pain in his stomach, as if something were torn there. And he could not keep still—he wanted to do something.

Jaz poured out a measure of whisky for himself and one for Richard. Then he went out, saying:

"You'd best stay here till I come back, Mr. Somers. I shan't be very long."

Jaz too was very pale, and his manner was furtive, like one full of suppressed excitement.

Richard looked at him, and felt very alien, far from him and everybody. He rose to his feet to rush out again. But the torn feeling at the pit of his stomach was so strong he sat down and shoved his fists in his abdomen, and there remained. It was a kind of grief, a bitter, agonised grief for his fellow-men. He felt it was almost better to die, than to see his fellow-men go mad in this horror. He could hear Jaz talking for some time to the one-armed caretaker, a young soldier who was lame with a bad limp as well as maimed.

"I can't do anything. I can't be on either side. I've got to keep away from everything," murmured Richard to himself. "If only one might die, and not have to wait and watch through all the human horror. They are my fellow-men, they are my fellow-men."

So he lay down, and at length fell into a sort of semi-consciousness, still pressing his fists into his abdomen, and feeling as he imagined a woman might feel after her first child, as if something had been ripped out of him. He was vaguely aware of the rage and chaos in the dark city round him, the terror of the clashing chaos. But what was the good even of being afraid?—even of grief? It was like a storm, in which he could do nothing but lie still and endure and wait. "They also serve who only stand and wait." Perhaps it is the bitterest part, to keep still through it all, and watch and wait. In a numb half-sleep Richard lay and waited—waited for heaven knows what.

It seemed a long time. Then he heard voices. There was Jack and Jaz and one or two others—loud voices. Presently Jack and Jaz came in to him. Jack had a big cut on the chin, and was pale as death. There was blood on his coat, and he had a white pocket-handkerchief round his neck, having lost his collar. He looked with black eyes at Richard.

"What time is it?" asked Richard.

"Blowed if I know," answered Jack, like a drunken man.

"Half-past eleven," said Jaz quietly.

Only an hour—or an hour and a half. Time must have stood still and waited.

"What has happened?" asked Richard.

"Nought!" blurted Jack, still like a drunken man. "Nought happened. Bloody blasted nothing."

"Kangaroo is shot," said Jaz.

"Dead?"

"No—o!" snarled Jack. "No, damn yer, not dead." Somers looked at Jaz.

"They've taken him home—shot in the belly," said Jaz.

"In his bloomin' Kangaroo guts," said Jack. "Ain't much left of the ant that shot 'im, though—neither guts nor marrow."

Richard stared at the two men.

"Are you hurt?" he said to Jack.

"Me? Oh, no, I scratched myself shaving, darling. Making me toilet."

There was silence for some time. Jaz's plump, pale face was still impassive, inscrutable, and his clothing was in order. Jack poured himself a half-glass of neat whisky, put in a little water, and drank it off.

"And Willie Struthers and everybody?" asked Richard.

"Gone 'ome to his missis to have sausage for tea," said Jack.

"Not hurt?"

"Blowed if I know," replied Jack indifferently, "whether he's hurt or not."

"And is the town quiet?" Somers turned to Jaz. "Has everything blown over? What has happened?"

"What has happened exactly I couldn't tell you. I suppose everything is quiet. The police have everything in hand."

"Police!" snarled Jack. "Bloody Johnny Hops! They couldn't hold a sucking pig in their hands, unless somebody hung on to its tail for them. It's our boys who've got things in hand. And hand them over to the Hops."

Somers knew that Johnny Hops was Australian for a police-man. Jack spoke in a suppressed frenzy.

"Was anybody killed?" Somers asked.

"I'm sure I hope so. If I haven't done one or two of 'em in I'm sorry. Damned sorry. Bloody sorry," said Jack.

"I should be careful what I say," said Jaz.

"I know you'd be careful, you Cornish whisper. Careful Jimmy's your name and nation. But I *hope* I did one or two of 'em in. And I *did* do one or two of 'em in. See the brains sputter out of that chap that shot 'Roo?"

"And suppose they arrest you to-night and shove you in gaol for manslaughter?" said Jaz.

"I wouldn't advise anybody to lay as much as a leaf of maidenhair fern on me to-night, much less a finger."

"They might to-morrow. You be still, and go home."

Jack relapsed into a white silence. Jaz went into the common room again, where members dropped in from the town. Apparently everything had gone quiet. It was determined that everybody should go home as quietly and quickly as possible.

Richard found himself in the street with Jaz and Jack, both of whom were silent. They walked briskly through the streets. Groups of people were hurrying silently home. The town felt very dark, and as if something very terrible had happened. A few taxi-cabs were swiftly and furtively running. In George Street and Pitt Street patrols of mounted police were stationed, and the ordinary police were drawn up on guard outside the most important places. But the military had not been called out.

On the whole, the police took as little notice as possible of foot-passengers who were hurrying away home, but occasionally they held up a taxi-cab. Jaz, Jack and Somers proceeded on foot, very quickly and in absolute silence. They were not much afraid of the city authorities: perhaps not so much afraid as were the authorities themselves. But they all instinctively felt it best to keep quiet and unnoticed.

It was nearly one o'clock when they reached Wyewurk. Victoria had gone to bed. She called when she heard the men enter. Evidently she knew nothing of the row.

"Only me and Jaz and Mr. Somers," called Jack. "Don't you stir."

"Of course I must," she cried brightly.

"Don't you move," thundered Jack, and she relapsed into silence. She knew, when he had one of his hell-moods on him, it was best to leave him absolutely alone.

The men drank a little whisky, then sat silent for some time At last Jaz had the energy to say they must go to bed.

"Trot off, Jazzy," said Jack. "Go to bee-by, boys."

"That's what I'm doing," said Jaz, as he retired. He was sleeping the night at Wyewurk, his own home being across the harbour.

Somers still sat inert, with his unfinished glass of whisky, though Jaz said to him pertinently:

"Aren't you retiring, Mr. Somers?"

"Yes," he answered, but didn't move.

The two were left in silence: only the little clock ticking away. Everything quite still.

Suddenly Jack rose and looked at his face in the mirror.

"Nicked a bit out of my chin, seemingly. It was that little bomb that did that. Dirty little swine, to throw a bomb. But it hadn't much kick in it."

He turned round to Somers, and the strangest grin in the world was on his face, all the lines curved upwards.

"Tell you what, boy," he said in a hoarse whisper, "I settled *three* of 'em—three!" There was an indescribable gloating joy in his tones, like a man telling of the good time he has had with a strange mistress—"Gawr, but I was lucky. I got one of them iron bars from the windows, and I stirred the brains of a couple of them with it, and I broke the neck of a third. Why it was as good as a sword to defend yourself with, see——"

He reached his face towards Somers with weird, gruesome exultation, and continued in a hoarse, secret voice:

"Cripes, there *nothing* bucks you up sometimes like killing a man—*nothing*. You feel a perfect *angel* after it."

Richard felt the same torn feeling in his abdomen, and his eyes watched the other man.

"When it comes over you, you know, there's nothing else like it. *I* never knew, till the war. And I wouldn't believe it then, not for many a while. But it's *there*. Cripes, it's there right enough. Having a woman's something, isn't it? But it's a flea-bite, nothing, compared to killing your man when your blood comes up."

And his eyes glowed with exultant satisfaction.

"And the best of it is," he said, "you feel a perfect *angel* after it. You don't feel you've done any harm. Feel as gentle as a lamb all round. I can go to Victoria, now, and be as gentle——" He jerked his head in the direction of Victoria's room. "And you bet she'll like me."

His eyes glowed with a sort of exaltation.

"Killing's natural to a man, you know," he said. "It is just as natural as lying with a woman. Don't you think?"

And still Richard did not answer.

The next morning he left early for Mullumbimby. The newspaper gave a large space to the disturbance, but used the wisest language. "Brawl between Communists and Nationalists at Canberra Hall. Unknown anarchist throws a bomb. Three persons killed and several injured. Ben Cooley, the well-known barrister, receives bullets in the abdomen, but is expected to recover. Police, aided by Diggers, soon restored order."

This was the tone of all the newspapers.

Most blamed the Labour incendiaries, with pious horror— but all declared that the bomb was thrown by some unknown criminal who had intruded himself into the crowd unknown to all parties. There was a mention of shots fired: and a loud shout of accusation against the mounted police from the Labour papers, declaring that these had fired on the crowd. Equally loud denials. A rigorous inquiry was to be instituted, fourteen men were arrested. Jack was arrested as the leader of the men who had counted-out Willie Struthers, but he was released on bail. Kangaroo was said to be progressing, as far as could be ascertained, favourably.

And then the papers had a lovely lot of topics. They could discuss the character and persons of Struthers and Ben Cooley, all except the Radical paper, the *Sun*, praising Ben for his laudable attempt to obtain order by the help of his loyal Diggers. The *Sun* hinted at other things. Then the personal histories of all the men arrested. Jack, the well-known V.C., was cautiously praised.

What was curious was that nobody brought criminal charges against anybody. Jack's iron bar, for instance, nobody mentioned. It was called a stick. Who fired the revolvers, nobody chose to know. The bomb-thrower was an unknown anarchist, probably a new immigrant from Europe. Each side vituperated and poured abuse on the other side. But nobody made any precise, criminal accusations. Most of the prisoners—including Jack—were bound over. Two of them got a year's imprisonment, and five got six months. And the affair began to fizzle down.

A great discussion started on the subject of counting-out. Tales were told, how the sick men in a hospital, from their beds, counted-out an unsympathetic medical officer till the man dared not show his face. It was said the Aussies had once begun to count-out the Prince of Wales. It was in Egypt. The Prince had ridden up to review them, and he seemed to them, as they stood there in the sun, to be supercilious, "superior". This is the greatest offence. So as he rode away like magic they started to count him out. "One! Two! Three!" No command would stop them. The Prince, though he did not know what it meant, instantly felt the thing like a blow, and rode back at once, holding up his hand, to ask what was wrong. And then he was so human and simple that they said they had made a mistake, and they cheered him passionately. But they had *begun* to count him out. And once a man was counted-out he was done: he was dead, he was counted-out. So, news-paper talk.

And Somers, looking through the *Bulletin*, though he could hardly read it now, as if he could not *see* it, in its one level, as if he had gone deaf to its note—was struck by the end of a paragraph:

"This tendency may be noted in the Christianised Melanesian native, in whom an almost uncontrolled desire to kill some-times arises without any provocation whatever. Fortunately for the would-be victim the native often has a premonition of the impending nerve-storm. It is not uncommon for a white man to be addressed thus by his model houseboy, walking behind him on a bush track: 'More better, taubada (master), you walk behind me. Me want make you kill!' In five minutes (If the master has been wise enough to get out of the way) a smiling boy will indicate that his little trouble has been weathered. In these cases Brother Brown is certainly a gentle-man compared to the atavistic white."

CHAPTER XVII

KANGAROO IS KILLED

"DEAR Lovat, also Mrs. Lovat: I don't think it is very nice of you that you don't even call with a tract or a tuberose, when you know I am so smitten. Yours, Kangaroo.

P.S.—Bullets in my marsupial pouch."

Of course Richard went up at once: and Harriet sent a little box with all the different strange shells from the beach. They are curious and interesting for a sick man.

Somers found Kangaroo in bed, very yellow, and thin, almost lantern-jawed, with haunted, frightened eyes. The room had many flowers, and was perfumed with eau-de-Cologne, but through the perfume came an unpleasant, discernable stench. The nurse had asked Richard, please to be very quiet.

Kangaroo put out a thin yellow hand. His black hair came wispily, pathetically over his forehead. But he said, with a faint, husky briskness:

"Hello! Come at last," and he took Somers' hand in damp clasp.

"I didn't know whether you could see visitors," said Richard.

"I can't. Sit down. Behave yourself."

Somers sat down, only anxious to behave himself.

"Harriet sent you such a silly present," he said. "Just shells we have picked up from the shore. She thought you might like to play with them on the counterpane——"

"Like that sloppy Coventry Patmore poem. Let me look."

The sick man took the little Sorrento box with its inlaid design of sirens and peered in at the shells.

"I can smell the sea in them," he said hoarsely.

And very slowly he began to look at the shells, one by one. There were black ones like buds of coal, and black ones with a white spiral thread, and funny knobbly black and white ones, and tiny purple ones, and a bright sea-orange, semi-transparent clamp shell, and little pink ones with long, sharp points, and glass ones, and lovely pearly ones, and then those that Richard had put in, worn shells like sea-ivory, marvellous substance, with all the structure showing; spirals like fairy staircases, and long, pure phallic pieces that were the centres of big shells, from which the whorl was all washed away: also curious flat, oval discs, with a lovely whorl traced on them, and an eye in the centre. Richard liked these especially.

Kangaroo looked at them briefly, one by one, as if they were bits of uninteresting printed paper.

"Here, take them away," he said, pushing the box aside. And his face had a faint spot of pink in the cheeks.

"They may amuse you some time when you are alone," said Richard, apologetically.

"They make me know I have never been born," said Kangaroo, huskily.

Richard was startled, and he didn't know what to answer. So he sat still, and Kangaroo lay still, staring blankly in front of him. Somers could not detach his mind from the slight, yet pervading sickening smell.

"My sewers leak," said Kangaroo bitterly, as if divining the other's thought.

"But they will get better," said Richard.

The sick man did not answer, and Somers just sat still,

"Have you forgiven me?" asked Kangaroo, looking at Somers.

"There was nothing to forgive," said Richard, his face grave and still.

"I knew you hadn't," said Kangaroo. Richard knitted his brows. He looked at the long, yellow face. It was so strange and so frightening to him.

"You bark at me as if I were Little Red Riding-hood," he said, smiling. Kangaroo turned dark, inscrutable eyes on him.

"Help me!" he said, almost in a whisper. "Help me."

"Yes," said Richard.

Kangaroo held out his hand: and Richard took it. But not without a slight sense of repugnance. Then he listened to the faint, far-off noises of the town, and looked at the beautiful flowers in the room : violets, orchids, tuberoses, delicate yellow and red roses, Iceland poppies, orange like transmitted light, lilies. It was like a tomb, like a mortuary, all the flowers, and that other faint, sickening odour.

"I am not wrong, you know," said Kangaroo.

"No one says you are," laughed Richard gently.

"I am not wrong. Love is still the greatest." His voice sank in its huskiness to a low resonance. Richard's heart stood still. Kangaroo lay quite motionless, but with some of the changeless pride which had lent him beauty, at times, when he was himself. The Lamb of God grown into a sheep. Yes, the nobility.

"You heard Willie Struthers' speech?" said Kangaroo, his face changing as he looked up at Somers.

"Yes."

"Well?"

"It seemed to me logical," said Richard, not knowing how to answer.

"Logical!" Even Kangaroo flickered with a surprise. "You and logic!"

"You see," said Richard very gently, "the educated world has preached the divinity of work at the lower classes. They broke them in, like draught-horses, put them all in the collar and set them all between the shafts. There they are, all broken in, *workers*. They are conscious of nothing save that they are workers. They accept the fact that nothing is divine but work : work being service, and service being love. The highest is work. Very well then, accept the conclusion if you accept the premises. The working classes are the highest, it is for them to inherit the earth. You can't deny that, if you assert the sacredness of work."

He spoke quietly, gently. But he spoke because he felt it was kinder, even to the sick man, than to avoid discussion altogether.

"But I don't believe in the sacredness of work, Lovat," said Kangaroo.

"No, but they believe it themselves. And it follows from the sacredness of love."

"I want them to be men, men, men—not implements at a job." The voice was weak now, and took queer, high notes.

"Yes, I know. But men inspired by love. And love has only service as its means of expression."

"How do you know? You never love," said Kangaroo in a faint, sharp voice. "The joy of love is in being with the beloved —as near as you can get—'And I, if I be lifted up, will draw all men unto me.'—For life, for life's sake, Lovat, not for work. Lift them up, that they may live."

Richard was silent. He knew it was no good arguing.

"Do you think it can't be done?" asked Kangaroo, his voice growing fuller. "I hope I may live to show you. The working men have not realised yet what love is. The perfect love that men may have for one another, passing the love of women. Oh, Lovat, they still have that to experience. Don't harden your heart. Don't stiffen your neck before your old Jewish Kangaroo. You know it is true. Perfect love casteth out fear, Lovat. Teach a man how to love his mate, with a pure and fearless love. Oh, Lovat, think what can be done that way!"

Somers was very pale, his face set.

"Say you believe me. Say you believe me. And let us bring it to pass together. If I have you with me I know we can do it. If you had been with me this would never have happened to me."

His face changed again as if touched with acid at the thought. Somers sat still, remote. He was distressed, but it made him feel more remote.

"What class do you feel that you belong to, as far as you belong to any class?" asked Kangaroo, his eyes on Richard's face.

"I don't feel I belong to any class. But as far as I *do* belong— it is to the working classes. I know that. I can't change."

Kangaroo watched him eagerly.

"I wish I did," he said, eagerly. Then, after a pause, he added: "They have never known the full beauty of love, the working classes. They have never admitted it. Work, bread has always stood first. But we can take away that obstacle. Teach them the beauty of love between men, Richard, teach them the highest—greater love than this hath no man—teach them how to love their own mate, and you will solve the problem of work for ever. Richard, this is true, you know it is true. How beautiful it would be! How beautiful it would be! It would complete the perfect circle——"

His voice faded down into a whisper, so that Somers seemed to hear it from far off. And it seemed like some far-off voice of annunciation. Yet Richard's face was hard and clear and sea-bitter as one of the worn shells he had brought.

"The faithful, fearless love of man for man," whispered Kangaroo, as he lay with his dark eyes on Richard's face, and the wisp of hair on his forehead. Beautiful, he was beautiful again, like a transfiguration.

"We've got to save the People, we've got to do it. And when shall we begin, friend, when shall we begin, you and I?" he repeated in a sudden full voice. "Only when we dare to lead them, Lovat," he added in a murmur. "The love of man for wife and children, the love of man for man, so that each would lay down his life for the other, then the love of man for beauty, for truth, for the Right. Isn't that so? Destroy no love. Only open the field for further love."

He lay still for some moments after this speech, that ended in a whisper almost. Then he looked with a wonderful smile at Somers, without saying a word, only smiling from his eyes, strangely, wonderfully. But Richard was scared.

"Isn't that all honest injun, Lovat?" he whispered playfully

"I believe it is," said Richard, though with unchanging face. His eyes, however, were perplexed and tormented.

"Of course you do. Of course you do," said Kangaroo softly. "But you are the most obstinate little devil and child that ever opposed a wise man like me. For example, don't you love me in your heart of hearts, only you daren't admit it? I know you do. I know you do. But admit it, man, admit it, and the world will be a bigger place to you. You are afraid of love."

Richard was more and more tormented in himself.

"In a way, I love you, Kangaroo," he said. "Our souls are alike somewhere. But it is true I don't *want* to love you."

And he looked in distress at the other man.

Kangaroo gave a real little laugh.

"Was ever woman so coy and hard to please!" he said, in a warm, soft voice. "Why don't you want to love me, you stiff-necked and uncircumcised Philistine? Don't you want to love Harriet, for example?"

"No, I don't want to love anybody. Truly. It simply makes me frantic and murderous to have to feel loving any more."

"Then why did you come to me this morning?"

The question was pertinent. Richard was baffled.

"In a way," he said vaguely, "because I love you. But love makes me feel I should die."

"It is your wilful refusal of it," said Kangaroo, a little wearily. "Put your hand on my throat, it aches a little."

He took Richard's hand and laid it over his warm, damp sick throat, there the pulse beat so heavy and sick, and the Adam's apple stood out hard.

"You must be still now," said Lovat, gentle like a physician.

"Don't let me die!" murmured Kangaroo, almost inaudible, looking into Richard's muted face. The white, silent face did not change, only the blue-grey eyes were abstract with thought. He did not answer. And even Kangaroo dared not ask for an answer.

At last he let go Richard's hand from his throat. Richard withdrew it, and wanted to wipe it on his handkerchief. But he refrained, knowing the sick man would notice. He pressed it very secretly, quietly, under his thigh, to wipe in on his trousers.

"You are tired now," he said softly.

"Yes."

"I will tell the nurse to come?"

"Yes."

"Good-bye—be better," said Richard sadly, touching the man's cheek with his finger-tips slightly. Kangaroo opened his eyes with a smile that was dark as death. "Come again," he whispered, closing his eyes once more. Richard went blindly to the door. The nurse was there waiting.

Poor Richard, he went away almost blinded with stress and grief and bewilderment. Was it true what Kangaroo had said? Was it true? Did he, Richard, love Kangaroo? Did he love Kangaroo, and deny it? And was the denial just a piece of fear. Was it just fear that made him hold back from admitting his love for the other man?

Fear? Yes, it was fear. But then, did he not believe also in the God of fear? There was not only one God. There was not only the God of love. To insist that there is only one God, and that God the source of Love, is perhaps as fatal as the complete denial of God, and of all mystery. He believed in the God of fear, of darkness, of passion, and of silence, the God that made a man realise his own sacred aloneness. If Kangaroo could have realised that too, then Richard felt he would have loved him, in a dark, separate, other way of love. But never this all-in-all thing.

As for politics, there was so little to choose, and choice meant nothing. Kangaroo and Struthers were both right, both of them. Lords or doctors or Jewish financiers *should* not have more money than a simple working man, just because they were lords and doctors and financiers. If service was the all in all it was absolutely wrong. And Willie Struthers was right.

The same with Kangaroo. If love was the all in all, then the great range of love was complete as he put it: a man's love for wife and children, his sheer, confessed love for his friend, his mate, and his love for beauty and truth. Whether love was all in all or not, this was the great, wonderful range of love, and love was not complete short of the whole.

But—but something else was true at the same time. Man's isolation was always a supreme truth and fact, not to be forsworn. And the mystery of apartness. And the greater mystery of the dark God beyond a man, the God that gives a man passion, and the dark, unexplained blood-tenderness that is deeper than love, but so much more obscure, impersonal, and the brave, silent blood-pride, knowing his own separateness, and the sword-strength of his derivation from the dark God.

This dark, passionate religiousness and inward sense of an in-welling magnificence, direct flow from the unknowable God, this filled Richard's heart first, and human love seemed such a fighting for candle-light, when the dark is so much better. To meet another dark worshipper, that would be the best of human meetings. But strain himself into a feeling of absolute human love, he just couldn't do it.

Man's ultimate love for man? Yes, yes, but only in the separate darkness of man's love for the present, unknowable God. Human love, as a god-act, very well. Human love as a ritual offering to the God who is out of the light, well and good. But human love as an all-in-all, ah, no, the strain and the un-reality of it were too great.

He thought of Jack, and the strange, unforgettable up-tilted grin on Jack's face as he spoke of the satisfaction of killing. This was true, too. As true as love and loving. Nay, Jack was a killer in the name of Love. That also has come to pass again.

"It is the collapse of the love-ideal," said Richard to himself. "I suppose it means chaos and anarchy. Then there will have to be chaos and anarchy: in the name of love and equality. The only thing one can stick to is one's own isolate being, and the God in whom it is rooted. And the only thing to look to is the God who fulfils one from the dark. And the only thing to wait for is for men to find their aloneness and their God in the darkness. Then one can meet as worshippers, in a sacred con-tact in the dark."

Which being so, he proceeded, as ever, to try to disentangle himself from the white octopus of love. Not that even now he dared quite deny love. Love is perhaps an eternal part of life. But it is only a part. And when it is treated as if it were a whole, it becomes a disease, a vast white strangling octopus. All things are relative, and have their sacredness in their true relation to all other things. And he felt the light of love dying out in his eyes, in his heart, in his soul, and a great, healing darkness taking its place, with a sweetness of everlasting alone-ness, and a stirring of dark blood-tenderness, and a strange, soft iron of ruthlessness.

He fled away to be by himself as much as he could. His great relief was the shore. Sometimes the dull exploding of the waves was too much for him, like hammer-strokes on the head. He tried to flee inland. But the shore was his great solace, for all that. The huge white rollers of the Pacific breaking in a white, soft, snow-rushing wall, while the thin spume flew back to sea like a combed mane, combed back by the strong, cold land wind.

The thud, the pulse of the waves: that was his nearest throb of emotion. The other emotions seemed to abandon him. So suddenly, and so completely, to abandon him. So it was when he got back from Sydney and, in the night of moonlight, went down the low cliff to the sand. Immediately the great rhythm and ringing of the breakers obliterated every other feeling in his breast, and his soul was a moonlit hollow with the waves striding home. Nothing else.

And in the morning the yellow sea faintly crinkled by the inrushing wind from the land, and long, straight lines on the lacquered meadow, long, straight lines that reared at last in green glass, then broke in snow, and slushed softly up the sand. Sometimes the black, skulking fin of a shark. The water was very clear, very green, like bright green glass. Another big fish with humpy sort of fins sticking up, and horror, in the green water a big red mouth wide open. One day the fins of dolphins, near, near, it seemed almost over the sea edge. And then, suddenly, oh, wonder, they were caught up in the green wall of the rising water, and there for a second they hung in the watery, bright green pane of the wave, five big dark dolphins, a little crowd, with their sharp fins and blunt heads, a little sea-crowd in the thin, upreared sea. They flashed with a sharp black motion as the great wave curled to break. They flashed in-sea, flashed from the foamy horror of the land. And there they were, black little school, away in the lacquered water, panting, Richard imagined, with the excitement of the escape. Then one of the bold bucks came back to try again, and he jumped clean out of the water, above a wave, and kicked his heels as he dived in again.

The sea-birds were always wheeling: big, dark-backed birds like mollyhawks and albatrosses with a great spread of wings: and the white gleaming gannets, silvery as fish in the air. In they went, suddenly, like bombs into the wave, spitting back the water. Then they slipped out again, slipped out of the ocean with a sort of sly exultance.

And ships walked on the wall-crest of the sea, shedding black smoke. A vast, hard, high sea, with tiny clouds like mirage islets away far, far back, beyond the edge.

So Richard knew it, as he sat and worked on the veranda or

sat at table in the room and watched through the open door.
But it was usually in the afternoons he went down to it.

It was his afternoon occupation to go down to the sea's edge
and wander slowly on the firm sand just at the foam-edge.
Sometimes the great waves were turning like mill-wheels white
all down the shore. Sometimes they were smaller, more confused, as the current shifted. Sometimes his eyes would be on
the sand, watching the wrack, the big bladder-weed thrown up,
the little sponges like short clubs rolling in the wind, and once
only, those fairy blue wind-bags like bags of rainbow with long
blue strings.

He knew all the places where the different shells were found,
the white shells and the black and the red, the big rainbow
scoops and the innumerable little black snails that lived on the
flat rocks in the little pools. Flat rocks ran out near the coal-
jetty, and between them little creeks of black, round, crunchy
coal-pebbles, sea-coal. Sometimes there would be a couple of
lazy, beach-combing men picking the biggest pebbles and putting them into sacks.

On the flat rocks were pools of clear water, that many a
time he stepped into, because it was invisible. The coloured
pebbles shone, the red anemones pursed themselves up. There
were hideous stumpy little fish that darted swift as lightning—
grey, with dark stripes. An urchin said they were called toads.
"Yer can't eat 'em. Kill yer if y' do. Yer c'nt eat black fish.
See me catch one o' these toads!" All this in a high shrill
voice above the waves. Richard admired the elfish self-
possession of the urchin, alone on the great shore all day,
like a little wild creature himself. But so the boys were: such
wonderful little self-possessed creatures. It was as if nobody
was responsible for them, so they learned to be responsible for
themselves, like young elf creatures, as soon as they were
hatched. They liked Richard, and patronised him in a friendly,
half-shy way. But it was they who were the responsible party,
the grown-up they treated with a gentle, slightly off-handed
indulgence. It always amused friend Richard to see these
Australian children bearing the responsibility of their parents.
'He's only a poor old Dad, you know. Young fellow like me's
got to keep an eye on him, see he's all right." That seemed to
be the tone of the urchins of ten and eleven. They were charming: much nicer than the older youths, or the men.

The jetty straddled its huge grey timbers, like a great bridge,

across the sands and the flat rocks. Under the bridge it was
rather dark, between the great trunk-timbers. But here Richard
found the best of the flat, oval disc-shells with the whorl and
the blue eye. By the bank hung curtains of yellowish creeper,
and a big, crimson-pink convolvulus flowered in odd tones. An
aloe sent up its tall spike, and died at its base. A little bare
grassy headland came out, and the flat rocks ran out dark to
sea, where the white waves prowled on three sides.

Richard would drift out this way, right into the sea, on a
sunny afternoon. On the flat rocks, all pocketed with limpid
pools, the sea-birds would sit with their backs to him, oblivious.
Only an uneasy black bird with a long neck, squatting among
the gulls, would wriggle his neck as the man approached. The
gulls ran a few steps, and forgot him. They were mostly real
gulls, big and pure as grey pearl, suave and still, with a *mâte*
gleam, like eggs of the foam in the sun on the rocks. Slowly
Richard strayed nearer. There were little browner birds
huddled, and further, one big, dark-backed bird. There they
all remained, like opalescent whitish bubbles on the dark, flat,
ragged wet-rock, in the sun, in the sea sleep. The black bird
rose like a duck, flying with its neck outstretched, more timid
than the rest. But it came back. Richard drew nearer and
nearer, within six yards of the sea-things. Beyond, the everlasting low white wall of foam, rustling to the flat-rock. Only
the sea.

The black creature rose again, showing the white at his side,
and flying with a stretched-out neck, frightened-looking, like a
duck. His mate rose too. And then all the gulls, flying low in
a sort of protest over the foam-tips. Richard had it all to himself—the ever-unfurling water, the ragged, flat, square-holed
rocks, the fawn sands inland, the soft sand-bank, the sere flat
grass where ponies wandered, the low, red-painted bungalows
squatting under coral trees, the ridge of tall, wire-thin trees
holding their plumes in tufts at the tips, the stalky cabbage
palms beyond in the hollow, clustering, low, whitish zinc roofs
of bungalows, at the edge of the dark trees—then the trees in
darkness swooping up to the wall of the tors, that ran a waving
skyline sagging southwards. Scattered, low, frail-looking
bungalows with whitish roofs and scattered dark trees among.
A plume of smoke beyond, out of the scarp front of trees.
Near the sky, dark, old, aboriginal rocks. Then again all the
yellowish fore-front of the sea, yellow bare grass, the home-

stead with leafless coral trees, the ponies above the sands, the pale fawn foreshore, the sea, the floor of wet rock.

He had it all to himself. And there, with his hands in his pockets, he drifted into indifference. The far-off, far-off, far-off indifference. The world revolved and revolved and disappeared. Like a stone that has fallen into the sea, his old life, the old meaning, fell, and rippled, and there was vacancy, with the sea and the Australian shore in it. Far-off, far-off, as if he had landed on another planet, as a man might land after death. Leaving behind the body of care. Even the body of desire. Shed. All that had meant so much to him, shed. All the old world and self of care, the beautiful care as well as the weary care, shed like a dead body. The landscape?—he cared not a thing about the landscape. Love?—he was absolved from love, as if by a great pardon. Humanity?—there was none. Thought?—fallen like a stone into the sea. The great, the glamorous past?—worn thin, frail, like a frail, translucent film of shell thrown up on the shore.

To be alone, mindless and memoryless between the sea, under the sombre wall-front of Australia. To be alone with a long, wide shore and land, heartless, soulless. As alone and as absent and as present as an aboriginal dark on the sand in the sun. The strange falling-away of everything. The cabbage-palms in the sea-wind were sere like old mops. The jetty straddled motionless from the shore. A pony walked on the sand snuffing the scaweed.

The past all gone so frail and thin. "What have I cared about, what have I cared for? There is nothing to care about." Absolved from it all. The soft, blue, humanless sky of Australia, the pale, white unwritten atmosphere of Australia. Tabula rasa. The world a new leaf. And on the new leaf, nothing. The white clarity of the Australian, fragile atmosphere. Without a mark, without a record.

"Why have I cared? I don't care. How strange it is here, to be soul-less and alone."

That was the perpetual refrain at the back of his mind. To be soul-less and alone, by the Southern Ocean, in Australia.

"Why do I wrestle with my soul? I have no soul."

Clear as the air about him this truth possessed him.

"Why do I talk of the soul? My soul is shed like a sheath. I am soulless and alone, soulless and alone. That which is soulless is perforce alone."

The sun was curving to the crest of the dark ridge. As soon as the sun went behind the ridge, shadow fell on the shore, and a cold wind came, he would go home. But he wanted the sun not to sink—he wanted the sun to stand still, for fear it might turn back to the soulful world where love is and the burden of bothering.

He saw something clutch in a pool. Crouching, he saw a horror—a dark-grey, brown-striped octopus thing with two smallish, white beaks or eyes, living in a cranny of a rock in a pool. It stirred the denser, viscous pool of itself and unfurled a long dark arm through the water, an arm studded with bright, orange-red studs or suckers. Then it curled the arm in again, cuddling close. Perhaps a sort of dark shore octopus, star-fish coloured amid its darkness. It was watching him as he crouched. He dropped a snail-shell near it. It huddled closer, and one of the beak-like white things disappeared; or were they eyes? Heaven knows. It eased out again, and from its dense jelly mass another thick dark arm swayed out, studded with the sea-orange studs. And he crouched and watched, while the white water hissed nearer to drive him away. Creatures of the sea! Creatures of the sea! The sea-water was round his boots, he rose with his hands in his pockets, to wander away.

The sun went behind the coal-dark hill, though the waves still glowed white-gold, and the sea was dark blue. But the shore had gone into shadow, and the cold wind came at once, like a creature that was lying in wait. The upper air seethed, seemed to hiss with light. But here was shadow, cold like the arm of the dark octopus. And the moon already in the sky.

Home again. But what was home? The fish has the vast ocean for home. And man has timelessness and nowhere. "I won't delude myself with the fallacy of home," he said to himself. "The four walls are a blanket I wrap around in, in timelessness and nowhere, to go to sleep."

Back to Harriet, to tea. Harriet? Another bird like himself. If only she wouldn't speak, talk, feel. The weary habit of talking and having feelings. When a man has no soul he has no feelings to talk about. He wants to be still. And "meaning" is the most meaningless of illusions. An outworn garment.

Harriet and he? It was time they both agreed that nothing has any meaning. Meaning is a dead letter when a man has no soul. And speech is like a volley of dead leaves and dust stifling the air. Human beings should learn to make weird, wordless cries, like the animals, and cast off the clutter of words.

Old dust and dirt of corpses: words and feelings. The decomposed body of the past whirling and choking us, language, love, and meaning. When a man loses his soul he knows what a small, weary bit of clock-work it was. Who dares to be soulless finds the new dimension of life.

Home, to tea. The clicking of the clock. Tic-tac! Tic-tac! The clock. Home to tea. Just for clockwork's sake.

No home, no tea. Insouciant soullessness. Eternal indifference. Perhaps it is only the great pause between carings. But it is only in this pause that one finds the meaninglessness of meanings—like old husks which speak dust. Only in this pause that one finds the meaninglessness of meanings, and the other dimension, the reality of timelessness and nowhere. Home to tea! Do you hear the clock tick? And yet there is timelessness and nowhere. And the clock means nothing with its ticking. And nothing is so meaningless as meanings.

Yet Richard meandered home to tea. For the sun had set, the sea of evening light was going pale blue, fair as evening, faintly glazed with yellow: the eastern sky was a glow of rose and smoke blue, a band beyond the sea, while from the dark land-ridge under the western sky an electric fierceness still rushed up past a small but vehement evening star. Somewhere among it all the moon was lying.

He received another summons to go to Kangaroo. He didn't want to go. He didn't want any more emotional stress of any sort. He was sick of having a soul that suffered or responded. He didn't want to respond any more, or to suffer any more. Saunter blindly and obstinately through the days.

But he set off. The wattle-bloom—the whitish, mealy ones— were aflower in the bush, and at the top of huge poles of stems, big, blackish-crimson buds and flowers, flowers of some sort, shot up out of a clump of spear-leaves. The bush was in flower. The sky above was a tender, virgin blue, the air was pale with clarity, the sun moved strong, yet with a soft and cat-like motion through the heavens. It was spring. But still the bush kept its sombreness along all the pellucid ether: the eternally unlighted bush.

What was the good of caring? What was the point of caring? As he looked at the silent, morning bush grey-still in the translucency of the day, a voice spoke quite aloud in him. What was the good of caring, of straining, of stressing? Not the slightest good. The vast lapse of time here—and white men thrown in like snow into dusky wine, to melt away and disappear, but to cool the fever of the dry continent. Afterwards —afterwards—in the far-off, far-off afterwards, a different sort of men might arise to a different sort of care. But as for now— like snow in aboriginal wine one could float and deliciously melt down, to nothingness, having no choice.

He knew that Kangaroo was worse. But he was startled to find him looking a dead man. A long, cadaverous yellow face, exactly the face of a dead man, but with an animal's dark eyes. He did not move. But he watched Richard come forward from the door. He did not give him his hand.

"How are you?" said Richard gently.

"Dying." The one word from the discoloured lips.

Somers was silent, because he knew it was only too true. Kangaroo's dark eyebrows above his motionless dark eyes were exactly like an animal that sulks itself to death. His brow was just sulking to death, like an animal.

Kangaroo glanced up at Somers with a rapid turn of the eyes. His body was perfectly motionless.

"Did you know I was dying?" he asked.

"I was afraid."

"Afraid! You weren't afraid. You were glad. They're all glad." The voice was weak, hissing in its sound. He seemed to speak to himself.

"Nay, don't say that."

Kangaroo took no notice of the expostulation. He lay silent.

"They don't want me," he said.

"But why bother?"

"I'm dying! I'm dying! I'm dying!" suddenly shouted Kangaroo, with a breaking and bellowing voice that nearly startled Richard out of his skin. The nurse came running in, followed by Jack.

"Mr. Cooley! Whatever it is?" said the nurse.

He looked at her with long, slow, dark looks.

"Statement of fact," he said in his faint, husky voice.

"*Don't* excite yourself," pleaded the nurse. "You *know* it hurts you. Don't think about it, don't. Hadn't you perhaps best be left alone?"

"Yes, I'd better go," said Richard, rising.

"I want to say good-bye to you," said Kangaroo faintly, looking up at him with strange, beseeching eyes.

Richard, very pale at the gills, sat down again in the chair.
Jack watched them both, scowling.

"Go out, nurse," whispered Kangaroo, touching her hand
with his fingers, in a loving kind of motion. "I'm all right."

"Oh, Mr. Cooley, *don't* fret, *don't*," she pleaded.

He watched her with dark, subtle, equivocal eyes, then
glanced at the door. She went, obedient, and Jack followed
her.

"Good-bye, Lovat!" said Kangaroo in a whisper, turning his
face to Somers and reaching out his hand. Richard took the
clammy, feeble hand. He did not speak. His lips were closed
firmly, his face pale and proud looking. He looked back into
Kangaroo's eyes, unconscious of what he saw. He was only
isolated again in endurance. Grief, torture, shame, seethed low
down in him. But his breast and shoulders and face were hard
as if turned to rock. He had no choice.

"You've killed me. You've killed me, Lovat!" whispered
Kangaroo. "Say good-bye to me. Say you love me now you've
done it, and I won't hate you for it." The voice was weak and
tense.

"But *I* haven't killed you, Kangaroo. I wouldn't be here
holding your hand if I had. I'm only so sorry some other
villain did such a thing." Richard spoke very gently, like a
woman.

"Yes, you've killed me," whispered Kangaroo hoarsely.

Richard's face went colder, and he tried to disengage his
hand. But the dying man clasped him with suddenly strong
fingers.

"No, no," he said fiercely. "Don't leave me now. You must
stay with me. I shan't be long—and I need you to be there."

There ensued a long silence. The corpse—for such it seemed
—lay immobile and obstinate. Yet it did not relax into death.
And Richard could not go, for it held him. He sat with his
wrist clasped by the clammy thin fingers, and he could not go.

Then again the dark, mysterious, animal eyes turned up to
his face.

"Say you love me, Lovat," came the hoarse, penetrating
whisper, seeming even more audible than a loud sound.

And again Lovat's face tightened with torture.

"I don't understand what you mean," he said with his lips.

"Say you love me." The pleading, penetrating whisper seemed to sound inside Somers' brain. He opened his mouth to say it. The sound "I——" came out. Then he turned his face aside and remained open-mouthed, blank.

Kangaroo's fingers were clutching his wrist, the corpse-face was eagerly upturned to his. Somers was brought to by a sudden convulsive gripping of the fingers around his wrist. He looked down. And when he saw the eager, alert face, yellow, long, Jewish, and somehow ghoulish, he knew he could not say it. He didn't love Kangaroo.

"No," he said, "I can't say it."

The sharpened face, that seemed to be leaping up to him, or leaping up at him, like some snake striking, now seemed to sink back and go indistinct. Only the eyes smouldered low down out of the vague yellow mass of the face. The fingers slackened, and Richard managed to withdraw his wrist. There was an eternity of grey silence. And for a long time Kangaroo's yellow face seemed sunk half visible under a shadow, as a dusky cuttle-fish under a pool, deep down. Then slowly, slowly it came to the surface again, and Richard braced his nerves.

"You are a little man, a little man, to have come and killed me," came the terrible, pathetic whisper. But Richard was afraid of the face, so he turned aside. He thought in his mind, "I haven't killed him at all."

"What shall you do next?" came the whisper. And slowly, like a dying snake rearing itself, the face reared itself from the bed to look at Somers, who sat with his face averted.

"I am going away. I am leaving Australia."

"When?"

"Next month."

"Where are you going?"

"To San Francisco."

"America! America!" came the hissing whisper. "They'll kill you in America." And the head sank back on the pillow.

There was a long silence.

"Going to America! Going to America! After he's killed me here," came the whispered moan.

"No, I haven't killed you. I'm only awfully sorry——"

"You have! You have!" shouted Kangaroo, in the loud, bellowing voice that frightened Richard nearly out of the window. "Don't lie, you have——"

The door opened swiftly and Jack, very stern-faced, entered.

He looked at Somers in anger and contempt, then went to the bedside. The nurse hovered in the doorway with an anxious face.

"What is it, 'Roo?" said Jack, in a voice of infinite tenderness, that made Somers shiver inside his skin. "What's wrong, Chief, what's wrong, dear old man?"

Kangaroo turned his face and looked at Somers vindictively. "That man's killed me," he said in a distinct voice.

"No, I think you're wrong there, old man," said Jack. "Mr. Somers has never done anything like that. Let me give you a morphia injection, to ease you, won't you?"

"Leave me alone." Then, in a fretful, vague voice, "I wanted him to love me."

"I'm sure he loves you, 'Roo—sure he does."

"Ask him."

Jack looked at Richard and made him a sharp, angry sign with his brows, as if bidding him comply.

"You love our one-and-only Kangaroo all right, don't you, Mr. Somers?" he said in a manly, take-it-for-granted voice.

"I have an immense regard for him," muttered Richard.

"Regard! I should think so. We've got more than regard. I love the man—love him—love him I do. Don't I, 'Roo?"

But Kangaroo had sunk down, and his face had gone small, he was oblivious again.

"I want nurse," he whispered.

"Yes, all right," said Jack, rising from bending over the sick man. Somers had already gone to the door. The nurse entered, and the two men found themselves in the dark passage.

"I shall have to be coming along, Mr. Somers, if you'll wait a minute," said Jack.

"I'll wait outside," said Somers. And he went out and down to the street, into the sun, where people were moving about. They were like pasteboard figures shifting on a flat light.

After a few minutes Jack joined him.

"Poor 'Roo, it's a question of days now," said Jack.

"Yes."

"Hard lines, you know, when a man's in his prime and just ready to enter into his own. Bitter hard lines."

"Yes."

"That's why I think you were a bit hard on him. I *do* love him myself, so I can say so without exaggerating the fact. But if I hated the poor man like hell, and saw him lying there in that state—why, I'd swear on red-hot iron I loved him, I would. A man like that—a big, grand man, as great a hero as ever lived. If a man can't speak two words out of pity for a man in his state, why, I think there's something wrong with that man. Sorry to have to say it. But if Old Harry himself had lain there like that and asked me to say I loved him I'd have done it. Heart-breaking, it was. But I suppose some folks is stingy about sixpence, and others is stingy about saying two words that would give another poor devil his peace of mind."

Richard walked on in angry silence. He hated being condemned in this free-and-easy, rough-and-ready fashion.

"But I suppose chaps from the old country are more careful of what they say—might give themselves away or something of that. We're different over here. Kick yourself over the cliff like an old can if a mate's in trouble and needs a helping hand, or a bit of sympathy. That's us. But I suppose being brought up in the old country, where everybody's frightened that somebody else is going to take advantage of him, makes you more careful. So you're leaving Australia, are you? Mrs. Somers want to go?"

"I think so. Not very emphatically, perhaps."

"Wouldn't want to if you didn't, so to speak? Oh, Mrs. Somers is all right. She's a fine woman, she is. I suppose I ought to say lady, but I prefer a woman, myself, to a lady, any day. And Mrs. Somers is a woman all over—she is that. I'm sorry for my own sake and Vicky's sake that she's going. I'm sorry for Australia's sake. A woman like that ought to stop in a new country like this and breed sons for us. That's what we want."

"I suppose if she wanted to stop and breed sons she would," said Richard coldly.

"They'd have to be your sons, that's the trouble, old man. And how's she going to manage that if you're giving us the go-by?"

Richard spent the afternoon going round to the Customs House and to the American Consulate with his passport, and visiting the shipping office to get a plan of the boat. He went swiftly from place to place. There were no difficulties: only both the Customs House and the Consulate wanted photographs and Harriet's own signature. She would have to come up personally.

He wanted to go now. He wanted to go quickly. But it was

no good, he could not get off for another month, so he must preserve his soul in patience.

"No," said Richard to himself, thinking of Kangaroo. "I don't love him—I detest him. He can die. I'm glad he is dying. And I don't like Jack either. Not a bit. In fact I like nobody. I love nobody and I like nobody, and there's the end of it, as far as I'm concerned. And if I go round 'loving' anybody else, or even 'liking' them, I deserve a kick in the guts like Kangaroo."

And yet, when he went over to the Zoo, on the other side of the harbour—and the warm sun shone on the rocks and the mimosa bloom, and he saw the animals, the tenderness came back. A girl he had met, a steamer acquaintance, had given him a packet of little white extra-strong peppermint sweets. The animals liked them. The grizzly bear caught them and ate them with excitement, panting after the hotness of the strong peppermint, and opening his mouth wide, wide, for more. And one golden brown old-man kangaroo, with his great earth-cleaving tail and his little hanging hands, hopped up to the fence and lifted his sensitive nose quivering, and gently nibbled the sweet between Richard's finger. So gently, so determinedly nibbled the sweet, but never hurting the fingers that held it. And looking up with the big, dark, prominent Australian eyes, so aged in consciousness, with a fathomless, dark, fern-age gentleness and gloom. The female wouldn't come near to eat. She only sat up and watched, and her little one hung its tiny fawn's head and one long ear and one fore-leg out of her pouch, in the middle of her soft, big, grey belly.

Such a married couple! Two kangaroos. And the blood in Richard's veins all gone dark with a sort of sad tenderness. The gentle kangaroos, with their weight in heavy blood on the ground, in their great tail! It wasn't love he felt for them, but a dark, animal tenderness, and another sort of conscious-ness, deeper than human.

It was a time of full moon. The moon rose about eight. She was so strong, so exciting, that Richard went out at nine o'clock down to the shore. The night was full of moonlight as a mother-of-pearl. He imagined it had a warmth in it to-wards the moon, a moon-heat. The light on the waves was like liquid radium swinging and slipping. Like radium, the mystic virtue of vivid decomposition, liquid-gushing lucidity. The sea too was very full. It was nearly high tide, the waves

were rolling very tall, with light like a menace on the nape of
their necks as they bent, so brilliant. Then, when they fell,
the fore-flush rushed in a great soft swing with incredible
speed up the shore, on the darkness soft-lighted with moon,
like a rush of white serpents, then slipping back with a hiss
that fell into silence for a second, leaving the sand of granulated silver.

It was the huge rocking of this flat, hollow-foreflush moon
—dim in its hollow, that was the night to Richard. "This is
the night and the moon," he said to himself. Incredibly swift
and far the flat rush flew at him, with foam like the hissing,
open mouths of snakes. In the nearness a wave broke white
and high. Then, ugh! across the intervening gulf the great
lurch and swish, as the snakes rushed forward, in a hollow
frost hissing at his boots. Then failed to bite, fell back hissing
softly, leaving the belly of the sands granulated silver.

A huge but a cold passion swinging back and forth. Great
waves of radium swooping with a down-curve and rushing up
the shore. Then calling themselves back again, retreating to
the mass. Then rushing with venomous radium-burning speed
into the body of the land. Then recoiling with a low swish,
leaving the flushed sand naked.

That was the night. Rocking with cold, radium-burning
passion, swinging and flinging itself with venomous desire.
That was Richard, too, a bit of human wispiness in thin overcoat and thick boots. The shore was deserted all the way.
Only, when he came past the creek on the sands, rough, wild
ponies looking at him, dark figures in the moonlight lifting
their heads from the invisible grass of the sand, and waiting
for him to come near. When he came and talked to them
they were reassured, and put their noses down to the grass to
eat a bit more in the moon-dusk, glad a man was there.

Richard rocking with the radium-urgent passion of the night:
the huge, desirous swing, the call clamour, the low hiss of re-
treat. The call, call! And the answerer. Where was his
answerer? There was no living answerer. No dark-bodied,
warm-bodied answerer. He knew that when he had spoken a
word to the night-half-hidden ponies with their fluffy legs. No
animate answer this time. The radium-rocking, wave-knocking
night his call and his answer both. This God without feet or
knees or face. This sluicing, knocking, urging night, heaving
like a woman with unspeakable desire, but no woman, no

thighs or breast, no body. The moon, the concave mother-of-pearl of night, the great radium-swinging, and his little self. The call and the answer, without intermediary. Non-human gods, non-human human beings.

CHAPTER XVIII

ADIEU, AUSTRALIA

KANGAROO died and had a great funeral, but Richard did not go up. He had fixed his berths on the *Manganui*, and would sail away in twenty days. To America—the United States, a country that did not attract him at all, but which seemed to lie next in his line of destiny.

Meanwhile he wandered round in the Australian spring. Already he loved it. He loved the country he had railed at so loudly a few months ago. While he "cared" he had to rail at it. But the care once broken inside him it had a deep mystery for him, and a dusky, far-off call that he knew would go on calling for long ages before it got any adequate response, in human beings. From far off, from down long fern-dark avenues there seemed to be the voice of Australia, calling low.

He loved to wander in the bush at evening, when night fell so delicately yet with such soft mystery. Then the sky behind the trees was all soft, rose pink, and the great gum trees ran up their white limbs into the air like quicksilver, plumed at the tips with dark tufts. Like rivulets the white boughs ran up from the white trunk: or like great nerves, with nerve-like articulations, branching into the dusk. Then he would stand under a tall fern tree, and look up through the whorl of lace above his head, listening to the birds calling in the evening stillness, the parrots making a chinking noise.

Sitting at the edge of the bush he looked at the settlement and the sea beyond. He had quite forgotten how he used to grumble at the haphazard throwing of bungalows here and there and anywhere: how he used to hate the tin roofs, and the untidiness. It recalled to him the young Australian captain, "Oh, how I liked the rain on the tin roofs of the huts at the war. It reminded me of Australia."

"And now," thought Richard to himself, "tin roofs and

scattered shanties will always remind me of Australia. They seem to me beautiful, though it's a fact they have nothing to do with beauty."

But, oh, the deep mystery of joy it was to him to sit at the edge of the bush as twilight fell, and look down at the township. The bungalows were built mostly on the sides of the slopes. They had no foundations, but stood on brickwork props, which brought them up to the level. There they stood on the hillsides, on their short legs, with darkness under their floors, the little bungalows, looking as if they weighed nothing. Looking flimsy, made of wood with corrugated zinc roofs. Some of them were painted dark red, roofs and all, some were painted grey, some were wooden simply. Many had the white-grey zinc roofs, pale and delicate. At the back was always one big water-butt of corrugated iron, a big round tank painted dark-red, the corrugation ribs running round, and a jerky, red-painted pipe coming down from the eaves. Sometimes there were two of these tanks: and a thin, not very tidy woman in a big straw hat stooping to the tap at the bottom of the tank. The roof came down low, making a long shade over the wooden verandas. Nearly always a little loggia at the back, from which the house door opened. And this little veranda was the woman's kitchen; there she had a little table with her dirty dishes, which she was going to wash up. And a cat would be trotting around, as if it had not an enemy in the world, while from the veranda a parrot called.

The bungalows near the bush edge had odd bits of garden nipped out of the paddocks and carefully railed in: then another little enclosure for the calf. At the back the earth was scratched, there was a rubbish-heap of ashes and tins slipping into the brambles, and very white fowls clustering for bed-time. In front of the house, in another bit of garden with wooden palings, two camellia trees full of flowers, one white and one red, like artificial things, but a bit seared by the wind. And at the gate the branching coral trees still flowering flame from their dark, strong-thrusting, up-curving buds.

So, with evening falling. There were green roads laid out in the wild, with but one lost bungalow to justify them. And a lost horse wildly galloping round the corner of this blind road, to quiet down and look around. A belated collier galloping stiffly on his pony, out of the township, and a woman in a white blouse and black skirt, with two little girls beside her,

driving a ramshackle little buggy with a quick-legged little
pony, homewards through the trees.

Lights were beginning to glint out: the township was
deciding it was night. The bungalows scattered far and wide,
on the lower levels. There was a net-work of wide roads, or
beginnings of roads. The heart of the township was one tiny
bit of street a hundred yards long: Main Street. You knew
where it was, as you looked down on the reddish earth and
grass and bush, by the rather big roof of pale zinc and a sandy-
coloured round gable of the hotel—the biggest building in the
place. For the rest, it looked, from above, like an inch of street
with tin roofs on either side, fizzling out at once into a wide
grass road with a few bungalows and then the bush. But there
was the dark railway, and the little station. And then again
the big paddocks rising to the sea, with a ridge of coral trees
and a farm-place. Richard could see Coo-ee with its low, red
roof, right on the sea. Behind it the rail-fences of the paddocks,
and the open grass, and the streets cut out and going nowhere,
with an odd bungalow here and there.

So it was all round—a far and wide scattering of pale-roofed
bungalows at random among grassy, cut-out streets, all along
the levels above the sea, but keeping back from the sea, as if
there were no sea. Ignoring the great Pacific. There were knolls
and pieces of blue creek-hollow, blue of fresh-water in lagoons
on the yellow sands. Up the knolls perched more bungalows,
on very long front legs and no back legs, caves of dark underneath. And on the sky-line, a ridge of wiry trees with dark
plume-tufts at the ends of the wires, and these little loose
crystals of different-coloured, sharp-angled bungalows cropping
out beneath. All in a pale, clear air, clear and yet far off, as it
were visionary.

So the land swooped in grassy swoops, past the railway,
steep up to the bush: here and there thick-headed palm trees
left behind by the flood of time and the flood of civilisation
both: bungalows with flame trees: bare bungalows like pack-
ing-cases: an occasional wind-fan for raising water: a round
well-pool, perfectly round: then the bush, and a little colliery
steaming among the trees. And so the great tree-covered
swoop upwards of the tor, to the red fume of clouds, red like
the flame-flowers of sunset. In the darkness of trees the strange
birds clinking and trilling: the tree ferns with their knob-scaly
trunks spreading their marvellous circle of lace overhead

against the glow, the gum trees like white, naked nerves running up their limbs, and the inevitable dead gum trees poking stark grey limbs into the air. And the thick aboriginal dusk settling down.

Richard wandered through the village, homewards. Horses stood motionless in the middle of the road, like ghosts, listening. Or a cow stood as if asleep on the dark footpath. Then she too wandered off. At night-time always these creatures roaming the dark and semi-dark roads, eating the wayside grass. The motor-cars rushing up the coast road must watch for them. But the night straying cattle were not troubled. They dragged slowly out of the way.

The night in the township was full of the sound of frogs, rattling, screeching, whirring, raving like a whole fairy factory going at full speed in the marshy creek-bottom. A great grey bird, a crane, came down on wide soft wings softly in the marshy place. A cream-coloured pony, with a snake-like head stretched out, came cropping up the road, cropping unmoved, though Richard's feet passed within a few yards of his nose. Richard thought of the snaky Praxiteles horses outside the Quiriline in Rome. Very, very nearly those old, snaky horses were born again here in Australia: or the same vision come back.

People mattered so little. People hardly matter at all. They were there, they were friendly. But they never entered inside one. It is said that man is the chief environment of man. That, for Richard, was not true in Australia. Man was there, but unnoticeable. You said a few words to a neighbour or an acquaintance, but it was merely for the sake of making a sound of some sort. Just a sound. There was nothing really to be said. The vast continent is really void of speech. Only man makes noises to man, from habit. Richard found he never wanted to talk to anybody, never wanted to be with anybody. He had fallen apart out of the human association. And the rest of the people either were the same, or they herded together in a promiscuous fashion. But this speechless, aimless solitariness was in the air. It was natural to the country. The people left you alone. They didn't follow you with their curiosity and their inquisitiveness and their human fellowship. You passed, and they forgot you. You came again, and they hardly saw you. You spoke, and they were friendly. But they never asked any questions, and they never encroached. They didn't care. The profound Australian indifference, which still is not really apathy. The disintegration of the social mankind back to its elements. Rudimentary individuals with no desire of communication. Speeches, just noises. A herding together like dumb cattle, a promiscuity like slovenly animals. Yet the basic indifference under everything.

And with it all, toiling on with civilisation. But it felt like a clock that was running down. It had been wound up in Europe, and was running down, running right down, here in Australia. Men were mining, farming, making roads, shouting politics. But all with that basic indifference which dare not acknowledge *how* indifferent it is, lest it should drop everything and lapse into a blank. But a basic indifference, with a spurt of excitement over a horse-race, and an occasional joy in a row.

It seemed strange to Somers that Labour should be so insistent in Australia—or that Kangaroo should have been so burning. But then he realised that these men were all the time yoked to some work, they were all the time in the collar. And the work kept them going a good deal more than they kept the work going. Nothing but the absolute drive of the world's work kept them going. Without it they would have lapsed into the old bushranging recklessness, lapsed into the profound indifference which was basic in them.

But still, they were men, they were healthy, they were full of energy, even if they were indifferent to the aim in front. So they embraced one aim or another, out of need to be going somewhere, doing something more than just backing a horse. Something more than a mere day's work and a gamble. Some smack at the old-established institution of life, that came from Europe.

There it is, laid all over the world, the heavy established European way of life. Like their huge ponderous cathedrals and factories and cities, enormous encumbrances of stone and steel and brick, weighing on the surface of the earth. They say Australia is free, and it is. Even the flimsy, foundationless bungalows. Richard railed at the scrappy amorphousness, till two nights he dreamed he was in Paris, and a third night it was in some other city, of Italy or France. Here he was staying in a big palazzo of a house—and he struggled to get out, and found himself in a high old provincial street with old gable houses and dark shadow and himself in the gulf between: and at the end of the street a huge, pale-grey bulk of a cathedral, an old Gothic cathedral, huge and massive and grey and beautiful.

But, suddenly, the mass of it made him sick, and the beauty was nauseous to him. So strong a feeling that he woke up. And since that day he had been thankful for the amorphous scrappy scattering of foundationless shacks and bungalows. Since then he had loved the Australian landscape, with the remote gum trees running their white nerves into the air, the random streets of flimsy bungalows, all loose from one another, and temporary seeming, the bungalows perched precariously on the knolls, like Japanese paper-houses, below the ridge of wire-and-tuft trees.

He had now a horror of vast super-incumbent buildings. They were a nightmare. Even the cathedrals. Huge, huge bulks that are called beauty. Beauty seemed to him like some turgid tumour. Never again, he felt, did he want to look at London, the horrible *weight* of it: or at Rome with all the pressure on the hills. Horrible, inert, man-moulded weight. Heavy as death.

No, no, the flimsy hills of Australia were like a new world, and the frail *inconspicuousness* of the landscape, that was still so clear and clean, clean of all fogginess or confusion: but the frail, aloof, inconspicuous clarity of the landscape was like a sort of heaven—bungalows, shacks, corrugated iron and all. No wonder Australians love Australia. It is the land that as yet has made no great mistake, humanly. The horrible human mistakes of Europe. And, probably, the even worse human mistakes of America.

"Then why am I going?" he asked himself.

"Wait! Wait!" he answered himself. "You have got to go through the mistakes. You've got to go all round the world, and then half-way round again, till you get back. Go on, go on, the world is round, and it will bring you back. Draw your ring round the world, the ring of your consciousness. Draw it round until it is complete."

So he prepared with a quiet heart to depart.

The only person that called at Coo-ee was Jaz.

"You're leaving us, then?" he said.

"Yes."

"Rather suddenly at the end."

"Perhaps. But it's as well I should go soon if I'm going."

"You think so? Taken against the place, have you?"

"No—the contrary. If I stay much longer I shall stay altogether."

"Come quite to like it!" Jaz smiled slowly.

"Yes. I love it, Jaz. I don't love people. But this place—it goes into my marrow, and makes me feel drunk. I love Australia."

"That's why you leave it, eh?"

"Yes. I'm frightened. What I want to do is to go a bit farther back into the bush—near some little township—have a horse and a cow of my own—and—damn everything."

"I can quite understand the 'damn everything' part of it," laughed Jaz. "You won't do it, though."

"I never was so tempted in my life. Talk about Eve tempting man to a fall: Australia tempts me. *Retro me*——"

Jaz was silent for a few moments.

"You'd repent it, though," he said quietly.

"I'll probably repent whatever I do," replied Somers, "so what's the odds. I'll probably repent bitterly going to America, going back to the world: when I want Australia. I want Australia as a man wants a woman. I fairly tremble with wanting it."

"Australia?"

"Yes."

Jaz looked at Somers with his curious, light-grey eyes.

"Then why not stop?" he said seductively.

"Not now. Not now. Some cussedness inside me. I don't want to give in, you see. Not yet. I don't want to give in to the place. It's too strong. It would lure me quite away from myself. It would be too easy. It's *too* tempting. It's too big a stride, Jaz."

Jaz laughed, looking back at Richard's intense eyes.

"What a man you are, Mr. Somers!" he said. "Come and live in Sydney and you won't find it such a big jump from anywhere else."

"No, I wouldn't want to live in Sydney. I'd want to go back in the bush near one of the little townships. It's like wanting a woman, Jaz. I want it."

"Then why not do it?"

"I won't give in, not yet. It's like giving in to a woman; I won't give in yet. I'll come back later."

Jaz suddenly looked at Richard and smiled maliciously.

"You won't give in, Mr. Somers, will you? You won't give in to the women, and Australia's like a woman to you. You wouldn't give in to Kangaroo, and he's dead now. You won't give in to Labour, or Socialism. Well, now, what will you do? Will you give in to America, do you think?"

"Heaven preserve me—if I'm to speak beforehand."

"Why, Mr. Somers!" laughed Jaz, "seems to me you just go round the world looking for things you're not going to give in to. You're as bad as we folk."

"Maybe," said Richard. "But I'll give in to the Lord Almighty, which is more than you'll do——"

"Oh, well, now—we'd give in to Him if we saw Him," said Jaz, smiling with an odd winsomeness he sometimes had.

"All right. Well, I prefer not to see, and yet to give in," said Richard.

Jaz glanced up at him suspiciously from under his brows.

"And another thing," said Richard. "I won't give up the flag of our real civilised consciousness. I'll give up the ideals. But not the aware, self-responsible, deep consciousness that we've gained. I won't go back on that, Jaz, though Kangaroo did say I was the enemy of civilisation."

"You don't consider you are, then?" asked Jaz, pertinently.

"The enemy of civilisaiton? Well, I'm the enemy of this machine civilisation and this ideal civilisation. But I'm not the enemy of the deep, self-responsible consciousness in man, which is what *I* mean by civilisation. In that sense of civilisation, I'd fight for ever for the flag, and try to carry it on into deeper, darker places. It's an adventure, Jaz, like any other. And when you realise what you're doing, it's perhaps the best adventure."

Harriet brought the tea-tray on to the veranda.

"It's quite nice that somebody has come to see us," she said to Jaz. "There seems such a gap, now Kangaroo is gone, and all he stood for."

"You feel a gap, do you?" asked Jaz.

"Awful. As if the earth had opened. As for Lovat, he's absolutely broken-hearted, and such a trial to live with."

Jaz looked quickly and inquiringly at Somers.

"Sort of metaphysical heart," Richard said, smiling wryly. Jaz only looked puzzled.

"Metaphysical!" said Harriet. "You'd think to hear him he was nothing but a tea-pot brewing metaphysical tea. As a matter of fact, Kangaroo went awfully deep with him, and now he's heart-broken, and that's why he's rushing to America. He's always breaking his heart over something—anything except me. To me he's a nether millstone."

"Is that so!" said Jaz.

"But one feels awful, you know, Kangaroo dying like that. Lovat likes to show off and be so beastly high and mighty about things. But I know how miserable he is."

They were silent for some time, and the talk drifted.

In the newspapers Somers read of a big cyclone off the coast of China, which had engulfed thousands of Chinese. This cyclone was now travelling south, lashing its tail over the New Hebrides, and swooping its paws down the thousands of miles of east coast of Australia. The monster was expected to have spent itself by the time it reached Sydney. But it hadn't—not quite.

Down it came, in a great darkness. The sea began to have a strange yelling sound in its breakers, the black cloud came up like a wall from the sea, everywhere was dark. And the wind broke in volleys from the sea, and the rain poured as if the cyclone were a great bucket of water pouring itself endlessly down.

Richard and Harriet sat in the dark room at Coo-ee, with a big fire, and darkness raging in waters around. It was like the end of the world. The roaring snarl of the sea was of such volume, the volleying roar of the wind so great as to create almost a sense of silence in the room. The house was like a small cave under the water. Rain poured in waves over the dark room, and with a heaviness of spume. Though the roof came down so far and deep over the verandas, yet the water swept in, and gurgled under the doors and in at the windows. Tiles were ripped off the veranda roof with a crash, and water splashed more heavily. For the first day there was nothing to do but to sit by the fire, and occasionally mop up the water at the seaward door. Through the long, low windows you saw only a yellow-livid fume, and over all the boom you heard the snarl of water.

They were quite cut off this day, alone, dark, in the devastation of water. The rain had an iciness, too, which seemed to make a shell round the house. The two beings, Harriet and Lovat, kept alone and silent in the shell of a house as in a submarine. They were black inside as out. Harriet particularly was full of a storm of black chagrin. She had expected so much of Australia. It had been as if all her life she had been waiting to come to Australia. To a new country, to a new, unspoiled country. Oh, she hated the old world so much. London, Paris, Berlin, Rome—they all seemed to her so old, so ponderous with ancient authority and ancient dirt. Ponderous, ancient authority especially, oh, how she hated it. Freed once, she wanted a new freedom, silvery and paradisical in the atmosphere. A land with a new atmosphere, untainted by authority. Silvery, untouched freedom.

And in the first months she had found this in Australia, in the silent, silvery-blue days, and the unbreathed air, and strange, remote forms of tree and creature. She had felt herself free, free, free, for the first time in her life. In the silvery pure air of this undominated continent she could swim like a fish that is just born, alone in a crystal ocean. Woman that she was she exulted, she delighted. She had loved Coo-ee. And she just could not understand that Richard was so tense, so resistant.

Then gradually, through the silver glisten of the new freedom came a dull, sinister vibration. Sometimes from the interior came a wind that seemed to her evil. Out of the silver paradisical freedom untamed, evil winds could come, cold, like a stone hatchet murdering you. The freedom, like everything else, had two sides to it. Sometimes a heavy, reptile-hostility came off the sombre land, something gruesome and infinitely repulsive. It frightened her as a reptile would frighten her if it wound its cold folds around her. For the past month now Australia had been giving her these horrors. It was as if the silvery freedom suddenly turned, and showed the scaly back of a reptile, and the horrible paws.

Out of all her bird-like elation at this new-found freedom, freedom for her, the female, suddenly, without warning, dark revulsions struck her. Struck her, it would seem, in her deepest female self, almost in her womb. These revulsions sent her into a frenzy. She had sudden, mad loathings of Australia. And these made her all the more frenzied because of her former great, radiant hopes and her silvery realisations. What, must it all be taken back from her, all this glisten of paradise, this glisten of paradise, this silvery freedom like protoplasm of life? Was it to be revoked?

There was Richard, that hell-bird, preaching, preaching at

her, "Don't trust it. You can't have this absolved sort of freedom. It's an illusion. You can't have this freedom absolved from control. It can't be done. There is no stability. There will come a reaction and a devastation. Inevitable. You must have deep control from within. You must have a deep, dark weight of authority in your own soul. You must be most carefully, sternly controlled from within. You must be under the hand of the Lord. You can't escape the dark hand of the Lord, not even in free Australia. You'll get the devils turning on you if you try too much freedom. It can't be done. Too much freedom means you absolve yourself from the hand of the Lord, and once you're really absolved you fall a prey to devils, devils. You'll see. All you white females raging for further freedom. Wait, wait till you've got it and see how the devils will bite you with unclean, reptile sort of mouths. Wait, you who love Australia and its freedom. Only let me leave you to the freedom, till it bites you with a sort of sewer mouth, like all these rats. Only let me abandon you to this freedom. Only let me——"

So he had preached at her, like a dog barking, barking senselessly. And oh, how it had annoyed her.

Yet gradually, quite apart from him, it had begun to happen to her. These hateful revulsions, when Australia had turned as it were *unclean* to her, with an unclean sort of malevolence. And her revulsions had possessed her. Then the death of Kangaroo. And now this blackness, this slew of water, this noise of hellish elements.

To Richard it was like being caged in with a sick tiger, to be shut up with Harriet in this watery cave of gloom. Like a sullen, sick tiger, she could hardly get herself to move, the weight of her revulsion was so deep upon her. She *loathed* Australia, with wet, dark repulsion. She was black, sick with chagrin. And she hated that barking white dog of a Richard, with his yap-yap-yapping about control and authority and the hand of the Lord. She had left Europe with her teeth set in hatred of Europe's ancient encumbrance of authority and of the withered, repulsive weight of the Hand of the Lord, that old Jew, upon it. Undying hostility to old Europe, undying hope of the new, free lands. Especially this far Australia.

And now—and now—was the freedom all going to turn into dirty water? All the uncontrolled gentleness and uncontaminated freedom of Australia, was it going to turn and bite her like the ghastly bite of some unclean-mouthed reptile, an iguana, a great newt? Had it already bitten her?

She was sick with revulsion, she wanted to get out, away to America which is not so sloppy and lovey, but hard and greedy and domineering, perhaps, but not mushy-lovey.

These three days of dark wetness, slew, and wind finished her. On the second morning there was an abatement, and Richard rushed to the post. The boys, barefoot, bare-legged in the icy water, were running to school under mackintosh capes. Down came the rain in a wind suddenly like a great hose-pipe, and Richard got home a running, streaming pillar of water. Home into the dark room and the sulky tiger of Harriet.

The storm went on, black, all day, all night, and the next day the same, inside the house as well as out. Harriet sulked the more, like a frenzied sick tiger. The afternoon of the third day another abatement into light rain, so Richard pulled on thick boots and went out to the shore. His grass was a thin surface stream, and down the low cliffs, one cascade stream. The sea was enormous: wave after wave in immediate succession, raving yellow and crashing dull into the land. The yeast-spume was piled in hills against the cliffs, among the big rocks and in swung the raving yellow water, in great dull blows under the land, hoarsely surging out of the dim yellow blank of the sea. Harriet looked at it for a few moments, shuddering and peering down like a sick tigress in a flood. Then she turned tail and rushed indoors.

Richard tried to walk under the cliffs. But the whole shore was ruined, changed: a whole mass of new rocks, a chaos of heaped boulders, a gurgle of rushing, clayey water, and heaps of collapsed earth.

On the fourth day the wind had sunk, the rain was only thin, the dark sky was breaking. Gradually the storm of the sky went down. But not the sea. Its great yellow fore-fringe was a snarl of wave after wave, unceasing. And the shore was a ruin. The beach seemed to have sunk or been swept away, the shore was a catastrophe of rocks and boulders. Richard scrambled along through the dank wetness to a bit of sand, where seaweed was piled like bushes, and he could more or less walk. But soon he came to a new obstacle. The creek, which formerly had sunk at the edge of the beach in a long pool, and left the sloping sand all free and beautiful, had now broken through, levelled the sand, and swept in a kind of snarling river to the snarling waves, across the cut-out sand. The fresh-water met the waves with a snarl, and sometimes pushed on into the sea, sometimes was shoved back and heaped up with a rattle of angry protest. Waters against waters.

The beach never recovered, during the Somers' stay, the river never subsided into the sand, the sandy foreshore never came back. It was a rocky, boulder-heaped ruin with that stream for an impasse. Harriet would not go down to the sea any more. The waves still raved very high, they would not go back, and they lashed with a venomousness to the cliffs, to cut a man off. Richard would wander cold and alone on this inhospitable shore, looking for shells, out of the storm. And all the time the waves would lash up, and he would scramble out. It seemed to him female and vindictive. "Beastly water, beastly water, rolling up so high. Beastly water, beastly water, rolling up so high, breaking all the shells just where they lie"— he crooned to himself, crooning a kind of war-croon, malevolent against the malevolence of this ocean.

Yet it was August, and spring was come, it was wattle-day in Sydney, the city full of yellow bloom of mimosa. Richard and Harriet went up to the United States Consul, to the shipping office: everything very easy. But he could not bear to be in Sydney any more. He could hear Kangaroo all the time.

It was August, and spring, and hot, hot sun in a blue sky. Only the sea would not, or could not, return to its old beauties. Richard preferred to go inland. The wattle trees and the camellia trees were full in bloom in the bungalow gardens, birds flew quickly about in the sun, the morning was quick with spring, the afternoon already hot and drowsy with summer. Harriet, in her soul, had now left Australia for America, so she could look at this land with new, relieved eyes again. She never more passionately identified herself with it as at first.

Richard hired a little two-wheeled trap, called in Australia a sulky, with a little pony, to drive into the bush. Sometimes they had gone in a motor-car, but they both much preferred the little, comfortable sulky. There sat Harriet full and beaming, and the thin Richard beside her, like any Australian couple in a shabby sulky behind a shabby pony, trotting lazily under the gum trees of the high-road and up the steep, steep, jungle-dense climb of the mountain to the pass.

Nothing is lovelier than to drive into the Australian bush in spring on a clear day : and most days are clear and hot. Up the steep climb the tree-ferns and the cabbage-palms stood dark and unlighted as ever, among the great gums. But once at the top, away from the high-road and the sea face, trotting on the yellow-brown sandy trail through the sunny, thinly scattered trees of the untouched bush, it was heaven. They splashed through a clear, clear stream, and walked up a bank into the nowhere, the pony peacefully marching.

The bush was in bloom, the wattles were out. Wattle, or mimosa, is the national flower of Australia. There are said to be thirty-two species. Richard found only seven as they wandered along. The little, pale, sulphur wattle with a reddish stem sends its lovely sprays so aerial out of the sand of the trail, only a foot or two high, but such a delicate, spring-like thing. The thorny wattle with its fuzzy pale balls tangled on the banks. Then beautiful heath plants with small bells, like white heather, stand in tall, straight tufts, and above them the gold sprays of the intensely gold bush mimosa, with here and there, on long, thin stalks like hairs almost, beautiful blue flowers, with gold grains, three-petalled, like reed flowers, and blue, blue with a touch of Australian darkness. Then comes a hollow, desolate bare place with empty greyness and a few dead, charred gum trees, where there has been a bush-fire. At the side of this bare place great flowers, twelve feet high, like sticky dark lilies in bulb-buds at the top of the shaft, dark, blood-red. Then over another stream, and scattered bush once more, and the last queer, gold red bushes of the bottle-brush tree, like soft-bristly golden bottle-brushes standing stiffly up, and the queer black boys on one black leg with a tuft of dark-green spears, sending up the high stick of a seed-stalk, much taller than a man. And here and there the gold bushes of wattle with their narrow dark leaves.

Richard turned and they plunged into the wild grass and strange bushes, following the stream. By the stream the mimosa was all gold, great gold bushes full of spring fire rising over your head, and the scent of the Australian spring, and the most ethereal of all golden bloom, the plumy, many-balled wattle, and the utter loneliness, the manlessness, the untouched blue sky overhead, the gaunt, lightless gum trees rearing a little way off, and sound of strange birds, vivid ones of strange, brilliant birds that flit round. Save for that, and for some weird frog-like sound, indescribable, the age-unbroken silence of the Australian bush.

But it is wonderful, out of the sombreness of gum trees, that seem the same, hoary for ever, and that are said to begin to wither from the centre the moment they are mature—out of the hollow bush of gum trees and silent heaths, all at once, in spring, the most delicate feathery yellow of plumes and plumes and plumes and trees and bushes of wattle, as if angels had flown right down out of the softest gold regions of heaven to settle here, in the Australian bush. And the perfume in all the air that might be heaven, and the unutterable stillness, save for strange bright birds and flocks of parrots, and the motionless-ness, save for a stream and butterflies and some small brown bees. Yet a stillness, and a manlessness, and an elation, the bush flowering at the gates of heaven.

Somers and Harriet left the pony and clambered along the stream, past trees of the grey, feathery-leaved wattle, most sumptuous of all in soft gold in the sky, and bushes of the grey-hard, queer-leaved wattle, on to the thick green of strange trees narrowing into the water. The water slithered rushing over steep rocks. The two scrambled down, and along after the water, to an abrupt edge. There the water fell in a great roar down a solid rock, and broke and rushed into a round, dark pool, dark, still, fathomless, low down in a gruesome dark cup in the bush, with rocks coming up to the trees. In this tarn the stream disappeared. There was no outlet. Rock and bush shut it in. The river just dived into the ground.

It was a dark, frightening place, famous for snakes. Richard hoped the snakes were still sleeping. But there was a horror of them in the air, rising from the tangled undergrowth, from under the fallen trees, the gum trees that crashed down into the great terns, eaten out by white ants.

In this place already the Christmas bells were blooming, like some great heath with hanging, bright red bells tipped with white. Other more single bell-flowers, a little bit like foxgloves, but stiff and sharp. All the flowers stiff, sharp, like crystals of colour come opaque out of the sombre, stiff, bristly bush plants.

Harriet had armfuls of bloom, gold plumage of many branches of different wattles, and the white heather, the scarlet bells, with the deep-blue reed-blobs. The sulky with all the bloom looked like a corner of paradise. And as they trotted home through the bush evening was coming, the gold sun slanting. But Richard kept jumping out from among the flowers, to plunge into the brake for a new flower. And the little pony looked round watching him impatiently and displeased. But it was a gentle, tolerant, Australian little beast, with untold patience. Only Harriet was frightened of the coming dusk.

So at length they were slipping down the steep slopes again, between the dense, creeper-tangled jungle and tree-ferns, dark, chilly. They passed a family moving from nowhere to nowhere, two colts trotting beside the wagon. And they came out at last at the bottom, to the lost, flickering little township at nightfall.

At home, with all the house full of blossom, but fluffy gold wattle-bloom, they sat at tea in the pleasant room, the bright fire burning, eating boiled eggs and toast. And they looked at one another—and Richard uttered the unspoken thought:

"Do you wish you were staying?"

"I—I," stammered Harriet, "if I had *three* lives, I'd wish to stay. It's the loveliest thing I've *ever* known."

"I know," he answered, laughing. "If one could live a hundred years. But since one has only a short time——"

They were both silent. The flowers there in the room were like angel-presences, something out of heaven. The bush! The wonderful Australia.

Yet the day came to go: to give up the keys, and leave the lonely, bare Coo-ee to the next comers. Even the sea had gone flowery again at last. And everybody was so simple, so kindly, at the departure. Harriet felt she would leave behind her for ever something of herself, in that Coo-ee home. And he knew that one of his souls would stand for ever out on those rocks beyond the jetty, towards Bulli, advanced into the sea, with the dark magic of the tor standing just behind.

The journey to Sydney was so spring-warm and beautiful, in the fresh morning. The bush now and then glowed gold, and there were almond and apricot trees near the little wooden bungalows, and by the railway unknown flowers, magenta and yellow and white, among the rocks. The frail, wonderful Australian spring, coming out of all the gummy hardness and sombreness of the bush.

Sydney, and the warm harbour. They crossed over once more in the blue afternoon. Kangaroo dead. Sydney lying on its many-lobed blue harbour, in the Australian spring. The many

people, all seeming dissolved in the blue air. Revolution—
nothingness. Nothing could ever matter.

On the last morning Victoria and Jaz's wife came to see the
Somers off. The ship sailed at ten. The sky was all sun, the
boat reared her green paint and red funnel to the sun. Down
below in the dark shadow of the wharf stood all those who
were to be left behind, saying good-bye, standing down in the
shadow under the ship and the wharf, their faces turned up to
the passengers who hung over the rail. A whole crowd of
people down on the wharf, with white uplifted faces, and one
little group of quiet Chinese.

Everybody had bought streamers, rolls of coloured paper
ribbon, and now the passengers leaning over the rail of the
lower and middle decks tossed the unwinding rolls to their
friends below. So this was the last tie, this ribbon of coloured
paper. Somers had a yellow and a red one: Victoria held the
end of the red streamer, Jaz's wife the end of the yellow.
Harriet had blue and green streamers. And from the side of
the ship a whole glittering tangle of these colours connecting
the departing with the remaining, a criss-cross of brilliant
colour that seemed to glitter like a rainbow in the beams of
the sun, as it rose higher, shining in between the ship and the
wharf shed, touching the faces of the many people below.

The gangway was hoisted—the steamer gave long hoots.
Only the criss-crossing web of brilliant streamers went from
the hands of the departing to the hands of those who would be
left behind. There was a sort of silence: the calling seemed to
die out. And already before the cables were cast loose, the gulf
seemed to come. Richard held fast to the two streamers, and
looked down at the faces of the two women, who held the
other ends of his paper threads. He felt a deep pang in his
heart, leaving Australia, that strange country that a man might
love so hopelessly. He felt another heart-string going to break
like the streamers, leaving Australia, leaving his own British
connection. The darkness that comes over the heart at the
moment of departure darkens the eyes too, and the last scene
is remote, remote, detached inside a darkness.

So now, when the cables were cast loose, and the ship slowly
left the side of the wharf and drew gradually towards the
easier waters of the harbour, there was a little gulf of water
between the ship and the wharf. The streamers lengthened out,
they glittered and twinkled across the space almost like music,

so many-coloured. And then the engines were going, and the crowd on the wooden quay began to follow slowly, slowly, holding the frail streamers carefully, like the ends of a cloud, following slowly down the quay as the ship melted from shadow to the sun beyond.

One by one the streamers broke and fluttered loose and fell bright and dead on the water. The slow crowd, slow as a funeral, was at the end, the far end of the quay, holding the last streamers. But the ship inexorably drifted out, and every coloured strip was broken: the crowd stood alone at the end of the wharf, the side of the vessel was fluttering with bright, broken ends.

So, it was time to take out handkerchiefs and wave across space. Few people wept. Somers waved and waved his orange silk kerchief in the blue air. Farewell! Farewell! Farewell, Victoria and Jaz's wife, farewell, Australia, farewell, Britain and the great Empire. Farewell! Farewell! The last streamers blowing away, like broken attachments, broken heart-strings. The crowd on the wharf gone tiny in the sun, and melting away as the ship turned.

Richard watched the Observatory go by: then the Circular Quay, with all its ferry-wharves, and a Nippon steamer lying at her berth, and a well-known, big buff and black P. and O. boat at the P. and O. wharf, looking so like India. Then that was gone too, and the Governor's Palace, and the castellated Conservatorium of Music on its hill, where Richard had first seen Jack—the Palace Gardens, and the blue inlet where the Australian "Fleet" lay comfortably rusting. Then they drifted across harbour, nearer to the wild-seeming slope, like bush where the Zoo is. And then they began to wait, to hang round.

There ahead was the open gate of the harbour, the low Heads with the South Lighthouse, and the Pacific beyond, breaking white. On the left was Manly, where Harriet had lost her yellow scarf. And then the tram going to Narrabeen, where they had first seen Jaz. Behind was the great lobed harbour so blue, and Sydney rather inconspicuous on the south hills with its one or two sky-scrapers. And already, the blue water all round, and a thing of the past.

It was midday before they got out of the Heads, out of the harbour into the open sea. The sun was hot, the wind cold. There were not very many passengers in the first class: and nobody who looked possible to the Somers pair. Richard sa

ADIEU, AUSTRALIA

in the sun watching the dark coast of Australia, so sombre, receding. Harriet watched the two seamen casting rubbish overboard: such a funny assortment of rubbish. The iron sank in the deep, dark water, the wood and straw and cardboard drearily floated. The low Sydney Heads were not far off.

Lovat watched till he could see the dark of the mountain, far away, behind Coo-ee. He was almost sure of the shape. He thought of the empty house—the sunny grass in front—the sunny foreshore with its new rocks—the township behind, the dark tor, the bush, the Australian spring. The sea seemed dark and cold and inhospitable.

It was only four days to New Zealand, over a cold, dark, inhospitable sea.